Penguin Books
Allen Lane The Penguin Press

The Life and Times of Private Eye 1961-1971

The Life and Times of

# PRIVATE EYE

1961-1971

*Edited with an introduction by* Richard Ingrams

Penguin Books
Allen Lane The Penguin Press

*Dedicated to* CLAUD COCKBURN *and* MALCOLM MUGGERIDGE

Penguin Books Ltd, Harmondsworth, Middlesex, England
Penguin Books Inc., 7110 Ambassador Road, Baltimore, Maryland 21207, U.S.A.
Penguin Books Australia Ltd, Ringwood, Victoria, Australia
Allen Lane The Penguin Press, Vigo Street, London W1

Paperback: ISBN 0 14 00.3357 2
Hardback: ISBN 0 7139 0255 8

First published 1971
Copyright © Pressdram Ltd, 1971

Designed by Philip Thompson

Almost all the photographs used in *Private Eye* are
supplied by Keystone Press Ltd, with whose permission
they are used

Made and printed in Great Britain by
Hazell Watson & Viney Ltd, Aylesbury, Bucks

# Contents

# ÆSOP revisited

*Reproduced from* Private Eye on London
*Weidenfeld & Nicholson, 1963*

The first issue of *Private Eye* appeared ten years ago in October 1961. But its foundations were laid nearly ten years before that at Shrewsbury School, where I started a long partnership with William Rushton, then aged 13 and already a cartoonist of talent. Our juvenile efforts appeared in the school magazine *The Salopian*, a dull and pompous periodical given over in the main to long accounts of sporting fixtures. This schoolboy satire was not of any great distinction, though we can I think claim to have invented the word 'pseud'; and there was one occasion when hordes of old boys wrote to complain about some smutty remarks which had been printed referring to a past headmaster, Sir John Wolfenden, then engaged on his Herculean investigation of homosexuality.

It would be nice to say that the harsh authoritarian air of public-school life nurtured the first seeds of savage indignation in the breasts of the young satirists, but this was not really the case. The school was no worse than most public schools at that time and we conformed along with the other pupils. When I left in 1955 to join the Army I left *The Salopian* in the hands of Rushton, and two young recruits, Christopher Booker, a tousle-haired intellectual, and Paul Foot, who was widely suspected of taking things too seriously.

Arriving in Oxford some three years later, almost the first person I met was Foot. It turned out we were in the same college. Like most others who had done National Service, neither of us felt like returning to academic work and we looked around for diversions. The journalistic scene was bleak. *Isis* had fallen into the hands of the infant New Left. The only bright spot on the horizon was a little magazine called *Parson's Pleasure* (named after the stretch of the river Isis where men were allowed to bathe in the nude), edited from Christ Church by one Adrian Berry and entirely given over to savage insults and abuse of everyone in the University. Foot and I quickly signed up with Berry and eventually he passed the paper over to us. Suffering perhaps from a fit of 'Après Moi Le Deluge', Berry asked to be included in our first issue a piece he had written which began: 'The relationship between — and — (*here were named two prominent undergraduates*) is becoming so scandalous as to merit the attention of the authorities.' This led to our first experience of libel and in the end Berry was forced to pay up. But, as his parents owned the *Daily Telegraph,* the blow was not too severe.

*Parson's Pleasure* was a prototype of the later *Private Eye*. It included joke leaders and parodies, as well as gossip and reports of the Oxford Union debates written by Foot. It was banned by W. H. Smith. Though I did not know it at the time, the magazine was kept going by Paul's uncle Michael, who inserted a full-page advertisement for *Tribune* in each issue paid for out of his own pocket. But this generous subsidy could not go on for ever and when it was withdrawn the magazine folded. The Oxford satire scene then shifted to Balliol College, where an embryonic whizz-kid called Peter Usborne was formulating plans to start a joint Oxford and Cambridge humorous magazine called *Mesopotamia*. The Cambridge contribution never materialized but Usborne managed to recruit enough Oxford talent to fill a decent-sized paper, including Foot and me, Rushton (who came from London to do the drawings), Andrew Osmond and John Wells.

The heroes of the day in addition to James Bond, Lawrence Durrell and Ingmar Bergman were the cast of *Beyond the Fringe* who by producing a highly successful revue at the Edinburgh Festival in 1960 had shown that it was possible to sell university humour (the word 'satire' had not yet been invented) as a national commodity. If it could be done with a revue, why not a magazine? Usborne with his eternal optimism was sure it was only too easy. He went to London to meet Christopher Booker, then working on the

*Liberal News,* an improbable nursery of satirical talent which also printed an anarchic strip cartoon by Rushton. Everyone was keen on the idea and it was fun to sit around in pubs discussing the possibilities. But after closing time, difficulties began to loom, like where was the money going to come from? As the Oxford euphoria was dissipated by the outside world, the *Mesopotamia* team started to split up. Foot had gone to Glasgow to work on a newspaper, Wells was, of all things, a schoolmaster at Eton, I myself became involved in theatrical activities, Osmond was in Paris learning French and Usborne in America working for *Time-Life.*

Then one day when all hope had faded Usborne suddenly re-appeared in London, determined to have one more go at getting things moving. A telegram was sent to Osmond summoning him back from his dilettante activities in Paris. Returning in a state of dazed shock, he agreed to put up £300 towards the launching of the paper. There were more meetings in pubs, at which interminable discussions took place about what the magazine should be called. The suggestions ranged from *Bladder, Finger* and *Tumbril* to *The Flesh is Weekly* and *The British Letter.* It was Osmond who suggested *Private Eye* and by that time everyone was so bored with trying to think up titles that they fell in with his conviction that *Private Eye* was far and away the best idea.

During the next two months the first three issues of *Private Eye* were published. They were almost entirely the work of Booker and Rushton, the latter doing all the illustration and the layout. (The manner of production for *Private Eye* has never changed since then. It consists of typing out the copy on a typewriter and sticking it on a piece of paper with any illustrations. This is then photographed and the plate printed.) The work was done mainly in Rushton's bedroom in the large Kensington house where he lived with his mother. Everyone lived in Kensington, Knightsbridge or Chelsea, and the early *Private Eyes* have a flavour of that world. Five hundred copies of the first three issues were printed on orange-coloured paper and sold in fashionable restaurants like Nick's Diner and cafes like the Troubador where bearded CND men gathered to listen to folk-songs. Other copies were sent free to selected VIPs in the hope that we might get some publicity. Kenneth Tynan sent a note of encouragement, Peter Cook suggested we should try putting funny bubbles on photographs, and a small announcement appeared in *The Times:*

'The first copies of a magazine called *Private Eye* edited from London by a group of recent Oxford and Cambridge graduates have been published. The staff, mostly former writers for the Oxford undergraduate magazine *Mesopotamia,* are waiting to see how the sales go before launching the magazine as a national weekly next year. *Private Eye* concentrates on satirical comment.'

*These orange coloured dummies, now 'priceless collectors' items' (Lord Gnome), were printed in Cricklewood by Rank Xerox. When Lord Rank found out about this he put a stop to it at once. Osmond then went to John Thorpe, a retired army band leader printing sheet music in Wembley, who set up a limited company in his son Leo's name which has printed the Eye ever since.*

**S**atire was all the rage. *Beyond the Fringe* was the West End success of the year and in the same month that *Private Eye* crept tentatively out into the Chelsea bistros, the *Establishment,* 'London's First Satirical Night Club', opened in Greek Street, Soho, with a fanfare of publicity. Within eight months it had a membership of 11,000, and it was almost inevitable that *Private Eye,* though very different in tone from the slick sick satire of the *Establishment,* should enjoy a similar success. In February 1962 the magazine began to appear at regular fortnightly intervals and was distributed to newsagents by a fledgeling tycoon, Charles Harness. An approach made to W. H. Smith at this time met with a prompt rebuff, since when the firm has consistently refused to sell the *Eye.* We got our first big publicity in *Time & Tide* (then a Liberal magazine) and the *Observer;* there was even a takeover bid from an eccentric Welsh publisher called Gareth Powell of the Seymour Press. Luckily his fellow directors vetoed the suggestion, but Powell loaned us free of charge a cavernous office in Neal Street, Covent Garden, just a stone's throw from Seven Dials, the breeding ground of pamphlets and lampoons in the 18th century.

After six months the circulation had reached 15,000 and subscribers ranged from Lady Violet Bonham Carter to several inmates of H.M. Prisons. But the magazine was nowhere near to paying its way. A further injection of capital was needed and Osmond for reasons best known to himself was eager to leave to join the Foreign Office. In May 1962 he sold *Private Eye* to Peter Cook and Nick Luard, the proprietors of the *Establishment*, for £1,500. Luard was the Brian Epstein of the satire boom, a Wykenamist ex-Guards officer and the only satirist to wear a suit, who having hit the jackpot with his first venture the *Establishment* was eager to expand his empire. So Booker, Rushton and I and our two secretaries Mary Morgan and Elizabeth Longmore (who later became Mrs Ingrams and Mrs Luard respectively) moved round to the *Establishment*, where we produced two or three issues in the waiters' changing room before settling down the road in 22 Greek St.

Luard's idea was that the *Establishment* and *Private Eye* would pool their talents to the advantage of both. He laid on regular weekly 'satirical lunches' at the club at which he hoped to tap a rich vein of jokes. But there was a deep mutual suspicion between the two camps and the lunches were awkward affairs from which few jokes emerged. Everyone was suffering from the consequences of being fashionable. While it was nice to be successful, there was also a feeling that it was not quite right for satirists to inspire such general acclaim. When Malcolm Muggeridge wrote in the *New Statesman*: 'One is struck, at the *Establishment*, by the general air of affluence. One looks around instinctively for Princess Margaret, or at any rate the Duke of Bedford,' he touched an exposed nerve. The tendency, as a result, was to go to yet greater lengths to shock people, to silence the gale of laughter that greeted each outrageous sally.

*Private Eye* was not immune from this temptation. About this time we created a bit of a stir by describing Mr Butler, then Home Secretary, as 'a flabby faced old coward', which was hailed by some critics as, at last, a return to the fruity free speech of the 18th century. But others were offended by personal remarks and a reference to C. P. Snow's failing eyesight drew a lofty rebuke from the chief guru of the satire movement, Michael Frayn. Another to complain was Kenneth Tynan, who accused the magazine of 'male-chauvinism' and bluntly asked: 'When are you going to develop a point of view?'

Sooner or later, too, we were bound to run into legal trouble. In the very early days of *Private Eye* Osmond had asked a lawyer friend to cast his eye over the paper before it went to press, but as the man said that every single article was libellous, it was felt that we should dispense with his services. All went well until issue 27, which described the Liberal candidate in the Rotherham by-election as 'keener on the good things in life than the bad things in Rotherham'.

The man took offence and issued a writ; but some two weeks later he died. This looked like an omen which would deter others from following his example. Not, alas, so. Hardly a month passed before we found ourselves up against a much more formidable plaintiff, Mr Randolph Churchill.

The article that caused the trouble was in fact about Winston Churchill. It took the form of a strip cartoon (see page 72) in which it was suggested that Randolph, then working on the official biography of his father, would gloss over the many discreditable incidents in the old man's career and concentrate on his hour of glory during the war. The only slur on Randolph himself was the suggestion that his books were the work of a team of hacks. Nevertheless Randolph's filial piety was so pronounced that he felt obliged to defend Sir Winston's good name from any attack. He

*The first issue*

therefore issued a writ against every single person connected with *Private Eye*, right down to the girls working in the office.

The issuing of the writs was treated by us as a colossal joke and in the display window outside the office at 22 Greek St we mounted a collection of exhibits – the offending article, the writ and a special Rushton cartoon called The Great Boar of Suffolk showing Randolph as a pig. Little did we know that every movement at No 22 was being watched by private detectives. Within a few hours, an injunction was issued compelling the removal of the exhibits from public display. Our lawyers, already spluttering with rage at the thought of anyone stooping so low as to attack Sir Winston Churchill, could now scarcely contain themselves. 'You did not inform us that the pig was excreting,' they wrote with reference to the Rushton cartoon. After a ten-minute session at the law courts the exhibition was removed to be replaced by the simple announcement 'Killjoy was here'.

*Private Eye* had finally met its match. The climax came when Peter Usborne left the dossier containing all the details of our defence in a restaurant, only to have it returned a few days later with a pencilled note: 'I think this is yours. Randolph Churchill'. After this we had to sue for peace. Rushton and Luard were invited down to the Churchill mansion in Suffolk where they were presented with an ultimatum – a full-page apology in the *Evening Standard* to be paid for by the *Eye*, or certain defeat in the law courts. After they had agreed to the former, the tension eased, Randolph produced whisky and introduced some of his 'hacks'. He even admitted to liking *Private Eye*. He had been intrigued, he said, to learn from one of his spies that when the writs were delivered at 22 Greek St, the writ server had been greeted with delighted catcalls and laughter.

*Randolph Churchill* v. *Gnome : seen outside the law courts (left to right) : Ingrams, Rushton, Booker and Luard*

(The spy had gained admission to the office posing as a buyer of back numbers.)

The Randolph action was always a matter for regret. Had it not been for the animosity it created, Randolph, I am sure, would have ended up as a regular contributor to *Private Eye*, which is more than can be said of many of the subsequent litigants. Contrary to popular belief these have not been politicians, who, for the most part, take their medicine like men. In ten years *Private Eye* has been sued by about 50 different individuals, a good half of whom have been journalists. They include the editors of the *Daily Express* (twice), the *Daily Mirror*, the *New Statesman* and the *Times Review of Industry* (dec'd), the late Robert Pitman, the proprietor of the *Spectator* and other smaller fry. In 1968 a libel action brought by two junior reporters on the *People* resulted in payments of well over £10,000 in damages and costs. All in all, *Private Eye* must have paid out nearly £50,000 to aggrieved parties.

In November 1962 came the climax of the Satire Boom, when the BBC moved in on the act with *That Was The Week That Was*. The lure of the telly with its fat cheques proved too much even for *Private Eye* and Booker became the programme's chief script writer and Rushton one of the team of performers, specializing in a superb impersonation of Harold Macmillan. Somehow, I was excluded from the pay roll, though Mary and I used to go along regularly on Saturday nights to the BBC's TV Centre in Shepherd's Bush, where something like an enormous cocktail party would be taking place. Here were to be seen the stars who had become famous overnight – Roy Kinnear, Lance Percival, Millicent Martin, recruits from journalism like Bernard Levin and the cartoonist Timothy Birdsall; the producer Ned Sherrin, pale-faced and frantic, the bustling BBC whizz-kid Donald Baverstock and at the centre of it all the programme's 'anchor man' David Frost, who had emerged from almost total obscurity as a night-club performer to the instant nation-wide notoriety that only the telly can bestow.

From the start Frost evinced a profound animosity from the founding fathers of the satire movement. There was something ungentlemanly about a man who was so obviously on the make. His astonishing industry ran counter to the spirit of public-school amateurism which characterized *Beyond the Fringe* and *Private Eye*. At the same time there was a strange charm about his barefaced ambition which was somehow endearing. In that respect he strongly resembled that other great showbiz figure of the Sixties who was emerging at the same time, Harold Wilson.

*TW3* has now passed into the realm of legend and it would be difficult if not impossible for anyone to discover what it was really like. As with the early issues of *Private Eye* one suspects that it would be hard to explain what all the fuss was about. Originally started as a late-night 'minority programme', it soon had an audience of 12 million and the BBC was becoming worried by its success, as it blatantly defied the Corporation's obligation to be fair and provide balance. From that point of view it was doomed from the start, and for all the subsequent disclaimers, the BBC was obviously relieved when it was taken off the air.

**D**uring an Oxford vacation I had spent some weeks at Sefton Delmer's farm in Suffolk tutoring his son Felix. Delmer was at that time writing his memoirs, a colourful account of the great days as the *Daily Express*' Chief Foreign Correspondent. In the evening over dinner he would read out his day's work and ask for helpful criticism and comment. I was rather snooty about his efforts and must at some time have expressed the view that no good journalist could write a good book. By way of reply Delmer gave me a book called *In Time of Trouble* by someone called Claud Cockburn. This fascin-

MAURICE RICHARDSON

*Claud Cockburn*

ated me, for it contained an account of how Cockburn had started a paper in the early Thirties, *The Week,* without money, printer or distributor. This paper, if Cockburn was to be believed, had built up a circulation of several thousand and was read by all the top people in the country. Claud Cockburn immediately became one of my heroes.

About two years later whilst on honeymoon in Ireland Mary and I went to see him. We had obtained an introduction from Donald McLachlan, then editor of the *Sunday Telegraph.* From McLachlan I gained a picture of Cockburn as a highly eccentric recluse living on the edge of the civilized world in conditions of extreme climatic change. (Later I learnt how his romantic view of Cockburn's existence had taken a hold. It was Claud's habit to ring McLachlan once a week to discuss possible topics for his column in the *Sunday Telegraph.* 'Did you see that piece in Thursday's *Times*?' McLachlan would ask. Claud: (who had not seen *The Times* but did not wish to seem deliberately out of touch): 'Appalling floods here, Donald. No papers getting through.' As the months passed Claud would invent increasingly bizarre reasons for his failure to spot a particular item of news or comment in some paper which, in McLachlan's view, no good journalist should do without. Eventually, having run the gamut of floods, droughts, pestilences and strikes all combining to prevent the free flow of communications in Youghal, he took to saying in a very authoritative tone: 'Oh, yes, I saw that, Donald. Absolute balls.')

Claud lived up to all my expectations, being highly amusing and full of charm. He is, despite his eminence, entirely without pretensions, and, despite his intense commitment, always amusing. I could not understand why he was so little in demand, unless it was the general feeling in Fleet Street that anyone who lives outside London cannot possibly know what is going on and that Cockburn in County Cork must be totally ignorant of all contemporary developments.

Claud, too, was a victim of the Youth Cult. The view was then widespread that the over-forties were fit only for the scrap-heap. The battle in all walks of life was between the whizz-kids and the fuddy duddies. It seemed to me that what *Private Eye* wanted was some old blood. Accordingly, with Booker and Rushton now heavily committed to *That Was The Week That Was* and all of us needing a holiday, we decided to give way to an older man. At Alan Brien's instigation we asked Claud if he would become guest editor for one issue. Rather to our surprise, he agreed.

By now, in 1963, the political scene was beginning to get out of hand. Looked at in retrospect, the Profumo affair seems only the logical climax to a long series of disasters. A scandal can only flourish in the right soil. There must be a prevalent atmosphere for an incident, which might in other circumstances be totally ignored, to emerge as a sympton of all that is wrong with the times.

In 1963 conditions were perfect. At the back of it all was the growing feeling that the Macmillan government was steeped in favouritism and corruption. (From there it was only a short step to the wilder rumours about sexual corruption which came to be so widely believed.) Macmillan's weakness was that he was a snob. In some ways he was a radical figure, but he had, like so many of his class, a fatal weakness for country houses and the people who live in them. Though it has been said by many that Macmillan's 'Edwardian image' was a sham cleverly designed to appeal to the strong nostalgia of the British people, it is nevertheless the case that his government and his appointments revealed a degree of old-world snobbery and favouritism that make Asquith's cabinet look revolutionary. The government ranks were thick with Earls and Marquesses, the Cabinet gave the impression of being a grown-up Etonian 'Pop' and it was obvious that Macmillan revelled in this anachronistic state of affairs, even boasting at one point that his powers of patronage made all those years of reading Trollope seem worth while.

It was against this backcloth of old-fashioned

privilege that the scandals of 1962–3 were to stand out with special relief. There were, in fact, three trial run-throughs before Profumo: In March 1963 a junior minister at the Home Office, Charles Fletcher-Cooke, resigned in unusual circumstances, writing a public letter to Macmillan in which he admitted having lent his car to a former inmate of a Borstal. Macmillan seemed to agree that this was ample ground for resignation (see page 69). Next came Vassall and the rumours of homosexuality; thirdly there was the Duchess of Argyll's divorce action. Although on the face of it the Duchess had no connection with politics, in the climate of 1963 it was enough for someone to be a Duke or Duchess for them to be associated in the public mind with Mr Macmillan and his cabinet. Rumours immediately began circulating which connected the Duchess with one or other member of the Cabinet.

In addition to these manifestations of upper-class decadence there was the important ingredient of Mr Henry Brooke, the Home Secretary. This unfortunate man, no doubt well-meaning and tolerant at heart, seemed incapable of putting a foot right. As Home Secretary he presided over a succession of blunders that brought the police force and the judiciary into the firing line. It was the behaviour of the Home Office, the police and the courts which constituted the real scandal of the Profumo affair. Profumo's peccadillo might have been quickly forgotten – and the security issue was an obvious non-starter – if it had not been for the behaviour of Brooke and the police force. It was Brooke who, perhaps unintentionally, instigated the police inquiries about Stephen Ward which led to Ward's hamfisted attempt to blackmail the government with a threat to reveal the truth about Profumo, which in turn led to Profumo's admission that he had lied to the House of Commons. The subsequent trial of Ward bore all the appearance of a primitive act of vengeance by the authorities and had the effect of implicating the police and the judiciary (including Lord Parker, the Lord Chief Justice) in the scandal.

Meanwhile it became obvious that the Press was failing abysmally in its duty to instruct the public. It had made an idiot of itself over the Vassall affair in its attempts to convict ministers of homosexual liaisons with Vassall; now, with Profumo, it was keeping mum despite the fact that it had proof in the shape of letters from Profumo to Christine Keeler that Profumo had lied when he stated that their relationship was entirely innocent.

The whole 1963 scene is well summed up in *The Last Days of Macmillian* (see page 76) written by Booker and illustrated by Tim Birdsall. Published in April, it brought Dr Stephen Ward hurrying round to Greek St convinced that we knew all. At that time he was still maintaining that Profumo had told the truth in his House of Commons statement and firmly resisted my attempts to extract a confession. As for us, we were little better informed of the situation than anyone else though we had printed on 22 March under the heading 'Idle Talk' a summary of the current rumours which went further than any of the national papers (see page 74). The day that article appeared, George Wigg first raised the matter in the House of Commons.

It was only natural that *Private Eye*, now only one and a half years old, should feel swamped by this plethora of scandal. The pack of cards was collapsing about our ears in an unexpected and lurid manner, and events themselves had overtaken satire. At the same time the strain of producing a fortnightly magazine and writing scripts for *That Was The Week That Was* was beginning to tell. An unhealthy air of neurotic excitement was evident in Greek St as elsewhere.

It was at this point that Claud Cockburn appeared

---

## THE NEW DAILY

The Only Daily Newspaper in Great Britain Independent of Combines and Trade Unions

No. 1,040 • • INLAND POSTAGE 3d. WEDNESDAY, AUGUST 28, 1963 REGISTERED AT THE G.P.O. AS A NEWSPAPER 3d. net

### These Outrageous Libels Are Not In The Public Interest

Vicious Smears Against The Prime Minister, Lord Avon, Lord Parker, Mr. Duncan Sandys, And Mr. Griffith-Jones

### Outrageous Contempt Of Court

THE new issue of *Private Eye* is a thoroughly scurrilous publication. In particular it contains gross libels against

**Mr. Harold Macmillan, the Prime Minister.**
**Lord Avon, Ex-Prime Minister of Great Britain**
**Lord Parker, the Lord Chief Justice.**
**Mr. Duncan Sandys M.P., Minister for Colonial Affairs**
**Mr. Mervyn Griffith-Jones Q.C., First Senior Prosecuting Counsel to the Crown.**
**The Police Force as a whole**

It also contains an outrageous contempt of court in connection with a case awaiting trial.

IT is not in the public interest that this kind of muck should continue to be published. *Private Eye* has no special rights or privileges, yet it has, in a life of only forty-four issues been allowed to get itself into a position where it can apparently say anything it likes about anybody and remain unscathed. So far only Mr. Randolph Churchill has hit back, and the publishers at once crawled before him.

THE Prime Minister, Lord Avon, Lord Parker, Mr. Duncan Sandys and Mr. Griffith-Jones should all of them immediately issue the writs that would already have been served if any other paper had said less than half that *Private Eye* says and implies about them.

UNLESS such steps are taken (and nobody except those libelled has the power to do anything) *Private Eye* will do tremendous and growing harm to our public life.

It is since *Private Eye* was established that we have entered upon the era of rumour and scandal which blights reputations and undermines respect for the nation's leaders and its established institutions, without bringing any compensating advantages.

*Private Eye* is part of the vicious attack upon the nation's moral standards and our way of life. Silence will not kill it. Proper reaction by those it smears will.

*The* Eye's *most vociferous critic: Edward Martell, editor of the* New Daily, *lashes out*

on the scene to take charge of one issue of the *Eye*. With his shambling gait, battered hat and long blue overcoat Claud looked like the last man to grapple with the complexities of the Profumo period. In answer to Press queries that he was a bit old for the job Claud pointed out that he was ten years younger than Macmillan. 'I think everyone realizes there's a rough time coming for the land of hope and glory' he said, 'and perhaps some people think that some of the real old roughs from the 1930s – it is fashionable to allege that we were starry-eyed idealists but we certainly knew where to put the razor blades in the potato when it came to a fight – might come in handy about now.' Almost as he spoke, the trial of Stephen Ward was opening at the Old Bailey.

It was always our intention with *Private Eye* that it should be a paper of information as well as jokes. The only trouble was that we had precious little information to print. Partly, no doubt, our youth and inexperience were to blame, but it was also true that neither Booker nor Rushton nor I were information-gatherers by nature. This is not just a question of getting stories but rather of knowing that there are stories to get, which demands a certain state of mind rather than a string of contacts. Claud had put the matter very well in *In Time of Trouble*. 'To hear people talking about the facts you would think that they lay about like pieces of gold ore in the Yukon days waiting to be picked up – arduously, it is true, but still definitely and visibly – by strenuous prospectors whose subsequent problem was only to get them to market. Such a view is evidently and dangerously naive. There are no such facts. Or if there are, they are meaningless and entirely ineffective; they might, in fact, just as well not be lying about at all until the prospector – the journalist – puts them into relation with other facts: presents them, in other words . . . . In that sense all stories are written backwards – they are supposed to begin with the facts and develop from there, but in reality they begin with a journalist's point of view and conception, and it is the point of view from which the facts are subsequently organized.'

Some doubts were expressed on the wisdom of inviting Claud Cockburn to edit the *Eye* on the grounds that having lived in an out-of-the-way corner of Ireland for the last few years he must inevitably be out of touch with what was going on. The doubters were confounded when he produced a story about an artist, Hal Woolf, that became front-page news in all the papers (see page 85). Mrs Woolf, the widow of the artist, had trudged round Fleet St with her story but had been dismissed as just another crank with a grievance. Finally she went to see Claud in Ireland and he, realizing at once that it was a good story, included it in his guest issue of *Private Eye*. It created an immediate furore and the Home Office were forced to set up an inquiry in response to the clamour of newspapers and Labour MPs. It wasn't bad for an Irish backwoodsman who was so out of touch.

The other thing Claud did was to name the head of MI6. Apparently this had never been done before and when I got back from holiday I was rather alarmed to be informed that all hell had broken loose, that the matter had been referred to the Prime Minister and that we would probably end up in prison for breach of the Official Secrets Act. By this time Claud, having laid his trail of havoc, had gone back to Ireland, leaving us to cope with any repercussions. These came soon in the shape of a visit from Colonel Sammy Lohan, secretary of the 'D' Notices Committee (who was later ignominiously sacked by Harold Wilson). The Colonel, a jovial figure with a bristling Kitchener moustache, seemed relieved to find that he had to deal not with the veteran trouble-maker Cockburn, but with a pack of obviously terrified overgrown schoolboys. After several drinks we were asked round to the Ministry of Defence, where Lohan read us a long lecture on the Red Peril and other topics relating to the National Interest. The object of all this was to persuade us to accept 'D' Notices – that is, printed details of secret matters which one is sent but not allowed to print. Eventually, which was no doubt the object, I became so bored that I agreed to accept the things. But the Ministry must have had second thoughts about it, for no 'D' Notices ever arrived. Perhaps someone thought that they would immediately be printed in *Private Eye*.

This was the only occasion on which the Government made any attempt to interfere with *Private Eye*.

**I**t takes some time to realize that the printed word has no effect at all on the behaviour of politicians. Important editors in ivory towers still like to think that their words can topple governments and change the course of events. It may be important for their self-respect that they should think this, but, in reality, nothing of the sort occurs.

To us in late 1963 it seemed almost incredible that Harold Macmillan should still be Prime Minister. We had done everything short of assassinating him. We had called him mad, senile, mangy and buck-toothed – we had accused him of lying, of megalomania, of treason. And none of it seemed to have had the slightest effect. The old fellow continued on his way as bland and unflappable as ever. It really was intolerable.

The end when it occurred was due entirely to chance. Macmillan had decided that despite all his difficulties he would lead the party at the 1964 election. But then he fell ill, and as had happened with his predecessor Sir Anthony Eden, the medical profession stepped in to decide the fate of the nation. Macmillan, convinced that he was very seriously ill and that he would be out of action for weeks following a major operation, decided finally to pack it in. He was said to be considerably annoyed when he was up and about in a matter of days, even more so when a few weeks later De Gaulle had exactly the same operation without even taking time off from his labours.

The ensuing appointment of Lord Home as Prime Minister produced an outbreak of hysterical rage in the *Private Eye* office which has never been paralleled. It seemed like Macmillan's final gesture of contempt for democracy to elect this half-witted Earl who looked and behaved like something out of P. G. Wodehouse.

Words were no longer enough; direct action was called for. In a euphoric lunchtime session at the Coach and Horses Rushton agreed to stand for Parliament against Home, who now had to resign his peerage and get elected as an MP. Within hours Peter Usborne had acquired an agent in the shape of Mark Heathcoat-Amory, a press release was made and offers of help were pouring in, most notably from John Calder, the publisher, who gave over his house for use as election headquarters.

It was an act of utter folly. The constituency of Kinross and West Perthshire where Home was standing was the third safest Tory seat in the country and consisted of 2,000 square miles of bracken inhabited in the main by sheep and pheasants. Pausing only to put together an issue of *Private Eye* wholly given over to the most savage personal attacks on Home, the entire staff adjourned to Scotland, where we found Rushton already installed in Calder's mansion. Calder himself had wisely decided to vacate the house for the duration of the campaign, leaving it in the hands of his butler, a man in comparison with whom Jeeves himself was an incompetent bungler. Whilst the girls dispatched the election address, a fine piece of invective written by Bernard Levin, Rushton and the rest of us (including Paul Foot, who had driven over from Glasgow) set out in a Landrover to make contact with the voters. There seemed to be very few of them about and they were certainly outnumbered by journalists who had poured in from all over the world to see the 14th Earl go through the democratic motions. Of Home himself there was no sign, though one could gather from the press that he was in

*Car sticker from the Rushton election campaign*

PROTEST VOTE RUSHTON

DEATH TO THE TORIES

Published by Mark Heathcote Amory, Agent, Ledlanet, Milnathort, and printed by David Philips, 16-18 Comrie Street, Crieff.

his element, receiving posses of loyal lairds and tenants. 'I just wanted him to meet my glenfolk,' said one lady.

Rushton's first public meeting had been arranged at the village of Killin by a local hotel-keeper of Irish descent. For the occasion a magnificent speech had been prepared containing not only jokes but a serious, well-documented account of how Home had been foisted on the nation by Macmillan in order to keep Butler out. All this was later to be confirmed by Iain Macleod in his famous *Spectator* article. But the seriousness of the occasion was spoilt by the Irish hotelier, who introduced Rushton with a highly incoherent speech during which he was observed to be swaying noticeably from side to side. When Rushton finally got up to speak he took a gulp of water from the carafe of water on the table, only to find, too late, that it contained pure Malt whisky. Despite this the speech went well, so well in fact that a few Tory lairds who were sitting up front felt obliged to try and demolish it at question time. But afterwards the Press were only interested in the identity of the meeting's sponsor, how to spell his name, how old he was and did he always behave like that.

It was the first time we had seen the Press in action and it was hardly an edifying sight. Rushton had had a rude introduction to them when he arrived at the Calder mansion late at night to find two well-known political journalists ensconced in Calder's sitting room drinking Calder's drink. Finding no one at home they had invited themselves in. In a way it was gratifying to discover that Lunchtime O'Booze really did exist. Though none of us dreamed of the lengths he would go to in order to bolster up Home's image as a democratic superman. A lot of this could have been excused on the grounds that they were 'only obeying orders', but there was and still is a strong element of sycophancy in the average Fleet St man who, when confronted by a figure like Home, instinctively tugs the forelock.

There was, too, a good deal of self-deception in the air. A lot of people find it difficult to accept that their political leaders are knaves and fools. They shy away from the thought and its uncomfortable consequences. So in 1963 they refused to face the possibility that the Prime Minister was a bumbling ass who had got his job as the result of a trick, and set about reassuring themselves and everyone else that the country was in safe hands.

In the event they were astonishingly successful. The prestige of Sir Alec (or Baillie Vass, as *Private Eye* readers came to know him) persisted throughout the decade, surviving all his ignominies and humiliations. In Tory circles the myth gained ground that the narrow defeat of 1964 would have been much greater had it not been for the Baillie's efforts, and when he was finally forced out of office as Leader of the Opposition in 1965 it was widely believed that he had stepped down of his own accord like the fine old gentleman he was. When he returned as Foreign Secretary in the Heath government of 1970 there was not a murmur of protest, despite the fact that he immediately perpetrated the first big clanger of the new administration by blurting out that arms sales to South Africa were to be resumed. It really was most odd, particularly since, when one thought about it, there was nothing whatever to be said in the Baillie's favour. In every political crisis of his career he had been on the wrong side: with Chamberlain at Munich, with Eden at Suez. During the thirties he had proposed, as a solution to the problem of unemployment, that out-of-work miners should be recruited into domestic service. Now he had become a Cold Warrior of almost Foster Dulles proportions – like so many of his generation who had lived through Munich, determined not to be caught out twice. Unable to face the fact that Britain was no longer a world power, he continued to subscribe to the view that it was our duty to keep the rest of the world in order and this meant, as he put it so well 'To carry weight we must be in the First XI and not only that, but one of the four opening batsmen.'

Rallying to the call, the voters of Kinross returned

*Poster by Barry Fantoni*

THE MAGAZINE THE MEN READ
PRIVATE EYE

him to Parliament with an enormous majority and the *Private Eye* candidate got only 45 votes (though this was no doubt due to the fact that at an eve-of-poll rally Rushton had told his myriad supporters to vote for the Liberal candidate, he being the man most likely to beat the Baillie).

**B**y the end of 1963 it was generally agreed by those who decide such things that satire was over. Nick Luard's *Establishment* Club and satire empire had collapsed in the summer. In November Sir Hugh Carleton Greene, Director General of the BBC, announced that *That Was The Week That Was* would not continue because of the forthcoming election. Exhausted by the long chain of excitements in 1963, culminating in the assassination of President Kennedy, the public underwent an inevitable reaction. At the *Eye* we entered a difficult period and the circulation, which had topped 80,000, the highest ever, during the Profumo period, now fell to about 20,000.

In the meantime, the original *Private Eye* team of Booker, Rushton and Ingrams had split up. In April 1963 Booker had gone off for three months to write a book. When the time had elapsed he wrote to Rushton and me asking if he could come back. We replied rather rudely saying no. The fact was that relations between us had grown increasingly strained. At the same time I felt that a strongly abusive note should be sounded and that Booker's rather more restrained approach was inadequate to cope with the horrors of 1963. His departure marked an abrupt change in the style of *Private Eye*. Booker had given the early issues their distinctive flavour – witty, sophisticated and urbane. In the ensuing months the tone became more strident, abusive and Left Wing.

The early *Private Eye* had been a fashionable success, owing its astonishing rise as much to the mood of the public as to the brilliance of its contents. We now had to survive solely on merit. It was equally clear that a diet composed solely of anti-Tory jokes was no longer acceptable. What was needed was the kind of thing Cockburn had done with his issue – scoops like the Woolf story. But Claud himself had gone back to Ireland and there didn't seem to be anyone else willing or able to take up where he had left off.

Luckily at this point, the nadir of *Private Eye*'s fortunes, Peter Cook returned from America, where he had been performing in *Beyond the Fringe*. By now Cook was the sole owner of *Private Eye,* having bought out Nick Luard when the latter's business empire collapsed. He set about the urgent business of salvaging the magazine's finances, contributing a hefty loan of some £2,000 and raising £100 donations from show-business friends. These subsequently were given £1 shareholdings in the paper, so that anyone who wishes to investigate *Private Eye*'s share structure at Companies House will find the following bizarre list of shareholders: Bernard Braden, Oscar Lewenstein, Dirk Bogarde, Bryan Forbes, Jane Asher and Lord Faringdon.

In addition, Cook became a regular contributor to *Private Eye*. Although he had acquired the reputation of a savage political satirist during the satire boom, Cook's talent has always been for outrageous nonsense fantasies. When he first came to *Private Eye* in the Neal Street days he would stalk about the room saying 'Good evening!' in an intense way and then embarking on lectures about enormous snakes 'many of them millions of miles long'; or he would impersonate a zoo keeper attempting to recapture a very rare type of bee which had become lodged in a lady's knickers. Cook bequeathed to *Private Eye* certain of its best-known expressions like 'not a million miles from the truth' or 'my lady wife, whose name for a moment escapes me'. Perhaps his finest creation was Sir Basil Nardly Stoads, head of the Seductive Brethren (see page 94). (This was the only occasion Cook actually *wrote* a piece for *Private Eye*. Normally he would walk up and down dictating.)

*Peter Cook*

Around this time, too, there appeared the first instalment of a strip cartoon entitled Barry McKenzie, written by Barry Humphries and drawn by Nicholas Garland. This was mainly remarkable for the astonishing expressions used by its hero, McKenzie, an Australian immigrant to London with rather basic tastes and an unusual vocabulary. I have never been quite sure how much of this is authentic Australian slang and how much is invention by Humphries. It includes a wide variety of expressions for urinating ('splashing the boots', 'shaking hands with the wife's best friend', 'pointing Percy at the porcelain') and vomiting ('chunder', 'liquid laugh', 'technicolour yawn', 'the big spit', etc). In between bouts of these two activities Barry's energies have been mainly directed at 'getting a Shiela to come across'. But despite what amount now to seven years of trying he has never once been successful.

Another brain child of Peter Cook's was *Mrs Wilson's Diary*, the first instalment of which appeared in November. Despite Lord Gnome's frenzied campaign to keep the Conservatives in, which included a series of election posters, a gramophone record (the first of a series) and a 'Stuff your own Quintin Hogg' cushion, the Labour party had won the election a month before, though with a much smaller majority than had previously been expected.

To those like me who had been brought up on the idea that the troubles of Britain sprung from the fact that the Tories were in charge and that they would largely disappear once the Labour Party got in, the advent of Harold Wilson to Number Ten was a climactic event. It took some time to adjust to the new situation. Consciously or not, the satire movement had been working with Wilson in undermining the fuddy duddies. The Wilson line, which was also inherent in much of the satire, was that for 13 years the country had been ruled by aristocratic amateurs – he used the cricketing analogy of Gentlemen and Players – and that he, the self-made professional economist, would soon set things to rights. This propaganda struck a chord at *Private Eye* and it took some time before we really got to grips with Wilson. The early *Mrs Wilson's Diary* concentrated on the social side of the new Prime Minister and the ridiculous contrast between the grandiose phrase borrowed from John F. Kennedy and Wilson's own suburban ambience. Slowly a composite picture of Wilson emerged, as a political Walter Mitty playing the part of Kennedy or Churchill as the mood took him, obsessed as any actor with his own publicity and neurotically suspicious of his colleagues. The *Diary* became *Private Eye*'s most successful feature. Two books were published (one of which was held up by Lord Goodman acting on behalf of Mrs Wilson on the grounds that people might think it had actually been written by her) and in 1967 Joan Littlewood put on a play which ran for nine months in the West End and was later seen on TV, though only after the ITA had deleted some of George Brown's lines. As far as I know Mrs Wilson never went to the play, but Wilson himself must have responded to the saga in some way, for in February 1970 he invited me and my wife to a reception at Downing St. It was disconcerting on entering not to find a dingy corridor leading down to the lounge and Harold's den. But any fears that the real thing bore no relation to the *Diary* were dispelled when we were introduced to Wilson by Gerald Kaufman. 'Y'know,' he said earnestly, looking round at the extraordinary assortment of guests that included Cliff Michelmore, Iris Murdoch and Morecambe and Wise, 'There are people here from all walks of life – artists, musicians, sculptors. Jack Kennedy's parties at the White House had nothing on this!'

It was not until the financial crisis of July 1966 that the real disillusionment with Wilson set in. It was then that his grandiose economic policy was seen to have been a sham. The resulting anger was more intense for the wild hopes that had preceded it. People were annoyed with themselves for having been deceived and this only intensified their vicious dislike of Wilson. *Private Eye* now dubbed him Wilsundra, after Dr Emil Savundra, whose mammoth Fire Auto and Marine Insurance Company crashed at about this time. From then on the magazine's attacks on Wilson were as savage as any on the Tories. Sell-out succeeded sell-out, culminating in early 1968 with Mr Callaghan's Kenyan-Asian immigration bill which finally destroyed any claim that Wilson might make to moral superiority over the Tories. *Private Eye* then published an obituary of the Labour Party.

**B**ut this was to come later. At the beginning of 1966, Wilson, who had been pulling out all his Churchillian stops over Rhodesia, won a resounding victory in the General Election in March. Meanwhile *Private Eye* was going through yet another crisis. The immediate cause was a libel action brought by Lord Russell of Liverpool. Though this only came to a head now, the article which caused all the trouble had appeared in issue 13 published in July 1962 at the time of the Eichmann trial. Russell waited for over a year before issuing a writ and the case dragged on for three years before it came to court. It was the first occasion on which we failed to reach an out-of-court settlement, and due to our inexperience of the workings of the law we had allowed it to drag on until it was too late to back out. Our lawyers advised us not to call any evidence and not to employ a QC. The advantages were, they said, that our counsel would have the last word with his speech to the jury and that by appearing to be not able to afford a QC we would win the court's sympathy. This advice proved to be mistaken. Lord Russell produced a seemingly endless stream of witnesses, including eminent dons and crippled war heroes, whose cumulative assertions were too much for our counsel to fight against with his single speech. In addition, Russell's lawyer made much of the fact that the *Private Eye* staff had not dared to go into the witness box and despite our obvious presence in the court, suggested we were skulking in our squalid Soho offices like the mean sneaky cowards that we were.

At the end of it all the jury awarded Russell £5,000 in damages, a colossal sum, far beyond our means. The situation was made worse when Russell's lawyers refused to accept payment over a period and demanded an immediate cheque. To many it looked like the end of the magazine. But once again Peter Cook came to the rescue. He set about organizing a mammoth Charity Matinee entitled *Rustle of Spring*, with tickets ranging from 10 guineas to three. An impressive array of stars offered their services free, including, in addition to Cook himself and Dudley Moore, Peter Sellers, Spike Milligan, Manfred Mann, George Melly (as compère), Roy Hudd and John Bird. Even the much-maligned David Frost volunteered to perform and was at once enlisted. A little difficulty presented itself when the Lord Chamberlain and the Lord's Day Observance Society objected to a Sunday performance, but eventually the show went on at the Phoenix Theatre (kindly lent by Bernard Delfont) on 6 May. The theatre was packed out and we raised over £3,000. Another £1,000 came from readers who sent in the money, often in small amounts, and by June we had enough to pay Lord Russell his £5,000.

There were still the costs, estimated at £3,000, and as if this were not enough we were now facing a bill of £1,000 from Quintin Hogg as the result of an out-of-court settlement. There is a traditional understanding that Ministers do not issue writs. The danger is of course that they will wait until they are out of office and then sue. Luckily for us Hogg did not demand his money immediately but agreed to accept payment by instalments. (Most litigants will do this, for the alternative is to bankrupt the magazine thereby killing the goose and its golden eggs.) After the settlement Hogg told reporters: 'I have absolutely no comment to make except that I am a generous man.'

1966 was a bad year for writs. In June the editor of the *Daily Express* issued nine and a newspaper report that this constituted a record against *Private Eye* drew an angry retort from Randolph Churchill, who claimed the all-time highest score with 13. It says a lot for the improved fortunes of the *Eye* that even with the help of the appeals and the concert we were able to stagger on in the face of this barrage of litigation. Certainly things were better; the circulation was up to 40,000 and the magazine was finally beginning to take shape as a combination of jokes and information – the shape it has preserved ever since.

At the back of the *Eye* Paul Foot had taken over the 'Illustrated London News' page which Claud Cockburn had contributed on and off since 1963. John Wells had left Eton and joined the editorial board; and Booker had returned to the fold in 1965, contributing a series of profiles called *Pillars of Society*, in which he singled out some fashionable idols for savage attack. In his new manifestation, Booker appeared as the sworn enemy of all that was new, dynamic and trendy – the Swinging London craze, Wilson's 'New Britain', the wretched Anthony Wedgwood Benn and the cult of dynamism and technology. At the same time Foot, his left-wing commitment hardened by years in darkest Glasgow where he had been working on the *Daily Record*, was attacking Wilson from the left – on Rhodesia, immigration and economic policy. Foot had come to London to join Hugh Cudlipp's *Sun*, as fine an example of the 'New Britain' as you could wish to find. The paper 'born of the age we live in', was typical of the botched efforts of old institutions like *The Times* and the Tory party, who during this period tried to get 'with it' and be young and classless, almost always with farcical results.

As well as Foot's page at the back we now had a thriving little gossip column at the front called the 'Colour Section'. This originated in an issue in 1964 which had been edited by Malcolm Muggeridge. Muggo, or the Guru, as we called him, had been introduced to *Private Eye* in 1963 by Claud Cockburn. He came to Greek Street with some reluctance, determined that he was an inveterate fuddy-duddy who had no part to play in the youthful satire movement. He was at once adopted as a kind of uncle to the magazine, to be rung up for advice about a tricky cover or a nasty libel action. It was he, for instance, who mediated between us and Quintin Hogg when the latter seemed bent on bringing *Private Eye* to its knees. At all times his advice has been invaluable, for he is one of the few journalists who has a genuine contempt for power and the people who pursue it. He had rightly seen in the early *Private Eyes* a tendency to view authority as 'a schoolmaster who when his back is turned can be pelted with paper darts and mocked with mimicry and funny faces'. It was largely thanks to him that we acquired a more mature approach.

A permanent reminder of Malcolm is contained in the heading of the 'Colour Section', in the shape of a small priapic gentleman riding on a donkey, an adoring young lady at his side. This Rabelaisian gnome was one of the figures in the frieze by 'Dicky' Doyle which had once adorned the old cover of *Punch*. He survived the Victorian period, unnoticed by any Mrs Grundy, and was only brought to light by Malcolm, who printed him on the cover of *Private Eye* in a 'blown up' version by Gerald Scarfe (see page 69). Later, when Bernard Hollowood, then editor of *Punch*, dropped the last remnant of the Doyle frieze from *Punch*, *Private Eye* adopted the little gentleman, and he remains on our masthead, a symbol of the vigorous satirical *Punch* of the old days which Malcolm had fleetingly revived.

*Punch's prick*

**W**ith Foot's invaluable help, the information side of *Private Eye* now began to snowball (he became a member of the staff in 1967). Starting with a few free-lancers and left-wing malcontents from the *New Statesman,* we began to build up a supply of sources. A regular Wednesday lunch was established in an upstairs room of the pub opposite the office, to which we invited possible informants – journalists, trade unionists, MPs (naturally I can mention no names). The existence of a Labour government was helpful to this endeavour. The Labour party gossips much more than the Conservatives who tend to keep their lips firmly sealed in deference to the concept of loyalty which has been instilled in them from their earliest years. But the average Labour MP will tell you two or three malicious stories about his colleagues within five minutes of acquaintance. The Labour party, too, conducts its disputes in public. Even the Wilson Cabinet found it hard to have any discussion without someone leaking the whole agenda to the press. At one point the situation got so bad that Wilson's Gestapo chief George Wigg was said to be going round asking which MPs had attended the *Private Eye* lunch.

Not that all our sources came from the Left. There are, we discovered, people in every organization with a strongly developed anarchic streak, mischief makers, mavericks, who like nothing better than to throw a few spanners in the works now and then. These people exist in Fleet Street, the BBC, the Civil Service and the City – even the Conservative party. They are people who are against the Establishment – whatever party it may subscribe to – and it is from their ranks that the *Eye* draws its informants and its readers.

As time went on, Foot developed from being simply a purveyor of gossip about politics and Fleet St and began to venture into other fields. It became evident that there are wide acres of territory into which the national newspapers do not go. There is, for example, the notorious lobby system whereby groups of journalists gang together and are 'briefed' by the authorities, on condition that they abide by certain rules like not revealing the source of their information. This system is not confined to political reporters. Industrial, crime, shipping, aviation and motoring correspondents are all to some extent prepared to sell their independence in exchange for a guaranteed supply of information. In some cases these journalists are little better than PR men for the organizations they report. It follows that several stories are never fully reported. There are other pressures on journalists which spring from the fact that the press has become part of the Establishment, maintaining a very close relationship with politicians and big business. Newspaper proprietors are made peers; city tycoons sit on their boards; the process may be observed in large newspapers as well as in intellectual weeklies.

So almost by accident *Private Eye* became a receptacle for all kinds of information which for one reason or another was being kept out of the papers. But not all our stories were Fleet St 'rejects', passed on to us by their disgruntled authors. There was most notably the Heart Transplant saga, when Foot, alone among British journalists, bothered to find out what was going on at Groote Schuur. There was Ronan Point – another technological disaster – and the long saga of the Concorde aeroplane; Israel, Greece and Northern Ireland; the Biafran civil war; the drugs industry; police and local government corruption; Porton Down – all these are stories which for one reason or another the national press do not report as fully as they might. *Private Eye* was the first to name the Kray Brothers in 1964 (see page 105), the first to reveal the facts about Dr Walter Adams when he was appointed principal of the LSE (see page 142) and the first to report that the South African government had told the MCC that D'Oliveira would not be acceptable as a member of the touring team of 1968.

It may sound as if we are blowing our own trumpet, but really these are only a tiny fraction of the stories that might have been printed in the period. With that in mind I have the feeling that the history of *Private Eye* as a journal of investigation is only just beginning. Some people seem to think that after ten years *Private Eye* has become 'part of the Establishment', whatever that may mean. In fact, in so far as it means anything, *Private Eye* has become more than ever before a thorn in the flesh of the authorities. To the trendies, currently bemused by the so-called Underground Press and the cult of Revolution and Pot, *Private Eye* may seem fuddy-duddy and old-fashioned. The authorities, judging by the number of writs and the continuing boycott by the distribution trade, take a different view. There are disturbing signs that *Private Eye* is at last being taken seriously.

It would no doubt be nice to look back over the ten years and make some meaningful remarks about the Sixties and the role of *Private Eye* as the vital influence that helped to shape the outlook of a generation. I do not intend to try.

*Private Eye* has made a living out of jokes and stories. We have eschewed, I hope, opinions, leaders, sermons, pontifications and other boring propaganda. What follows is simply a scrap book. If there is any moral or message the reader can decide for himself what it is. I can only echo Lord Gnome's words: 'This book traces the rise of the most consistently brilliant, amusing and informed periodical in the long history of journalism.'

Richard Ingrams *March 1971*

*The present nucleus (left to right): Fantoni, Foot, Ingrams and Booker*

*Authors*

From the beginning the jokes in *Private Eye* have been composed by a team. One person writes or types while the others contribute orally in the appropriate accent. Roughly speaking, the original team was Booker, Rushton and Ingrams and from 1964–6 Ingrams, Wells and Cook and since then Ingrams, Booker and Barry Fantoni, who first came to *Private Eye* as an artist in 1962. (In 1963 he and Rushton entered a painting, 'Nude Reclining', for the Royal Academy under the name of Stuart Harris, which excited a major artistic controversy).

Mrs Wilson's Diary was written by Ingrams and Wells from an idea by Cook.

The Footnotes are by Foot. The Colour Section by Foot, Patrick Marnham and one or two anons.

Contributors in the period 1963–6 included Bernard Levin and Alan Brien.

Additional jokes by Spike Milligan

*Artists*

Rushton did all the drawings in the early issues. He was later joined by Gerald Scarfe, Timothy Birdsall, Ralph Steadman and Barry Fantoni. Trog (Wally Fawkes and George Melly) joined the *Eye* after their Thalidomide cartoon (see page 63) was rejected by the *Spectator*. Other artists include Michael Heath, Bill Tidy, Frank Dickens, Larry, Hector Breeze and Nicholas Garland.

Lay-out by Tony Rushton, chief dogsbody and box-wallah. Photos by Maurice Hatton, Lewis Morley, Keystone Press.

*Notes for the Uninitiated, Foreigners, etc.*

LORD GNOME

The proprietor of *Private Eye*. He first appeared in Issue 4 as a press tycoon bearing a marked similarity to Lords Beaverbrook and Thomson. Since then his business interests have 'diversified' to include commercial TV and radio, washing machines, insurance, carpets, etc. A Conservative supporter, he was a prominent member of the 'I'm Backing Britain' campaign of 1968.

EMMANUEL STROBES

Personal Assistant to the above.

'GROCER' HEATH

The sobriquet was first used in November 1962 when Heath was conducting the Common Market negotiations in Brussels, determining the price of New Zealand butter, Kangaroo meat etc. He next came to prominence when he masterminded the abolition of Resale Price Maintenance in 1964. In 1970 he won the election on a pledge to reduce the price of groceries.

BAILLIE VASS

Sir Alec Douglas Home. See page 104.

LUNCHTIME O'BOOZE

*Private Eye*'s chief reporter. Invented by William Rushton in Issue No 7. Several Fleet St men claim to be his original.

GLENDA SLAG

A female columnist.

HANS KILLER

A Viennese-style music critic.

NEASDEN

An area of North London first mentioned in Issue 5. Used to denote the contemporary urban environment.

KNACKER OF THE YARD

A police inspector of very little brain and pronounced venial tendencies.

THE TURDS

A popular singing group invented by Peter Cook. Any resemblance to real live pop groups is purely coincidental.

WISLON

A frequent misprint.

THE GRAUNIAD

Ditto (sic)

"Lloyd George knew my mother"

FILM MAN DEAD (see page 17)

• • • • • •

"Josiah Berrington, who played small parts in several pre-war British film comedies, threw himself off Waterloo Bridge while "his balance of mind was disturbed" a South London coroner found today. Mr. Berrington was 58 and unmarried.

# BORE of the WEEK

**Q.** What exactly is new about old Punch these days?

**Mr.Punch.** Well, I must admit that when we took over a few years back, things looked pretty bleak. Lot of our oldest readers were actually threatening to cancel. Of course, the paper had been going a little too far --- politically I mean. Fellow Muggeridge never knew quite where to stop --- particularly over the Eden business, sick man and so on.

**Q.** But you soon got things ironed out again?

**P.** Oh yes, a clean sweep my dear fellow. Circulation chaps tell me things have never looked better. Got some of these layout boys in to spruce things up --- two columns instead of three, that sort of thing. And advertising too --- as I often say, the paper would be pretty empty without the ads.

# Mr Punch looks at Old Punch

**Q.** And what about your staff?

**P.** Oh, much the same you know. Still got Figgis the librarian, for instance --- been with us since 1899 --- checks the jokes to see whether they've been in before . . .

**Q.** No, I meant the writers . .

**P.** . . oh, the writers. Yes. Well, I do a lot myself, of course. Then we've got Boothroyd, Ellis, B.A.Young --- all veterans, can turn their hands to anything. And this new fellow E.S.Turner --- awfully good on anything that needs a bit of research.

**Q.** And the artists?

**P.** Well, I do a lot of course. Then there's Brockbank, who does the cars, Thelwell, does the horses --- and old Langdon, jolly good topical stuff. And, of course, we had to get rid of Illingworth --- apart from the expense. We've got this fellow Mansbridge for the political cartoon now --- may not be quite such an artist,but at least he can make a point without getting across people.

**Q.** You mentioned a clean sweep. Can you enlarge on that?

**P.** Well,even an old dog must learn new tricks. Magazines have changed a lot recently - gone in for all this glossy paper and so

on. Well,we felt something new was called for - new features and so on.Like our "Then as Now" column - marvellous how some of these old jokes stand up to the passage of time.

**Q.** Any other innovations?

**P.** Oh yes. We brought in our Toby Competitions - they've been a great success.

**Q.** But you no longer have the Toby Competitions.

**P.** Do we? I mean, don't we? No we don't, do we?

**Q.** You have that "First Appearance" feature.

**P.** Ah, yes. Bit short of writers - so what about the readers having a go?

**Q.** Mr.Punch,how do you see the function of your paper in our society today?

**P.** I'm glad you asked me that one. As the only humourous magazine in Britain,we feel a very real sense of responsibility to our readers. We've got to keep abreast of the times,take a cool, straight-from-the-shoulder look at contemporary fads and so on. We're particularly keen on keeping up with this lively younger generation we're always reading about.

**Q.** Isn't all this rather serious for a humourist?

**P.** Oh, dear me no. You see we are essentially funny about serious things. Punch is nothing if it's not bang up-to-date. Rock 'n roll, expense accounts, teddy boys, hula hoops - there s nothing going on we don't take a good laugh at.

**Q.** But surely,you're sometimes serious about serious things also?

**P.** Heavens yes. Serious comment is one of the things we're particularly proud of having introduced into the paper. My own Charivaria, for instance. Not without its spice of humour,but basically hardhitting comment on all the little follies of the Twentieth Century. Then there are these series we're always running about the things that really matter - the Affluent Society and so on.

**Q.** And finally, Mr.Punch,what of the future?

**P.** Ah.well. Doesn't always do to look into the future these days,does it? Find the present confusing enough sometimes.But I don't see why we shouldn't carry on much as we've always done in the past. As someone once said - and I think it's so very true - humour is a serious business. We've been in that business now for one hundred and twenty years. We know our humour.

"What with Selwyn's pay pause and Schedule A, we'll soon be playing cricket against the Common Market"

# PRIVATE EYE

incorporating THE FLESH'S WEEKLY

VOL I No 4        Wednesday 7th February 1962        Price 6d.

BRITAIN'S
FIRST
MAN
INTO
SPACE

ALBERT GRISTLE
AWAITS
BLAST-OFF

Ho Ho Very Satirical

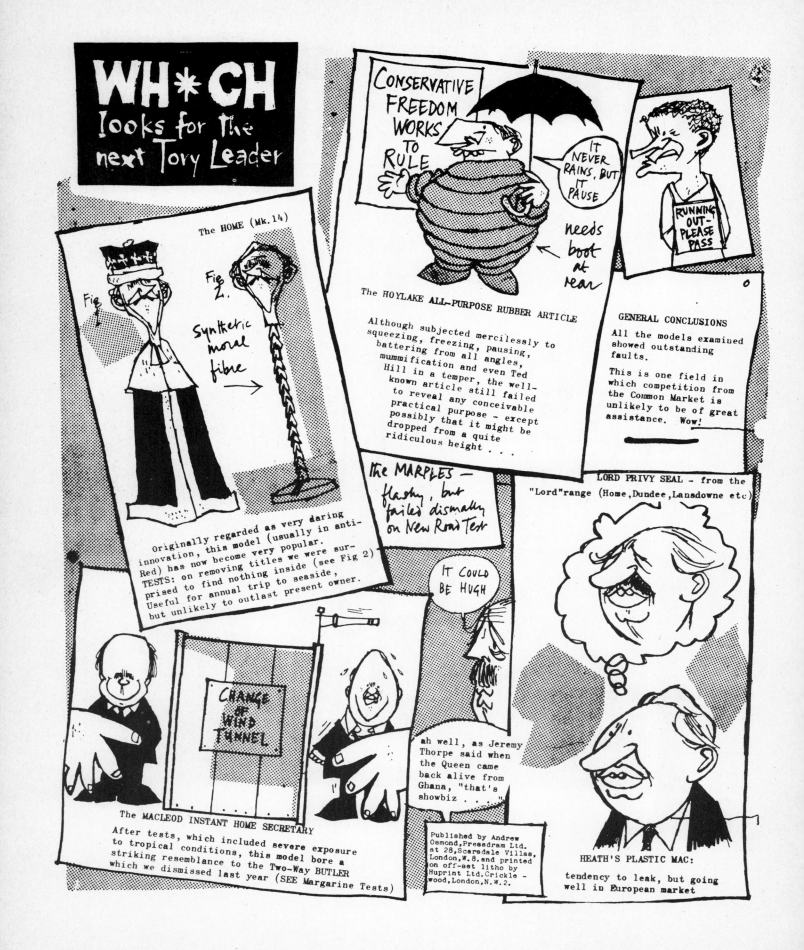

# WH*CH looks for the next Tory Leader

**CONSERVATIVE FREEDOM WORKS TO RULE**

"IT NEVER RAINS, BUT IT PAUSE"

needs boot at rear ←

RUNNING OUT - PLEASE PASS

**The HOYLAKE ALL-PURPOSE RUBBER ARTICLE**

Although subjected mercilessly to squeezing, freezing, pausing, battering from all angles, mummification and even Ted Hill in a temper, the well-known article still failed to reveal any conceivable practical purpose - except possibly that it might be dropped from a quite ridiculous height . . .

**GENERAL CONCLUSIONS**

All the models examined showed outstanding faults.

This is one field in which competition from the Common Market is unlikely to be of great assistance. Wow!

**The HOME (Mk.14)**

Fig 1

Fig 2.

Synthetic moral fibre →

Originally regarded as very daring innovation, this model (usually in anti-Red) has now become very popular. TESTS: on removing titles we were surprised to find nothing inside (see Fig 2) Useful for annual trip to seaside, but unlikely to outlast present owner.

the MARPLES — flashy, but failed dismally on New Road Test

**LORD PRIVY SEAL - from the "Lord" range (Home, Dundee, Lansdowne etc)**

IT COULD BE HUGH

CHANGE of WIND TUNNEL

ah well, as Jeremy Thorpe said when the Queen came back alive from Ghana, "that's showbiz . . . . ."

**The MACLEOD INSTANT HOME SECRETARY**

After tests, which included severe exposure to tropical conditions, this model bore a striking resemblance to the Two-Way BUTLER which we dismissed last year (SEE Margarine Tests)

Published by Andrew Osmond, Pressdram Ltd. at 28, Scarsdale Villas, London, W.8. and printed on off-set litho by Huprint Ltd. Crickle-wood, London, N.W.2.

**HEATH'S PLASTIC MAC:**

tendency to leak, but going well in European market

# ÆSOP revisited 1. The Satirist

Young Jonathan Crake shows early talent for raising laughs in School Play ...

... at Cambridge his gay, witty, little pieces in all the mags have the chaps in fits ...

... sparkling revue " Short Back and Sides " mentions Prime Minister. Crake acclaimed as biting satirist of our time ...

... instantly beseiged by press, TV men seeking views on Monarchy, Mr. Gaitskell, Common Market, Schedule A, the Bomb ...

... stage, TV, film offers pour in. Featured in five glossies simultaneously. Opens satirical nightclub in Fulham .. strain becomes terrific ...

... cannot open his mouth without everyone collapsing at brilliant satirical comment...

MORAL:

HUMOUR IS A SERIOUS BUSINESS

# You won't find us THERE

BUT you will from our business manager, ("a tall man with ginger knees"*) who resides at 37a Clephane Road, London N.1. Private eYe is now obtainable in the laughable Yearly package (twenty-six fortnight's worth) for 18/6, and a mere ten shillings for the handy six-monthly ECONOMY OFFER.

NAME

ADDRESS

Cheques, P.O.'s, betting slips payable to Pressdram Ltd.

*the poet milligan

"Nigel, I think we're going to have an abortion'

## THE WEEK'S GOOD CAUSE

It seems like only yesterday - those dear dead days when a packet of fags was only 4/6, when a pint and a box of matches still cost little more than half-a-crown, when you could have the night of your life down the Tottenham Court Road and still come home with change from a five-pound note.

How we danced - when Helen Shapiro was topping the bill at the old Palladium, there was 13/4 in every pound and good Queen Liz was firmly on the throne. It was in that Golden Age that out of a 6 guinea-a-week garret and a few pieces of string Private Eye was born.

Terylene-bound, hand-written copies of a new treasure for every family library "Private Eye Looks Back Over Two Weeks" will be available just as soon as the Editor recovers his ball-point pen. But meanwhile YOU TOO can be there - on the ball with the latest, up-to-datest satirical comment in Private Eye - the new comical weekly which is to appear in this experimental format every fortnight from now on.

Send just 5/-, repeat FIVE shillings, for an unrepeatable three-month, post-free, no-questions-asked subscription to:

The Circulation Manager,
Private Eye,
37a Clethane Road,
Islington, London N.1.
Cheques, postal-orders, betting slips payable to PRIVATE EYE.

Aristides P.Gnome.Proprietor.

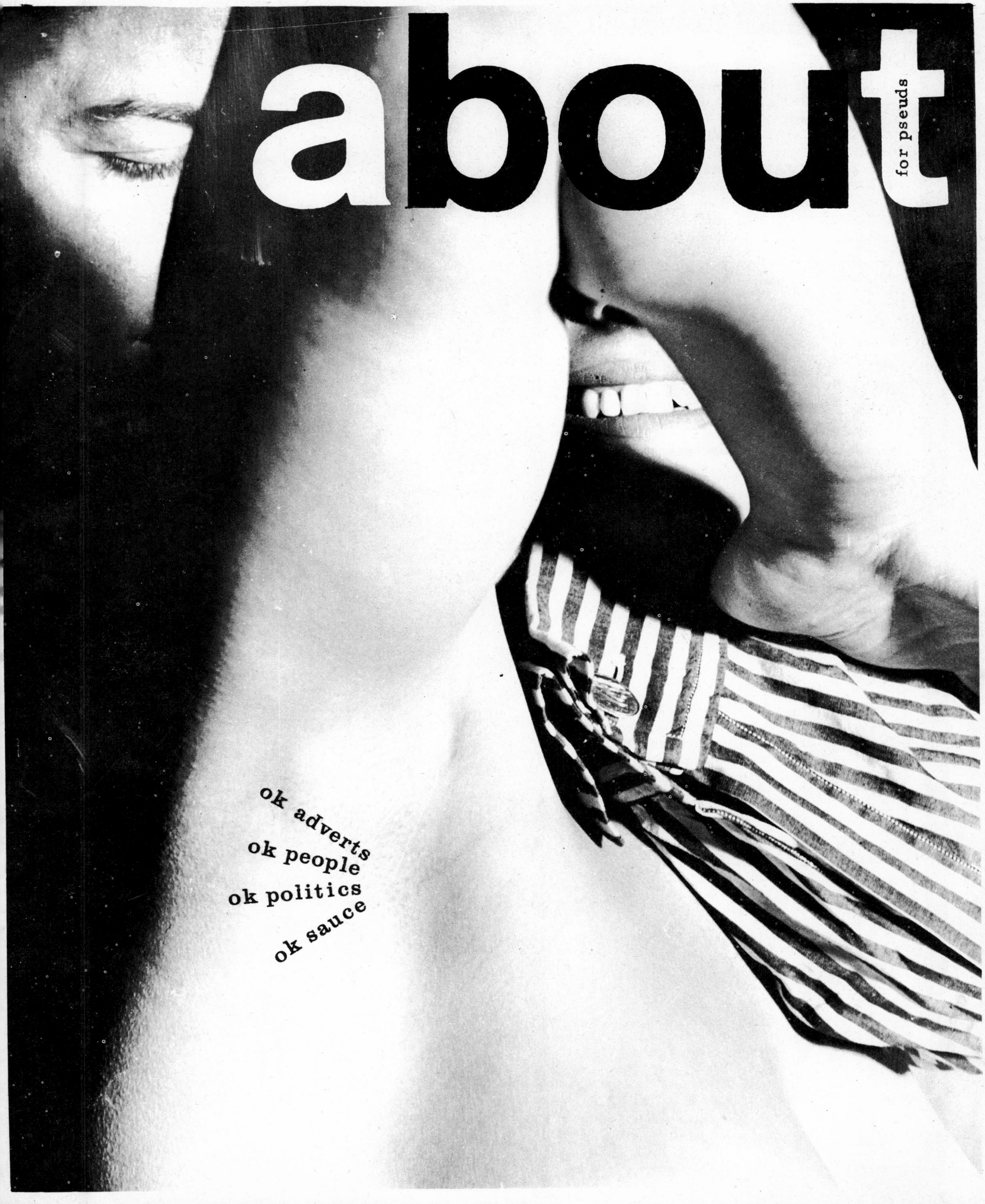

# about

ok adverts
ok people
ok politics
ok sauce

PUBLISHER Clive Brilliantine
EDITOR Clive Brilliantine
LAYOUT AND ARTISTIC DIRECTOR
Thom Woolsack
ASSISTANT LAYOUT AND ARTISTIC
DIRECTOR Brennan LeSmoothe
DESIGN ASSISTANT Denis Teeth
PHOTOGRAPHIC ADVISOR Norman
Plantaganet-Smith
ADVERTISING DIRECTORS Martyn
Martyns, Janitte Collingham-Gardens

writer: fred harbottle

# about

THORNTON WEEDS who
contributes the remarkable
series of photographic
self-portraits on pages
76-98 took up photography
two months ago. Success
has not blinded him - he
still uses Boots for his
developing.

MERRYMAN TUBE has
just come down from Cam-
bridge, and has already
had 17 novels published
by the avant-garde House
of Rupture and Tube. He
usually writes about Mada-
gascar where he was born
but writes on Eaton Square
on p. 216.

HARRY GASH has spent
28 of his 33 years in Her
Majesty's Prisons. This
has never been allowed
to interfere with his regular output of verse-plays
- his latest sucess which
has just completed its first
year in the West End being
"Arnty's Froats So Bleeding
Tuff it blunt me Razer". He
writes on the poems of Sir
Henry Newbolt on p. 326.

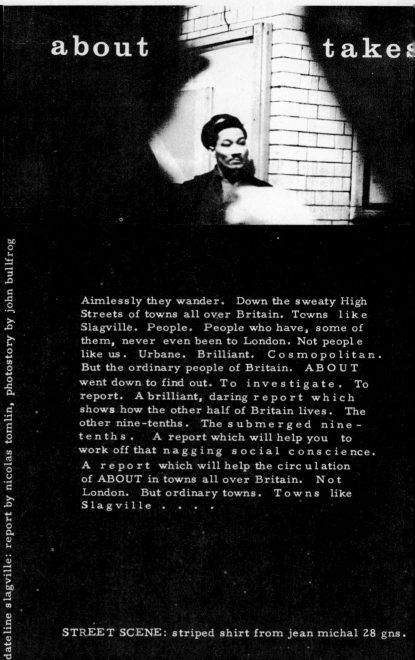

about                  takes

dateline slagville: report by nicolas tomlin, photostory by john bullfrog

Aimlessly they wander. Down the sweaty High
Streets of towns all over Britain. Towns like
Slagville. People. People who have, some of
them, never even been to London. Not people
like us. Urbane. Brilliant. Cosmopolitan.
But the ordinary people of Britain. ABOUT
went down to find out. To investigate. To
report. A brilliant, daring report which
shows how the other half of Britain lives. The
other nine-tenths. The submerged nine-
tenths. A report which will help you to
work off that nagging social conscience.
A report which will help the circulation
of ABOUT in towns all over Britain. Not
London. But ordinary towns. Towns like
Slagville . . . .

STREET SCENE: striped shirt from jean michal 28 gns.

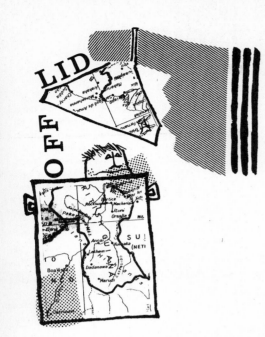

OFF LID

S
LAGVILLE

"NOT REALLY A PLACE
for old people Slagville -
they all die off in the fumes"
said an espresso-addict
in El Kardoma, the town's
most fashionable resort
for the younger set.
(sweater in pearl pearl
from Relaxinit of Chel-
sea at £32: 19: 11½.)
(three-quarter length
raincoat in beige from
Puddleware 64 gns.)

SATURDAY NIGHT
singsongs in the
pubs of Slagville
are famous where-
ever "a mickle maks
a muckle".

# PACE SETTERS OF 196TWO

We found him relaxing at home, the young man who is setting young London afire with his daring, brilliant ventures in magazine-publishing and money-making. In the Regency drawing-room of his riverside Chelsea pied a terre he sipped a daiquiri and listened to Dave Brubeck on the hi-fi. But there isn't much time for playing in the crowded life of Clive Brilliantine, the young man who brought off his first big property deal (in Stepney) when he was still a short-trousered young prep school boy. "They were exciting times" he remembers, "I kept on having to sneak out of school to appear before the Rents Tribunal". It was at Oxford that Clive first fell for politics. Today he is one of the best-connected and most brilliant members of the Bow Group. He is by no means an orthodox Conservative, "I do feel that race prejudice and the plight of the old people are the two most exciting challenges of our time" he said.

Today Clive, who is shortly to marry top model Gloria Gershwin, is well-known as one of London's best-dressed, best-looking, most brilliant men-about-town. "I have over 48 pairs of hand-painted ski boots alone" he said modestly. But Clive's most exciting venture yet started only two years ago when he bought ABOUT. "I thought it was time that brilliant, smart young people had something to read of their own" he says. It is almost entirely due to him that ABOUT is today the most exciting, daring, challenging, brilliant magazine in its field. And what of tomorrow? "I would like to be Prime Minister" he told us, with a shy smile.

# VAGUELY NOUVEAU

**DEREK HULL**

What a bore they are, aren't they? Those awful know-alls at parties who've read their Gilliat and their Lindsay Anderson, who can quote Sight and Sound at you from cover to cover, who've almost certainly "just flown back from Paris" where they saw Marienbad six months before it got to London. Whatever films you've seen, they're always one ahead. Whatever names you drop, they've always met the actual Director or Actress or critic in question.

Well, don't worry. For however little you know about films, you can easily (continued p. 78)

## DINING 'IN'

(continued from p. 87)

If you want to impress your friends with a knowledge of fashionable Tibetan delicacies, I strongly recommend the Bistro Lhasa which has just opened in the Kings Road. The House speciality is Buttered Yak's Hide on Charcoal which really ought to be eaten with a flagon of snow-washed Potala betel-juice (very intoxicating!). Your host who is most amusingly dressed as the Dalai Lama was in fact until last month Victor Emmanuel of the Terazza Via Appia in Frith Street.

Lastly, of course, there is always the Les Poissons du Nicholas II in Wilton Place, very chic at the moment with debs escorts, the smarter PR boys and the Belgravia arty set. The decor, by Sean Kenny, is based on a "fish and chip shop" in the North of England. The menu is starkly simple, being limited only to Fillet de Cod et Pommes Frites. Prices also are steep, working out with drinks (not licensed, I'm afraid!) at around three pounds a head. But remember - English cooking is coming back!

## More About Talk

(continued from p. 3)

money.
Today his ceramic designs for the pine-high soaring walls of New York skyscrapers have the art world at his feet. His latest commission, "Grandmother and Child", in grey-green amberglass, for the Executive Suite of a San Francisco toiletware manufacturer, will fetch him little short of $40,000,000. It is indeed pleasing to reflect that our age must be the only one in history in which artists have received their proper material due and recognition from their contemporaries.

# GNOME HOUSE historical survey

ABOVE: architects' drawing, as widely publicised on hoardings, in press etc. Particularly note harmonious blending of the building's sweeping line with natural surroundings.

BELOW: as building actually looks when built and fuss is over.

May 1961. Lord Gnome reveals at Annual General Meeting that Universal Products expansion plans are to include 105-storey new Office Block. "Everyone else is building them so why shouldn't we?"

June. First difficulties over choice of St. Pauls site. Lord Gnome finds he owns 51% share in Church Investments Inc. Difficulty overcome at Special Board Meeting.

July. "Save St. Pauls For The Nation" Fund opens, headed by John Betjeman, Nikolaus Pevsner, the Earl of Drift-wood and Lady Violet Bonham Carter. Gnome hires Public Relations firm.

August. PRO's advise 2-point plan:
1. That Gnome should offer accomod-ation to National Theatre in basement.
2. That design for new block should be thrown open to £5000 International Competition, with lucrative offers to sculptors and other artists.

October. Prix de Gnome awarded to Blowlamp and Partners for most flattering design (see left), reprinted in Times and Guardian.

November. Objection placed before L.C.C. Planning Committee that 678-foot Gnome Tower would cast 3000 acres of City into perpetual shadow, and that no provision was made in new building for parking. Gnome has L.C.C. Planning Com-mittee to lunch at Gnome Park, Surrey. Objections overruled.

December. Public Enquiry into loss of St. Pauls opens. Agreed after two weeks expert evidence that St. Pauls was "completely out of tune aesthetically with its surroundings". Prime Minister refuses to see deputation led by John Betjeman on grounds that "he really mustn't keep pestering me".

January. First sod cut by Lord Gnome.

February. Gnome discovers he hasn't enough employees to fill new building when finished. "Well, go out and hire some" he barked.

(So here we are.)

# SCALE MODEL DISPLAYED ON SITE

RIGHT: A young assistant explains the scale model to Sir Basil Blowlamp, the Architect of Gnome House

The erection of Gnome House will undoubtedly be the biggest single construction operation of its kind since the building of the advertisement for "King of Kings". It is, for instance, officially estimated that, during construction:

○ no less than 654,000 working days will be lost through unofficial strikes alone

○ the braces of the 22,846 foremen employed, if laid end to end, would stretch from here to Southend on an August Bank Holiday

○ more cups of tea will be drunk by Irishmen every hour than are drunk in Dublin every year. (If you think how many Irishmen are drunk in Dublin every year, you should have some idea)

It is also estimated that when the building is completed, no less than 17% of the people who enter it will never find their way out again.

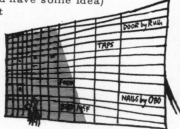

"Now, where did we leave that damn Foundation Stone?"

stage door of national theatre

ROYAL FESTIVAL HOLE

6. Basement includes swimming pools, bars, rifle-ranges, Bowling Alleys, Bingo Halls, and National Theatre, the "Princess Anne". Six-inch wings and discreetly hidden projection room make it particularly suitable for revival of "Ben Hur" six months after opening.

SPECIAL 'ROYALTY' STAGE designed to vanish after Premiere

1. Buckingham Palace Observation Platform
(special fees for Paris Match photographers)

frosted glass
(By Order of
Lord Chamber-
lain)

2. Note complete elimination of
windows. "Don't want employees
wasting my time looking at the
view" says Gnome, "why give
'em windows as well as Daylight
Lighting?" Walls are thus freed
for advertising of a suitably
tasteful character.

3. 53rd Floor reserved for Staff Fallout
Shelters. "We must not minimise the
danger from underground explosions"
says Gnome. Special Individual Shelters reserved for each Director (and
one Secretary). Mass-Shelter for
typists' pool - "it reminds me of the
Blitz" said Ivy Scroggs.

4. Another startling innovation,
architecturally years ahead of
its time, is the Elevated Pedestrian
Way two storeys up - keeping
main corridors of building free
of traffic.

5. Equestrian Statue of Lord Gnome
and family (symbolising, in the words
of sculptor Hugo Prayermat, "Fecundity")
sets off splendid All-Steel Entrance
Doors, leading into 800-foot Reception
Hall (with built-in Platinum Blondes)
in Spanish Rococo style favoured by
Lord Gnome.

Phalace of
Westminster

Proposed Site
of Gnome House

New Office Block
(name and purpose
have yet to be de-
cided)

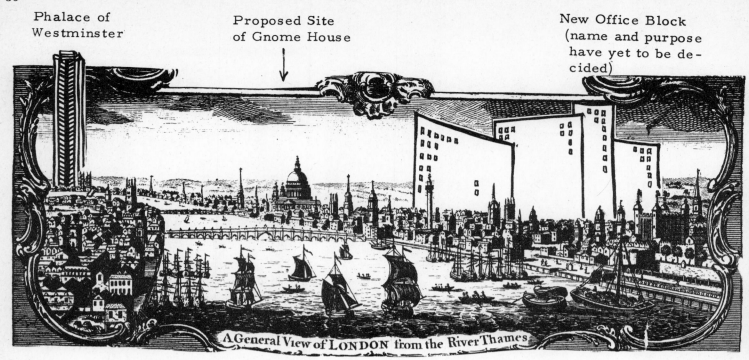

A General View of LONDON from the River Thames

# eYe views

# GNOME HOUSE

TEXT OF A GRACIOUS MESSAGE FROM LORD GNOME AT THE CEREMONIAL
LAYING OF A FOUNDATION STONE  FOR GNOME HOUSE:

It was truly remarked by one of our island poets, as he gazed at London's noble
skyline, "Earth hath not anything to show more fair".  It has been for every Age
to make its own contribution to London's indomitable character.  From the First
Elizabethans, Westminster Abbey and St. Pauls.  From our Victorian forbears,
our great stations.  And in our own age perhaps the noblest contribution of all -
the mighty Shell Building, the gracious Vickers Tower and the stately black
palace of one of my competitors in Fleet Street.  It is only fitting that the contribution of our generation should vie in splendour and size with that of  e v e r y
preceding one.  And that is why I do not think we should dwell unduly today on
the fact that in order to make possible our truly fine 105-storey Tower, designed
after the most exhaustive competition by many of the leading architects of the
day, and enhanced by the finest sculpture and most attractive mural-designs
that money could buy, it was unfortunately necessary to eliminate some fragments of our more ancient heritage.  But I am sure I am speaking for you all
when I say that, when Gnome Tower looks proudly out over London, and when
generations yet to come gaze up at its massive commemoration of the Se c o n d
Elizabethan Age, neither St. Pauls nor the Tower of London will, in truth, be
unduly missed.

# ÆSOP revisited

2. The Tele-Pundit

IT IS INDEED AN IGNORANT MAN WHO IS NOT FAMILIAR WITH THE WORKS OF SCHLEIST.

SO MUCH THEN FOR JEAN-JACQUES PISSOIR, THE WORLD'S GREATEST PLAYWRIGHT

For millions he is a fortnightly life-line to the world of books, art and Instant Culture - Hew Wellbread the omniscient compere of "Minotaur"..

...MOUTH MUSIC OF THESE IRISH PEASANTS WHO ARE STILL FREE TO MAKE THEIR OWN ENTERTAINMENT..

WISH WE HAD TV.

...from Schoenberg to Shakespeare, from Adamov to Zen, never at a loss for a name to drop or a life's work to summarise with a margarine smile..

BRILLIANT... WHAT A MIND... KNOWS MORE THAN C.P. SNOW... ...COO!

HOW DID ONE HEAD...?

...millions ask during Epilogue "How did one head come to carry all he knows?"...

LLANDISWL Y TWMGOCH BETTWS Y COE DAI BACH

WHAT'S HE ON ABOUT?

← CELTIC FRINGE

...Wellbread's career in culture begins as teacher of Lithuanian for Arts Council in Wales...

WHAT PRECISELY DO YOU MEAN, 'WHERE'S THE SKYLON'?

...as PRO to Festival of Britain first shows talent for disguising ignorance by quick comeback with the suave question...

I AM TRULY SORRY, MADAM LIVID OF HOUNSLOW, BUT MR MICHELMORE WAS NOT AWARE THAT HE WAS IN CAMERA...

...impresses BBC interviewers, particularly Arts Council tie, and taken on as PRO in complaints department ...is promoted to...

IN THE NEXT ¼-hour, CHILDREN, WE ARE GOING TO LEARN ALL ABOUT ART

...children's programmes as Uncle Hew, and so obvious choice in BBC eyes for new prestige programme "Minotaur".

MORAL:
THERE IS NO SUBSTITUTE FOR WOOL (so long as it's pulled with a will)

RESEARCH DEPT.

HURRY UP, WITH MY INTRODUCTION TO SCHLEIST, WILL YOU?

**66** On a high pinnacle of Israel's Mount Sinai stood a solitary, suntanned, 31-year old Jew. Behind him hovered the wiry little monster whom he knew only as 'Satan'. Together they looked out over the world.

" I will give you all this if you will bow down and worship me " said the Devil

Slowly and sadly the Jew shook his head.

JESUS CHRIST HAD MADE HIS FIRST BIG MISTAKE **99**

Only a man who himself has controlled the destinies of millions could tell such a story. Only a man who has shared the same temptations could relive the personal tragedy of

# The Divine Propagandist

Next week - Exclusive to the DAILY EXPRESS
LORD BEAVERBROOK'S LIFE OF CHRIST, AS TOLD TO GODFREY WINN

"Someone once asked me why I married the Queen. And I replied "Because she was there"".

# the last 5 years ?

HULLO - THEIR MISSILE

Aha - OUR ANTI-MISSILE MISSILE

Oh - THEIR ANTI-ANTI-MISSILE-MISSILE MISSILE

BRAVELY DONE LADS, OUR ANTI-THEIR ANTI-ANTI-MISSILE-MISSILE MISSILE

GOD, THEIR ANTI-OUR-ANTI-THEIR-ANTI-ANTI-MISSILE-MISSILE-MISSILE-MISSILE

SPLENDID SHOW! THERE GOES OUR—

OH!

OH, DEAR FIFTEEN - LOVE

# PRIVATE EYE

## A FORTNIGHTLY LAMPOON

Vol. 1 No. 10      Friday 4th. May 1962      Price 1/-

The poet Milligan speaks — page 9

# AESOP revisited

5. WORKER'S PLAYWRIGHT

1956. Osborne, Wilson, Lard burst upon cultural scene. "At last a real breath of the slagheap" lauds Cyril Connolly, who has never seen one except from train window on way north to Edinburgh Festival.

I MUST HAVE A SINK IN MY DRAWING-ROOM

COLIN WILSON SWEPT HERE

*!?ω!?

WARDEN SPARROW!

SINKS

PETER

Meanwhile in East End kitchen Ambrose Weskit gathers material for new play. "What do these men know of genuine working-class life?" he muses, "Osborne even went to a fee-paying school".

BOTHER!

ROOTS

BARLEY

JERUSALEM

CHICKEN SOUP

Weskit's play "Boots in My Soup" opens in Midlands. Instantly acclaimed as "at last a real breath of Stepney" by Kenneth Tynan who lives in Hampstead ...

Capri

..AND THEY'RE NOT EVEN JEWISH

...Weskit observes Osborne etc. lunching at Caprice, becoming tycoons, wearing suits. Determines to remain true to working-class so..

...approaches T.U.C. chiefs with plan to bring genuine culture to workers (plays by Weskit etc.) through nation-wide network of Festivals, shopstewards etc.

THINK!

STRIKE NOW

.. BUT WOULD IT BE GOOD FOR OUR "IMAGE?"

CENTRE £

Murder by the RED BARD a melodrama for the people
Φ Φ with Φ Φ
Sir J. Gottlieb
Sir S. Milligan
Sir L. Bart
Fred Nacker
÷ ÷ ÷ ÷ ÷

TONIGHT

... Centre For-Ward becomes intellectual rage. Charity Matinee of Victorian melodrama given in old music hall to raise funds ...

FOLK OFF

FOLK MUS

Foden Mot

FOLK ODE

FOLK OFF

FOLK DRAMA

FOLK SONG

FOLK DANCING

TAKE FIVE

...at last Weskit opens Grand Consolidated Festival of Folk Arts and Crafts in Scunthorpe - ceremony coincides with Coronation Street - only three people present ...

moral

ART IS A BOURGEOIS CONCEPT

# a taste of living

NOW SHOWING

cert **X**

## HOW WE MADE 'TASTE' by Karl Ritzinger

**I**t all began when Tony rang me one morning to suggest lunch. "I've got an idea here that might interest you" he said. We met at the Caprice, and after a Truite Ronay and some excellent Balsacher '47 we got down to coffee and cigars. "I thought we might do something on the lines of a film" he suggested. I was definitely interested. We met again the following week at the Trattoria via Appia in Frith Street, and after some of their superb Veal Valpolicella Tony took up the subject again. "About this film" he said, "I've been looking at the takings of Karel and John's latest, and I definitely think there's something in it". We discussed the various problems involved, such as distribution and budgeting, but I told him that I liked the idea a lot.

Within a matter of days we had the luck to beat Woodfall to the rights of Stan Blister's little known novel "A Waste of Living" - by a mere £50, as it turned out - and although we knew that the generally drab, pessimistic tone of the book would have to be changed for the screen, by changing the title and cutting the double-suicide ending, we felt that we had here the raw material of a really down-to-earth portrayal of life as it is actually lived in the North of England, by the great mass of the people who actually live there.

We were lucky enough to find two exciting new cheap unknowns in Alfred Weights and Shirley-June Tush to play the lead parts of the latently homosexual professional lacrosse player Arthur Sidmouth, and Doreen, **the** girl who watches sympathetically from a bar stool in the film's opening shots as Arthur vomits up his half-pint of ginger shandy. (CONT .)

"There's only one way to put pace into a picture: that's to keep your characters running".

KARL RITZINGER

The next day Arthur goes to the park on a lonely long-distance training run.

As he runs he muses to himself: "Twenty-five quid a bloody week and what've you got to show for it at the bloody end but a cupboard full of filthy bloody shirts and a hangover from Saturday night. Being alive these days you might as well be bloody dead, what with the Government and the price of beer".

At this moment he meets Doreen, who has been down to the corner to get a packet of fags for her Mum

A. Hullo then.
D. Hullo.
A. What'yer doing then?
D. Bin down to corner to get some fags for me Mum.
A. My name's Arthur.
D. I'm Doreen.

Within minutes they are on Art and 'reen terms. They walk innocently hand in hand through the park, high above the smoke and the squalid terraces - in another, cleaner, purer world of their dreams . . .

A. 'Reen?
D. Yes, Art?
A. What you say we go over to my place - me Mum's out and me Dad's over at Club.
D. Really, I don't think my Mum would go much on that.

But the waiting millions at the box-office would, and cannot be denied, and soon the couple are on their innocent way, past little laughing groups of white and coloured children playing together in the mean streets . . . .

... and they run ... and they run ... and they run ...

The next scene speaks for itself.

Naturally, since it's her first time and since this is a British movie, the following scene ensues some weeks later . . .

D. Arthur?
A. Yes, love, what is it?

D. Arthur, something hasn't happened that should have happened.
A. What do you mean, something hasn't happened that should have happened?
D. What I mean is that unless the something that should have happened and hasn't happened doesn't happen soon, something that shouldn't happen's going to to happen.
A. But are you sure love that just because the something that hasn't happened that should have happened hasn't happened, it really means that what shouldn't happen's going to happen?
D. All I know is if something that should happen doesn't happen soon, something else has got to happen.
A. I just don't know what on earth you're on about woman.
D. What I mean, Arthur, is . . . . we're going to have a . . .
A. . . .bloody hell. Alright, I better go and see my Aunty. She knows what to do about these things . . .

. . . and so, when all else has failed, and the thing that shouldn't have happened finally happens, Arthur and Doreen get married
. . . and live squalidly . . .
. . . ever . . .
. . . after.

THE END

# AESOP revisited

Young Arthur Philistine arrives in Fleet Street from provinces. Instantly bewitched by Romance, Glamour, Adventure of the Street...

...catches eye of the Lord. Becomes youngest Editor on Street...

...by stopping at nothing and obeying everything becomes wild success ... sales in Rhyl soar ...

...regardless of the Lord's opinions sales continue to soar ...

...but eventually Philistine is forced to retire. Writes autobiography "Dead Lines All My Life", packed with Romance, Glamour, Adventure of the Street. Stars as himself in filmed version "The Day The Daily Express Caught Fire" ...

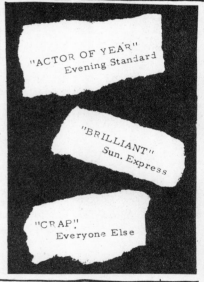

"ACTOR OF YEAR" Evening Standard

"BRILLIANT" Sun. Express

"CRAP" Everyone Else

...joins TV company as Special Advisor on Romance, Glamour, Adventure of the Street ...

...forced to "resign" for personal reasons. Wildly misquoted by reporters as to real reasons ...

MORAL:
ONCE YOU'VE GONE ON THE STREET, YOU'VE GOT TO STAY THERE

# AESOP revisited

7. T.V. COMIC

After undistinguished career blowing own trumpet in army, Tony Halfcock opens at Windmill. Spotted one lunch hour by talent-spotting BBC producer . . .

. . . 'alfcock's 'alf 'our opens with Kenneth Williams . . . wild success . . .

. . . Williams dropped . . .

. . . 'alfcock moves to TV with Sid James . . . wild success . . James dropped . . .

. . . having turned down film offers for years until right one came along, Tony finally makes "The Rabble". A right one it is. After showing at five film festivals it fails to make general release . . . Tony forced despite artistic convictions back to TV . . .

. . . given entirely new character by scriptwriters Simpson and Galton . . series wild success . . . acclaimed by intellectuals . . .

. . . Simpson and Galton dropped . . decides to write own scripts . . .

. . . BBC forecasts wild success. BBC dropped. 'alfcock disappears to evolve new image . . .

MORAL:
To Thine Own Self Be True

. . . 'alfcock disappears.

# The un-Making of the President

## CHAPTER ONE - THE GRAND DESIGN

"The best way to win a democratic election is to get more votes than your opponents." This old adage of American political folklore became a fast favourite with John F. Kennedy during his campaign for the Presidency.

But now all this lay behind him. As the dawn slanted down over the Appalachians and the first snow flurries of January ran down the frosted, leafless lanes of New England and the Pacific breakers rolled in on the golden beaches of California Kennedy sat up through the night with some of his top aides - O'Brien[1] O'Donovan[2], O'Sorensen[3] and analyst Lou Harris - pondering the next moves.

As always in conferences of this kind, John F. Kennedy was superb. For twenty minutes he talked, giving a complete rundown on the situation as he saw it and only breaking off from time to time to bounce an old football round the room. "As Jefferson used to say, we're not going to get very far just by sitting still. I told the American people they were facing a grave crisis. And although they elected me, they obviously didn't believe the bit about the crisis, otherwise they wouldn't have so damn nearly elected Dick Nixon. Now I am elected it is vital I appear as a man of my word. We must find that crisis, we must create it if necessary, and we must project it to the nation with all the vigour and skill at our command."

## Chapter Two - FORECAST OF TOMORROW'S PAST

The day is short and light/the night is long and dark". This quotation from the great American poet Robert Frost became a fast favourite with John F. Kennedy during his first few months in the White House.

[1] now Executive Personal Assistant to the President
[2] now Personal Executive Assistant to the President
[3] now Assistant Personal Executive to the President

The Oval Room in the White House is long and rectangular in shape. It contains a desk, a chair, and most important of all to John F. Kennedy, a telephone. Kennedy is the first President to have been born since the invention of the telephone, and he probably makes as much use of the instrument as any President in history.

From that wan January day, the Grand Design of Hyannisport evolved inexorably towards its end, stage by stage, with clockwork Kennedy efficiency.

The first step was to create artificially a critical situation so vast, so ridiculous, so incredible that no one would possibly blame it on the President. Something that would therefore be blamed on somebody else, on anybody else - such as the Russians, or the previous Administration or the C.I.A. The answer, finally arrived at after analyst Harris had taken sampling returns from thirteen predominantly Protestant precincts in Des Moines, Iowa, was Cuba. Invade Cuba, with a force so pitifully small that the expedition could end in nothing but disaster, and the nation would rally to the President as the only man strong enough to save the U.S.A. from Fidel Castro.

## Chapter Three - PRESIDENT FOR KENNEDY, Round SEVEN

The morning sunlight was slanting down on the plasterboard offices of a small town newspaper deep in the heart of Texas, as a large white Cadillac drew up to deposit a certain local cotton farmer and the newspaper's proprietor.

A thousand miles away in Washington John F. Kennedy was busily scanning the columns of the New York Herald Tribune as he prepared for the coming day's engagements.

The two events had outwardly little in common. But slowly, inexorably, inevitably the lives and the names of the two men were to be drawn together across the great anonymous gulf that is American democracy.

For the cotton farmer's name was Billie Sol Estes. And the part he had to play in the Grand Design was by no means small. For after analyst Harris had obtained sampling returns from no less than three predominantly negro precincts in Nashville, Tenn., it was agreed in the White House that nothing was so likely to produce a sense of national unease as the realisation that half the Administration, right up to and including two members of the Cabinet, was under strong suspicion of having been connected with bribery, corruption and fraud on a vast scale, almost unparallelled in American history.

## Chapter Four - WAITING FOR WALL STREET

"If you get enough people worried, you may start a panic". These words of Emerson's, with which John. F. Kennedy used frequently to regale newsmen on his private plane during the 1960 campaign, came back to the President many times at this stage of building the crisis.

It was at this stage that, on the advice of analyst Harris and speechwriters Sorensen and Schlesinger, he warned America in his by now immortal words "we are about to invade Siam". It was at this time, too, that he put in his shrewd blow to look as ridiculous as possible by cancelling his subscription to the Herald Tribune.

But the final stage of the Kennedy crisis came with his deliberate slapping down of the steel companies. Analyst Harris's sampling returns showed John F. Kennedy that nothing would be so likely to cause widespread lack of economic confidence than the realisation that the Administration and Big Business did not see eye to eye. Sure enough, Kennedy's carefully calculated move paid off. Within a matter of weeks the market was sliding as it had never slid before in the great history of the American democracy.

By 1963 America was in the grip of total crisis - abroad, at home, and in every field. She was involved in war over Siam, her missiles failed to work, her economy had come to a dead stop.

In the prevailing mood of crisis the great American people turned at last to the single man, the prophet in the wilderness who had warned that this would happen. John F. Kennedy was unanimously acclaimed as the only man who could save America from itself.

I admit the Immigration Bill ran counter to all my principles . . .

Of course I shared everyone's doubts about Hanratty's sanity . . .

And I know that flogging lunatics in gaol doesn't do anybody any good . . .

The fact remains - I'M JUST A FLABBY FACED OLD COWARD

P.S. And what's more, he's such a flabby faced old coward he won't even sue us.

P.P.S. And even if he does sue us he's STILL a flabby faced old coward.

This is why people like Adverts least ... soft pretty
Adverts, soft absorbent adverts produced by once talented
men with soft absorbent brains.  There's only one use for Adverts
like these.

ERIC BUTTOCK WRITES
.HOME . . .

Dear Mummy

larst wek transport house (thats Gaters house) had
there house Fate in the park.  it was called the
festival of Laber ha ha and evryone had to mak
flotes of there one, to sho there House Spirit Spirit.
It was orl joly xpensive about £700 per flote
so george Brown he's the Skool Buly think how
can we pay for it orl.  he also think how can i be
more poplar at the sam time, sinc he hav ben
somewot in the doghouse recerntly.

then he com up with this brite weeze why dose
he not get old bert rusell to pay for it.  so he
sa 'bert' i see you hav not paid up yore 6d.
sub. to the deb.soc.  and anihow you are just
a peenut and a komunist.  so were going to
xpel you or else.

then he find that old Gaters hav not paid up
either so quikly he get gaters to pay up,  then
he find that old Bertie hav frends, Chorley
and Colins (he's the Skool Chaplin) and Matron
wooton but Ruthless Gorge disregard them orl
and stil go on trying to tak the Mikey out of
Bert.  then he find that 150 thousand other men
hav not paid up for Deb.Soc either but StILL
he go on with his litl game.  Finerly Bert sa
"but i hav paid up", so anyone with sens would
think Gorge mite pull out and xxxxx save his
face wots left of it.  but he kik out old bert
anihow and dosnt even get his 6d.

now George is evn more in the doghouse xh than
ever almost as bad as Ian macloud in tories
house, xxxx so old mac, hes Hed of Skool,
sa joking to Gaters why do we not xchange
George brown and macloud.  but noone is having
ani so it look as if noone is going to win the nex
elekshun at orl xept posserbly the xxxx scotish
xxxxxxx Nashnerlists ha ha

me  luv eric

← Old Black Gaters he say:
'I kno all about defence
I've been sitting on it foryears

What on earth does he know about it ?

"Of course, we modern Christians have got
a long way beyond thinking of God simply as
a kindly old gentleman, with a long white
beard and blue eyes, sitting on a cloud somewhere vaguely above us . . . "

Richard Burton to teach English at Oforxd
*SCOTSMAN*

"TAKE YOUR SEATS FOR THE LAST SUPPER"

# PRIVATE EYE

No. 15
Friday
13 July 62

1/6

Price 1/-

# MAC - NEW BULLETIN

**HE'S O.K!**

# SATISFACTORY !!!!

### YES, THE PRIME MINISTER'S CONDITION IS 'SATISFACTORY' - AND THAT'S OFFICIAL!

MR. MACMILLAN WAS STATED LAST NIGHT TO BE 'SATISFACTORY' AFTER AN OPERATION HAD BEEN CARRIED OUT ON HIS MOUSTACHE.

Tension mounted all day outside the Basingstoke County and General Hospital as vast crowds gathered anxiously in the forecourt - crowds of photographers and newsreel cameramen anxiously jostling for shots of the seventh-floor window behind which the full drama of the Prime Minister's operation was being enacted.

From time to time one could see a nurse passing the window, in full nurse's uniform of white cap, starched apron and blue dress. From time to time one could see her pass back again.

The Prime Minister arrived at the hospital yesterday in a horse-drawn vehicle. Crowds gathered round the entrance as he was carried in to the operating theatre, shouting "Get well Mac" and other encouraging slogans.

#### HOME ON THE MANGE

Fears in the medical profession that the mange which had attacked Mr. Macmillan's moustache might have spread to his brain are now lessening.

OUR POLITICAL CORRESPONDENT writes:

It is understood in political circles that Mr. Macmillan was anxious to go to the country as soon as possible after his operation, to allow the wave of popular sympathy which has welled up some more tangible form of expression. But he has been restrained from this course by his medical advisers who state that he is in no condition to do anything but convalesce - which he will probably do, encased in plaster, propped up on the Front Bench alongside the stuffed effigies of Mr. Selwyn Lloyd and Mr. R.A. Butler which have, of course, been there for some time.

OUR MEDICAL CORRESPONDENT writes:

It is quite usual for a man of such advanced senility as Mr. Macmillan to suffer from mange. This eventually results in the head of the patient falling down into his body. However doctors are now able to deal with the disease with a simple operation whereby the head, having been located, is readjusted on the shoulders by a metal framework which joins above the upper lip and can be concealed by a false moustache.

Behind the window was the hint of a curtain, of a sort of gauze material, and looking bravely out on the dramatic scene - a single drooping aspidistra.

Get well messages to the Prime Minister had been pouring in all day from world leaders past and present - such as Chancellor Adenauer, Sir Winston Churchill and President Eisenhower.

MR. MACMILLAN'S ROOM (ARROWED) ON THE SEVENTH FLOOR.
The County and General Hospital at Basingstoke was endowed by private donation in 1917.

Early this morning he was reported as having sat up and asked for chicken and the Earl of Home sat with him for several hours.

# PRIVATE EYE

No. 16
Friday
27 July 62

Price 1/-

# NATIONAL GALLERY STOLEN

A COUNTRYWIDE police search for the National Gallery, missing since last Tuesday, may have stumbled across a vital clue.

The clue arrived at Sotland Yard yesterday in the shape of a Picture Postcard from Scarborough, bearing four views of the municipality from different angles and the legend Greetings from Rhyl. The card, which was postmarked Bognor Regis, also carried the following message in block capitals:

THE GALLERY IS SAFE. IT IS IN GOOD HANDS, SLIGHTLY DAMP. YOU WILL GET IT BACK IN XCHANGE FOR FREE PARDON, MATEY. AND RAIL FARES RETURN.

The postcard was addressed to Sir Philip Hendy, the ex-Gallery's Director, who was, of course, kidnapped last week and has since been returned in a brown paper package to the Arts Council with a note reading 'Sorry, Our Mistake'.

A spokesman for Scotland Yard said last night:

"It is plainly the intention of the thieves to hoodwink the police into thinking that the National Gallery is in Scarborough or Rhyl. Of course the Bognor Regis postmark gives them away."

Police have issued the description of a man answering to the name of the Earl of Crawford and Balcarres. Tall and scarfaced, with a tattoo of the Leonardo Appeal Fund on his left knee, he was last seen on a No.73 bus carrying a large bag. It is thought that the bag may contain the missing Gallery.

OUR ART CORRESPONDENT WRITES: (and indeed draws, but only for a fee)

Following the Bridges Report, this latest theft has only served to reinforce the view, held by some, that all pictures should in future be kept in storage, and only be seen by the public on the production of a written affidavit signed by the Trustees of the Gallery concerned. Sir John Rodent, the Director of the Tate Gallery, said recently:
"The time has come when some pictures are too valuable to be viewed by the public. We at the Tate, however, have deterred potential thieves by including a large quantity of worthless reproductions, forgeries and other artistic jokes on our walls. The result is that no one here is quite sure how much the pictures are worth, or indeed whether they are in fact pictures at all.

The absence of the Gallery, which was not officially noticed until Friday of this week, has caused something of an uproar in artistic circles.

## LEGEND

(a) The site of the theft.
(b) Route believed to have been taken by thieves.
(c) Police are baffled by the fact that the thieves totally ignored St. Martin's-in-the-Fields.
(d) An omnibus of the type from which the theft was first observed.
(e) The spot from which Pigeon-fancier Tradethroat observed the theft actually taking place, and
(f) the pigeon he fancied.

Despite the fact that the police search for the missing building has so far proved futile, the authorities are confident of an early development for redevelopment by Cotton. "All airports are being subjected to a rigorous scrutiny," said the Yard spokesman, "and it is most unlikely that the thieves will succeed in smuggling the Gallery out of the country. Our art correspondent explains: The very size of the Gallery is sufficient to render such a feat improbable.

Rumours that it had been broken up and smuggled out of the country as Northamptonshire Brick have been discounted. No brick is made in Northamptonshire.

# anatomy of Sampson

INTRODUCTION.

Eighteen months ago I was rash enough to embark on an investigation as to who really runs Britain. I wrote to 200 Top People and invited them to lunch with me, which, with the exception of Mr. Charles Clore who could afford his own, they all did. I also read a few memoirs and odd newspaper clippings, and picked up a lot of old Whitehall gossip. I then had to produce the book as fast as possible, before it became out of date. The result is as follows.

CHAPTER ONE        DUKES

"Better a young Duke than an old windbag"
Disraeli.

In 1933 there were 45 Dukes in the United Kingdom. Today there are 36 (including the Irish Barons). Most of them are men and their average age is 45.7. On the whole they keep themselves to themselves, are very rich (only three of them actually have jobs, all in the Government) and live in Southern Rhodesia. The others are landowners and live quietly on their estates. In some cases these estates are very large. An estimate of the annual bag on the estate of the Duke of Throstle gives some idea of its size:

Grouse       273
Partridges  164
Deer          72
Pigeons   5,789
Peasants      6

But by and large Dukes as a race are on the way out. This is evident from the decrease in the number of butlers employed by the Dukes. In 1925 there were 703 butlers in service. Today there are 62 (4 of them Dukes.)

CHAPTER TWO        THE MONARCHY

"The days when a Sovereign could order the chopping off of Ministers' heads are long since gone".

Walter Bagehot.

In 1900 there were 84 Kings in Europe alone. Today there are only 5, including the Queen of England. She is closely related to them all, and most of the 84 Kings in 1900 have turned out to be her Great Grandfathers. The Queen is a shy woman, with a high-pitched voice and few close friends. They include Lord Rupert Nevill, Prince Philip and her horse. She lives in a flat at the back of Buckingham Palace, and during last year took part in:
    4 State Visits (Malagassey Republic,
                         Tonga, Nicaragua)
    1 Trooping the Colour

She also spent:
    6 weeks at Ascot
    4 weeks at Goodwood
    6 days at Epsom

and Launched:
    1 ship
    457 plaques
    5 regiments

It is evident from this list that the Queen does not run Britain.

CHAPTER THREE        THE CIVIL SERVICE

"In the Corridors of Power there are many doors but few windows".
C.P.Snurd

In 1920 there were only 245 Civil Servants in the whole country. Today there are 15,673,825. When one considers the decline in Britain's position in the world during this period, this represents a remarkable increase.

Civil Servants live in a closed world of their own, a world of teacups and discreet whispers. The senior ones are quite highly paid, and many of them went to Oxford or Cambridge. The lower grades tend to be paid rather little.

Some Ministers tend to take a great interest in the affairs of their Departments. Others, quite wisely, when faced with their top Civil Servants take to the grouse moors.

CHAPTER FOUR        CONCLUSION

Who then runs Britain? Where is the true seat of power? Does it lie beneath the Italianate cupolas of Whitehall, or the Gothic pinnacles of Westminster? In the glossy boardrooms, or the ducal palaces? Or does it lie perhaps in the strange, indefinable, almost mystic link which binds them all? As Sir Charles Snurd once said: "The face of power is a grey man, walking down a grey corridor, and murmuring "we'll fix it later"". Perhaps we shall never know who that man is. Certainly, after eighteen months as a glorified gossip-columnist, I myself haven't a clue.

The Duke of Bedford = Nancy Mitford

The Duchess of Kent | Lord Beaverbrook (Minister of Aircraft Production) | O = Harold Macmillan (Chancellor of the Exchequer) | O = Evelyn Waugh

Sir Malcolm Sargent = THE EARL OF HOME | Norman Mailer | Nancy Mitford    CROMER | John Betjeman

H.M.Queen Elizabeth = O | | Hugh Carleton-Greene

LORD GNOME | John F.Kennedy= CHARLES CLORE | Nancy Mitford = The Earl of Waldegrave (MINISTER OF AGRICULTURE)

Unity Mitford | Randolph Churchill | The Marquess of Salisbury (PUBLIC HOUSE) | 45th Duke of Abercorn

SYMBOLS
O= Deceased Wife (of)
△ = GOVERNOR GENERAL or above

(Compiled from Observer Cuttings Library)

# ÆSOP revisited

EVERYTHING SEEMED RIGHT FOR ROLLING STONE, THE FAMOUS RACING DRIVER . . . . FAST CARS . . . . TRAVEL . . . . . MONEY . . . . . BEAUTIFUL WOMEN . . . . AND EVERYONE SAID THAT HE WOULD SURELY BE THE CHAMPION DRIVER OF ALL THE WORLD . . .

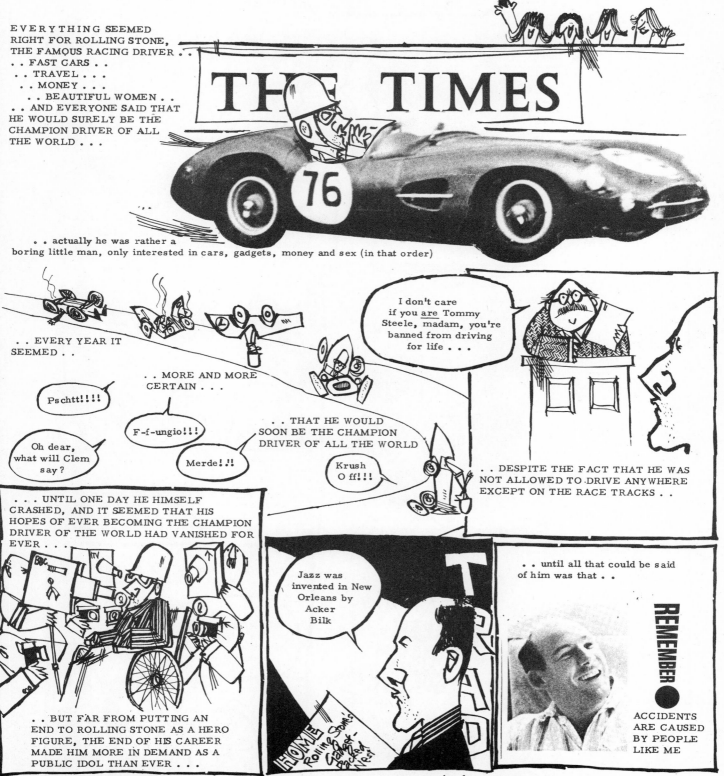

page 55

. . actually he was rather a boring little man, only interested in cars, gadgets, money and sex (in that order)

. . EVERY YEAR IT SEEMED . .

. . MORE AND MORE CERTAIN . . .

Pschtt!!!!

F-f-ungio!!!

Oh dear, what will Clem say?

Merde!.!!

. . THAT HE WOULD SOON BE THE CHAMPION DRIVER OF ALL THE WORLD

Krush O ff!!!

I don't care if you are Tommy Steele, madam, you're banned from driving for life . . .

. . DESPITE THE FACT THAT HE WAS NOT ALLOWED TO DRIVE ANYWHERE EXCEPT ON THE RACE TRACKS . .

. . . UNTIL ONE DAY HE HIMSELF CRASHED, AND IT SEEMED THAT HIS HOPES OF EVER BECOMING THE CHAMPION DRIVER OF THE WORLD HAD VANISHED FOR EVER . . .

. . BUT FAR FROM PUTTING AN END TO ROLLING STONE AS A HERO FIGURE, THE END OF HIS CAREER MADE HIM MORE IN DEMAND AS A PUBLIC IDOL THAN EVER . . .

Jazz was invented in New Orleans by Acker Bilk

. . until all that could be said of him was that . .

REMEMBER

ACCIDENTS ARE CAUSED BY PEOPLE LIKE ME

. . filling the gossip columns with trivia about his private life . . .

. . introducing TV programmes on subjects about which he knows nothing . .

. . and, of course, as always, he remained the inspiration of every young man with too much money, not enough sense, and a Sprite.

# ÆSOP revisited

Bored with pre-War life as City gent, IAN PHLEGM finds Glamour and Romance in Naval Intelligence . . .

I'd like you to cover this Jamaican Tour, Phlegm, and watch the exes will you?

THE SUNDAY TIMES

. . after War joins Sunday Times. Misses Glamour and Romance . . .

Jamaica, I'm afraid 00Bond, and kill anyone you like.

. . . Phlegm's fantasy goes to work - imagines himself as BASILDON BOND, Lover, Gambler, Conoisseur and Secret Agent Extraordinary...

Crumpet?

. . . writes brilliant thriller, packed with Sex, Gambling, Brand Names and Violence...

To: Editor, Spectator
Dear Sir,
I find the adventures of Mr. Bond utterly depraved, sadistic, snob-ridden and revolting and am much looking forward to the next.
yrs. etc

All pornography should be Bond

Attaboy.. kill 'em all

. . . adventures of Bond wild success in all quarters . . .

AAAAHH!

And send up another woman, who'll be stirred but not shaken

. . . Phlegm forced to churn out more and more adventures of Bond - each one more fantastic, more packed with Sex, Violence and Brand Names and worse than the last...

THE PLOT SICKENS...

It's a Colt .45 and I've had my 45

. . . finally Bond utterly exhausted by Sex and Sadism ... Phlegm accused of pinching plots ... in last book cannot raise more than 20 pages of Bond ...

CAN PHLEGM SURVIVE ?

SPLAT! ZUK! YAROOO! POW!

BATTERED, BLEEDING AND WRITTEN OUT, HE IS ENTIRELY AT THE MERCY OF HIS PUBLISHER, THE DREADED SIR JONATHAN RAPE ONLY A MIRACLE CAN SAVE PHLEGM....

..SUDDENLY!

**MORAL** YOU CAN ALWAYS PUT OLD WINE INTO NEW BROTHELS

It's all right, Phlegm, we've sold the film-rights. You won't have to write another for ten years

# THIS PICTURE COULD MEAN WAR

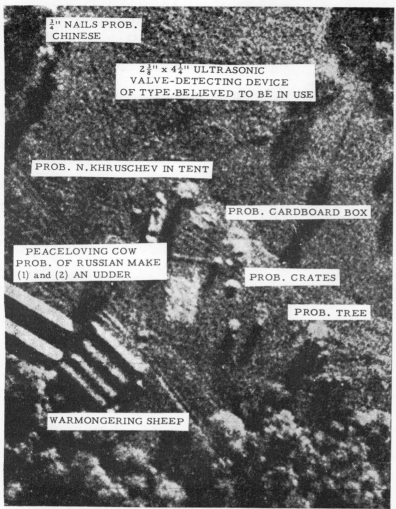

¾" NAILS PROB. CHINESE

2⅜" x 4¼" ULTRASONIC VALVE-DETECTING DEVICE OF TYPE BELIEVED TO BE IN USE

PROB. N. KHRUSCHEV IN TENT

PROB. CARDBOARD BOX

PEACELOVING COW PROB. OF RUSSIAN MAKE (1) and (2) AN UDDER

PROB. CRATES

PROB. TREE

WARMONGERING SHEEP

\*

16 FISHBEDS    9 FAGOTS    12 FISHBEDS    8 FAGOT

## LORD HOME AGREES

YES, THIS IS THE PICTURE THAT COULD MEAN WORLD WAR III.

To the ordinary peaceloving reader it may look just like an ordinary clump of trees in any old field. Which is, of course, what it is.

But the trained observer looks beyond the simple peaceloving blades of grass, the few freedom-hungry sheep. For when this picture is blown up 24,000 times it shows nothing less than an enormous underground missile site. On neat racks lie hundreds of nuclear missiles, each one carefully labelled with the name of an individual American city and the words "Made in Russia".

THESE ARE THE SECRETS REVEALED BY THE EVER-VIGILANT EYE OF THE PEACELOVING U2 PILOT AND THE CAREFUL USE OF WHITE INK IN THE PENTAGON PHOTOGRAPHIC SECTION.

● These are also the pictures, it was revealed last night by the Danish newspaper Dagbladet, that were taken last year of a Montana chicken-ranch for its millionaire owner Homer Q. Tilt.

\*    \*    \*

Miami, Florida

There is an air of indescribable tension in this waterfront town here tonight.

During the past few days, half the United States Army has moved into Florida to play its vital part in the forthcoming Naval blockade. "Operation Peaceloving", as it is known, is proceeding smoothly, despite last night's revelation that President Kennedy's pictures were all fakes.

Said Kennedy himself: "What the hell - the show must go on".

Commented cigar-chewing, grenade-throwing 7-star General Otis P. Kneethug, in charge of naval operations: "These Chinese must be taught a lesson".

Lord Home expressed concurrence with these sentiments. "It is quite right to point out that these pictures are fakes; but I am right behind the President in any move he cares to make".

Fig. 1
Harmful, warmongering Russian ship to be stopped at all costs.

Fig. 2
Harmless, peaceloving American ship that will do the stopping.

(The difference is apparent from the smoke)

---

Among the installations spotted by the U2 in Cuba are several 'Nests of Fagots' (or Pooves, as they are known in this country.) In Washington yesterday, I was shown pictures of the Pooves taken from 97,000 feet and magnified 4,500 times. (see picture above.)

"They are bearded little men" said the Washington spokesman, "wearing swimming trunks".

It was probable, he went on, that they were being trained by Soviet Fagots (flown into Cuba last month) to undermine the moral strength of the peaceloving Western hemisphere.

As the Vassall case demonstrated only this week, the Russians have employed the same devices to great effect in our own armed services.

President Kennedy stated in his speech last night:

"There can be no doubt at all

that these Fagots are of a hostel and offensive character, and as such constitute a definite threat to the peace of the Western world. It is our opinion that they are being trained in Cuber with the intention of eventual infiltration into the United States to subvert and sabotage the Constitution - as we have already seen from the film Advise and Consent, Communist influences in Hollywood have long since blueprinted the course such subversion may take".

OUR MEDICAL CORRESPONDENT Writes:

"The Washington pictures show very clearly the characteristics of the Fagotus Cubanus Castratus, or lesser bearded poove, one of the most deadly and carniverous species of poove. Any contact with this species causes moral decay, and eventually imprisonment and death".

The Earl of Home expressed full agreement with this view.

In view of our 'special relationship' I do think he might let me stand a little closer

"When I heard that President Kennedy had blockaded Cuba...

...I thought 'Christ! Now we're for it. This idiot is going to have us all blown up'...

THE QUESTION EVERYONE IS ASKING * * * * * * *

q●Why wasn't Macmillan told?

q●He was, but he forgot.

NEWS IN BRIEF * * * * * * *
The city of New York was today wiped out by a series of nuclear explosions. No Britons are reported as being amongst those killed - R.I.P.

... Now it looks as if things are going to be all right ...

... so I'm all for JFK. He was quite right to do what he did."

# Lord Home agrees

"I HAVE HEARD IT SAID . . .

. . THAT I AM NOTHING BUT A PUPPET. . .

. . . I SHOULD LIKE TO MAKE IT ABSOLUTELY CLEAR . . .

. . . THAT THIS IS NOT TRUE ".

Can't you see I'm busy

3 a.m. NEWS

Castro talks to "Sunday Telegraph"

**Anglo-Bulgar Wool-gathering**

# THE GAURDIAN

**Friday November 31 1962**    Price 4d

## SPRING COMES TO ULLSWATER

## Farming Community 'Unruffled'

From the PRESS ASSOCIATION

Ullswater, Wednesday

Spring has arrived in Ullswater, it was officially announced here tonight.  The official stated later that all seemed 'calm' and that demonstrations were unlikely.

Certainly the local inhabitants seem, outwardly at least, to be taking the events of the past twenty-four hours in their stride.  There is no air of panic or hysteria in the streets, and there would appear to be a strong feeling locally that this thing was inevitable.

At the same time, there is in certain quarters a strong undercurrent of suspicion about possible repercussions in fields other than the purely agricultural.  It is known, for instance, that events of this nature can be liable to trigger off further incidents of a more intimate, and ultimately even possibly compromising nature.

It is this factor which has alarmed the more conservative element of the population.

There is no sign yet of any Governmental response to the situation, but an official of the local Post Office stated last night that this would probably provide "greater opportunities for fishing".  The statement was taken here to mean possible international intervention, from what source or on what scale it is difficult as yet to assess.

The Tide of History, perhaps?  No, just a peaceful scene in Regent's Park

## E.E.C. Forty Years On

By LEONARD BEATEN, our Common Market Correspondent

The traditional Common Market negotiations are still dragging on here in Brussels, becoming daily more baffling in their complexity.

Particularly to myself, since, as a Canadian by birth, I am not really interested, and as a Defence Correspondent by profession, I have little knowledge of the issues involved. All I do know, is that only the Gradian would be silly enough to send a man of my qualifications off on a wild-goose chase like this.

## Go West, Old Man

From ALISTAIR CREAK
Miami, Florida
With Richard Nixon now gone to a villain's grave, unwept, unhonoured and unhung, with Washington once again flexing all its energy and subtlety for another round of skirmishing along the New Frontier, with the pavements of Fifth Avenue and Chicago's legendary Loop blistered by the oven-heat of an Indian summer, it seems a far cry from that wet and windy day some quarter century ago when first I stepped off a boatfull of rotting bananas with nothing but a typewriter and a flattened Liverpudlian accent to my name to cover the Land of Opportunity for The Gaurdian.
Now, of course, with all my other more lucrative commitments, I have little time to dash off more than the odd bit of election gossip to distant Manchester, while Max Freedman works overtime to keep you all posted on what's actually happening over here - but, of course, he's so boring that you probably never find out.  Still, I'm glad the paper can still take the credit for having my by-line from time to time.

### CHINESE ADVANCE CONTINUES

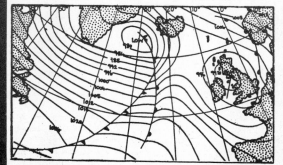

The Chinese today continued their advance.
(BBC News Bulletin)

### Tomorrow's paper

Much the Same

## THE GUARDINA

Manchester Friday
November 25

# "No News is Good News"

It was a celebrated dictum of C.P. Scott, Editor of The Guardian for over 90 years, that "comment is free, but facts are sacred". It is an axiom that might well be taken to heart at the present time by the rest of Fleet Street. Facts, the very stuff of news, are indeed sacred. And yet other newspapers, such as The Times and the Daily Telegraph, consistently scatter facts around their columns with what, in less grave a situation, might well be regarded as gay abandon. Facts are too sacred to be treated merely as fodder for the Press Barons.

The Garduian alone has consistently upheld the high standards of Scott, in ruthlessly ignoring such facts as may leak through to us. And yet, in certain sections of the press, we are bitterly reviled for our moral purpose. In last week's Spectator, for instance, appeared a vicious smear that for us today "comment is free, but facts are expensive".

While, as a paper of principle, the Garduian is not rich - it is indeed up to its ears in debt - it is not going to fritter away its valuable resources in a frivolous search for truth.

We have a small, but select band of correspondents, scattered across the world, of an extremely high calibre. Every one of them, in fact, is of such quality that they receive a by-line for their pieces. If facts should come the way of our correspondents, then we shall fearlessly publish them. If they don't, then quite properly we shall leave them out. That is honest journalism, in our finest tradition.

If, on the other hand, our readers should happen to buy another newspaper, and thus discover what they are missing - then that is their affair and not ours.

## mainly for women

### FIREWORKS IN THE HOME
#### by Alison Allovertheplace

The most important thing for a young mother to remember about Christmas is that it is quite the most dangerous time of the year for children.

The Christmas tree and its fairy lights may look quite charming as the centrepiece of your home decoration, glowing in the corner of the drawing room. But just one small tug - and a happy family festival can end in tragedy. For even fairy lights must use electricity - and we all know what that can lead to.

So I suggest that this year you try celebrating Christmas without a tree. After all, forethought is the best form of insurance.

The same goes, of course, for any old fireworks that may be left over from Guy Fawkes day. The safest thing here is to soak them all thoroughly in water before use - thus minimising any

## review

### SILVESTRI CONDUCTS

#### by NEVILLE BORDUS

Mahler's Fifteenth at the Festival Hall! A massive work, lasting well over five hours, and scored for a choir of 600 and an orchestra of 104 instruments.

It is a scandalously neglected work, and at the same time, one of the masterpieces of modern music. The towering genius of Mahler, illuminating even at its most banal, exciting and at the same time tedious, what can we say of it?

The Fifteenth is Echt Mahler. It contains some of the finest statements he ever made and it illustrates the profound romanticism of this great poet, at the same time it has been completely disregarded, except by warped old critics like myself.

Also in the programme were Bach's B Minor Mass and several new works. All seemed to be well performed.

### A COUNTRY DIARY

With the new one-way traffic system now in operation in Earl's Court, many visitors to the 43rd International Banking Congress are finding difficulty in parking their cars within walking distance of the hall. One Indonesian delegate, who arrived in Kensington High Street, asked a policeman to direct him and was advised to leave his car in the new underground car-park at Marble Arch. He arrived at the Congress twelve hours late.

### NEW PLAQUE

A small ceremony will take place a week on Thursday at Number 83, Graceneedle Street in Streatham. For over six months, in 1883, the house was occupied by Sebastian Stringling, the well-known archivist and bookbinder, who did some of his best work on his own home-made machinery in the basement. The Chairman of the L.C.C. Education Committee is to unveil a plaque in his memory.

### FISH INSTITUTE

The foundation stone of the New Commonwealth Institute for Re search into Tropical Fish will be laid today by the Burmese Ambassador, Mr. Bom Too. The building

## Furthermo

by W. J. Weatherby

It has taken a long time for th American public to recognise genius of Ferther Moore, the young novelist who has recentl published Nigger Man, a torri story of the south which goes f beyond Faulkner or Tennessee Williams.

## Mr Khrushchev's warning

By VICTOR ZSAZSA

The Albanian People's Daily yesterday revealed that the Baluchistan oat harvest had failed for the third year in succession. This is undoubtedly evidence that the rift between Moscow and Pekin is now wider than ever before.

The news, which was given full prominence on page 17, also confirms recent speculation that the more liberal faction in the Kremlin is losing ground again to the advocates of a tougher line in relations with the Western bloc, particularly in relation to a settlement over Berlin.

This latest move by Tirana also provokes speculation over the position of two other countries in the Warsaw Pact, Bulgaria and Rumania, both of whom recently sent delegates to the Albanian-Soviet International Friendship and Brotherhood Week celebrations.

One feature of this latest development that is puzzling Western experts is the fact that no oats are in fact grown in Baluchistan - but most Soviet

**WHAT? STILL AT IT?**

He has been compared by some American critics to Melville. Wrongly, I think, for there is more of Fenimore Cooper about him, and something even of Hawthorne.

But I recognised his genius as soon as I met him. At first meeting he is a shy, retiring man with a deprecating manner that belies his obvious stature as a writer. We sat for three hours in Hank's, a small Scandinavian bistro on the fringes of the Village, and after a few vodkas (Moore is a great admirer of Pasternak) he began to talk freely of his childhood.

"Mother was a cow, Pop was a drunk. I kinda went my own way". I mentioned Dostoievsky. He lit a cigarette. The waiter hovered, and refilled our glasses. I was reminded of O'Neill. I spoke about him for at least half an hour. When I had finished, Moore was gone.

## Impressive display by Germans

By Cyril Chapman
Aston Villa 0, Southampton 1

*The Guardian*

Mr Healey was still standing at the despatch box, engaged in the dispatch box, engaged in Powell when the debate adjourned until today.

*The Guardian*

No One Understands Us Either

JOSEPH ALSOP: As this correspondent said last week in the
New York Herald Tribune, and
he likes to repeat it here on
Mondays just for the extra £10..
FRANCIS BOYD: ...well, of
course, they never really intended me to have this Column
at all. But when they asked me
what I thought about someone
doing a political piece here on
Tuesdays, I jumped in quickly
and said "Yes, of course, I
think I can squeeze it in." But
there's nothing new for me to
say, you know, except about
the Hull University Liberals...

LORD ALTRINCHAM: I really
think after having to apologise
to President Kennedy for being
so rude, I'd better play safe by
not saying anything ...
RICHARD CROSSMAN: I find
it so different from being a
columnist on the Mirror. I
mean, here I can really
rake up some political dirt,
even if it's only what we
were gossiping about in
the Commons the night be-
fore . . .

A peaceful scene in Regent's Park? No, just
another bloody dull picture from the Gaurdian.

**STOP PRESS**

# MAC TELLS TERMS OF POLARIS DEAL

EVENING STANDARD

## It's packed with dynamite

BRITISH NUCLEAR SUBMARINE DREADNOUGHT - of the type which is unsuitable for the firing of Polaris missiles. As can be seen from this top-secret Admiralty diagram, the ship's motive-power plant leaves little room for armaments.

**OUR DEFENCE CORRESPONDENT EXPLAINS:**

Yes, Mr. Macmillan has done it again. He has returned from Nassau, not with the Skybolt, nor even with the Polaris - which will not be available until 1973, by which time, of course, it will be quite obsolete.

Instead, in his pocket, he carries a special intermediary Polaris - which will see Britain over the awkward intervening years during which she will be exceptionally vulnerable to Soviet attack.

\* \* \* \* \* \* \* \*

Why is this missile so special? Simply because it is not a complicated conventional nuclear device, triggered off by complicated technical machinery- but a simple rocket which any child, let alone Mr. Macmillan, could operate. BECAUSE IT IS FIRED BY SIMPLE OLD-FASHIONED DYNAMITE!!

As President Kennedy is believed to have told Mr. Macmillan personally - "LIGHT WHITE PAPER AND RETIRE IMMEDIATELY".

\* \* \* \* \* \* \* \*

Further controversy has been aroused by the statement of Defence Minister Peter Thorneycroft that "when the Polaris missile is eventually delivered it will be a British finger on the button. Even in the unlikely event of our being abandoned by all our allies we shall retain full independent control over the Polaris".

This statement is, of course, quite easily explained.

The only occasion on which, in a nuclear war, we are likely to be abandoned by all our allies is if we go to war with America.

In that case, we should, of course, be fully equipped to take on America on level terms - provided we had the President's permission first.

\* \* \* \* \* \* \*

## trog

I'm sorry but the ethical position is quite clear. Thalidomide was a legal prescription, but what you suggest is an illegal operation.

# WHAT'S MACMILLAN LIKE IN BED ?

see page 64

( This could be a New Art Form,
but we're not sure. )

# PRIVATE EYE

No. 29
Friday
25 January 63

Price 1/-

# design for living

# David Slick: MAKING THE BEST OF IT

David Slick, one of the most brilliant of our interior decorators, has never baulked at the offbeat commission. So we were not surprised when he received our suggestion that he should go and look over a really very ordinary little house in Camberwell, with delighted acceptance. "One does feel" he cried, as we motored in his pink Cadillac through the rather drab streets south of the river, "that the life of the lower orders is somehow frightfully exciting. Look at that Victorian church, for example. Absolutely appalling. But what a challenge!"

The house we picked at random for David's comments was the terrace-cottage of Mrs. Mabel Thrush. She was absolutely overcome at the thought that one of London's most fashionable decorators should be given a completely free hand with her home, and our promise that, as soon as the photographers had moved out, it would be returned exactly to its former state, at our expense. David, in his turn, was "simply delighted at the informal intimacy of this little nook — so refreshingly untypical" was his first comment.

David threw up his hands in delight as we entered the dark sitting-room. "Oh, what bliss! The worst possible taste. No attempt to set off the room, at all. No, I wouldn't do a thing with it. It's a perfect treasure-chest of anti-design. But I think the ceiling might perhaps be brought down". He prodded it gingerly with his umbrella. "Oh, there it goes. Well, that's more like it, isn't it? One feels, at once, the effect of space. So important".

... we cautiously made our way over the rubble and the apparently inanimate form of Mr. Thrush, out into the little backyard. David was thrilled by what he called "the delicious little al fresco loo in the corner". Though he added "I think a plastic seat might perhaps be more hygienic — it's rather my latest thing".

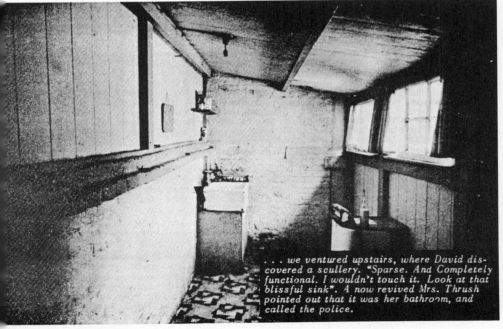

... we ventured upstairs, where David discovered a scullery. "Sparse. And Completely functional. I wouldn't touch it. Look at that blissful sink". A now revived Mrs. Thrush pointed out that it was her bathroom, and called the police.

# WHY ARE THERE NO ADS IN THIS TAKE OFF?

## BECAUSE THERE AREN'T ENOUGH IN THE SUNDAY TIMES COLOUR SECTION TO MAKE IT WORTH WHILE

# VASSALL TRIBUNAL :

# O'BOOZE IN COURT

Mr. Lunchtime O'Booze, a reporter of Private Eye Newspaper, today answered allegations before the Radcliffe Tribunal that some of his articles on the Vassall case had been 'misleading'.

The Attorney General began by referring to an article that had appeared under the headline "'ALRIGHT, SO I'M A HIDEOUS OLD POOVE" - ADMITS GALBRAITH'.

"Did you have any information to substantiate this allegation?"

"I did" replied O'Booze.

The Attorney General then asked Mr. O'Booze what had been the source of his information. "Could you" he said "tell us what was the source of your information?"

"My inspiration, sir?"

"Your information, Mr O'Booze".

Mr. O'Booze explained that he had spent the evening of October 23rd. with some 'colleagues' in a licensed establishment, 'El Vino's', at 47, Fleet Street, E.C.4., and had discussed the Vassall case with them at length.

The discussion had been "serious".

In the course of the evening, the allegations concerning Mr. Galbraith had been made.

"By whom were these allegations made, Mr. O'Booze?"

"Well, you see, we were all talking away'. . ."

"I suggest, Sir, that these insinuations were entirely dreamed up by yourself?"

"Oh, no, we were all making them. That is to say, one of our sources was more informed than others, and he was telling us about this place in Soho where men buy brassieres and so on..."

"Mr. O'Booze, would you tell the Court the name of this source, please".

"I am afraid, Sir, that you are asking something beyond my conceptions of ethics or principle".

Mr. O'Booze was then given 24 hours to cook up a more likely tale.

GLOSSARY OF TERMS OF THE TYPE USED BY IMAGINATIVE JOURNALISTS.

Reliable Source = Sober Colleague
Usually Reliable Source = Usually Drunken Colleague who happens to be sober at the time
Well Informed Source = Colleague who is completely drunk at the same time as you are
Whitehall Source = Put quotes round the most sensational thing you can think of
Usual Source = H.P.

It's all very well for de Gaulle getting bumped off - He doesn't have to rise again in three days

NOW SURELY, SIR PERCIVAL, IF YOU VISITED MR. VASSALL'S FLAT YOU MUST HAVE NOTICED HIS, WELL, UNNATURAL TENDENCIES . . . ?

NO, DEAR, HE SEEMED PERFECTLY NORMAL TO ME

timothy

# British Letters

Dear Prime Minister,

A certain amount of publicity has recently been given to the case of my daughter, who is alleged to have committed a parking offence while wearing a jersey I had lent her. At the Ministry of Teenage Welfare I have been particularly concerned with the freedom of self-expression of young people; and it was in this connection alone that I contemplated humouring my daughter in this way.

On reflection, I think that what I tried to do, though intended in a paternal and liberal way, involved a serious error of judgement, and that I could not possibly continue at the Ministry in view of the unhappy misconstruction that can undoubtedly be put upon this excessive indulgence.

In the circumstances, the only right and proper course for me is to resign my post.

yours earnestly,
WILBRAHAM LOBETHRUST
Assistant Under-Parliamentary Under-Secretary, Ministry of Teenage Welfare

Dear Lobethrust,

I read the letter which I asked you to write me with the deepest regret, and I say this from the bottom of a full heart. But you will appreciate that, while nepotism in the Government is one thing, incest is quite another. There have been occasions in the past when Ministers, such as Alan Lennox-Boyd and Lord Carrington, have offered me their resignations on the grounds that they had committed gross political blunders. I felt that their errors were the collective responsibility of the whole Government. On this occasion, however, your own offence can do nothing but bring us all into disrepute - and I am sure, therefore, that you have taken the right course, and I feel that it will only serve to bring the whole matter into the glare of further publicity if I accept your resignation. Which I do.

H. Macmillan

ugisəɹ oʇ
əʌɐɥ ɥʇoq p,ʎəɥʇ puɐ puə oʇ
puə pıɐ[ əɹəʍ ɯɐɥs[ıɐH
pɹoꞀ puɐ əɯoH pɹoꞀ ɟI

KENNEDY SALUTES THE GALLANT CHICHESTER

Nice to see you again, Jack.

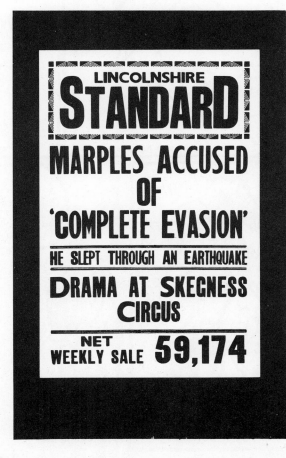

LINCOLNSHIRE STANDARD

MARPLES ACCUSED OF 'COMPLETE EVASION'

HE SLEPT THROUGH AN EARTHQUAKE

DRAMA AT SKEGNESS CIRCUS

NET WEEKLY SALE 59,174

# chatto

I must admit that lately I'd been having my doubts about the Market . . .

. . . talks not going too well . . .
. . Heath having a difficult time getting the right conditions . . .

. . . But when that bloody Frog de Gaulle says he'll do anything to keep us out . . .

. . . I think the time has come for us to get in AT ANY PRICE!

# ÆSOP revisited

This is the story of HAROLD WILLSOON, an extremely clever little politician. The reason why he is called Willsoon is that whenever someone has said "Oh, not even Harold would do a thing like that" you can be absolutely certain that he will soon..

... Harold's meteoric career first takes shape one Grammar School speechday . . .

...by 21 he is a briiliant young Oxford don - already learning the art of deception..

... by 31 - the youngest Cabinet Minister of century. Only three man stand now between him and his prize . .

...as loyal Minister, respect of Party for Willsoon soars. Government runs into crisis. Willsoon resigns with Bevan . . .

...as Bevan's loyal No.2, Willsoon's popularity in Party soars. Bevan resigns from Shadow Cabinet. Willsoon takes his place...

... schemes against Bevan to make Gaitskell Leader. As Gaitskell's loyal No.2 becomes one of Party's undisputed leaders...

...despite performance over Bank Rate . . .

...but at last sees Promised Land when Gaitskell runs into trouble over Bomb. Willsoon does not oppose rebels, does not oppose Bomb...

...but soon opposes Gaitskell for leadership. Although soundly beaten, Willsoon knows his time will come . .

MORAL:
If at first you don't succeed. .

**GENTLEMEN, GENTLEMEN! DISORDER, PLEASE, DISORDER!**

# ÆSOP revisited

OVER NOW to the factory in Suffolk, where the keel has just been laid of the 500-volume Official Biography of the Greatest Dying Englishman. The Great Bumpkin himself, Rudolph Rednose, is enthroned . . .

Here beginneth the First War

It's not me that's the hack - it's the people who write my books

W.S.C.

. . . never was so much written by so many for so little. But, as the Bumpkin and his hirelings pay nightly homage with readings from the Great Book, as fat offers for serialisation flow in from the scoop-hungry Sunday Telegraph - a dreadful doubt arises. That like all Official Portraits this one too will bear little resemblance to the original . . . that it will, for instance, forget to mention how the Greatest D.E. devoted his life to . . .

TONY·PANDY 1911

Let them eat coke!

PHOTO BY TONY PANSY

DADDY AT TREASURY 1926

Spend money on roads! Nonsense! It was the railways that made Britain Great!

MOTOR CARS ARE BUNK

DADDY AGAINST THE INDIANS 1936

Your Gandhi and Soda, sir

I have not become the Tory's First Rebel to watch over the liquidation of the British Empah

. . . smashing the workers (shooting Welsh miners, General Strike etc) . . .

. . . putting back clock in all directions (back to Gold Standard, Free Trade) . . .

. . . opposing every manifestation of 20th Century in favour of long-lost glories of 19th, 18th, 17th etc. . . .

DADDY AT WAR 1942

Disaster at Dieppe, sir

Only 5000 dead! You should have seen what we did at Gallipoli!

WSC

WD

You didn't think I meant all the United Europe rubbish, did you? Only did it to get the Freedom of Strasbourg

. . . wild and futile military gestures, regardless of cost . . .

. . . and that even when he chanced on a radical idea for the only time in his life - he was careful to betray it again as soon as he came into office . . .

. . . but it will concentrate instead on the one short period of his life from which he can be painted as the Great Patriot who did more for his countrymen than anyone else in the 20th Century.

You have now reached the end of this magazine. You are asked to rise and sing the National Anthem

The Editor,
Private Eye,
22, Greek Street,
London, W.1

Stour,
East Bergholt,
Suffolk.
14 February, 1963

Sir,

I write to call your attention to the lies and libels about my father and myself contained in your issue of February 8.

I   Your allegation that I am planning to write a biography of my father of a tendentious character amounting to a falsification of history is unfounded; and flies in the face of all the known facts (see transcript of my broadcast on B.B.C. Television, January 31, and article of Page 5 of the SUNDAY TELEGRAPH of February 3).

II  Your suggestions that I intend to omit or gloss over unpleasant alleged episodes in my father's life are abominable. I shall certainly paint a truer picture than you have done. Your further statement that I am not going to write the book myself is also false and constitutes a libel not only on myself, but on those who are associated with me in this enterprise.

The lies you tell about my father are exceptionally gross and offensive.

III  Your allegation that my father was responsible for "shooting Welsh miners" is not only a lie, but the reverse of the truth.

(See account of Tonypandy riots in Annual Register for 1910 and in Peter de Mendelssohn's THE AGE OF CHURCHILL.)

IV  Your suggestion that my father had a callous disregard for loss of British and Canadian lives in two world wars, and in particular that he made light of the casualties at Dieppe, is the vilest libel I have ever seen.

I only draw your attention to the lies you tell about my father since, being his official biographer as well as his son, I have a special responsibility for maintaining his reputation against defamations such as yours.

I shall be glad to have your observations on the foregoing as soon as possible.

yours faithfully,
Randolph S. Churchill.

---

*We the undersigned wish to withdraw the false allegations we made and implied against Sir Winston and Mr. Randolph Churchill, and the latter's assistants in the issue of Private Eye of February 8th.*

*Christopher Booker*    *Mrs. O'Morgo Ingrams*
*William Rushton*    *Anne Chisholm*
*Richard Ingrams*    *Sir Charles Harness*
*Nicholas Luard*    *Brian Moore*
*Peter Usborne*    *Pressdram Ltd.*
*Tony Rushton*    *Leo Thorpe Ltd.*

# Come off it . . .

. . . you can't seriously argue that this **une**mployment business isn't serious?

You've just been misled by the figures, that's all. I mean of that 800,000 you've been reading about in the papers, you've got to take off at least 50,000 for the usual seasonal increase.

So there are really only 750,000 out of work then?

Oh, no. Because you've got a lot of exceptional factors at work this year, you see. You've got to knock off at least another 150,000 chappies in the building trade, for example - chaps who say it's too bloody cold to be out brewing up tea and all that nonsense they do.

I see. So that leaves a mere 600,000?

Well, then, you've got to allow for the 100,000 people who happen to be moving from one job to another...

...so we're down to half a million?

Still sounds a lot, of course. But then you've always got to remember the 50,000-odd layabouts who never do any work anyhow - just sponge on the Welfare State. And just at the moment there happen to be about 100,000 teenagers on the dole who've never had a job anyway - so one can hardly describe them as having lost their jobs, can you?

No, I see. So, in fact, the true figure is only about 350,000 - which is pretty reasonable, I suppose?

Oh, no, it's much better than that. You see, if you take into account Selwyn's balls-up in the last Budget - when he warned that there might be too much demand by the end of 1963, and that personal spending would probably rise by 4% - then all the remaining 350,000 can be blamed directly on Selwyn's mismanagement . . .

...and he's already been given the sack, you mean ...

...exactly! So not only are there no unemployed! BUT YOU CAN'T PUT ANY BLAME ON THE PRESENT GOVERNMENT AT ALL !

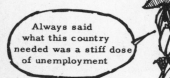

Always said what this country needed was a stiff dose of unemployment

# Idle Talk

REVEALS

## Lunchtime O'Booze

Mr. Silas Jones, a West Indian immigrant of no fixed adobe, was today sentenced at the Old Bailey to 24 years Preventive Detention for being in possession of an offensive water pistol.
The chief 'witness' in the case, gay fun-loving Miss Gaye Funloving, a 21-year old 'model', was not actually present in Court. She has, in fact, disappeared.
It is believed that normally, in cases of this type, a Warrant is issued for the arrest of the missing witness.

### 'Parties'

One of Miss Funloving's close 'friends', Dr. Spook of Harley Street, revealed last night that he could add nothing to what had already been insinuated.
Dr. Spook is believed to have 'more than half the Cabinet on his list of patients'. He also has a 'weekend' cottage on the Berkshire estate of Lord *, and is believed to have attended many 'parties' in the neighbourhood.
Among those it is believed have also attended 'parties' of this type are Mr. Vladimir Bolokhov, the well-known Soviet spy attached to the Russian Embassy, and a well-known Cabinet Minister.

### Resignation?

Mr. James Montesi, a well-known Cabinet Minister, was last night reported to have proffered his 'resignation' to the Prime Minister, on 'personal grounds'.
It is alleged that the Prime Minister refused to accept his alleged 'resignation'. Mr. Montesi, today denied the allegations that he had ever allegedly offered his alleged 'resignation' to the alleged 'Prime Minister'.

Mr. Silas Jones is serving his 24 - year sentence in a prison of the type it is believed is a long way from Fleet Street. Miss Funloving is still 'in hiding'.

### in the dark

The public is still in the dark.
And so am I, which is why I have had to compile this whole ridiculous story from other newspaper cuttings.
So what?

"Of course it's easy to see what's got to be done . . ."

"...oh, quite. Get the economy back on a really efficient, competitive footing . . ."

"...complete overhaul of our education - get rid of this class nonsense . . ."

"...complete clean-up of the legal system . . ."

"...and the constitution..."

"...new political leaders . . ."

"...we'd need a revolution to achieve all that . . . "

" . . . course, the great strength of the British way of life is that we don't have revolutions".

# PRIVATE EYE

No. 34
Friday
5 April 63

Price 1/-

INTERCONTINENTAL BALLISTA
Another of the Emperor Macmilian's humiliations at this time was the acquisition, at enormous expense, of large numbers of these weapons from his Persian allies. The missiles failed to leave their <u>cubicula jacenda</u> or launching pads.

# the last d
# MACMIL

AN EXTRACT FROM "THE DECLINE AND FALL OF THE BRITISH EMPIRE" WITH NO APOLOGIES TO MR. EDWARD GIBBON

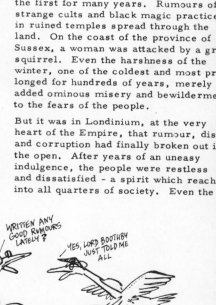

By the early days of the year 1963, the twilight of the British Empire provided a sorry spectacle of collapse and decay on every hand.

It is evident from history that there is no nation which, having extended its sinews and vigour in the conquest and administration of empire, can then, on relinquishing that empire, maintain its previous standards of morality and efficiency in the prosecution of its remaining activities.

\* \* \* \* \* \* \*

A strange mood walked abroad in Britain of that year, the eighth of the reign of the Emperor Macmilian. The ability and desire of the Emperor and his advisers to undertake the proper responsibilities of government seemed to have quite evaporated.

Throughout the country the broad roads went unpaved. The iron roads that had once been the proud arteries of a brilliant civilisation were uprooted to give way once again to the weeds of the forest.

Even in the furthest reaches of the Empire unrest was slowly ripening into bitter contempt for the symbols of authority that had for so long held sway. When Macmilian's consul, the horse Elizabetha, made a progress through the province of Australia, few bothered even to stop in the streets to observe the passing of the tattered imperial standards. Among the placid farms and latifundia of Rhodesia, black rebellion was brewing up in the hearts of the African slaves, exacerbated by the iron rule of the Governor Winstonius Ager, and unassuaged by the smooth ambivalence of Macmilian's proconsular envoy Butlerius Africanus.

\* \* \* \* \* \* \* \* \*

But it was in Britain itself, and in Londinium that the air was heavy with the smell of indulgence and decay, with searchings after strange Gods, with rumour and counter-rumour and with a drifting sense of doom.

The old faiths of the Republic had lost their hold. Even the High Priests no longer proclaimed the existence of the Gods. The legions had abandoned their once fierce bull-worship almost entirely. Only Son-Worship still flourished, in outlying regions of Suffolk.

In place of religion, there came at this time a great spate of omens. An outbre of the plague among travellers, one of the first for many years. Rumours of strange cults and black magic practiced in ruined temples spread through the land. On the coast of the province of Sussex, a woman was attacked by a gre squirrel. Even the harshness of the winter, one of the coldest and most pro longed for hundreds of years, merely added ominous misery and bewildermen to the fears of the people.

But it was in Londinium, at the very heart of the Empire, that rumour, dist and corruption had finally broken out in the open. After years of an uneasy indulgence, the people were restless and dissatisfied - a spirit which reache into all quarters of society. Even the

Vast tracts of the Northern provinces had fallen into desuetude. Along the great rivers of Tyne, Clyde and Mersey, the hammers of the shipyards were stilled. The busy workshops that had once provided the sinews of imperial prosperity were silent. The people moved in uneasy groups through the streets, deprived of bread, craving in vain for circuses, sensitive to that stirring of the instincts of the mob that finally erupted in open rioting outside the Senate at Westminster.

THE GEESE of the Via Fleeta who gave their name to the pamphleteers and satrists whose warnings of the evils of Macmilian were never heeded.

Labels in image: HORRID OLD POOVES PLOTTING — THINKS! — WHISPER WHISPER — HELLO FANS! — JUVENILE THE COURT SATYR WITH FAITHFUL AUDIENCE OF DAILY MAIL COLUMNISTS — MAKE FIRST FOLD HERE — FOOT INSURED FOR £5,000,000,000,000

flower of the legions, the Praetorian Guard, were in mutinous mood at their camp at Pirbrittius.

After his final defeat in the Gallic campaign, after the prolonged and tiring battle of Brussels upon which all his ambitions had been centred, the Emperor Macmilian himself lounged increasingly powerless at the heart of this drift and decay. His Ministers fought and intrigued over the succession, no longer mindful of the great perils that lay without. While the proper administration of the country languished utterly.

Wild rumours flew nightly through the capital. Of strange and wild happenings in country villas out in the country. Of orgies and philanderings involving some of the richest and most powerful men in the land. In the private diaries of a well-known courtesan of the times, we can read the names of many leading members of imperial society - ranged in order of sexual prowess.

But while natural debauchery became the small talk of a capital long sated with public offerings of vice and harlotry of every description, among the clerks and eunuchs of the administration the old standards of the Republic had vanished altogether. Men proclaimed their love not for their wives, but for each other- and the strange loyalties thus formed, stretching up into some of the highest places in the land, allowed laxity, indulgence and even treason to flourish unchecked.

At this time too, the Chief of the Praetorian Guard, Sextus Profano, came under widespread suspicion for his admission in the Senate that he had been acquainted with Christina, a beautiful girl known well to many of the great figures of society despite her lowly origins, and whose lover, a negro slave, had been sentenced to seven years in the sulphur mines for threatening to kill her in a fit of jealous revenge. It was a sign of the times that few expressed surprise at such an admission.

Labels in image: BAOR — FAECES

MUTIN'OUS LEGIONARY or Praetorian Guard of the type which rose in protest against an excess of official Bull-Worship.

All these happenings brought the capital into a frenzy of speculation that was far from healthy for the continued reign of Macmilian, and the scribes and pamphleteers were only the leaders and articulators of the widespread hostility and contempt aroused by the Government in the hearts of the great mass of the people.

But it was finally the sight of one of Macmilian's more despised advisers, Henricius Domus Secretarius, making himself a private triumph through the streets, leading from his chariot the proud and chained figure of a great African chief Enobarbo, that drove a weary people into deciding that the Emperor's tyranny and disregard for any sentiments but the cheap, the opportunist and the ignoble must be put aside for ever. And that these small men who had disgraced all the noble and glorious history of the British Empire with their petty deeds should be humiliated and forgotten.

Labels in image: CHIEF ENOBARBUS — BROOKE'S WEAPON

Absolutely shocking - papers
these days seem to be full of
nothing else . . .

   . . . oh, I know - high
places absolutely crawling
with 'em . .

. . . Civil Service riddled
with the fellows . . .

   . . . show business. . .

. . . even some of 'em in the
Cabinet. . .

   . . . oh, really?  Who?. .

. . . well, Mr. Macmillan, for
a start . . .

   . . . you don't really mean
it? . . .

. . . heterosexual?  Oh, yes, no
doubt about it.

# WE'VE NEVER HAD IT SO OFTEN

4rog

## DR. WARD WRITES TO BROOKE

**Dr.** Stephen Ward, the osteopath and portrait artist, has written to Mr. Henry Brooke, the Home Secretary, on an undisclosed matter.

The 'undisclosed matter' in question is believed to relate to the wage-scales of assistant osteopaths in rural areas.

\* \* \* \* \* \* \* \*

An evil and pernicious rumour has been circulating in Fleet Street, Westminster and other hives of idle gossip, to the effect that Mr. Stephen Ward has placed before the Home Secretary Mr. Brooke certain "new evidence" in the alleged Keeler-Profumo affair and has made a statement to this effect to the Press. We would like to state quite categorically that there is no truth whatsoever in this rumour, and we would also like to congratulate the Press for pretending to know absolutely nothing about the alleged "statement".

# Macmillan Confesses

IN RECENT MONTHS, BRITAIN HAS BEEN ROCKED BY A SERIES OF SCANDALS INVOLVING MANY OF THE LEADING FIGURES IN POLITICS AND SOCIETY. THE VASSALL AFFAIR. THE ENAHORO SCANDAL. THE PROFUMO CRISIS. THE DUCHESS OF ARGYLL DIVORCE. IN ALL OF THEM CABINET MINISTERS WERE INTIMATELY INVOLVED.

And running through all these scandalous sensations, they all had one thing in common.

Only one man in Britain was in a position to know the innermost truth of all these events.

Only one man was in a position to cover up for his friends.

### HAROLD MACMILLAN

Today 'Private Eye' starts publishing the full, exclusive confessions of 70-year old Mr. Macmillan, the humble crofter's grandson who rose to become on intimate terms with many of the most famous and fashionable names of our time.

Among the questions Mr. Macmillan has fully and frankly answered in this sensational 'Private Eye' series

O   Why I consistently lied to the House of Commons over the years

O   What I told Jack Profumo when he first came to me with the truth back in March

O   What I told the Security Boys they could do with themselves when they first came to me with the truth back in February

O   Why I always think I can get away with it

Little did I know, in those happy days back in 1957 when I at last attained my life's ambition - to be Prime Minister of Britain - how tragically and terribly the whole affair was going to end.

As I first walked into Number Ten, on that cold January day, everything looked bright for me. From my humble origins I had risen to be accepted in the highest ranks of society. By skilful manoeuvering at the time of the Suez crisis, I had achieved the highest honour my countrymen can bestow!

Little did I foresee how I was to betray that honour so grossly over the next seven years - until the final humiliation of my resignation!

The letter that fell into the hands of 'Private Eye' six months ago. Because we are gentlemen, we returned it, at once, to Mr. Macmillan (although keeping a photostat copy simply for our files.)

Admiralty House
Whitehall, S.W.1

Dear Jack—
In great haste and because I can't
get a reply from your phone
(Must have a wad nik Bevins
about that !!!)
Please be careful what you get
up to. If we play our cards right
no one need ever find out
about us.
Let it be our own precious
secret which no one else
need ever know
Love.    M

How the country was to be consistently betrayed by my lies and evasions.

How so many of my friends were to have their names dragged in the mud of public contempt and degradation. How my Government was to become notorious throughout the world for its incompetence, laxity and vile corruption. Little did I foresee, at that time, how every one of my policies - such as they were - would collapse in disaster through mismanagement and lack of conviction. And that eventually the little children would run through the streets, howling execration at my name and tweaking without mercy my already ludicrous moustache.

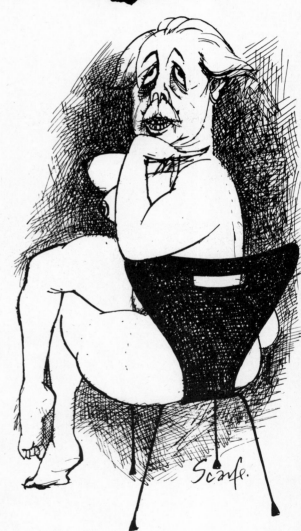

## THE HAPPY DAYS

NEXT WEEK: I flirt with Russian official 'Mr. K.' and am invited to Moscow - Henry Brooke lets me down - the night I was thrown over by de Gaulle - Henry Brooke lets me down again - the day I told Lord ████████ that I preferred 'a real MAN' - Henry Brooke lets me down for the last time

# Romantic
## ENGLAND
# The Taking of the Soundings

Although Britain is a 'democratic' country, many traditional procedures of government are not accompanied by the more vulgar 'manifestations' of democracy, such as 'voting', which flourish in other countries.

This is especially true of the traditional 'Conservative Party', an age old body of men who govern England. These men in the light of hallowed custom conduct their affairs according to 'gentlemen's agreements' and such is their great mutual loyalty and respect that all decisions are assumed to be 'unanimous' and traditionally 'democratic'.

No more so than at 'The Taking of the Soundings' - an ancient ceremony which takes place on those rare occasions when it is felt that the Party should 'elect' a new leader. (It should be explained that there is usually no need for the ceremony to take place at all, the new leader appearing out of the traditional 'Mists of History' to be acclaimed by all and 'sundry'.)

Unlike most new fangled organisations such as The College of Cardinals, the party does not 'vote' at such a time. What it does do is difficult to describe. Indeed, so ancient and time honoured is the ceremony that almost all living Conservatives have forgotten what it is.

Suffice it to say that 'the soundings' are 'taken' from the Body Politic by the traditional 'Sounding Fathers' each representing one portion of the Body - these include time honoured Lord Poole, 'elected' by the Prime Minister, and the traditional Lord Home. Other venerable men represent 'The Voice of History' and are thought to speak for all dead Conservatives and those who are yet to come.

The 'soundings' are then brought together in the traditional 'Carlton Club' - a secret meeting place of the Party, and once they have been 'weighed' (some, traditionally, are heavier than others) they are conveyed to The Great Oracle of Truth (or The Queen, as she is known).

By the mystical power invested in her she then speaks the name of the new leader, after passing over the rejected candidate, the traditional Mr. Butler.

To the untrained observer this procedure may seem hazardous, or even 'undemocratic', but such is the mystical sense of unity and justice which prevails that the right decision is inevitably taken and The British People are thus given the leader of their choice in accordance with the highest principles of democratic liberty.

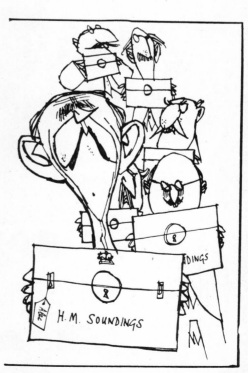

H. M. SOUNDINGS

# PRIVATE EYE

No. 42
Friday
26 July 63

Price 1/-

## Come to lovely London and find # HOW TO BECOME DEAD Without anyone knowing how

There are some sad little old sacks about who still try to miss their round in the bar while they hold the customers enthralled with the tale that a lot of the stories that appear in Private Eye are "merely" jokes - things that couldn't, ha-ha-heil, happen here. Just for the record, the following event was no joke, and it did happen here.

(Before everyone gets depressed, let's state that this is at least one bit of you-know-what which is not going to be swept under the carpet. Stephen Swingler M.P. has assured Private Eye that he is going to question and cross-question the Home Secretary - in the House and out of it - until some explanation of the bloody death of Harold Woolf emerges from the normal miasma of lies.)

This man Woolf (60 when he passed on) was in his day a good and fairly widely esteemed painter. In his later years he became what the French used to call "embourgoise" - he held down a good job in the Postal Department of London University. He was quiet, regular to the point of obsession in his habits. He had been a bit of a tearaway in his day - helped to kill a lot of Germans too, when duty called - but now the only relic of those old days was the fact the he smoked, every week-end, some marijuana.

This, in the opinion of this reporter, is a mistaken thing to do. But it is not a valid ground for having ones head split open and becoming sort of, as it were, if one may hazard the phrase, kidnapped.

So on November 10th of last year he went into Berlemonts pub in Dean Street to meet his ex-wife - still a close friend. They and a couple of other old friends used to meet there every Sunday for a drink.

His ex-wife says:-

"He explained that he was a little late becuse at about one o'clock, just before meeting us, he was waiting for a friend in Poland Street, outside a betting shop, when a flashy car stopped by him and the driver spoke to Hal and asked him if he had seen any police (he used a slang word I didn't know). Hal replied ' I don't know what you're talking about.' The car drove off and in a few minutes returned. The driver got out and looked around and said 'Have they been?'. Hal again did not respond and the man got back into the card and said to Hal 'You should get yourself a tin hat'. We took that as a joke and thought someone was going to blow up the betting shop."

As Woolf was in the habit of telephoning his former wife frequently and was particularly regular in all his habits she was bothered by not hearing from him on Monday, Tuesday, Wednesday, or Thursday.

He then walked out into a mystery. None of his friends saw him again until a fortnight later when they found him dead in the Atkinson Morley Hospital.

Mrs. Woolf then got in touch with a Mr. Cotton, a mutual friend of hers and Mr. Woolf, an antique dealer. He telephoned the Harrow Road Police Station and he was asked to go over and declare Mr. Woolf missing, this Mr. Cotton did and was told by the police that they would telephone him immediately if they had any news.

On Novemebr 17th Mr. Cotton and Mrs. Woolf again visited Harrow Road Police Station and were told that there was no news of their friend.

On the following day Mr. Cotton went to Mr. Woolf's rooms and found his passport. With this he went to Harrow Road Police Station and gave them a copy of the passport photograph which might help to trace him. The police said that his photograph and description would be transmitted to all London Police Divisions and two days later Mr. Cotton went to Bow Street Police Station, where they told him that they had seen a photograph and description of Mr. Woolf in the Police Gazette.

Mr. Cotton continued to make enquiries about his friend. Very early in the morning of November 24th an officer at the West End Central Police Station telephoned Mr. Cotton and told him that his friend Mr. Woolf "is very ill at the Atkinson Morley Hospital at Wimbledon. Your friend mixed Teacher's whiskey with Marijuana and got himself knocked down by an E-Type Jaguar in Park Lane. Mr. Cotton then telephoned the Atkinson Morley Hospital and was told by the Night Sister of Brodie Ward that in fact Mr. Woolf was dead.

Mrs. Woolf and Mr. Cotton went to the hospital and identified Mr. Woolf, whose face was bashed in and his head fractured. They there discovered the fact which to them was astounding, that throughout the period which Mr. Woolf had been dying in the hospital two police officers had been in permanent attendance at his bedside. On one occasion when Woolf seemed to gain consciousness he tried to give the Sister in the ward a telephone number which he wanted rung. The police intercepted the message and gave the Sister a number which proved to be that of a telephone booth at the local Underground Station.

What surprised these people very much was the fact that although he had been on the Missing Persons' List for nearly a fortnight, the police in fact, did not communicate with them until after the man was dead. Yet for reasons of their own the police were in fact sitting by the man's bed side all that time.

Alarmed and bewildered by this situation they attempted to trace what had really been the movements of Harold Woolf during those days. They found that he had indeed been knocked down by a car in Park Lane, had been taken to St. George's Hospital and had been discharged with "a lsight abrasion on his forehead and abrasions on his legs and shoulders". He was X-rayed and found to have no fractures.

As soon as he was discharged, the police picked him up at the hospital. On the following day he was brought back to the hospital in a condition which caused the hospital doctor to have him sent to the Atkinson Morley Hospital, where he died.

It is admitted that during the entire period from his first admission to St. George's to his death, the police knew exactly where he was.

He had among his posessions a note-book which gave the names and addresses of people to be telephoned "in the event of an accident". Yet nobody in fact rang those numbers until after he was dead.

His friends drew from all this the conclusions that you or I would draw. They went to a well-known solicitor - who is also a well-known politician - who agreed to take up the case. The head of the solicitor's firm being absent at the moment, he left the matter in the hands of an assistant. The assistant informed Mrs. Woolf and Mr. Cotton that they should of course be represented at the inquest. Within a few hours of the inquest the assistant suddenly informed them that he had been unable to obtain legal representation in time, but that they should themselves attend and ask for an adjournment in order that proper legal representation could be obtained. He said that this would be a relatively easy matter. However, when they got to the inquest the coroner refused to ajourn it. Soon after that, this same assistant quit or was dismissed from that particular solicitor's office and at the same time all the documents in the case which Mrs. Woolf - she was the executrix of Mr. Woolf's not inconsiderate will - had deposited with the solicitor, disappeared too. And from that dark day to the present nobody has been able to find out why this man was held inoommunicado during these days, why he was killed or who killed him.

This is the type of question which London citizens should ask and get answers to.

The fact that Mr. Woolf was an old friend of one of the close women friends of Christine Keeler and that the entire event occured at the moment when the Profumo case was about to break has exited some observers, but according to our information, may be entirely irrelevant.

# Not WANTED

This evil looking man, aged 54, is wanted by the Police for crimes involving 'obscenity, distortion, cant, snobbery, humbug, evasion and hypocrisy'.

His name: MERVYN GRIFFITH JONES Q.C.

Mr. Griffith Jones has until recently been thought to be a mere figure of fun, a harmless lunatic not capable of hurting a fly.

It was he, you will remember, who asked the Lady Chatterly jury: "Is it a book that you would even wish your wife or your servants to read ? "

It was he who made the immortal statement:

> The word "f✱ck" or "f✱cking" occ✱rs no less than thirty times. I have ✱dded them up, but I do not guarantee that I have✱dded them all up. "C✱nt" fourteen times; "b✱lls" thirteen times; "sh✱" and "ars✱" six times api✱ce; "c✱ck" four times; "p✱ss" three times, and so on.

Having become the laughing stock of Europe one hoped that he would at least have the decency to retire from the bar.

Or one hoped that his future appearances in court would be greeted with such shouts of mirthful derision that he would be compelled to resign.

But this was not the case. Mr. Griffith Jones is blissfully unaware of the ludicrous figure he presents to the nation.

And he knows that by exciting the subconscious fears and lusts of jurymen and by reminding them of the servants and nannies which they never had, he can still secure convictions for sexual offences.

It was this that helped him to secure a conviction against Dr. Ward. The jury did not laugh when Mr. Griffith Jones referred to Ward throughout his summing up as "this filthy fellow". They did not raise an eyebrow when he said that 'nothing improper had take place' to mean that a couple had not slept together. They listened intently when he remarked that 'the girl was quite respectable - not wanting to go to bed with anyone', inferring that to want to go to bed with someone entailed a lack of respect.

It is this man who is now wanted by the Police. And for once they are on to something.

Private Eye asks:

IS THIS A MAN YOU WOULD WANT YOUR SERVANTS TO GO TO BED WITH ?

THE ANSWER MUST BE NO

# Unpleasant Rumours Denied

Referring to what she termed a "smear campaign" against the Cities of the Plain, the Lady Mayoress of Gomorrah said yesterday that in fact living conditions had reached a new high level and there was no reason to expect any deterioration in the situation.

"I know I can speak for Sodom too" she said "when I say that we very much resent irresponsible criticisms of our way of life, and particularly suggestions that we are headed for some unspecified 'disaster'."

She pointed out that the smell of brimstone which has recently pervaded the area has been declared, by the local officer of Health, to be quite without injurious effect on human health.

She bluntly put responsibility for "disturbing rumours" on a man calling himself "Lot".

"Mr. Lot", she said, "is a married man with two daughters who has apparently been unable to adjust successfully to community life in Sodom. As a result he seems to have been conducting some kind of poll with the alleged object of finding out how many 'just men' there are there.

"He has sought to persuade fellow citizens that, through a man named Abraham he has information to the effect that our communities are in immediate danger of destruction by brimstone and fire.

"My latest information is that Mr. Lot is making preparations to leave town immediately.

"I am happy to say that in Sodom and here in Gomorrah public confidence is high, and very few are likely to follow his example."

# PRIVATE EYE

46
iday
Sept. 63

Price 1/-

Gerald Scarfe.

# DENNING IS SERVED

# PRIVATE EYE

No 49
Friday
1 Nov. 63

Price 1/-

In the autumn tranquillity of his days while the golden leaves fall silently to the ground an old man, his faithful wife by his side, sits peacefully in the park happy in the knowledge of a lifetime's work well done, a country served and an old colleague stabbed ruthlessly in the back…

MACMILLAN PROMISED BUTLER IN 1957 THAT HE WOULD
SUCCEED

BUTLER WAS THE OBVIOUS CHOICE

BUTLER HAD THE MOST EXPERIENCE

BUTLER WAS BEST QUALIFIED TO STAND UP TO WILSON

THE MPs WANTED BUTLER

THE PARTY WANTED BUTLER

THE CABINET WANTED BUTLER

THE PEOPLE AS A WHOLE WANTED BUTLER

# WHY WASN'T BUTLER CHOSEN ?

BECAUSE I HATE
BLOODY BUTLER'S GUTS

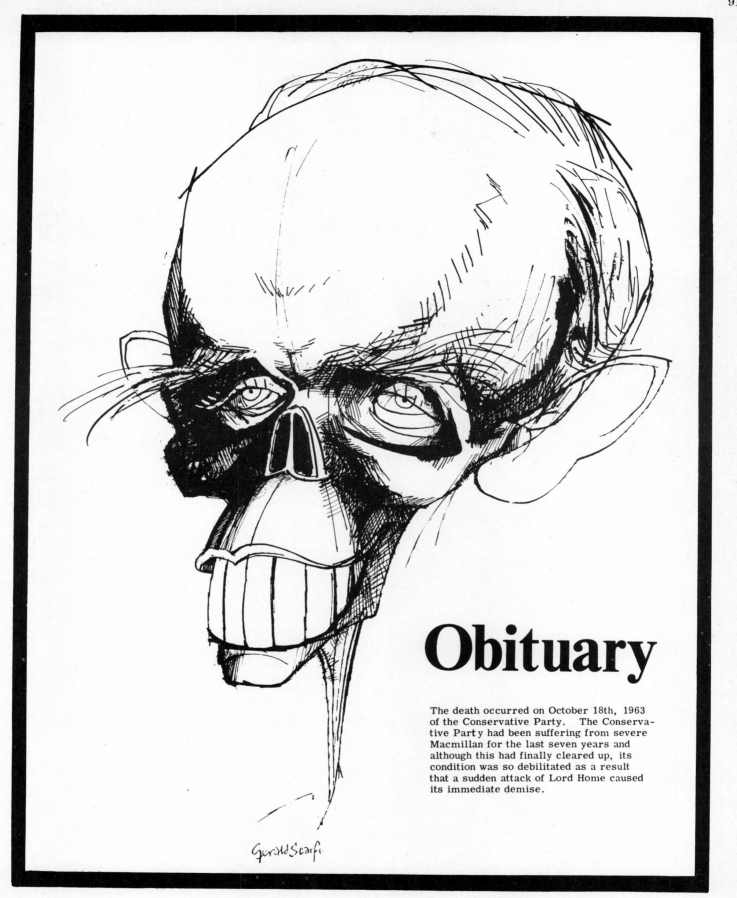

# Obituary

The death occurred on October 18th, 1963 of the Conservative Party. The Conservative Party had been suffering from severe Macmillan for the last seven years and although this had finally cleared up, its condition was so debilitated as a result that a sudden attack of Lord Home caused its immediate demise.

"I lived among miners for 20 years"

Lord Home B.B.C T.V.
Monday 21ST Oct '63

# ALL THIS NONSENSE...

about Home being an Earl is really rather childish. I mean the Earl of Arran is quite right - it doesn't <u>mean</u> anything. And he ought to know. After all he's got his <u>column</u> in the Evening News because he's a jolly good writer not because some high up thought wouldn't it be rather fun to have this silly old Earl (who's one of the Directors) shooting his gob in the Evening News, might even put the sales up in the suburbs. If his name was Fred Smith, he'd still be writing that rubbish - I mean that excellent column.

And the same goes for Lord Home - or just plain Sir Alexander Frederick Douglas Home, Knight of the Thistle, as he now is - I mean if he'd been born Fred Smith he'd still be where he is today. Of course he wouldn't have gone to Eton or Christ Church or anything like that - but there again people always get in a great state about Eton as if everyone who went there was somehow privileged. Of course they're not - it's a jolly tough life and lots of left wing rebels came out of Eton - George Orwell and . . . well George Orwell is only one example.

And I know that if you went to Eton in those days it was pretty easy to get into Christ Church, Oxford, on the old boy net. But there were lots of others who got in on academic merit. Lord Home wasn't one of them but that's not the point. Anyone else could have done what he did. Then again people say it didn't really matter what <u>class</u> of degree you got provided you had the right back ground. They say well Lord Home only got a third - and if he'd been anyone else he couldn't even have got a job in the Foreign Office. But that's not very logical is it? I mean he didn't want to get a job in the Foreign Office (I know he was Foreign Secretary but that was later). No, he wanted to stand for Parliament. There again you could say "Oh well it's easy enough to get nominated if you're one of the local gentry" - but then plenty of people get in who aren't local gentry. Look at all those Labour M.P.'s for instance.

The point is of course that being an Earl is just the same as being a black man - I mean a white man - it's a pure accident of birth and your chances of making a success of things are just as good as if you're an ordinary working class chap.

So let's have no more of this silly inverted snobbery.

For one thing it's so frightfully rude.

I think that's rather childish, even if it's true

# GOYA
## SCARFE
### AND THEIR TIMES

# SEDUCTIVE BRETHREN

### Sir Basil Nardly-Stoads explains

As chief **Rammer** of the Seductive Brethren, (writes Sir Basil Nardly-Stoads) it is often my pleasure and privilege to seize hold of young women and clamber hotly all over their bodies.

I am often asked, by those who want to know (continues Sir Basil Nardly-Stoads) what exactly the Seductive Brethren do and what they believe in: to this there is no simple answer but to say that the BODILY SEIZING OF YOUNG WOMEN is at least part and parcel of our belief would be no exageration.

### THE FUNCTION OF THE RAMMER

In my position, or rather in my numerous positions as Chief Rammer, (Sir Basil Nardly-Stoads writes) it is my solemn duty to uphold the traditions of the sect and deal with the thousand and one contingencies that need must occur in an organisation of this kind; in this I am assisted by the Holy Dragger (elected annually), Sir Arthur Starborgling. Sir Arthur saw service and, indeed, a number of other things in Dieppe. Between them the Rammer and the Dragger control the discipline of the Brethren.

### HOW MANY ARE THERE OF US

The exact number of the Brethren at any given time (Sir Basil goes on) is always hard to calculate but it can be safely said that a figure of two would be exact; it is our proud claim that we are far more exclusive than our religious competitors The Exclusive Brethren and their sinister affiliates, The Elusive Brethren.

### THE ORIGINS OF THE SECT

As long ago (in the words of Sir Basil) as 1961 Saint Basil (ne Nardly-Stoads) first discovered (or in the words of the Holy Stoadscript) came across the mystic words in the New Testament "Go forth and seize young women." This was taken by Saint Basil to be the essence of the message that God, in his infinite wisdom, was trying to get across. AND GO FORTH HE CERTAINLY HAS. In the words of Dragger, Sir Arthur Starborgling, "Sir Basil has certainly gone forth and seized them all right."

### AFTER THE SEIZURE

Once the seizing has taken place it is the sacred function of The Rammer and Dragger jointly to achieve the SPODE of AARON. What this is can never be revealed to those outside the Brethren, but I feel (writes Sir Basil Nardly-Stoads) that the words "Rumba", "Spreading" and "Hub" might well indicate to the sophisticated reader the nature of the ceremony.

Next week I hope to adumbrate on this and explain to the general pubic exactly how they can send us money.

# COMPETITION

ENTER NOW!

## IN VOGUE

The Douglas-Homes live lives which are homely, comfortable, with just enough of everything but with no luxury. The sort of life that is lived and understood by the majority of their fellow countrymen.

I don't see anything funny about that

---

# 1ST PRIZE

OH, JESSOP, WILL YOU NEVER LEARN

43, Leicester Way
Fenham
Newcastle-on-Tyne,5.

25th October,1964.

Dear Sir,

As the reputation of 'Private Eye' becomes more notorious, several M.P's have taken to writing letters to this nefarious publication.

1 would like your personal guarantee sir, that you do not intend to indulge in this form of indecent exhibitionism.

Yours faithfully

J. THOMPSON

9, Denton Road,
West Denton,
Newcastle-on-Tyne,5.

Dear Mr.Thompson,

Yours is a somewhat strange request.I do not hesitate however,to give you complete assurance that under no circumstances whatsoever will a letter bearing my signature appear in the pages of PRIVATE EYE.

Yours faithfully,
E.POPPLEWELL.

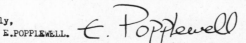

# OSBORNE RAUS !

We in Britain have long prided ourselves on the fact that we are without racial discrimination, that everyone in Britain, irrespective of race, creed or colour, is equal before the law. (That is, stands an equal chance of being beaten up by bent coppers who later give perjured evidence against him and are subsequently, having for once been very properly sacked, reinstated in the police force by Henry Brooke.)

But now, we regret to say, this fair picture is in danger of being besmirched by racialist fanatics who, although only a small minority in Britain, wield an influence wholly out of proportion to their numbers.

It has come to our notice that Sir Cyril Osborne, M.P., has been refused the lease of a house he wished to rent on the grounds that the lease contained a clause against the letting of it to 'a person of colour'. Sir Cyril, of course, is the owner (as is Mr. Selwyn Lloyd, ) of a large block of shares in a property company which exercises racial discrimination in its lettings. But, as this company only refuses accommodation to niggers, Sir Cyril naturally has no qualms about it.

The property company which has thus so shamefully broken with the traditions of England is Rakeoff and Sharke (Holdings) Ltd., with a registered address in the sleazier quarters of the House of Commons where all the hired PRO's masquerading as M.P.'s hang out. It is understood that Sir Cyril applied to this company in the normal way (or what passes for normal in the case of Sir Cyril Osborne) for the lease of a house on which he had had his eye for some time (with a view to dividing each of the rooms in eight and sub-letting them profitably to niggers) and was refused, the company drawing his attention to the clause which said that no 'person of colour' could take one of their houses.

'But I am not a person of colour' cried Sir Cyril, reasonably enough. 'Oh, yes, you are, you grubby little bastard', replied the spokesman. 'You are usually a rather repulsive pink, with yellow-grey blotches. When you are feeling queasy (as well you might) you are a horrible greenish-white, and when you have been at it rather over much, you are a kind of dirty, drained fawn colour. In the summer, you are apt to turn a singularly hideous brown, not unlike the more wretched specimens of the niggers you get so hysterical about, and the top of your bald head in particular is a riot of colours, all of them disgusting, and the general effect extremely so. Indeed, when the skin begins to peel, your head becomes a kind of mottled mess, with horrible red blotches, white-edged, sprinkled among the increasingly dirty and shiny brown of the rest. In short, you are a repulsive little tick.If you are not a person of colour, what are you?'

Sir Cyril thought long and hard, but was unable to answer this question. However, he refused to get rid of his shares in Oriel Property Trust.

Mr. Selwyn Lloyd was not available for comment, but you would have to be colour-blind to like the look of him.

## HALL OF FAME

# oh wotalotigot

says VISCOUNT "SMARTY-BOOTS" ECCLES

I was a worried man. I will admit it.   Thrown out of the Cabinet in 1962, I did not know where to turn.

One day I was a hopeless Minister of Education, the next I was nothing.

I was forced to roam the streets looking for work.

ALL I HAD TO MY NAME WAS A BARONY AND SEVENTEEN DIRECTORSHIPS !

But then Lord Home came along.

And Lord Home knows how an old snob's mind works. He knows you can't chuck out a Cabinet minister and only make him a Lord. For a New Year present he made me a Viscount.

SO NOW I   HAVE A VISCOUNTCY AND SEVENTEEN DIRECTORSHIPS !

# oh wotanorribleoldsnobiam

(Issued on behalf of Viscount Eccles by  Private Eye Promotions Ltd.)

# HOUSEWIVES RUSH TO JOHN BLOOM AFTER T.V. CLASH WITH ACID-TONGUED LEVIN

'Lynch the slippery little fellow', they cry, not meaning Levin.

John Bloom said on TWTWTW that it was essential to let the British housewife make up her own mind about trading stamps, and clearly acknowledged the success of his whole business to the ability of the housewife to decide for herself.

Yes - there's no doubt about it - John Bloom has proved that you can fool all the people most of the time, or at any rate that if you buy enough advertising space in the popular press the housewife's complaints can be used as tasteful and original wallpaper for Bernard Levin's outside lavatory

AND HERE'S THE PROOF!

1.   When you send in the coupon at the foot of this page, applying for a 39-guinea washing-machine PLUS fabulous free gifts, we will send you IMMEDIATELY two enormous salesmen who will hit you until you sign a form applying for a 60-guinea washing-machine of inferior make and NO FREE GIFTS AT ALL!

2.   How can we do this?  It's simple!  The salesmen we employ are told quite clearly that unless they can trick or bully SEVEN-TEEN housewives a week into buying rubbish they don't want at prices they can't afford, THEY WILL GET THE SACK!

Only Bloom's policy can show such results - that is why he is outdistancing old-fashioned, stick-in-the-mud firms that cling to outmoded policies of honest advertising and fair trading!

3.   But that's not all!  When the machine goes wrong, as in some cases they have done WITHIN TWELVE HOURS OF DELIVERY, you can write and telephone for our FABULOUS AFTER-SALES SERVICE until you are  blue in the face .  And the amazingly simple principle on which John Bloom has built up his super-successful business is that absolutely no notice whatever will be taken of you.   You see - the housewife must make up her own mind- if she buys a lot of scrap-iron from John Bloom, she is not an idiot - she knows it can't be expected to work.   So why should she bother to get anyone to come and repair it, especially since they won't?

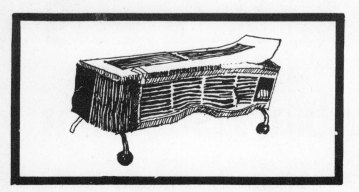

'IT'S UP TO THE PUBLIC TO MAKE UP THEIR MINDS WHETHER YOU OUGHT TO BE PROSECUTED OR ONLY SUED BY $1\frac{1}{2}$ MILLION DISSATISFIED CUSTOMERS' - BERNARD LEVIN TO JOHN BLOOM ON THAT WAS THE WEEK THAT NEVER WAS

4.   And those are only SOME of the advantages you get from buying a John Bloom washing-machine or refrigerator.  In addition, you get all the price-slashing advantages of our FABULOUS direct-from-factory sales system - which means that often the machines have broken down in transit BEFORE THEY EVEN REACH THE HOUSEWIFE !

5.   And - most FABULOUS offer of all - there is our part-exchange promise.   This is how it works.   Suppose you have an old washing-machine which, despite its battered and homely appearance, is a very great deal better than anything we could sell you, even if the claims in our advertising were true.   Our salesmen will visit you, and promise you £35 off the price of one of our machines for it.   They will then take it away to our factories, where experts will dismantle it to see if they can borrow any of other firms' ideas.   Months later, you will be sent the sum of £2, together with a bill for £178.10s. for our £45 washing-machine, PLUS - absolutely free! - a thinly-veiled threat to pour water all over your furniture under the pretence of giving you a demonstration.   SIMPLE, isn't it?

ONE WORD OF WARNING:  THE AVERAGE HOUSEWIFE REALLY IS AS BIG A BLOODY FOOL AS I BELIEVE HER TO BE.   SO THERE IS TREMENDOUS DEMAND FOR OUR SHODDY PRODUCTS AND NON-EXISTENT SERVICES.   IN ORDER TO ENSURE THAT YOU ARE DISAPPOINTED TOO, FILL IN THE COUPON BELOW AND POST IT TODAY!

**FREE**
Please send me a load of old junk and a blonde in a plain envelope.   I am over 21. Also please either grow a beard or shave.

NAME (Mr./Mrs.) _____

ADDRESS _____

_____ COUNTY _____

# SHOCK

# *PACK IT IN MR. C. !*

## THOMSON CALLS TITLES BAN 'NARROW'

**FROM OUR OWN CORRESPONDENT**

OTTAWA, Wednesday.

MR. ROY THOMSON, the publisher, said to-day that he " accepts with grace " the decision of the Canadian Government that he must give up his Canadian citizenship to become a British baron.

" It is with the greatest regret that I am now told I must give up my Canadian citizenship. I find it difficult to understand why this should be so.

### Prestige loss

" What object is served? Will it not deprive Canada of important favourable world prestige? "

# NO !

His face is wrinkled by the passage of time. His hair is turning white. He moves more slowly than in his youth. His back is stooped and his voice reduced to a senile pipe.

HE IS HUGH CUDLIPP, aged 53.

The men close to Mr. C. have been saying for years that it is time for him to retire to spend his last remaining years in 'peace with dignity'.

THEIR HINTS HAVE GONE UNHEEDED. Mr. C. intends to soldier on oblivious of his friends' advice.

What is more he plans to bring out a new paper this year. Ironically it is to be called "THE SUN". Significantly, it will appear in the autumn.

The new paper, says Mr. C., "will reflect the way young people think".

IT WILL NOT.

It will reflect the way Hugh Cudlipp thinks they think.

AND WE KNOW WHAT THAT MEANS.

In case you have forgotten, let us remind you of the sad story of the Sunday Mirror.

"Only a fool couldn't see it or sense it. This new Sunday newspaper is for THE MODERNS.

Of all ages. All classes. All politics and religions.

About time, too. The stuffier papers have clung too lovingly to traditions and taboos that mean precious little in the second half of this roaring expansionist century."

So wrote the aged Mr. C. on April 7th, 1963.

10 months later the new with-it, way-out, way-ahead Sunday Mirror has finally ground to a halt in the same old stuffy sea of 'sexy' rubbish that characterised the SUNDAY PICTORIAL.

Nothing daunted the white-haired 'rebel' launches out with a new paper. Once again the paper will appeal to the youth.

And once again the YOUTH OF ENGLAND shudder with boredom at the thought.

So Mr. C., as you sail down the Thames this weekend in your luxury cabin-cruiser, pause for a moment, stroke your long white beard and reflect:

In the words of the immortal husky person Ernest Q. Hemingway

"THE SUN ALSO SETS"     (Cert X.)

# SALUTE THE BRAVE !

Rejoice this morning that a clear, clean, courageous voice booms through the miasma of double-talk and parliamentary pussy-footing.

And for who? Colonel George Edward Cecil Wigg, Labour M.P. for Dudley, is whom. The gallant soldier is afraid to reveal nothing - except his age in "Who's Who" - in a ripe, rich, juicy language which turns blue the fusty, Old-School-Tie air of Westminster.

Salute the Billingsgate Battler. Applaud the Vitriolic Veteran. Three cheers for the Swashbuckling-Swaddy and hats off to the Red-faced Red-coat.

Who are the mealy-mouths, the tender-skins, the baby-talkers who blench at Wigg's wigging? The phrases he uses go back to the honest, outspoken, earthy tradition of 'Tom Jones' if not 'Fanny Hill'.

Who shrinks from being called 'a little, incompetent squalid creature'? Not our Prime Minister - no mean hand with a waspish tongue himself.

Who calls for protection at being addressed as 'a cheap skate and a phoney'? Not our Minister for Air

Does the Front Bench quail at being told that Polaris is 'a phallic symbol to make them feel like men'? Never!

Sir Alec and his virile team can face the insult that he is 'not fit to black the boots of the dirtiest private who ever took the Queen's shilling'.

If they could not, they would not be worthy of the Mother of Parliaments.

Colonel Wigg does not hide his aims. "If I am being offensive, by God, I am trying to be", he trumpeted. Can he take it as well as dish it out? Of course he can. When THE SPECT-ATOR called him a ' ********* ********* ******** ', did he run to his lawyers ?

YES, AS A MATTER OF FACT, HE DID.

What then this verbose and adjectival morning do we call Colonel George Edward Cecil Wigg?

We call him a slack-jawed, bleary-eyed bag of condemned offal. We call him a pot-bellied, weak-bladdered, beef-brained load of old crapulence. We say he looks like a camel, talks like a toucan, thinks like a stoat, and brays like a jackass. He is an offensive, reeky, fetid, mouldy, rancid, maggoty, scurfy, maculate, slimy, clinkerous, suppurating, dungy, putrid, overflow of a cesspool. He is a pompous, self-adoring, humourless BOGTROTTER who cannot bear to take one thousandth of the infantile abuse he hurls to his opponents under the cover of Parliamentary privilege.

# PRIVATE EYE

No 61
Friday
17 April 64

Price 1/-

# Goering Goering GONE

KILMUIR WAS HERE

Widespread interest has been aroused by Lord Killgoering's recently published autobiography. In particular his brief description of the historic encounter at Nuremberg with Hermann Goering has resulted in a demand for a fuller description of this momentous battle of wets. Here in a special article for Private Eye Sir David Maxwell House (as he then was) recalls those hectic days.

I shall never forget that electrifying moment at Nuremberg when the American prosecutor Newton Q. Bumwhistle put to Herr Goering the key question: "Are you guilty or not guilty?"

With his astonishing insight into the legal mind, the wily German fox replied with a smile: "Nein."

I have no wish to cast aspersions on the competence of my erstwhile American colleague, but it is only fair to say that he was bloody awful.

Nonplussed by Goering's brilliant outburst, the American burst into tears and hurriedly left the court.

In the silence that followed one could hear the hearts of the allied prosecutors sinking.

Was it possible that with this masterstroke the cunning Teuton might escape the processes of justice and retire to live a life of ease on the Riviera?

The thought appalled me.

It was clear that someone must come forward who would prove a match for the burly Herr. It was moreover clear that I was such a man.

Goering had never looked more offensively confident, as I faced him in the dock. A deathly thrush fell on the court and was quickly removed by two ushers, or thrushers as they were known.

I started my questions in a deceptively ingenuous manner.

"Herr Goering," I said, "what is your name?"

"Herr Goering," he replied, obviously ruffled.

"There's no need to repeat everything I say," I parried with a flash.

An audible sigh of relief went up in the crowded courtroom. At last an adversary had been found who could play the beastly Boche at his own game.

Without giving him a moment to gather his thoughts I thrust home with a new line of attack:

"Herr Goering," I said, "are you or are you not guilty of the murder of 7 million Jews?"

"Nein"

"Seven or nine, it makes no difference to me, you are guilty are you not?"

"Nein," he obstinately replied.

Here was my chance. I turned to the judge: "M'lud! I demand that the word 'Nein' be stricken from the record and the words 'Ja' inserted."

The judge readily assented.

I could see that the scheming Kraut had been thrown off his Guard.

Indeed throughout the Trial the Allied soldiers were forced to intervene as Herr Goering made no attempt to conceal his perverted desire for the warders who stood by him in the dock.

But this was the first indication I had that Herr Goering was not, to put it bluntly, altogether 'as other men tend to be'. I was determined not to dodge the issue.

"Sind Sie, oder sind Sie nicht eine outrägische Püff?"

He side stepped the question with a resounding "Jawohl!"

But I was not be so easily deterred.

"How then do you explain this picture of yourself on top of the Matterhorn waving a copy of the New Daily?"

"Nein," he said again.

A lesser man than I might well have despaired at the sheer audacity and legal brilliance of the fellow.

All the odds seemed weighted against the frail team of 167 allied lawyers and judges forced us as we were to make up our own rules as we went along, to grapple with the strategems of this one dastardly Prussian.

But then, by one of those accidents which can sometimes change the whole course of a trial, the judge, at a signal from myself, decided to intervene.

"Herr Goering," he declared, "it is my solemn duty by the powers invested in me to declare a true and impartial verdict. The fact that you have run rings round the prosecuting counsel in no way influences my decision. Your lot lost the war and you will therefore be shot."

But as the world knows Goering was to have the last word. A few days later he died by his own hand after concealing a quantity of cyanide up his arse, or arsenic up his side, I forget which.

..................................................

NEXT WEEK:
MODESTY, MY ONLY FAULT

For weeks the Foreign Office has been irked by foreign efforts to discover and interpret mysterious acts of British diplomacy in Panama - one of the world's sensitive trouble-spots. In March the British sent a new ambassador to Panama. After a month they recalled him for urgent consultations. A couple of weeks ago the man was abruptly and mysteriously retired from the Foreign Service "for reasons of health". Both Washington and Moscow considered the affair more than strange; international suspicion smouldered over the affair. The Foreign Office has remained silent.

The true facts show that the Ambassador - by name Randle Reid-Adam - behaved throughout with dignified determination. Arriving in March he was routinely abused by the local press, and a small bomb was thrown at him. He maintained his composure.

Then, after a month the Foreign Office was startled by a 3 a.m. call from Randle Reid-Adam demanding to speak with Sir Harold Caccia on a matter brooking no delay. Caccia was roused and took the call.

Reid-Adam said: "It's about my cats. Three of them. They've arrived and these Panamanians are trying to quarantine them." Caccia thought the Ambassador was talking in some kind of code. Suppose he was trying to say that the Americans were marching out of the Zone into Panama, or vice versa. Some sort of brink. He said: "Did you say cats?"

Reid-Adam said: "Of course I said 'cats'. Three cats. They have arrived and these people insist on quarantining them. I have protested in vain. I happen to be exceedingly fond of my cats. I must insist that you immediately take the most drastic possible action. They must be brought to their senses."

"You have brought me to the telephone at this hour to talk about your cats?"

"Well if Her Majesty's Ambassador can't save his cats from quarantine, the whole Service is reduced to absolute farce."

The conversation ended with Caccia instructing Reid-Adam to return to London immediately. But they had to wait a little while. When Reid-Adam did arrive he was asked for an explanation of the delay. He said that naturally he had to take time to break into the quarantine section at the port of the cats' arrival & rescue the three animals. He was happy to say that he had been able to arrange for a plane to convey them to Miami. According to the latest advices they were in excellent health.

So it seemed was Reid-Adam. But it took the Foreign Office only a few weeks to reach the strange conclusion that a staunch love of cats is a disease, and retired him from the Service.

# Astonishing Revelation by Scottish Newspaper

THE PROVO

PROVOST KNOWLES

BAILLIE VASS

THE new pr
unruly te
"They must h
Provost Fre
less than t
Every
teenage b
areas.
The i
little to
most

Mod terror not

spirit

# 'DOUGLAS-HOME' an Impostor

In an amazing report, the Aberdeen Evening Express last week revealed that the man known to the country as 'Sir Alec Douglas Home' is none other than the notorious Scottish impostor Baillie Vass.

Sir Alec (or Baillie Vass) last night said, "I have no idea who this Vass fellow is. All I can say is that I don't envy him his job as Prime Minister." When it was pointed out that Sir Alec (or Vass) was in fact Prime Minister he replied, "Don't bore me with statistics. I can't be expected to know everything."

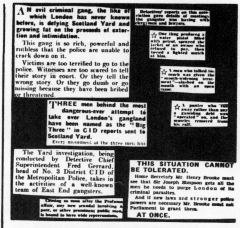

Reporters on some Fleet Street newspapers have refused to cover what everyone in the business calls "the Kray story".

They think it physically too dangerous.

This is the latest developement in a situation which gets more grotesque by the hour.

We have a state of affairs in which, if reports in the Sunday Mirror and Daily Mirror are true

Whole areas of London, east and west, are being terrorized, people who resist, ask questions or talk are maimed and liable to be murdered:

prominent public figures are blackmailed:

but

the victims are powerless,
the police are powerless
the newspapers are powerless.

The Sunday Mirror, which opened the ball on July 12th - and was followed by the Daily Mirror and Daily Express, was by July 19th, still unable to take the fluff out of its mouth and name plainly the men they are talking about. They, of course, know the names. So, of course, do the police. So of course does everyone except the unfortunate "general public". The men referred to have for a week been discussed and denounced in every bar in Fleet Street.

PRIVATE EYE considers this situation both farcical and intolerable. Either the charges are true, in which case the newspapers should have the guts to publish them, whatever the risk of libel action. Or they are untrue or grossly exaggerated, in which case they should stop scaring the people with this horror movie of London under terror.

PRIVATE EYE thinks it sensible and proper to print the names.

The two people being written and talked about are the twin brothers, Ronald and Reginald Kray.

For ten years both have been well known figures of London life.

They are rich.

They have criminal records.

They are credited in the underworld with immense power. Criminals have "authoritatively" told researchers that the Krays can whistle up 300 thugs for rough stuff and mayhem in half an hour. Or else it is that they can mobilize a thousand of the same in two hours.

The same sources say the Krays have at their disposal "suicide" squads" of dedicated goons, so loyal that they will risk life sentences in reckless acts of violence on behalf of their "leaders". The goons, criminals declared, specialize in blowing off the kneecaps of hostile elem-

# HAIL! HAIL! THE GANG'S ALL HERE

ents. Or they squirt a man with petrol and toss a lighted match on him.

The Krays are known to work energetically on behalf of many charitable causes. They have unquestionably done valuable work for spastics and retarded children. They have raised and contributed funds for cancer research.

They have been in business in the East End for approximately eight years, and in the West End for approximately two. They operate the Esmeralda's Barn nightclub.
There is no visible evidence that in the last couple of years they have been in any illegal business.

In 1958, the Krays were the central figures in a remarkable escape story. One of them, at the time in a place of confinement, was visited by his brother. At the end of the visiting period a twin walked out and disappeared to freedom. The authorities were then confronted with the other twin, raising hell and threatening to sue everyone in sight for illegal confinement.

■ The Krays have been with us for a long time.

■ So have the protection rackets.

■ The question is just why has the subject suddenly become a matter for such grave anxiety?

It may very well be that "protection" and the crimes that go with its enforcement are becoming more widespread and violent. So far as intimidation is concerned, since it is a fact that some reporters have been "pre-terrorized" it could be taken for granted that a lot of other people are too.

■ It that case, the most sinister aspect of the affair is that newspapers intimidate themselves with the libel laws to the point where they would rather muffle up the facts, at least until some gallant M.P. has ventured to put them into a "privileged" Parliamentary question, rather than pay out £25,000 or so for a lost libel action. (At that, £25,000 would be £10,000 less than one Sunday newspaper is hoping to arrange to pay the Kray brothers for their story.)■

In this connection a statement to PRIVATE EYE by Detective Chief Superintendent Fred Gerrard, head of No. 3 District C.I.D. of the Metropolitan Police, is of interest.

PRIVATE EYE telephoned to ask if he could say anything about investigations which the Mirror reported he was making. He referred to the statement from the Chief Commissioner published July 14th denying - among other things - that he was ordering or had conducted an investigation into alleged goings on between a homosexual peer, some clergymen and thugs.

P.E.: We realise that the Commissioner has denied that he has ordered such an investigation, but what about your investigations into the protection rackets and other charges?

Chief Sup: I am not making any investigations. I cannot help you.

P.E: Your statement is helpful in itself.

C.S: I am not here to help you.

Another explanation offered in some quarters for the uproar is that it is part of a general campaign to jolt the public into giving the police "wider powers". (This theory was strengthened by the timing and publicity handling of last week's official report showing crime rampant and rising and the police feeling "frustrated".)

The Mirror papers were vigorous in following up The People's exposure of the insanity and misbehaviour of ex-Detective Sergeant Challenor. Now they are astoundingly urging more powers for the police and - of all people - Henry Brooke.

PRIVATE EYE is not anxious to be sued for libel, have its kneecaps blown off, or get sprayed and burned as a sort of reluctant Buddhist. However, it must be recognised that if the Mirror reporting is accurate, this may quite probably be the last issue of PRIVATE EYE under the present management.

(Political Repercussions - Page 16)

Because his claim for injuries caused by the collapse of a pavement was dismissed as An Act of God, Mr. George Albright is suing God for £10,000 damages.

"God", he says, "is widely recognized as the creator of Heaven and Earth and the Churches are his appointed agents".

Mr. Albright has named 32 churches, synagogues, and chapels in his writ.

The Rev. Zilch of Palm Beach said: "I am prepared to give evidence in favour of the principal defendant".

Forty two years ago Mr. Albert Pember was ordered to pay his wife, Maud Pember, maintenance of two pounds a week. Recently he asked the magistrates to revoke the order.

Mr. Pember explained that after he married Maud in May, 1925, they went home to a wedding tea. At the end of the meal Maud's parents ordered him out of the house and that was the last time he saw her.

"I would have been willing to continue payments", he said, "but I was forced to retire and I can't get another job".

After hearing a thump outside her front door Mrs. Brogden of The Bay of Plenty, Wellington, NZ, found a kingfisher lying stunned on the footpath. She applied the kiss of life.

"It was quite difficult getting the air into his beak" she said, "but after some time he came round".

Last year Mrs. Brogden gave the kiss of life to a thrush.

Because she had lost her hair but not her passion for sea-bathing, Mme. Yvon Carbleu of Bordeaux could only enjoy herself to the full when, minus her wig, she swam from deserted beaches. Her husband did not consider solitude an adequate compensation for his wife's embarrassment. When she took her dip he would accompany her - without a costume.

Observed and arrested for immodesty by zealous constables, M. Carbleu told the Bastia Magistrate: "I swim nude because my wife is bald".

He was fined 300 NF.

*

A man who wished to build an hotel in Westville, South Africa, was shocked when the local town council informed him that in accordance with the apartheid laws he would have to install two completely separate sewage systems.

"It may sound strange to you," said the Chief Building Inspector, "but we have a fully segregated sewage system."

The Mayor, Mr R. E. Browne, said he knew of no law to that effect. "But I can see the sense in it."

The Borough Engineer said: "There is no such law - but I can see the sense in it."

The Town Clerk, Mr C.G.J. Coetzee said, "There is no such law - but it has become accepted practice over the years."

# TRUE STORIES
## CHRISTOPHER LOGUE

After boasting that he could kill a man and revive him, the villagers of Mando, Ghana, watched Kwaku Mark stab and bury Samuel Nuhu.

Samuel's relatives sent for the police and guarded the grave. The police arrived and warned Kwaku that he faced a murder charge.

However, when the coffin was raised and opened it was full of baked beans.

The crowd gave Kwaku the bird.

 The police have captured Anthony Smithers who escaped from a prison two and a half years ago. He was working as a labourer at Scotland Yard.

*

After crashing their car whilst on holiday in New Zealand, Messrs. Shepherd & Donaldson from the United States, were surrounded by pedestrians. Streaming with blood and badly bruised they faced a barrage of questions, like:

"Do you like it over here?"

"Who did you vote for at the last election?"

"Will Governor Romney become President?"

Those who are in the habit of dining out in style at The Golden Egg restaurant, Colchester, had their meals enlivened the other day when a young man picked up a large plastic tomato and squirted its sauce content all over a lady who was seated next to him. This done, he threw the tomato across the room, crossed the street, and entered the Wimpy Bar where other condemned souls were undergoing nourishment.

After looking about he climbed onto the bar and picked up a plastic cocoanut whose contents he squirted over the cakes and the barman, cried "Good Evening," (although it was only afternoon), and withdrew to a nearby pub.

Asked why he had done these things, he answered:

"I wanted to read something amusing in the local paper."

 A 44-years old Dubliner determined to show 'what an Irishman can do,' after having a few jars, started to bang his head against the wall of a hotel.

After some time his numerous audience saw him fall to the floor - stone dead.

Blonde, shapely, Elain Phillips, aged 23, boarded a Stockton to Saltburn bus, took a seat, and waited for the conductor.

When he came she asked for a half fare to Saltburn. This she was tended. Moments later the conductor realised his mistake and asked her for the rest of the money.

Miss Phillips produced a shilling and threw it on the floor.

"It was different when you went to bed with me," she said.

When the driver was called she said:

"It's all your fault, we'd still be engaged if it wasn't for you".

In court she strongly denied taking drugs.

A police spokesman said: "I'm baffled".

Mrs. Charlotte Warne, a Folkstone pensioner, has a bus stop outside her home. From the top of the bus passengers can see into her lavatory.

In order to secure privacy Mrs. Warne has to consult a bus timetable before relieving herself.

Mr David Mudd abandoned smoking during his employment as a television reporter. Now, as prospective Conservative candidate for the Falmouth Cambourne division of Cornwall, he has started to smoke again because he "feels it necessary to symbolise the freedom of the individual".

Suspecting that his wife was enjoying extra-marital pleasures, the driver of a cement-carrier parked his loaded vehicle in a street near his house and observed an E-type Jaguar standing at his door. The bedroom windows were drawn. Concluding the obvious he reversed his carrier up to the Jaguar and emptied four tons of wet cement into it. Then he resumed his watch. Twenty minutes later a young and good-looking man emerged from his house, kissed his wife goodbye, walked down the path, and rode away on a bicycle parked in front of the Jaguar.

*

In 1921 Shizo Kanakury was entered by Japan as a competitor in the Stockholm Olympic Games.

Shizo was present at the start of the race but missing at the finish. Officials and police searched for him, newspapers enquired after him; nothing was heard again.

Until last week, that is.

Then 54 years, eight months, six days, thirty two minutes, and 20.3 seconds after the gun, Shizo breasted the Stockholm tape, surrounded by amazed and somewhat elderly sports journalists.

On being congratulated Shizo said:

"Thank you. It's been a long race".

# PUNCH IN THE
# PRIVATE EYE

1/6

No 69   Friday   7 August 64

# The Rake's Progress: PUNCH

1. Born in penury, 1841. Meagre circulation and impertinent views. Inclined to Republicanism. Queen Victoria Not Amused. Financial stringency leads to takeover by printers, Bradbury & Evans.

2. Respectability achieved. Captions lengthened. Servants and Foreigners good for a laugh. Queen Victoria amused. Thackeray, too drunk to find editorial seat, carves initials on Table.

3. Tenniel Knighted. Partridge Knighted. Queen Victoria Knighted. A.P. Herbert blessed and Knighted. Dog Toby Knighted. Everything great fun. Circulation drops.

4. Muggeridge appointed Editor. Queen Victoria disgusted. Advertisers disgusted. Editorial office disgusted. Regular Readers disgusted. Paper improves. Advertising drops. Muggeridge dropped.

5. Dazed by 'sixties. Price increased. Economy cuts in Humour. Holloway gets 'with it'— starts Women's Page. Homosexuality mentioned twice. PRIVATE EYE lampooned.

6. Holloway Knighted, Bernard Holloway Knighted, A.B. Holloway Knighted, B. Holloway Knighted, A. Holloway Knighted, Boothroyd Knighted, Thelwell Knighted, Bradbury & Agnew Knighted, Publicity Manager Knighted, Doorman Knighted. Kate Greenaway Award, 1965.

'ONCE MORE INTO THE SHIT...'

The scramble at Kettering is over, and Sir Geoffrey de Freitas has made the grade. Meanwhile in the safe Labour seat of Shoreditch the ambitious swarms of possible Labour MPs are massing their forces.

In a special exclusive report PRIVATE EYE brings you a clear infallible guide on

# how to become a LABOUR MP

The guide starts from the moment a "safe" Labour seat falls vacant. Labour MPs can of course be elected from marginal constituencies, but this usually implies fighting an electoral campaign and bringing in politics. It is much easier and safer to concentrate on a seat where the Labour majority is more than 10,000.

Some 98% of all Labour candidates in safe seats belong either to the Old Left or the New Right. It is therefore vital to ally yourself to one of these groups.

For membership of the Old Left the following qualifications are necessary:

(1) Some 20 or 30 years' membership of a trade union, with at least some record of participation in the union affairs.

(The bigger the union the larger your support. It is much better, for instance to be a member of the Transport and General Union than of the Boot and Shoe Operatives Union.)

(2) A long record in local Government.

(3) A complete lack of interest in politics - apart from those of over twenty years ago. Hunger marches and Spanish Civil War are OK but for anything after that a record of absolute subservience to whatever the party, or the union were putting across at the time, is essential.

The NEW RIGHT demands different qualifications.

(1) Education at a good school and a university.

(2) Friendship with some high-up member of the National Executive. (This can be carried to extremes. Robert Maxwell, prospective candidate for South Buckinghamshire, and President of the New Right, takes George Brown to lunch with Isaac Wolfson at the Savoy Grill.)

(3) Absolute support for the Executive.

(4) Absolute opposition to the Young Socialists.

(5) (If possible) an off-hand knowledge of science. This can always be assumed. Dr. Jeremy Bray, for instance, Labour M.P. for Middlesborough West, describes himself as a scientist. In fact, like Harold Wilson, he is a statistician.

## THE NOMINATION

Nomination is the first step on the road to power.

Any of the local ward parties, the local Co-Op Party, the Young Socialists, the Women's section or any of the affiliated unions can nominate..

The Old Left Candidate has no problem. His union will nominate and he should bring pressure to bear on other unions to nominate him.

The New Right hopeful should get a letter from his friend or hero of the NEC (Sarah Barker is the best person) to the local organiser. He should then visit the organiser, buy him a few drinks, and go to see a few ward chairmen. An "amenable" chairman will soon be found, and the nomination is assured.

## THE MORE NOMINATIONS THE BETTER

### THE SHORT LIST

There may be as many as 70 nominations but only about six names will get on the short list drawn up by the Constituency Party.

Neither candidate has a real problem here. The Old Left will be forced on the list by the strength of his union (and their promised funds for the campaign). The New Right candidate should ensure that another letter or 'phone call goes from Transport House to the Constituency Chairman.

## THE SELECTION CONFERENCE

This is of course a crucial stage.

Each organisation affiliated to the local Constituency Party is entitled to a certain amount of delegates to a selection conference.

## THE MOST IMPORTANT ASPECT OF YOUR ENTIRE CAMPAIGN IS TO GET ALL YOUR DELEGATES TO THE CONFERENCE

The Old Left candidate should see that every possible delegate in his union in the area attends the conference. Each one should be visited and told about the conference.

The best method of getting them there is to pretend that they MUST go. Imply to the delegate that if he doesn't he will be slung out of the union and his job. If he says he votes Tory tell him that it doesn't make the slightest difference. He must do his duty and choose the local Labour candidate.

A particularly good method, perfected recently by the Transport and General Workers Union in Scotland, is to invite all the delegates of your union to tea at the Co-Op.

This brings them in in large numbers, and allows you to explain to the assembled company (after tea) what your name is and how to use the ballot papers.

The New Right should concentrate on the Women's Sections and the tame unions which Transport House officials can control by ringing up National leaders in London (the NUGMW is the best for this). The Fabian Society and the Socialist Medical Association are always good for two New Right delegates each.

In a safe seat, you should be absolutely sure of 100 delegates before the conference starts.

## THE SELECTION SPEECH

This does not matter very much since most of the votes are already assured. Here are a few tips for slogans for both candidates:

OLD LEFT:

Local Government is vital to the country's health. I have been in Local Government for 40 years.

NEW RIGHT:

The future of Britain depends on science and growth. As a teacher, I know how bad modern schools are. (These sentences should not follow each other).

Both speeches should contain a weak joke about the Tories, a long aside about the candidate's children and an enthusiastic reference to Aneurin Bevan (this last may win a few votes from the delegates who hated his guts when he was alive).

## THE ELECTION

This is of course totally unimportant. Try to keep a good image by wearing your rosette the right way up, and hugging your wife as the result is announced. Try not to discuss politics, as this may be held against you in later years.

## PARLIAMENT

Many people are saying that MP's are not getting well enough paid and have to work hard.

Don't be put off by this rubbish.

MP's are saying it because they want more - not because they haven't got it good already.

The fact is of course that an MP's job opens up enormous potential for a good life. There are binges galore.

You might even be lucky enough to get invited - as was Mr. Bob Mellish and a few friends recently - to Angola and Mozambique at the expense of the Portugese Government.

Make a few statements to the Press about how Fascism, torture and slave labour are not as bad as they were and you might even be asked again.

The Future Labour Offers You in Parliament is bright and rosy.

When you succeed, as you must, on our methods, don't forget to give us some of the credit.

# POP SCENE

*BY MAUREEN CLEAVAGE*

**'Are they ?'**

**" I SEE 'THOU SHALT NOT COMMIT ADULTERY' 'S DROPPED TO EIGHTH....."**

# Introducing the TURDS

I want you to meet four very young and very exciting Turds.

They're from the new Beat Centre of Rochdale and they're swinging into the charts with their first waxing "Chain Stagger".

### YOUNG

Yesterday, I popped into the studio and talked to them.

The Turds are something new. Ir-reverent, greedy, short and acned, there is a trendy look about them that sets a 60's pace, as up to date as next year's Courreges Underwear.

The leader of the group Spiggy Topes explained: "Actually we don't have a leader. In our eyes all Turds are equal."

### EXCITING

Spiggy regards the Turds' success philosophically. "What I say is I mean about this beat business well I shouldn't think we'll be around in a hundred years' time."

Spiggy is the lead singer and favours a grainy Bo Diddleyesque style that has the youngsters at shriek pitch excitement.

### PACEY

I asked him about the controversial microphone stroking that is the high point of his act. "Is it in any way sexually orientated?" His reply was revealing: "Of course it is you idiot dolly. Look are you a virgin or something?"

The Turds like everyone else in the world are classless and horrible. The Turds started at the bottom and are already dominating the thinking of pacey people.

I think the Turds are going to be with us for a long time.

(God help us all. Ed.)

# Turds to star in film

The news that Britain's leading pop group The Turds have signed a contract worth "well over one figure" to appear in a film (provisional title 'Lazarus - the Story of a Rising Pop Singer!) has been greeted with dismay in most circles.

The film is to be directed by Nathan ("The Knicker") Crisp, a 79 year old Canadian who was responsible for the very successful 'Eat More Brillo' series of T.V. commercials. He plans to start shooting early last week.

### REVOLTING

Mr. Crisp told me that most of the film will be improvised on location in a disused dart factory. "The Turdies are intrinsically humourous and they have a wonderful native wart" he said.

Also starring in the film: Anna Neagle and Sir Donald Wolfit who will provide the love interest. Sir Donald said: "It will be very refreshing to work with Turds and I know Anna's looking forward to it. It's a challenge for me. I hear the group are nauseating and nothing so mars a performance as a sudden attack of vomiting in a tender love scene."

### HORRIBLE

Miss Neagle, who is to star as Frieda Straster, a Bond-style prophetess, is to wear an amazing costume made entirely of margarine extract and wood shavings. She told me: "I have never got into margarine and wood shavings before. I think we're all going to have a lot of fun."

Spiggy Topes, who is to play Lazarus, was enthusiastic about the idea of working with experienced performers such as Sir Donald and Miss Neagle. "I'm sure I'll pick something up from those two old farts" he told me prior to diving down my blouse in search, he later explained, "of some hard stuff."

The Turdies' new record "Eat my Friend" is currently 9,482 in the 'Melody Maker' charts.

# PRIVATE EYE

No 75
Friday
30 October 64

1/6

## QUEEN OPENS PARLIAMENT

**HOW MANY POOVES ARE THERE IN WILSON'S GOVERNMENT?**

see page 3

# STOADS IN COURT

## 'Far from ordinary' scenes

The trial of Sir Basil Nardly Stoads charged with an "offence" against the person of the Rev. Knocker Prume opened yesterday before Justice Quarble at the Old Baillie.

Opening the case for the prosecution, Mervyn Grabely Stapps Q.C. related the events of the now famous night of December 20th. "It will be our solemn duty," he said, 'to show in the eyes of this court how on the aforesaid night the accused did wittingly and with intent, harbour and procure bodily substances of a loathesome nature against the parson heretofore, namely Rev. K. Prume."

Crossexamined by counsel, the Rev. Knocker Prume stated that whilst his religious principles were opposed to the application of unduly severe punishment which, he felt, should be reserved for the Almighty, he nonetheless expressed a desire to see the defendant "lashed to within an inch of his life".

Justice Quarble: Gentlemen of the Jury, I charge you to ignore this last piece of evidence.

(Cries of "What?", "Speak up!" etc from the Jury.)

Opening for the defence Sir Quentin Bloab Q.C. told the Jury that the very fact that he, a man of the utmost integrity and enormous income, had consented to take on the case was no small indication of the innocence of his client, Sir Basil Nudely Stopes.

Stoads: Nardly Stoads, your lunacy.

Bloab: That's as may be. Leave this to me, Fatface. (Continuing)

It shall be, gentlemen of the Jury, my submission that the accused, Sir Basil Nardly Stoads, did ipso volente and entirely without prejudice perform acts which in this day and age are considered to be of an 'artistic' nature and we shall call witnesses to this effect. Gentlemen of the Jury, I put it to you that we are no longer living in the 20th century –

(A note was then handed up to Sir Q. Bloab by Mr F.Q. Robinson, Solicitor in Ordinary, on the receipt of which Sir Quentin was seen to chuckle.)

Gentlemen, the days are gone when the sight of an unclothed sheep would cause amazement and despair amongst the populace at large. Call Denys Peans.

Clerk: Call Denys Peans!

Bloab: Denys Peans, you are, are you not, Professor of English Literature at Clibbard University?

Peans: No. I am just someone of the same name having a bit of a lark.

Bloab (roguishly): No eating in the court, please.

Justice Quarble: It is cold, isn't it?

Nardly Stoads: Good evening.

(Cries of "Grab", "Probe", "Grope" from Seductive elements).

The Dowager Wintisteria, 103 year old mother of the Clintistorit of Wintistering was then called.

Bloab: Would you not say, madam, that the bodily substances so slightingly referred to by the prosecution are of considerable literary merit which, on a close inspection, would reveal details of historical interest?

Wintisteria: No...

(A document issued by the Midland Bank was then passed to the witness, which she examined carefully.)

Wintisteria: That is to say Yes.

Quarble: Make up your mind woman. Yes or No?

Wintisteria: By all means, your absurdity.

Quarble: Pray continue, Sir Quentin.

Bloab: Would you not agree, madam, that the accused is a loathsome and despicable wretch who should be cast from hence into another place?

Stoads: Wait a minute, Bloaby, whose side are you on?

(After further consultation and an exchange of documents Sir Quentin resumed)

Bloab: Would you not agree, madam, that the accused is an upright and god-fearing citizen, whose bearing and deportment the young would do well to imitate?

Wintisteria: I think you had better ask my son about that.

The Clintistorit of Wintistering was then assisted into the box.

Bloab: How long have you known Sir Bummel Studely Goads?

C. of W.: If I were to mention the figure of 71 years, would that be of any interest?

Bloab: None at all, you foppish loon. Would you not agree that the accused is a man of firm postures and a supporter of many worthwhile movements?

C. of W.: Indeed, indeed. I have never known such a randy old bugger.

(Uproar. Cries of "Shame", "Withdraw the Gribling", etc.)

Stoads: Clinty - et tu ?

(Breaks down, sobs and swallows quantities of accessories. Uproar continues.)

Quarble: Gentlemen of the Jury, you have heard both sides of this unsavoury and appalling story. It is not for me to stress the loathsome repulsive and disgusting nature of the creature who cowers before you in the dock; it is solely my province to direct you on matters of law. If you take the view that the defendant despite the flagrant holes in the fabric of his evidence is in some way innocent of these heinous crimes then it is your duty to bring in a verdict of Guilty, that is to say, Not Guilty. But, contra, should you feel, as I do, that the accused has been overwhelmingly proven to be a shameless and perverted person fit only to be locked up with others of his ilk pending Her Majesty's pleasure, then it is your solemn duty to pronounce him Guilty. Pray consider your verdict and for God's sake be quick about it.

The Jury then retired, as indeed Justice Quarble should have done in 1903. As he left the court in an open Brougham, the Clintistorit of Wintistering was booed and jeered by Seductive elements in the crowd who threw matter of an 'unusual' nature in his direction.

# TRUE STORIES

## CHRISTOPHER LOGUE

The last wish of Miss Mary Foley was to be buried in Arran Island, the place of her birth.

Nothing stood between this wish and its fulfillment save 4,000 miles - the distance from the island to Boston, Mass., where Miss Foley passed to her reward.

The burial trip was organized by an undertaker named Sheehan. The fee was £300, door to door.

Being a son of Cork, undertaker Sheehan knew that Arran was a desolate and barren hunk of rock, approachable only by rowing boat. It was therefore arranged that the remains should travel to Shannon by jet, and thereafter by helicopter to Arran.

The coffin was due to arrive in time for eleven o'clock mass on Sunday morning.

Soon after touch down at Shannon, the fine American coffin was crated and attached by means of slings to the helicopter. The journey should have taken no more than twenty minutes.

However, a few minutes after take off something went wrong; the coffin and the remains of Miss Foley fell four hundred feet into the village of Paradise.

Some hours later the wreckage was collected by van, the remains were transferred to an Irish coffin, and at 10.30 on Monday morning they took to the air again from Lahinch Golf Club Car Park.

Prior to take off rigorous tests had been applied to the helicopter and its lifting device.

"We did everything except loop the loop," said Mr. Emby, a director of Trans World Helicopters, "we are licensed to carry all kinds of freight".

Undertaker Sheehan was enjoying his lunch in a Lahinich hotel when they brought him the news of a second disaster.

The helicopter's pilot had dropped the coffin into the sea off the cliffs of Moher.

At once a search was organized. The Kilronan lifeboat was contacted, but the crew refused to put out to sea because no life was at stake. Said Father McNamara, secretary of the lifeboat:

"We are holding discussions to see if an exception can be made in this case".

No such qualms beset Mr. Peter Hall, the helicopter's navigator. In order to help a Galway trawler pinpoint the spot where the coffin was last seen floating he dropped into the sea. "I was in the sea for ten minutes", he said, "it was freezing. There was no sign of the coffin".

Underwater television cameras, skin-divers, spotter planes, and the Galway fishing fleet, all failed to trace the coffin.

"We thought we had her once" said a frogman, "but it turned out to be a dead sheep".

*

Last week, Mervyn Sharpe, an eighteen year old garage mechanic swam the Channel in dense fog. "It was a nightmare", he said.

A young lady accused of shoplifting told the magistrate: "Well, I was working in this shop and they promised me £7, but when the time came I only got £3. Right, I said, and put on four jumpers, twenty-four pairs of knickers, four suspender belts, two brassieres, and five pairs of stockings.

"When I got home I told my mum: The old cow didn't pay me what she promised, and mum started going on. Just you wait I said, and started doing a strip.

"Mum was sitting there smoking her fag, laughing and shouting, Go on! Go on! .... I'll have that ... while I was taking the things off. And my old Nan, she's 84, was sitting there going hee-hee-hee ...."

*

A lady, suffering from an ulcer, was given a modern potion called duagastone. Some weeks after she began to take the drug she was admitted to hospital for an examination.

Two doctors were about to leave the ward in which she lay when, to their surprise, a report so loud it resembled a pistol shot, rang out from beneath her bed.

"We thought it might have been an expensive Christmas cracker," said the doctors, "however, when we questioned the patient she explained, somewhat shyly, that it was herself."

"Between three to seven hours after I take my pill," she explained, "my bowels emit a powerful shot.

"My husband and I have spent many sleepless nights waiting for the "shot" which, as we have our evening meal about seven, usually goes off at about two a.m.

*

○ The Abbé Berbard Gachet, a 44 year old priest, has been fined £710 for posing for obscene photographs with a governess, Adele Delaunay, aged 73.

The couple were among 31 people arrested by the Paris police after a raid on a religious bookshop.

An extraordinary Sicilian programme note; from the opera *La Bohème*.

Acto One: The poete Rodolph and the pain Marcel are half dead with cold in their eyrie. To give themselves something to do they are bourning a deama written by Rudolph. The philosopher Colline enters and standas astounded ta the splendour of the fireplace. Schuanard enters throwing some pieces of money on the ground. The lord who made Schuanard play until his parrot gave up his last breath the cunning of the musician who proposes to give the bird some poisonous parsley is of no interest to them. Schuanard suddenly has an idea. Why dine at

Act Two: Marcel isogling the girls when his old love Musette walks in with Alcidor. To get rid of Alcidor Musette pretends her fott is hurting while the Latin quarter is adorned with sausage and other delights ? One drinks at home but one dines out. The idea is accepted with publication, especially as the food before them will serve a gloomier day. As soon as Alcidor has gone Musette and Marcel exchange a passionate embrace. Some soldiers pass by to sound the retreat. The companions accomodeate theif etsps and march along with a military air among the joyous crowd.

Act Three: Rudolf sings: "Shall we ait till Springs ?" And the young girl replies: "I wish Winter would lasta for ever".

*

Mr and Mrs Robert Lynch met in a Mancunian bar.

At the time of their meeting Mrs Lynch was wearing corduroy trousers and a sweater. She called herself Paul.

"I was having a drink," she said, "when I saw Bubbles" (Mr Lynch's preferred name) "across the room. He was wearing a pink frock and a blonde wig. I could see his legs."

After a whirlwind courtship of three weeks, Bubbles and Paul were married.

The groom said: "I used to live as a woman until I found the man I love."

Paul was in the WRAF where she completed athletic, survival, and parachute courses - in Malaya. Recently she was discharged from the service for medical reasons. His maiden name was Bunn.

The best man at their wedding was called William Watson. His preferred name is Shirley. During the ceremony he wore false eyelashes.

Bubbles, the groom, wore a grey sports coat which went nicely with his red wavy hair.

The newly-weds, who are honeymooning in Liverpool, said : "We haven't changed. We still regard each other as opposites."

The bridesmaid was called Miss Ambler.

Information: The Times 11.9.67
Manchester Evening News 25.7.67

Monitors: Simon Watson Taylor
Keith Garnett

# 100s MASS IN SMITH SQUAR

A CONSTABLE POINTS THE WAY TO SMITH SQUARE

It is difficult to tell you how delighted I was by the excellent turn-out of readers and afficionados for my May Day Demonstration. Assembling in Parliament Square in warm spring sunshine, we were at once heartened and agreeably astonished by the truly magnificent band of young people of all ages who had gathered to pledge their support to the Rt. Hon. Baillie Vass, Knight of the Thistle, many in the company of their little ones.

After making contact with the charming constable who volunteered to lead us to the goal of our pilgrimage, we moved off, with banners flying, to the heartwarming strains of 'Colonel Bogey', provided on this occasion by the vassed bands of the Albert Brothers, gaily attired in their traditional uniforms. To the swinging beat of the big bass drum, the deep-throated braying of the sousaphone, and the bloodstirring clash of the cymbals our procession struck wonder and mute admiration into the many passers by, some of them foreigners to our shores, and with martial pomp and heads held high we moved by way of Smith Street into Lord North Street, scene of so many fine political novels of this decade. Those of Mr Maurice Edelbum being particularly worthy of recall.

What a sight we were ! I was particularly impressed by the industry and ingenuity, not to say political insight, shown by many of the placards. "DOWN WITH LEVIN" they read : a simple and direct attack on one of the most despicable figures of our epoch. "HIGH SPEED VASS GETS THINGS DONE" was another, or "THE VASS WITH THE DELICATE AIR" - a fitting tribute to the Conservative leader's masterly powers as a diplomat and as a father. "PRAVDA AND TASS BEHIND BAILLIE VASS", "UP THE BAILLIE THREE TIMES DAILY", "WHO'S A CRETIN?", "CONSERVATIVES DESERVE ALEC'S LEADERSHIP", "HANDS OFF THE RANN OF KUTCH", and many other apposite and boldly painted slogans.

It was while we were moving through Lord North Street that clouds obscured the face of the sun and we were struck with a sudden squall of what is normally referred to as rain, but our spirits remained undampened, and brandishing our soggy banners we turned proudly into Smith Square to the tune 'Onward Christian Soldiers !'. After a preliminary circuit of the square, one of my staff enquired of a nearby constable the whereabouts of the Conservative Party Cen-

tral Office, and we were
imposing building in the
ner, guarded on this occ
wart flatfoots, or as one
feet. While the band by
spiration moved through
of that grand old hymn '
final signatures were co
tion, and with due solem
staff approached the fro
ding, and rang the bell.
after a few moments by
and elderly gentlman , p
to the description of Mr

It is here that I feel
some comment on the ab
politician. Recently ap
good faith, by the Rt. Ho
seems to me, albeit a la
affairs, as in many othe
brought little but discred
ty and its unique leader.
use the unfortunate word
ference to the latter's a
television, but he has se
unworthiest aspersions
the present Prime Minis
must confess for the mo
Disastrous though I cons
be for the health and wea
it seems to me that his a
a life peerage on the gra
to millions as the wife o
ston Churchill, upon who
heaped, is the one spark
otherwise grey and most
Mr du Cann's comments
discordant and tasteless
of all right-thinking pers

" ABIDE WITH ME "
IN SMITH SQUARE

# Lord Gnome writes

...d to a tall
...t-hand cor-
... six stal-
...ut it, flat
...asteful in-
...talgic bars
...th me',
...or the peti-
...editorial
...of the buil-
...answered
...stooping
...ot answering
...du Cann.
...ity to make
...ntioned
...no doubt in
...e Vass, it
...these as
...he has
...great par-
...ly did he
...ng' in re-
...res on the
...cast the
...otives of
...ose name I
...cpaes me .
...s person to
...ur nation,
...conferring
...dy known
...e Sir Win-
...raise be
...ncy in an
...e career.
...y strike a
...the hearts

On this occasion, his conduct seems to me inexcusable. The details of the demonstration were in his hands a full week before our physical arrival in the sphere of his duties : the least he could have done to show his support for his great and glorious leader would have been humbly to receive in person this spontaneous gesture in the shape of many hundreds of signatures. As it was, I am certain that his absence will have done much to dampen those fires of enthusiasm that I myself have done so much to fan into flame with the bellows of my oratory. Wake up, Mr du Cann !

To return to the historic scene in Smith Square : having delivered the signatures into the humble but worthy hands of the caretaker, my editors led the waiting crowd in the singing of 'For he's a jolly good Baillie', and joined in giving three deafening cheers for our absent leader. A spontaneous movement in the crowd then called for three cheers for the Police, who had done so much to make our demonstration a success, and these were given, much to the astonishment of the bone-headed constabulary. The demonstrators then dispersed in an orderly manner, or, in the case of certain anarchist gentlemen, in a disorderly manner. These, I regret to say, saw fit to pursue the orchestra, still gallantly playing a rousing schottische, throughout at least two underground conveniences and finished up in an unsightly struggle with the police in Downing Street. I take no responsibility for what may have transpired, and refuse to allow this tiny minority to obscure the pure light of true purpose that suffuses this demonstration in my memory.

One other thing. Not only did I receive no reply to my personal letter to prominent Conservative spokesmen, among them Mr Maudling, Mr Heath, and Mr Macleod, but I was also disgusted to find no mention whatever of this historic event in the pages of the public prints. This merely serves to confirm the abysmally low opinion I have always held of the Conservative spokesmen, and of the so-called 'Gentlemen of the Press'. I can see little hope for this country so long as such people remain in positions of power, not to mention authority. It is for this reason that I would like to proffer my thanks to you, my loyal readers, for having lit a candle in this naughty world which my, who knows, and God willing, set such a fire alight within the hearts of men as will cause them to bless the very name of Gnome through ages yet unborn.

My obedient, not to say servile friend,

E. Strobes.
pp. Lord Gnome

...E CROWD

MEMBERS OF THE MILITARY BAND PAUSE FOR A "SMOKE" BEFORE THE DEMONSTRATION BEGINS

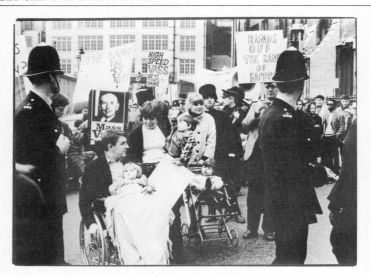

A DISABLED MUSIC HALL ENTERTAINER WITH HIS YOUNG FRIENDS PREPARES TO LEAD THE PROCESSION

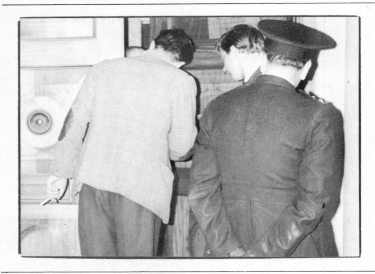

WATCHED BY A CURIOUS CONSTABLE, THE EDITORIAL STAFF PRESENTS THE PETITION AT THE CONSERVATIVE PARTY CENTRAL OFFICE

Strange as it may now seem to remember, barely five years ago the political party that now forms the Government of this country seemed both likely and determined to leave the centre of the political stage for ever. Defeated three times in a row, bereft of function or purpose, the Labour Party by the summer of 1960 seemed to have quite abandoned the search for new policies relevant to Britain's contemporary problems and given itself over wholeheartedly to the far more interesting diversion of tearing itself to pieces over unilateralism. But then, only two months after its disastrous Scarborough Conference, came the miracle: the event that, by twists and turns, was ultimately destined to bring the Party, albeit precariously, back to power. That event was the election as President of the United States of the 'young, dynamic, tough-minded' John F. Kennedy.

By the summer of 1961, the high noon of Selwyn's Pay Pause, a strange mood began to walk Britain. Precipitated by the fourth major economic crisis since the war, it became fashionable - particularly among 'progressive' middle-class 'intellectuals' of a political bent - to talk of Britain as a 'tired country', strangled by 'complacency' and 'the class system'. 'What's Wrong With Britain' became the cry, and the theme of a thousand Guardian leaders and articles in the New Statesman. And the answer was not far to see - or to be precise, it was only three thousand miles away to see; the trouble with Britain was simply that it didn't have a 'young, dynamic, tough-minded' Government like that of John F. Kennedy, full of 'young, dynamic, empirical whizz-kids' like Robert S. MacNamara, late of the Ford Motor Company. To a certain kind of political middle-class intellectual, the pallid young men who wrote for The Observer or worked for the Liberal and Labour Parties, 'Kennedy-ism' became at last their cause and their panacea for all Britain's ills. These young men, who pretended to be tough-minded realists, were in fact soft-minded romantics; they had found a comfortable high-minded faith in strutting about in the jack-boots of 'dynamism', talking 'tough' military jargon about 'making break-throughs', 'blasting aside the cobwebs of reaction and complacency' and 'getting Britain moving'.

An ideal candidate for initiation into this synthetic faith was the young 'blue-eyed boy' of the Labour Party, Anthony Wedgwood Benn - or 'Wedgie'. The essence of the attraction of 'Kennedy-ism' to its acolytes was its appeal to their priggish, middle-class masochism; it offered them an up-to-date version of that sort of 'smart' Uplift and sense of High-minded Self-Discipline that twenty years previously had been the stock in trade of Frank Buchman's Oxford Group. And ever since 'Wedgie' had got himself something of a reputation as a 'sneak' at Westminster School, he had certainly been the boy for priggish Uplift. As the son of a famous Labour politician, his early political career had been easy; in 1950 he was presented with a safe seat and became the youngest member of the House of Commons. He soon showed himself to be one of nature's Boy Scouts - like so many middle-class 'radicals'; he was an ostentatious teetotaller and liked nothing

## PILLARS OF SOCIETY 6. WEDGIE THE WHIZZ

so much about the Labour Party as the forced camaraderie it allowed him to indulge with his proletarian brothers - a great one for taking off his jacket to show his braces and for offering visitors to his rather smart Holland Park house steaming mugs of proletarian tea.

But not even his glamorous 'lone-fight' against the 'archaic' disqualification of hereditary peers from membership of the Commons gave our blue-eyed Boy Scout the 'tough-minded' faith he was looking for - until the second even took

place that was eventually to bring the Labour Party back to power. For a number of reasons which need not detain us, Hugh Gaitskell was never a man who could have embraced the gimmickry and trappings of 'Kennedy-ism' to win an election. But fortunately for the Labour Party, at just the right moment, he gave way to a man who recognised that the solution to the Party's problems was not to solve them by actually <u>doing</u> anything about them; but merely to give the Party a lick of new paint by <u>talking</u> differently, by talking the language of Kennedyism and by endless repetition of such empty slogans as 'we must get Britain moving'. The advent of Fuehrer Wilson was the moment Benn had been waiting for; here at last was his

leader and his faith. And in a series of articles in the Guardian, throughout the months leading up to the election, he spelt it out again and again. 'The Regeneration of Britain' was his theme - and again and again he goose-stepped his way through 'harsh realities', 'blasting holes' in 'the cotton wool complacency', talking of 'the big push' that lay ahead, of 'releasing energy', of 'tough, young New Frontiersmen' and 'huge New Frontier task forces. 'Wedgie The Blue-Eyed Boy Scout' had become 'Wedgie The Whizz-Kid', waiting for the New Britain, swatting up 'the technology of transport' in the hopes that he would become Transport Minister - and even getting a crew-cut to give him 'a tougher and more dynamic image'.

But when the magic moment and the New Britain finally came, it was far from being quite the paradise Wedgie had been led to expect. For a start he wasn't even put in the Cabinet. This was perhaps more of a disappointment than the fact that he didn't get the Ministry of Transport - the fact that half-way through 1964 he stopped writing endless articles in the Guardian about what should be done about transport and started to write about what should be done with the Post Office instead, indicates that he may have received some forewarning that he was to be made Postmaster General. And indeed for a whizz-kid bursting with energy, the Post Office was not a bad hunting ground; it would have been hard to find a Government Department in greater disarray after thirteen years of Tory rule; with the BBC, the telephone service and the delivery of letters being perhaps the three most prominent symbols of collapse and decay in contemporary Britain.

The only trouble is that after nine months of Wedgie the Whizz-Kid, every aspect of the Post Office's responsibilites is in even greater disarray than it was before. Even Marples may not have done a great deal - but at least he had a sure touch for gimmickry. Wedgie does nothing - and even his gimmickry is amateurish, as was shown when he chose to publicise the new 'telephone in your car' service at a time when one telephone call in every six is going astray and huge numbers of people can't even get a telephone in their homes. Dithering and self-contradiction over pirate radios, the mishandling of increased postal charges, Wedgie's record has been one of unmitigated disaster. But nothing tells so much the true quality of the 'dynamic, tough-minded, ruthless, efficient' British Kennedy-ite as Wedgie's behaviour in the one real battle he has so far had to fight as Postmaster General - over the postmen's demand for a 9% pay increase, which threatened to make a complete mockery of the Government's incomes policy. And what did our 'tough-minded' Whizz-Kid say to that? He gave in without a murmur - and without even consulting his Cabinet colleagues, whom he was thereby making look even wetter than they already looked. And what did our 'tough-minded' middle-class intellectual do when one of the few really tough, working-class members of this Government, Mr Ray Gunter, rang up to tell him what he thought of him? He burst into tears.

# DAILY GETSWORSE

Help!

FRIDAY AUGUST 6 1965    Weather: Snow

## The Biggest News of the Day

By SQUIRE BARROWBOY

The biggest news of today is to be found on page 16.

A FULL PAGE COLOUR ADVERTISEMENT FOR LOOSEBOWEL'S BAKED BEANS.

For many years Loosebowel Ltd. have carried the good name of Britain all over the world.

They have an unequalled reputation for craftsmanship, enterprise and baked beans.

They have done wonders for the export drive.

Their chairman, Sir Geoffrey Loosebowel, is rightly renowned as one of the outstanding figures in British industry today.

Their baked beans are the finest in the universe.

We will say the same for any company which takes a whole page colour advertisement in the DAILY GETSWORSE.

## UP

## UP

## UP

goes the price of the SUNDAY GETSWORSE.

In this Sunday's issue:

## How Mountbatten won the War

a sensational story which we have never been able to tell before.

also:

## The Duke of Windsor forgets

Part 17 (repeat): "Mr Baldwin speaks to the Nation".
ORDER YOUR COPY NOW TO ENSURE A FANTASTICALLY BORING SUNDAY not to mention more money in the pocket of Sir Max Aitken.

### BREAST POCKET CARTOON

"Possibly it is just a teeny bit risqué, Osbert, but only three hundred people in London will understand it and those illiterate people at the Getsworse certainly won't - anyway they can't afford to sack you - so why don't you just pop down to Fleet Street and by the time you get back I'll have made you a Martini and we might have a couple of hours together before that dreadful daughter of mine gets back from her protest march etc."

## A Great Day for Britain

# REJOICE !

GEORGE G. ALE
RENE McALCOHOLL
BOTTOM PINCHER

YES ! IT'S BOOM TIME FOR THE DAILY GETSWORSE !

That was the cheering news from London's busy Fleet Street last week.

In the past few weeks alone the circulation of the DAILY GETSWORSE has risen to no less than 4,000,000 copies a day !

This represents an advance of no less than 50,000 copies a day in the past six months alone.

### REJOICE AGAIN

It is also more than TWICE as many copies as were sold in the days when the circulation of the DAILY GETSWORSE was only 2,000,000.

This is good news for Fleet Street.

It is good news for all those who love newspapers.

It is good news for Britain, for the DAILY GETSWORSE is an entirely British owned newspaper.

### I SAY

It is also good news for Sir Max Aitken, the enterprising Chairman of Getsworse Newspapers, who has built up the DAILY GETSWORSE single-handed ever since he inherited it from his father over a year ago. For it means more money in his pocket.

### REJOICE

It is particularly good news since only four years ago the circulation of the DAILY GETSWORSE was 4,500,000 and this is the first time it has stopped going steadily downwards ever since.

## Fredericks-town - New Fake

A superb new Fake has been acquired for the Beaverbrook Art Gallery in New Brunswick.

The painting, which is believed to be at least five years old, has been examined by experts who are satisfied that it is a genuine Fake.

---

EXPORT DRIVE

THE LITTLE VILLAGE of Puerto del Sod in Venezuela wanted a new public convenience. Now comes the news that Grobbit and Slobes of Acton is to supply it - at a cost of £178.

The citizens of Puerto del Sod will attend to the needs of nature in a British toilet.

Now let our exporters make sure that the paper that is used is British paper - preferably old copies of the DAILY GETSWORSE.

## All the Knees that are fit to print

IT IS THE POLICY OF THE DAILY GETSWORSE NOT TO LET A DAY GO BY WITHOUT PRINTING AT LEAST ONE PHOTOGRAPH OF A WOMAN TAKEN FROM KNEE LEVEL.

And for why ?

Because our photographers are dwarves.

They are British dwarves.   And the knees are British knees.   From henceforth the Daily Getsworse will have a new policy.   It will no longer be printing photographs of women taken at knee level.

It will merely be printing photographs of knees.

In this way the readers of the Getsworse may be ensured of an even greater quantity of knees per page.

And the knees will be even larger.

YET ANOTHER FIRST FOR THE DAILY GETSWORSE !

## JUST FANCY THAT

Mr Peter Baker, once tipped to become Editor and until recently deputy Editor of the Getsworse, is now reduced to writing a series of articles for a woman's magazine.

Their subject: "The Manhood of Prince Charles".

# PRIVATE EYE

o. 95
riday
August 65

1/6

## WOMEN!   WIN MR. HEATH!

| | | |
|---|---|---|
| ★ | **TOUGH** | |
| ★ | **ABRASIVE** | |
| ★ | **DYNAMIC** | |
| ★ | **Superbly Professional** | |
| ★ | **MODERNISING** | |
| ★ | **Grammar School** | |
| ★ | **RUTHLESS** | |
| ★ | **Silvery Grey Hair** | |
| ★ | **ABRASIVE** | |
| ★ | **Trains run on time** | |

**2nd PRIZE**
⭐ A weekend with Mr. Maudling.

**3rd PRIZE**
⭐ A lifetime with Enoch Powell

 JUST PLACE THE ABOVE IN ORDER OF PREFERENCE, SNIP
AND SEND TO LORD GNOME, 22 GREEK ST., LONDON W. 1.

# COLOUR SECTION

George Brown's habit of kissing any woman he meets excited some comment in the public prints a few weeks ago. It has also excited some comment from his colleagues. At a recent party given for the 'New Establishment" by the enterprising publisher George Weidenfeld, Mr. Brown was introduced to the wife of the American Ambassador and warmly kissed her on the left cheek and then on the right. But this was not all. With a cry of "And one on the middle in the good old English fashion!" the Deputy Prime Minister lunged towards her lips. While the guests blinked in embarrassed disbelief, one of the Hungarian economists was heard to whisper to his neighbour "This is not the worst. He has done it also with Princess Margaret."

In all the accounts of the 'Beatles M.B.E.' story it has been assumed that the whole thing was a vote-winning stunt on the part of H. Wilson and that it was pretty poor form to involve Her Majesty in that kind of "squalid political manoevre".

Not, we are reliably informed, so. Last week at one of those informal off the record get-togethers, this time on the lawn at Marlborough House, Wilson was asked by a curious journalist why he had made the controversial award. He replied that it was not his decision. Her Majesty had insisted.

Which, of course, takes some swallowing.

A man came into the offices of one London newspaper last week with a story which might, if it had been printed, have cast something of a gloom over the Dublin festivities in connection with the Casement funeral. He said he had been in Pentonville between the wars, and had at one stage been a member of a work party engaged in building a wall. During the preliminary excavations several bodies had to be moved, and there was no doubt in his own mind that prison officers poking about in February of this year with only a pencilled sketch-map on an old piece of paper had in fact made a grisly mistake: Dublin had in all probability, he thought, gathered to pay homage to the remains of Dr Crippen.

## Claud Cockburn
### Down Memory Lane
# THAT BOUNDER BYERS

For ungentlemanly bad-thought dispenser of the month must be nominated Lord Byers. He had the extraordinarily bad taste to state - somewhere in Somerset - that Sir Alec Douglas Home had been 'pushed out by niggling behind-the-back gossip and denigration'.

It certainly goes to show how untrue it is that all of us 'needs must love the highest when we see it'. True, the vast majority of our fellow countrymen recognised the sheer, altruistic goodness of Sir Alec. Not so the man Byers. Lord, forsooth. One would have supposed his high rank would have impelled him to suppress, at least, his own coarse thought and set an example to his inferiors - particularly the Jacobin yokels of Somerset, ever prone to put the worst construction on the actions of their betters.

The so-called Byers must have had a rude awakening indeed on the Sunday when he opened his Sunday Express and read the truth which he, in his insensate determination to throw mud on all that should be sacred, had so wantonly sought to distort, nay conceal.

Rightly heading its leading article with the words - so simple, yet so direct in their appeal to all that is best in all of us - 'The Good Man', the Express wrote that Sir Alec "quits the Tory leadership for the same reason that he reluctantly assumed it . Simply because that is how he sees his duty. Sir Alec, through his kindliness and dignity had attracted many devoted followers. He had but to raise his hand and they would have rallied round him. He could have gone on indefinitely, calculating that the opposition to him was bound eventually to wither and die.... The glittering prize that most politicians would scramble for and cling to, Sir Alec freely hands over to another man because that man may be better for the Tory party'.

The Sunday Express did but utter in the finest imaginable prose - of a quality customarily permitted to be handled only by the writers of obituaries - sentiments put on record by, thank God, many and many a leader writer and political commentator.

Gratifying indeed was the message they conveyed: He did not fall, he was not pushed, he jumped for the good of the Party.

No doubt Lord Byers and his ilk are all too well accustomed to getting behind people's backs, niggling till ready, and then making a big push with the old denigration. Not so the leaders of the Tory Party. Not so, indeed in the good old days, the leaders of the (then) noble Liberal Party of which Byers purports, reportedly, to be a member.

Naturally, they had their differences of opinion, their essentially friendly contests and tussles. And very uplifting they were to watch from Tring, Herts in the years just before World War I.

A Gallup Poll of opinion in Tring at that time - naturally we had no such thing and would have regarded it as an unwarranted intrusion upon etc etc etc. - would have shown three main categories of thought among the members of the adult male population

One group of thinking males showed certain affinities to what we may call the Byers mentality. They niggled. They denigrated. While decent people saw in Lloyd George the embodiment of all those homespun virtues which have ever sprouted from the soil of Welsh Noncomformism, these tittle-tattlers did not scruple to make low jokes about his sex life, and with any encouragement would produce nasty little calculations supposed to show how much certain of his cronies had made out of the manipulation of the Marconi shares.

You would have thought they would at least have let Asquith alone. He was fighting the suffragettes fearlessly and set his face like sandstone against those who wanted serious action taken against Army officers at the Curragh whose only offence had been mutiny. Yet just because the man sometimes staggered and stumbled as he steamed towards his place on the front bench of the House of Commons after dinner, they put about tales that he drank. Like a fish, old boy, they used to say.

The second opinion-group consisted of people who not only declared that all our Public Men were pure in heart and noble of intellect, but actually believed their own declarations. This group was, admittedly, rather small, but made up for that by being immensely happy.

Some people, it appears, have only recently found out just what it means to have God on your side. These people in Tring, Herts, knew it then. And was it likely that, such being the case, God was going to let a lot of blabber-mouthed scoundrels and titled degenerates get their paws on the tiller of our Ship of State? Not on your Nellie, he wasn't. Whoever was in charge was in charge because God asked him to be, and was therefore a good man, who would bring peace and prosperity to Tring. And so they did, right up to the time around midsummer 1914, when God saw - and all other understanding people saw - that the nation needed a tonic, like a real big killing and maiming of millions.

The third group was the largest. It was made up of people who in little secret conclaves over the port and brandy, and assured that no informers were present, not only agreed with everything Group I said publicly, but added a lot of even more damaging information about the goings-on of public men of all parties. But the difference between Groups I and III was that Group III knew that the right thing to do was, in public, to voice the sentiments of Group II.

This, they knew, was the way to Maintain Public Confidence, Combat a Spirit of Creeping Cynicism and Unrest among the Masses, and Deter the Kaiser by showing that Britain Stood United.

Had it not been for the brave face put on things by Group III something awful might have happened.

Lord Byers should take note of that fact and think twice before he suggests that such things as niggling and denigration play any role in our British political life.

It is ironic that, at a time when England is supposedly setting the cultural style for the world, it should have taken an American, Richard Lester, to be the first man to capture and reflect the mood of the New England on film. As the queues still lengthen outside 'Help!' and 'The Knack', this has undoubtedly been Lester's summer. He has been hailed by pubescent Beatle-fans and Sunday-newspaper intellectuals alike; by the Sunday Times' sober Dilys Powell as 'ambitious, audacious, sophisticated, dazzling'; by the Observer's crackerjack Ken Tynan as 'brilliant'; by the Sunday Telegraph as 'one of the best things to have happened to film comedy for thirty years'. How the Beatle-fans reacted has not, on the whole, been recorded - but there is no question that, in Lester's hectic, frenetic, pyrotechnic, gagpacked style, they have caught the dry, pacy, up-to-the-minute authentic echo of their own zeitgeist as never in films before.

Lester is the first British film-maker of the age of Pop Art and the Colour Section. He wants his films to have instant impact - to dazzle, to amuse, to amaze - but not to last. He is quite unashamed when he says that they are meant to be totally ephemeral - "for me", he says, "there is nothing really lasting." His nonstop piling on of gag after boff after pratfall means that you hardly have time to realise whether a joke is funny or not - if it isn't, then here's another one! And above all, he woos his audience with the visual image, with his firework photography, with all the expertise he learned in his years of directing television commercials - the secret of which, after all, is to cram as much into as short a space as possible, never to let the audience get bored. Much of his photography is indeed beautiful - in 'Help!' alone there are at least 100 frames that could be frozen to make the cover of a Sunday Times Colour Section. And certainly it all makes those old 'New Wavers' of the dear, dead days of Woodfall - the working-class romanticism of Schlesinger, the historical romanticism of Tony 'Tom Jones' Richardson - look like something from another age.

But for all Lester's simple aim to provide Instant Amusement for the Here and Now and Nothing More, is there not a nagging doubt in the minds of many who see his films? What is this strange feeling that although 'Help!' wasn't exactly boring, it was a little ...well, boring? When it comes down to it, underneath all the jazzy photography, and the colour filters, and the zooms and speedups and the hypnotic sound-track - what was going on? Was anything going on? The fact is that 'Help!' is in fact two films - a fast-moving surface and a lumbering, painful, boring B-picture with a lousy, jokeless script going on underneath - the aim of the first being, by legerdemain, to draw attention away from the second which no one would pay 2d. to see. Mr Lester has learned his lessons from his years of making commercials well - for 'Help!' is in fact nothing more than one huge, glossy, 90-minute commercial with slightly less connected plot than is usually crammed into 30 seconds of Having a Tiger in Your Tank.

TRENDY!

I AM A BORE

POP

PILLARS OF SOCIETY 8

LESTER SQUARE

It would be rash, however, to dismiss Mr Lester merely on the strength of one film in which any director's hands would necessarily be tied by the brief of having to weave a coherent and plausible masterpiece around the non-Thespian talents of the Beatles. Obviously he must rather be judged on a film like 'The Knack', in which he starts with the advantage of a carefully-written theme and professional actors through which to speak. Certainly 'The Knack' is a much better film. It still contains vestiges of an imaginative play in its script. There are moments, such as that when the regular Casanova intoxicates and hypnotises a girl into virtual submission, as a stoat hypnotises a rabbit, which will be long memorable. But the nagging doubt is never far away -

and as soon as the film is considered in retrospect it returns; that, like 'Help!', it is little more than a feat of cinematic legerdemain to distract attention from a ceaseless unremitting, piledriving cornucopia of half-remembered silent film gimmicks, unfunny sexual double-entendres, lumbering, ill-timed pieces of slapstick and the sort of corny, repetitious jokes that one might expect from a fairly humourless ex-student of psychology at an American University - like the 'Buckingham Palace Joke', that recurs in both films, and is vaguely reminiscent humourwise of Mr Bernard Hollowood. *

Now, of course, it will be said that so long as the legerdemain succeeds, so long as the eye deceives the mind, then Mr Lester's purpose as a film-maker is secure. He only claims, after all, to provide Instant Amusement for the Here and Now. But the tragedy of Mr Lester is he thinks, as do his intellectual admirers, that he will go on being able to provide Instant Amusement for the Here and Now for ever. He may espouse ephemerality. He may eschew the desire to be remembered in years to come. But he will still, himself, wish to go on eating and making films in the years to come. And he will be hoist by his own petard. For what he doesn't yet realise is that his whole style of making films, his recurring jokes, his ebullient plagiarism from every original film-maker there has ever been without any real original contribution of his own, are as ephemeral as the films themselves. He is a craze, a trend, a delusion. And his day will soon be over.

* The Editor of 'Punch' - a magazine.

## NEW LONDON CRIES.1

NON-STOP STRIP! TWELVE LOVELY BIG TITTIES AND BUMS!

NAKED LUNC REAK

STEADman

## NEW LONDON CRIES. 6

'ERE 'RENE, LOOK AT 'IM! DONT 'E LOOK QUEER?

STEADman

# JOURNAL OF YE PLAGUE YEER NINETEEN HUNDRED AND SIXTY FIVE

## BEING SOME EXTRACTS FROM YE DIARY OF SAM. PEEPS ESQ.

**Jan 8th.** Returned to London where I hear talk of a great sickness having taken root in the city. Many are already stricken by it and particularly the young people.

**Jan 21st.** I walked this day in the village of Chelsea, where I did for the first time see many in the streets afflicted with the sicknesse and for the first time also did see the houses where plague had struck, marked out by blue-painted doors, wrought iron work, carriage lamps, bowls of geraniums hung from windows and the like.

**February 16th.** Down the river to Fleet Street where I did meet old friends in the alehouse of Ale Vino. Much talk of the nature of the sicknesse and of how those affected soon begin to gibber strange sounds, 'with-it', 'dynamic', and the like, and attire themselves in bright shoddy materials, transported into some nervous ecstasy.

**March 17th.** The pest houses are now everywhere, some called boutiques, some trattorias, some bistros, where the unfortunate sufferers may gather to find comfort in each other being like afflicted. It is a particularly sad sight to see the young girls, their faces pale and drawn with the plague, their skirts raised above the knee as a sign that they are stricken.

**April 19th.** Had long converse with a company of gentlemen as to the original causes of the plague, some saying one thing, some another. A common conclusion was that the chief carriers of the pest appeared to be certain chronicles and journals which, allowed freely into the homes of rich and poor alike, do spread th'infection daily; these being glossy magazines and Coloured Sections. On contact with these vile effulgences, the reader eventually lapses into a kind of wild madness and a delusion that only the present time is of any importance and that he must present the right appearance to the world by donning strange garbs, filling his house with op-art tablecloths and drivelling his need for 'dynamic' Government. Eventually the poor sufferer, having worked himself into a frenzy with the constant need to change his garb and opinions every few minutes, wastes away and dies.

**May 17th.** Did make my way to Southwark Church, there hoping at least to find some respite from the infection which is gripping the town. Only to discover that the preacher himself had been only too obviously afflicted, dressed up in thigh length bootees and proclaiming loudly that for the Estab-lished Church to survive it must 'get with it', by abandoning any pretence at belief in the existence of the Almighty. A distressing experience.

**July 28th.** The pest is now striking at even the mightiest in the land. For today the Conservative Party, meeting in solemn conclave to choose their new leader, did all at once throw themselves into a terrible dance and with horrid cries of 'dynamic', 'abrasive', and 'ruthless' did elect as their king the most boring of their number, a Mr Heath, for that he struck the right 'image' of the moment. I have little doubt that within a twelvemonth their fashion will have changed and they will all be heartily sick of him, for having seen the reality of the man.

**August 27th.** The town is now nothing but plague pits and pest houses and wandering crowds of the diseased, there now being fewer who are whole than those afflicted. A strange sight in Marylebone, where hundreds of brightly dressed young people plunged simultaneously into a new plague pit to be known as 'The In Place' with apparent pleasure as they expired. There is intelligence from outside the town that the plague has now spread throughout the countryside, and does ravage the land at will. Never can there have been such a pestilence in all history and I see no recovering from it.

Bring out your freuds!

Plague & go

Rushton

Desecrating my column with rumours issuing from Hammersmith police station, a notoriously liberal station, filled with near-barrister constables and sergeants who attend poetry readings IN THEIR VERY LIMITED SPARE TIME, I report a fight. On the one hand, the elderly bobbies, outraged by their daughters' boy-friends and the (to them) common knowledge that smoking cannabis is now so widespread that their legal excuses for searching nubile female drug fiends are soon to be curtailed; on the other, the young fuzz, not unaware that every piddling pot bust makes them look ridiculous in the eyes of their non-uniformed mates - to say nothing of their wives.

Late one Saturday night, the eternal, anonymous, and abominable landlady phones in to say that the drug fiends are whooping it up in her basement flat. Most of the fuzz are about to leave for what remains of the weekend. They ask: are they doing any damage? Is there a fight? Have you actually seen the fiends? Well, no, she hasn't, BUT. But what? But they are playing records very loud AND they are dancing NUDE. Has she actually seen anyone dancing nude? YES! That does it.

Six guys pile into a white Jag, roust out a tame magistrate, get his name on the break-in order, and roar up to the address. The front door is open. In they charge, plus Ruby (sister of Sam the wonder-dog) who can detect a grain of hash at a distance of four hundred and fifty yards, with the naked nose.

Inside are about twenty people whizzing round and round the room like tops, the record player is going full blast with Turkish zither music, though you can hardly hear it for the elemental shrieks of the whizzers. Everyone is wearing leotards. Brought back to their Hammersmith basement by Ruby's barks, the leading whizzer explains that he is giving a class in "whirling" and that the company are a West London Branch of the Ombas, or Whirling Dervishes, a religious group, who are absolutely opposed to any form of pleasurable activity whatsoever - save whirling.

By now there are about fifteen policemen in the room. The old school are in favour of arresting the lot, taking them down to the station, and dusting out their pockets to find the grain that has been wrinkling Ruby's nose. The young school are for turning it in - and just wait till that old buzzard calls us again.

Youth prevails. Back at the station, a tremendous theoretical argument develops. In five minutes it has escalated, and - once again - the old are laying into the young, who are defending themselves sturdily.

The phone rings in the Putney cop-shop. The Putney boys - also looking forward to an early night - have to pile into their Jags and whizz round to Hammersmith, there to forcibly separate the rival factions. Just wait till "Uncle Jo" Simpson hears about this.

## TRUE STORIES
### Christopher Logue

● For many years the resident gravedigger of Wotton-Under-The-Edge has been Mr Maurice Pick. This autumn, the parish council decided on an efficiency drive. They consulted a firm of Time & Motion experts who offered to send down a team to watch, measure and record Mr Pick while he interred his fellow villagers. Their fee was £45 per day.

After consultation the councillors decided they could not afford the experts. Nor could they afford Mr Pick - who was costing £1 a day.

Mr Pick was sacked.

People, however, continued to die. The council advertised for a new gravedigger. Nobody answered the call - except Mr Pick. His application was rejected.

As increased efficiency is, as often as not, a euphemism for loading the cost onto somebody else, the council informed all local undertakers that they would have to include gravedigging costs in their interment charges.

The local undertakers advertised for a free-lance gravedigger. Mr Pick offered his services and was accepted - his charge is a flat £12 per grave.

Under the old (or inefficient) system the charge per grave worked out at £2.15.0.

Mr Pick is better off. The undertakers are involved in more paper work. The villagers, including the council, have to pay more for their last rights.

★

After hearing a case in which a prize chihuahua had been raped by a boxer, the Fairfax County judge said:

"I dislike dog cases. There's always a horde of witnesses. And I have to spend half an hour over a piddling little dog. Furthermore, it grieves me to see decent middle class people in the courts. I'm used to handling a different class of person altogether."

★

The RSPCA has been left 14 brothels by Mr Joe Borg, known in Sydney as "The King of Vice."

Mr Borg was blown to smithereens by a bomb planted in his car.

In addition to these valuable properties, Mr Borg left the Society $500,000.

"He was a great animal lover," said an RSPCA spokesman.

After being gaoled for forgery, Mr Richard Scoby found himself occupying the cell immediately above that of Anna Holmes, who was being held on a charge of possessing illegal alcohol.

During their incarceration, Mr Scoby proposed to Miss Holmes by shouting "Will you marry me?" down the lavatory pipe that connected their two cells.

They were married in handcuffs. The best man was doing life for wife slaying.

★

Last year an unusual Christmas party was held near Stoke-on-Trent. Forty nude housewives washed down mince-pies with whisky in the Hanley Steam Rooms, danced to rock'n'roll among the rubberised paper chains and "really let go" according to the organisers, Mrs B Shufflebottom and her neighbour Flo Simcock.

Park Superintendent Walter Barmy said: "A nosh up in the nude is a very good idea."

★

Emerging from the courtroom where he had just accepted a fine of some £18 for using a car without a current road license, Mr Michael Wallis noticed another car whose license had expired. It belonged to Mr Craven-Smith Willes, the Magistrate who had just imposed the fine.

★

Back to playtime kiddiewinks. A man, Milivoja Ristic, 76, a Serbian from Bor (see your atlas) has bought a derelict bus which he plans to eat over a period of two years.

Mr Ristic has already consumed 22,500 razor blades, two and a half hundred-weight of glass, eight pounds of lead shot and a jeep.

"I've always been like this," he said, "during the war I ate ordinary food but it ruined my stomach."

★

Mr and Mrs Windle of Shipley, Yorkshire, could not have been surprised when the police stopped their car. One wheel was lacking a tyre, a second tyre was deflated, and the bonnet coachwork was severely dented.

When the police asked Mrs Windle - who was driving - to produce her license, her husband grabbed a wallet from the dash board and leapt out of the car screaming: "My leg! My leg! It's gone again!"

Then he fell to the ground and writhed in agony, at the same time dropping the wallet down a drain.

Once the wallet had vanished Mr Windle made a complete recovery; indeed, he even helped the police to push the car into a side road.

The wallet, which contained a provisional driving license was recovered by Shipley's Highway Department.

Mr Windle was fined £5.

## CLAUD COCKBURN

# Let Sewers be Sewers

*L*ot to be said for a sewer smelling like a sewer. That way, you decide to take the effluvia or leave them alone. As is known, chemists can make that outlet smell like springtime in the Rockies. But they do that, and what happens? You go out in a boat on a party of pleasure, breathing the supposed ozone through your hock and sandwich, and you have been poisoned.

The above paragraph is penned in grateful tribute to Eldon Griffiths, MP.

Since whoever has survived to read this must have lived through the reports of the Labour Conference and the Tory Conference, that reader will know that the business of disguising sewers as drinking fountains has achieved results which are nearly miraculous.

Naturally the process is a technological secret. But roughly speaking what they do is spray something on. So that while the man is spewing out at Blackpool some jet of racialist filth, the spray transmutes it into an eloquent plea for common sense not forgetting our full commitment to the brotherhood of man.

Every brother and sister takes another sandwich and four thousand million deadly germs. Delicious. When the causes of the painful death are finally established, it will be too late.

Similar situation with the Tories. A man speaks who, on the evidence of his performance in Government during the past thirteen years, would be incapable of selling a refrigerator to the Upper Volta or a bullet-proof vest to Soekarno.

The stench of his remarks would, in natural state, be nauseous. But comes the spray. And that funny looking scum which seems to have formed on the top of the beer and light wines turns out to be a few crumbs of hard-hitting, forthright criticism of Labour's ineptitude and inability to give the export drive the dynamism, dynamism, dynamism.

More applause and happiness. More deadly germs consumed. Same result. Diagnosis comes too late.

So the people to applaud and cherish are the ones that someone forgot to spray. Or else their natural odour overcomes all these chemical tricks. With the result that you get the authentic whiff of it, even after it has been filtered through a newspaper column.

Prominent among these should be named Eldon Griffiths MP. He is not, obviously, prominent as a person. Who in God's name would want to read a profile or biography of Eldon G ?

But prominent as a phenomenon.

Just in case anyone actually does want to know anything else about him, he was the man who for a quite long while was London Correspondent of the American magazine Newsweek. His successors there will be happy to fill you in on Eldon.

THE MAN GRIFFITHS

At one point he informed various colleagues and acquaintances that he deemed it his duty to join the Labour Party. It was the effective, (they gathered) and therefore the righteous thing to do.

He joined the Tories and became a speech-constructor for Baillie Vass.

On second thoughts, it is not quite certain that those counsels were wiser. Had he joined the Labour Party he might have been out in a little cold for a while. But right now he might quite well have been speech-writing for Wilson.

Still, man can't have everything. So there he was at the Tory Brighton Conference talking about patriotism, talking about confidence in our great people and nation, talking about how utterly rotten, rotten, satirists are who denigrate. That's what they do. Denigrate.

His proposition - important simply because it is what 70 percent of Tories and 68 percent of Labour people really think - is that what we need is more patriotism, more confidence, more hard work by all sections of the community, and less satire. Said he:
"We have been going through a period of national self-denigration: where once it was said that Britain is best, now we are told so often it is worst. The satirists are turning our weekend television screens into a never-ending commercial tearing Britain down.

"By all means let us continue to have fun at our own expense, but is it not time that national self-denigration was matched by national self-assurance? What is so wrong with Britain - besides its socialist Government ?

"What I am calling for is a new kind of patriotism: not the old flagwagging variety - though that was not all bad - but a new

old kind that has to do with each one of us doing his best in his job as a coalminer, a bus conductor, a businessman, or a politician; because in addition to what we get out of it ourselves we can also benefit our neighbour, and in benefiting our neighbour, our country."

If the boys at the back of the hall will just stop shuffling their feet and barracking our distinguished leaders, everything may take a quick turn for the better.

For it seems that the satirists, the critics, are our downfall. If they would only keep their traps shut, not keep pointing at that lavatory shared by twenty-three slum-dwelling members of the affluent society and that villager in Vietnam with the napalm coming, our Great Old Country would be all right.

A reasonable person, on reading such a thesis as advanced by honest Eldon, could be excused a small smile, even a loud guffaw.

Nobody, such a reasonable person would say, is going to take this ape seriously. Surely we all know that from - let us say - the Crimean War through the Boer War, through the horrors of two World Wars, the satirists, the critics, have been the people who in fact saved the nation's bacon?

But the reasonable person would be wrong. People do take the Griffithery quite seriously. Worse than that, they take it for granted.

So they did in Tring, Herts, before, during and after World War I.

Anyone there who, in 1913, said that if all those fools in London and Berlin and elsewhere went on the way they were going, there was going to be a bloody awful war and smash-up was treated to the Eldon treatment.

"Confidence" was what we ought to have. People who said the Irish ought to be taken seriously, people who said that the Tories were virtually mutineers, and Asquith a fraud, were seen as narking the Best of Britain. They got the Eldon treatment too.

Consequence was, that satire and criticism were often reduced to quite a low level around Tring, Herts at that time. And throughout the country too.

The ancestors of Eldon Griffiths prevailed. People had confidence. Such deep, profound confidence that a breath of satirical criticism gave them the shuddering heebie-jeebies.

The results are a matter of record.

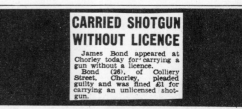

# PRIVATE EYE

No. 102
Friday
12 Nov. 65

1/6

# SOCIAL SCENE

Apparently there was this man in bed with this woman...

**1**

and the man said: "Do you smoke after intercourse?"

**2**

and she said: "I don't know. I've never looked"

**3**

Go on! What happened next?

Good evening!

**4**

"I'll have to hang up, Dora . I've got a real kink here"

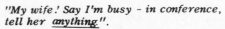

"My wife! Say I'm busy - in conference, tell her *anything*".

"He's on the couch with Miss Burnham".

# UNDER PLAIN COVER

Seven years ago, the Harrow East Conservative Association were forced into the embarrassing position of choosing a new Conservative candidate to replace their former Member, Mr Ian Harvey. Mr Harvey had resigned after being convicted of indecent offences with guardsmen in a public park.

They chose as Mr Harvey's successor Commander Anthony Courtney - then fifty years old - a retired naval commander who worked in a subsidiary role in Naval Intelligence during the war and spoke Russian fluently. For good measure he had been heavyweight champion for the Navy for several years. No doubt in the many mansions of Harrow East, the local Conservatives felt that sober respectability had returned for ever to their politics.

Last August however, the local Constituency Officers were perturbed to receive through the post a brochure in plain wrapper which contained details of one of the Commander's visits to Moscow and was illustrated by photographs - one of the Commander in his naval uniform, another showing him in a state of undress helping a woman off with her blouse and the third completely naked, walking away from a bed in which the woman reclined in a state of some disarray. The fact that the photographs were wittily subtitled "I'm no Profumo but..." (looking to one observer "like something out of Private Eye"), and, in addition, that in the third picture the Commander's pudenda had been tastefully whited out, suggested to all concerned a Russian plot of staggering dimensions.

Others to receive the brochure included Mr George Wigg, a number of Tory MPs, Courtney's Labour opponent in Harrow, and The News of the World which in the best tradition of that fearless newspaper decided to do nothing about it.

Now the Commander is not concerned with denying the authenticity of the pictures. They were taken in Moscow and they depict an incident which did take place. The woman was a friend of his. What he quite rightly objects to is the Russians taking pictures of him with hidden cameras and trying to besmirch his reputation. What he does in Moscow bedrooms is his own affair, and if the Russians want to make personal capital out of it then they should be attacked. The Government should make the strongest possible protest to Moscow.

Unfortunately the Government does not see it that way. Possibly if the pictures were faked there would be grounds for protest. But the official point of view is that the Commander has asked for it and that if he is going to make visits to Moscow then he should behave like other VIPs - go to bed at half past eight and restrain his natural desires for the duration.

Protests apart however, the incident puts the Conservative Leadership in an embarrassing (so they think) position. They do not view it with the Commander's Bond-like candour. Terrified of anything which smacks of Profumo, Grocer Heath and his lieutenant Edward du Cann are doing their

ILLUSTRATED LONDON NEWS

damnedest to shut the fellow up. But the Commander is determined, in the best naval tradition, to stick to his guns and give the matter a full hearing. He intends to raise it in the House of Commons during the debate on the Queen's speech.

While the nation waits in trembling suspense for the next instalment of the drama, Private Eye can only reflect ruefully on the utter incompetence of the Russians as scandal-mongers. Why send the brochure to The News of the World? They've never published anything interesting in their lives. Private Eye would have published the picture immediately - perhaps even on the front page.

# AUNTIE'S BIAS

The Prime Minister's rage at BBC interviewers attacking Labour Ministers on the screen has ended in a truce between the Party leaders which indicates, fairly enough after all, that from now on attacking any Party leader on the screen will be banned. The pity about the whole business is that the real complaints about the BBC political coverage have been lost in a silly sectarian quibble. What few people seem to have noticed is the control of political coverage on both channels by, of all things, The Economist.

For some time now Alistair Burnett has been, in effect running the Parliamentary and party political coverage on the Independent channels. As Editor of The Economist most people look on Burnett as the ideal, eminently reasonable "independent" commentator.

Do they know, however, that the BBC's top pundit on political matters - a man who not only acts as link-man in most political programmes but also insists on playing a leading part in scripting and programming them - is a colleague of Burnett's? Do they know that Ian Trethowan, formerly deputy political correspondent of The News Chronicle, is Political Correspondent of The Economist?

Try as he does to preserve his impartiality, Trethowan finds it impossible to disguise his sympathies for the Tory Party. At a recent municipal election week, as results flooded in showing gains for Labour, Trethowan's face grew longer and longer. Eventually, it brightened. "Here's a better result," he exclaimed. "The Tories have gained a seat in ..." and his voice trailed away as he desperately tried to make amends.

Then there was the famous instance of the Oxford Vietnam teach-in when Trethowan gave vent to some ideas about the Foreign Secretary's performance which led on quite logically from the subtly cut edition of the teach-in which the BBC transmitted. Trethowan could hardly disguise his delight at

what he called the "drubbing" of the Left.

Trethowan does not keep his political allegiances to himself. Sir Michael Fraser, Deputy Chief of the Conservative Party, is godfather to one of his children.

Small wonder, with this impassioned Tory at the helm, that The Economist's political line, though it makes the necessary obeisances to Labour's plans for modernisation, is generally pro-Tory, and regards the Labour Party as a necessary evil to keep wages down for the next two years, after which the Tories can come back and get on with the job. That's the Trethowan view, and the Burnett view, and therefore, unhappily, the view that we've all got to watch on our telly screens while these two pompous reactionaries remain in charge.

# HANGING UP AGAIN

What on earth has come over the police in their attitude to the extraordinary campaign now being waged on the telephone against anyone remotely responsible for the excellent book recently written by Lord Russell of Liverpool on the A6 murder? In the book, Lord Russell comes to the conclusion, backed with a mountain of detailed research, that Hanratty was not guilty.

The first victim has been Lord Russell himself. Over the eighteen months he has been writing the book he has been plagued with hundreds of anonymous calls, most of which result in a click as the receiver goes down the other end. Some, however, have threatened him with all manner of horrors if the book ever got into print.

Mr Fred Warburg, who agreed to publish the book after the brave, fearless Leftwing Gollancz, who commissioned it, had dropped it like a hot brick, was immediately plagued with a series of abusive calls. Like the caller to Russell, the man described himself as Peter Alphon and made it clear he held strong Fascist views.

Similarly, Professor Hugh Trevor-Roper who reviewed the book sympathetically and who suggested that the case might be reopened is constantly answering the phone to be asked by the operator if he will pay for a call from Mr Borman ringing from a Langham callbox. The caller simply puts down the receiver.

Although the police have been contacted several times in this affair, and although they have been presented with a mountain of evidence, (in particular the transcript of a 50 minute conversation with Warburg and the caller taken down by the Primrose telephone exchange), they have refused to do anything about it. As Scotland Yard told Lord Russell: "If we acted, it would only give further publicity to your book."

The other argument of the police is that there is no criminal offence which covers such calls. In fact, they know full well that they can and do charge such a menace with abusing electricity (penalty: a £10 fine, or a month in prison).

Could it be that the police in general are afraid that Hanratty might turn out to be another Timothy Evans, and that they will be held largely responsible for an innocent being hanged? Could it be that such a fear obstructs them in the course of their duty?

# Breakfast at the Connaught Hotel 1966

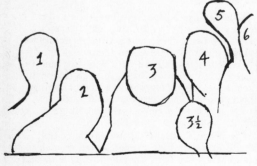

The above picture has not been hung in the Royal Academy Summer Exhibition which opened at Burlington House last week.

The picture refers somewhat allegorically (our Art Critic writes) to the breakfast party given earlier this year by Dr. David Frost, the television personality. It shows some of the many eminent persons present:

1. LORD LONGFORD, the witty Irish peer.

2. MR. CECIL KING.

3. MR. H. WILSON.

3½. DR. DAVID FROST, the television personality, (host).

4. MR. DONALD BAVERSTOCK, the Welsh person.

5. JACK ROBINSON, Bishop of Woolwich.

6. SIR JOSEPH LOCKWOOD, Chairman of E.M.I.

# PRIVATE EYE

No. 103
Friday
26 Nov. 65

1/6

LORD GNOME SAYS:

# KITH-MY ARSE!

# COLOUR SECTION

The formidable task of providing Lord Thomson of Fleet with the trappings of a liberal education continues apace.

On a recent visit to Paris to mark the opening of a new Hilton Hotel the chubby Canadian was whisked around the Louvre in little more than 20 minutes. After rather a blurred impression of the Venus de Milo, the Mona Lisa and the Winged Victory he was asked for his impressions. "It didn't interest me," was his sole comment.

Later in the day he was observed to be seated alone, morosly brooding in a corner of one of the new hotel's many eating areas. An hospitable group of journalists invited the great man to join them, and began to question him on the somewhat public and belated manner of his education. One of these, a graduate and greatly daring, asked him if he did not think that he had missed rather a lot by not going to a university.

"If I'd gone to a university" replied Thomson, "I'd be working today for someone like me."

---

Something that seemed to sum up the election campaign was seen in a BBC studio last week.

Mr. Heath was rehearsing for his party political broadcast. On the tele-prompter could be seen the words:

I CARE DEEPLY ABOUT . . . . .

The word 'deeply' was underlined no less than three times.

---

Many would think from a perusal of Richard Dimbleby's obituaries that as far as Royal Occasions were concerned, Dimbleby was a mere spectator standing in the wings, describing the scene for the absent public.

Most people for example probably assumed at the very climax of the Coronation Service, when the Archbishop raised the crown and held it for several seconds before finally lowering it onto the Queen's head, that this dramatic pause was part of the hallowed ritual, time-honoured for centuries.

Not so. Before the service Dimbleby instructed the Archbishop to count ten before bringing the crown down so that he would have time to fit in the requisite amount of commentary.

"CIGARETTES BY ABDULLA . . . . CONTRACEPTIVES BY DUREX ?"

# PRIVATE EYE

NUMBER 115   FRIDAY 13 MAY 1966          PRICE ONE SHILLING & SIXPENCE

## PERSONAL

"They that change for the sake of change are as chaff blown by the wind: they shall perish utterly from the face of the earth." PROVERBS.

Moral issues required. W.H. The Times.

Dr. David Frost seeks missing volumes Punch 1936-1937 to complete script.

E11R where were you last Friday? H.W.

Jonathan Miller seeks Cheshire Cat. William Rushton need not apply.

John Bird requires role in any spectacular T.V. production of Alice in Wonderland.

Old man seeks raddled bum.

Lost between 21st June 1965 - and - Aug. 1966 - Maidenhead in perfect condition. Reward £50.

George Brown requires staff to run country's economy. Object: No money.

Sir W.H. requires competent gossip columnist.

Grateful thanks to St. John Stevas for favours received. J.C.

BUM 1. number plate for sale. Any offers? B. of M.

Fat ex-Tory M.P. Excellent connections, experience with pigs. Old Etonian, will do anything, go anywhere for money.

Tall, fairly fat, rosebud-lipped ex Tory M.P., Old Etonian will do anything, go anywhere.

Wealthy duchess (ex) seeks interesting position.

IS MALCOLM MUGGERIDGE DEAD? God hits back in this week's NEW STATESMAN.

Desperately wanted. Manuscripts on Moors Murder Trial. Anything accepted. G. Weidenfeld.

Pay no attention to above. Send to me. V. Gollancz.

Old jokes refurbished. Send to Dr. David Frost, c/o Connaught Hotel.

A.F. come back. I need you more than ever. Tony.

Your Pen can Earn You Money. Send to Second Hand Pen Mart., S.E.17.

That treasured old snapshot can become a beautiful portrait in oils. Send it to Sir Charles Wheeler. P.R.A. (Retd.)

If any more of my staff are found telling stories to Private Eye, they will be sacked. M.P.

Unseemly spots? Use Dr. ALAN BRIEN'S PATENT ELIXIR BALM.

Don't miss this week's PUNCH. Articles by Oginga Odinga, President Ntulu Zambi, the Guru of Zat, Professor E. L. Stards.

MURDERS? Popular Sunday Newspaper will pay good money for confessions, evidence, photographs, etc.

T.C. You snivelling two-faced little ponce. K.T.

Royal Court Theatre urgently seeks Director. Must be Orthodox Left Wing. Theatrical experience not vital.

MANAGING Director req'd for large-scale electrical firm. Honest Man preferred.

Don't miss the RT. HON. SELWYN LLOYD's appeal on behalf of Distressed Toryfolk. B.B.C. Home Service. Sunday May 16. 6.30 p.m.

Experienced housemaid for Government House - Apply J.H.

K.T. You are such a smarmy-faced niggling little coward you dare not even reveal your full name. You flea-ridden old skunk. T.C.

Rubicunt stupid ex-Tory Minister seeks peerage. North London area preferred. No coloureds.

Barman wanted for small New Hebrides hotel, live in, good rates of pay. Write, with photo.

Ex-Naval Intelligence Man. Old Harrovian, excellent references seeks model work. Photographs available on request from Russian embassy.

Three former Tory defence ministers seek equally boring companion for mystery tour S.E. Asia.

L.M. You bastard. R.C.

In Memoriam. Somerset Maugham. "Funny the way you used to behave. Now we're dancing on your grave." B.N., N.C.

WANTED Two tickets for any performance by Lisa Shane in Funny Girl.

Producer required for late-night T.V. conversation programme. Experience inessential.

R.C. Same to you. L.M.

Layout man wanted for reputable Fleet St. concern. Write Box No. 5600.

AD money paid for articles, poems, reviews. Send enclosing S. A. E. The Spectator, 99 Gower St.

Relatively young, ex Eton, jazz pianist with good political connections, seeks journalistic post. Write R. D-H. c/o Daily Express.

FOYLES Literary Luncheon Wed. May 18. Guests of honour: Hank Jansen, Carter Brown and the Editor of 'Spank'. Tickets 2gns. from Christina Foyle.

L.M. I shall issue writs. R.C.

Conservative Party requires LEADER. Preferably Public School. Box 6100.

JAN It was just one of those things. God bless you D. F.

Editor of left wing weekly urgently requires first class gamekeeper. Write P.J. Iver, Bucks.

Old clothes, cast-offs desperately wanted. Send: Cookieboutique, Kings Rd. S.W.3.

Kensington family seek chef. Preferably foreign, deaf, dumb and illiterate. Box No. 0066.

Successful but shy Tory politician would like to meet sociable lady. Friendship view marriage. E.H. The Albany.

BORN FREE - the touching life story of the Marquess of Bath, now a film. Premiere in the gracious presence of H. R. H. Uffa Fox. May 27. Tickets 15gns. All proceeds to Marquess of Bath Investments Ltd.

POP People Read the Times.

THE Youth A photographic study of boyhood. 2,000 studies of nude laddies in characteristic poses. Send 89gns to: 'Screw the Pooves', Wigmore St., W.1.

L of C. Loved your work. I.B.

Pathetic case, recently out of hospital, job in jeopardy. Will anyone help? Write D. E. A.

Ned. Those dear dead days. How much I miss you. Caryl.

For the appallingly greedy. Chocolates filled with gnat's pee. Stuff these black gobbets into your maw and you'll be the envy of other snobs. Send 88gns. for illustrated catalogue to: Boris Chocolates, Bumhole St. W8

## OLD BOREY'S

GARDENING TWADDLE NO.1,675

Fifty years ago her Majesty the Queen was a mere twinkle in her Uncle's knee. Today she is a thriving symbol of all we hold most often. How has this come about? NOT by these idiotic meanderings to be sure. But you know when I look around me and see puny figures beating their ironical bladders against the powers that pee, I sometimes wonder whether the war was worth fighting after all.

The other day I popped into a chemist to buy my month's supply. A man was standing at the counter long-faced and woe-begone. "What's the matter with you?" I cried. He answered "Constipation". Four minutes later he was dead. Now that wouldn't have happened fifty years ago.

### CHOICE OFFER

50 lovely glads for only 3/6d. Beautiful bloomers. Will flower in 1981.

1 old bulb, possibly turnip, 1/2d.

---

Peter Cook wishes to announce that he is no longer responsible for the debts of his wife - Wendy Elizabeth Cook.

Casino Royale. Four directors desperately wanted. Ideas welcome. Postcards only please.

Small thatched cottage in remote area of Ireland wanted by Daily Telegraph satirist shortly to undergo nervous breakdown.

Enlightened bishops, aristocrats, establishment figures required to lend tone to tawdry second rate Bunny Club. Write to R.D-H. c/o Kensington Palace.

Wanted. Back numbers of The Times. Not you, Sir William!

Will the Editor of Private Eye please contact his solicitors, Rubinstein, Nash where he will learn something more to his disadvantage.

Pathetic case. G.P. earning £32,000 a year cannot hold out for delayed pay-rise. Cheques welcome. Dr. E. St.J. Framlingham. The Palace, Walton-on-Thames.

Old Penguins required by senile bird fancier and pervert.

# PRIVATE EYE
# All-purpose Titillation Supplement

## SWINGING ENGLAND!

A MESSAGE FROM LORD GNOME:

It has been brought to my attention that there are still a very small number of American periodicals which have not yet produced their twenty-four page survey of the Swinging, Vibrant, Thrusting New England Where Even The Hovercraft Wear Mini-Skirts etc. etc. For the benefit of the export drive my gifted staff have at vast expense produced this lavish All-Purpose Swinging England Pull-Out Supplement for reproduction at a modest fee. Cheques, OBE's etc. to be sent to the above at usual address.

ALL-PURPOSE GROUP PHOTOGRAPH OF LONDON'S SWINGING 'IN' SET: PERM ANY THIRTEEN FROM FOLLOWING AND CAPTION ACCORDINGLY

1. George Weidenfeld   or/ Lord Goodman
2. Arnold Wesker       or/ Lady Antonia Fraser
3. William Rushton     or/ Terence Donovan
4. Peter Hall or/ Peter Brook or/ Bill Gaskell etc.
5. Princess Margaret   or/ Mick Jagger
6. Maureen Cleave      or/ Terence Stamp
7. Joan Littlewood     or/ The Queen Mother
8. Christopher Booker  or/ Dr. Jonathan Miller
9. Harold Pinter       or/ General de Gaulle
10. David Bailey       or/ Lord Harlech
11. Mary Quant         or/ David Warner
12. Paul McCartney     or/ Mark Boxer
13. Jocelyn Stevens    or/ someone who just happened to be passing at the time

Photograph taken either on top of Hilton Hotel or/ on top of GPO Tower or/ inside Tony Snowdon birdcage by either/ Lord Snowdon or/ Dr. Jonathan Miller or/ someone who just happened to be passing at the time.

or/ the West Indies cricket team throughout

# THEATRE *CONTINUED*

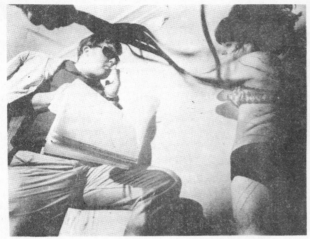

Brilliant, gifted, searing young director Dick Dexter (National Theatre) on set of latest Osborne epic THE KISS OF THE LASH. Freely adapted from mediaeval morality play, Osborne paints tragic picture of man who battles to find truly personal morality through incest, rape, homosexuality and killing his mother, but fails to find lasting happiness.

Her 'old man' may be one of Premier Wilson's top aides but Helen's right out there swinging. One of the swinging, way-out-ahead-of-the-crowd Kray twins who have set London's 'up' crowd by the ears, mini-skirted Helen Kray, daughter of Finance Minister Douglas Kray, photographed down Carnaby Road in the heart of London's Chelsea.

# THE ENGLISH PRESS: boring, hack-ridden, the best in the world

### by KARL J. PIPESUCKER

Headlines blister and crackle like D-Day machine gun bullets. Editorials thunder and lacerate their victims in a nonstop Spanish-style auto da fe. Even the words themselves are seared in ink onto virgin pages of newsprint. To the poor American correspondent, accustomed to think of the press only as mere newspapers produced by ordinary human beings, Britain's jumping Fleet Street is bewildering indeed.

Where else in the world could you find sportswriters who spin phrases that would have put Will Shakespeare himself to shame? A press columnist like swinging Dave Frost of the Spectator who can invite the Prime Minister to breakfast in the morning and turn in 750 lacerating words in the afternoon? In one recent issue of the Daily Telegraph alone I found such words as 'meaningless' (used of Harold Wilson's speeches), 'schizophrenic' (used in a review of a book on psychology) and 'kipper' (used in a story on the smoked herring industry). Each in its context had the effect of a 70-megaton H-Bomb exploding on New York.

The great London Times, edited with magisterial omniscience by lantern-jawed Sir William Haley, and its traditions going right back to the coffee houses of Roman London, is quite unique in the universe. When Sir William turns in an editorial (known in Fleet Street's 'in' pub Al Vino's as 'a thunderer'), full of richly ripened phrases as finely turned as a Chippendale chair leg, the Government literally totters.

But nothing can compare to the experience of Sunday morning, when critics such as corrosive Alan Brien and keen-eyed Kenneth Tynan tear into their victims with flamethrower reviews that literally burn off the page. Even as ı sit here I am surrounded by thick clouds of black smoke. I am just turning to Robert Robinson's feared film column in the Sunday Telegraph. The heat is unbearable, the paint is blistering on the walls ... (contd. p. 94)

'JEWELLED PHRASES SPARKLE FROM THE PAGE LIKE A GOBELIN TAPESTRY'

*CORRECTION*
In the sale of Old Masters at Sotheby's on Wednesday a landscape with the Judgment of Paris by Claude was bought by Agnew's, not Leggatt Bros.

# FOOD

EVEN THE ROAST BEEF SWINGS TO A BEATLE BEAT
Drools
John Q. Crosby

In New York it's nothing but rush; in Rome, it's nothing but spaghetti; in Paris, restaurant prices are so astronomical that the French are literally starving in the streets. Suddenly - it's London that's (continued p. 94)

---

DECADENT ENGLAND
Note to editors

The Swinging England Supplement may be easily transformed into a Decadent England Supplement merely by simple reversal of key phrases. e.g. for

'The pound may be sinking, but down Chelsea way the mini-skirts are flying in a town that has suddenly become young at heart etc.'

read:

'The mini-skirts may be flying down Chelsea way, but the pound is sinking and London has become obsessed with juvenile trivia etc.'

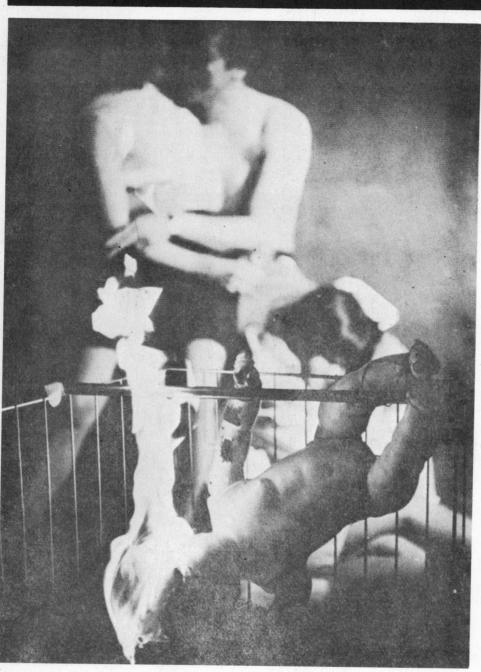

A HURRICANE OF EXCITEMENT IS TODAY BLOWING ACROSS THE ENGLISH STAGE, THE MOST BRILLIANT, SEARING, COURAGEOUS AND REFRESHING IN THE WORLD. BRILLIAN SEARING YOUNG PLAYWRIGHTS ARE BLASTI DOWN THE STUFFY BARRIERS OF AN OUT-DATED, CLASSRIDDEN MORALITY AND FORG ING A NEW FREEDOM FOR THE THEATRE IN THE WHITE-HEAT OF SEARING REVOLUTION

It all began ten years ago. The English theatr was almost literally dead. At the Haymarket Theatre audiences of white-bearded old men and ninety year-old women drank tea and slept quietly while ancient plays written by forgotten playwrights were enacted by teams of octogen-arian knights and dames. (Indeed without a title it was almost impossible to get a job in the class-ridden halls of Shaftesbury Avenue). And then one fine summer evening the revolution began. From the stage of the Royal Court John Osborne's Jimmy Porter poured his biting, lacerating stream of corrosive poison right into the heart of the British class-system. The monarchy tottered. The knights and dames, laden with their ill-gotten honours, skulked off into the shadows. The stuffy, aged, upper class audiences who had regarded the theatre merely as a sop to their threadbare prejudices and class hatred, were literally killed off by the burning, scathing, refreshing irreverence of the new play wrights. From the slums of Manchester and the downtrodden masses of the East End, genius after genius poured in an unending stream. Alongside the names of Shakespeare and Marlowe a new roll of honour seared its way into history in letters of fire - Shelagh Delaney, Bernard Kops, Fred Harbottle, Harold Pinter, Solly Gold Sid Bellings. It was a new Renaissance. But that was 1959. Today, of course, many of these names are forgotten. But their legacy remains. Today the British theatre, corrosive, audacious, shock-filled, knows no barriers. Today the theatre has the courage to investigate burning social problems - homosexuality, lesbianism, incest, rape, lesbianism - in an audacious, searing battle to keep up the flood of sensational-ism. The old taboos have been toppled - but as brilliant, young, corrosive 59-year old Peter Hall of the Royal Shakespeare Company defiantly states: 'We shall soon find new ones'.

Truly can it be said that such plays as A Baby Barbecued (see sensational picture) by James Bond and 14-year old Trevor Neasden's searing, controversial The Rapists are a lacerating indictment of a society which can produce such men as Bond and Neasden themselves. The swing ing, audacious, irreverent playwrights of today have been recognised at last. They are even honoured by the state. The revolution has won. Today at the new, swinging Haymarket, young, irreverent actors like Ralphie Richardson play in dramas deeply relevant to our own time, such as Bernard Shaw's You Never Can Tell.

(continued page 94.)

A BABY BARBECUED (Royal Court) in which a baby nightly blazed before the audience was so searing, vile, unspeakable and deeply concerned with human values that hardly anyone dared to see it and after only three days it was taken off. Wrote critic Penelope Gilliat: 'At last a play with the courage to exploit the kind of searing violence which made Shakespeare great'.

Harold Pinter's THREE
AUTHORS IN SEARCH OF AN
ORGASM (Aldwych). What
seems an everyday tale of
mass-rape by four brothers
in an ordinary suburban home
suddenly flares into com-
passionate drama when it is
discovered that they are all
impotent. Play ends on
deeply questioning note with
three brothers attempting
to masturbate, while fourth
(in girl's undies) irons
quietly in foreground (brilliant
echo of Osborne classic Look
Back). Wrote critic Penelope
Gilliat: 'This is not a mastur-
batory play but a play about
masturbation, which is something quite different'.

Says brilliant, corrosive, young
Peter Hall: *'We have put an end
to complacency. We have killed
off the middle-aged fuddy duddies
who only came to the theatre as a
sop to their prejudices. Today we
have the finest young theatre in
the world, filled with the swinging
young people of today who come to
the theatre as a sop to our
prejudices'.*

Central scene from brilliant new
interpretation of HAMLET by
young American Charles Marowitz. Shakespeare's longwinded
classic is compressed into
just five searing minutes.
Hamlet is revealed as transvestite homosexual deeply
frustrated by lesbian relationship between his mother and
Ophelia, vividly conceived as
swinging Kings Road dolly.
Marowitz' latest project - an
action-packed, twenty-minute
version of all Shakespeare's
plays compressed into one,
played in Carnaby gear by
Soho strippers, with excerpts
from big speeches flashed on
theatre walls by seventeen
projectors shooting simultaneously. Says Marowitz:
"In the twentieth century it's
time we really worked out what
the old bore was on about".

# BRIEFIN

## THEATRE

BORING-BORING (Duchess). Torrid
promiscuity combined with topical
assault on chaotic airline scheduling
to make searing document of our time.

THE IDEAL HUSBAND (Strand). Irish
homosexual's bitter tirade against
social taboos, marriage, heterosexual-
ity, Michael Denison and Dulcie Gray,
as deeply relevant today as when it was
written.

OTHELLO DOLLY (Dreary Lane). Sex-
starved middle-aged nymphomaniac and
her search for satisfaction with two
young boys. Copraphagic finale to Act
One stops show.

MOSES AND THE FLYING DUTCHMAN
(Covent Garden). Music and words
take second place to spectacular all-
electronic space-age orgy staged by
Sean Kenny and Peter Hall. Bestiality
triumphs.

ARSENIC AND OLD MOUSETRAP
(Vaudeville). Slinky Sybil Thorndike
plays mass-murderer in lesbian/
incestuous partnership with her sister,
outwitted at final curtain by butler
Lewis Casson pulsating in Cary Grant's
old role. Abrasive.

BLACK AND WHITE MENSTRUAL
(Victoria Palace). Half-naked white
showgirls succumb to clutches of
kinkily dressed negroes in searing
attack on racist immigration laws.
Makes Othello seem tame.

# TIGHTNITS IN OBSERVERSNEER

The most extraordinary aspect of the "red plot" allegations was that the Prime Minister should talk vaguely about the "tightly-knit body of men" on Monday, 20th June, but wait until Tuesday, 28th June before outlining his evidence for the charge. The ensuing week was a tough one for newspapers and commentators. Obviously the charges left a mystery which had to be explored. And clearly Wilson stood to benefit enormously if the newspapers could substantiate his charges.

Unhappily for him, however, the daily newspapers did not take the bait. Until the Sunday (26th) nothing appeared which indicated any substantial support for the Prime Minister. On that Sunday the *Sunday Times* in a full, thoroughgoing inquiry carried out by five reporters who trailed the key executive members all week and interviewed every single EC member, threw the charges right out of court. Peter Paterson of the *Sunday Telegraph*, who has as many contacts as anyone, plainly regarded them as utterly ill-founded. The only newspapers to print anything in support of Wilson were the *News of the World* (with a smallish, not very serious account) and, much more seriously - in a huge article on the facing-leader page entitled "The Plot Behind the Strike" - *The Observer*.

The *Observer* story, "by our industrial and political staff", was divided roughly into two halves. The first purported to reveal a shady deal whereby "in return for allowing outside direction of the strike, members of the executive were offered a guarantee of phased and unofficial strike support from other unions". The deal was called off, according to the article, when the industrial support was not forthcoming

For these assertions there was not one scrap of intelligible evidence. The names of the "influenced" members of the executive were n _ stated. The people who were doing the deal outside the union were not identified in any way. The leaders were not told where this deal was conducted, by whom, or on what occasion.

Instead the article quoted a headline in the *Morning Star* indicating that there might be a general strike if the Navy moved in to sort out the docks - a point that was made in headlines by every other capitalist newspaper at the same time. A declaration of support from the Communist World Federation of Trade Unionists was offered in evidence - although the W.F.T.U. declares solidarity with every large official strike all over the Western world. Finally it was said that some dockers in Hull had supported the seamen. Since the Hull dockers are among the most militant in the country, that is hardly surprising.

Having made these allegations about nobody in particular, with no evidence to support them the *Observer* then took a series of names and proceeded to smear them. The names were familiar: Norris; Coward; Gollan; Ramelson; Goodwin.

The technique is to name a name and present facts about his past which link him

with the Communist Party or some "sinister" activity. There is no argument as to whether such activity is right or wrong. It is simply a catalogue of association. Thus we read in the *Observer* of a Mr. McWhinnie:

"He also bring out occasional issues of *Transport Workers of the World*, the review of the Trade Unions International of Transport, Port and Fishery Workers, and a similar journal on behalf of the Mineworkers".

That the *Observer* used this sort of technique is, perhaps, not surprising since their reporters on the story were in contact with the Economic League, who, no doubt, were only too keen to help as much as possible.

The article bragged about its knowledge of the Prime Minister's information. It referred in definite terms, on more than one occasion, to "information placed before the Prime Minister".

The *Observer* had shown a keen interest in the Prime Minister's original declaration. Several leading reporters including Eric Clarke, David Howarth and Ivan Yates were pushed out on the story early in the week. They concentrated mainly on combing the doss-houses in the East End and Liverpool looking for a chance contact who might spill the non-existent beans. The *Sunday Times* reporters, who in the words of one of them "lived in the pocket of the NUS Executive all week", never once saw an *Observer* man.

By Thursday night, when the *Sunday Times* through more legitimate reporting methods, was already convinced that the charges were absurd, the *Observer* inquiry had appeared to come to nothing.

Soon after the Prime Minister had made his opening speech about tightly-knit subversives, Lord Goodman, Wilson's solicitor, chairman of the Arts Council and trustee of the *Observer*, had dined with Sir William Carr, proprietor of the *News of the World*. In the course of conversation, Carr offered to tell the whole truth about the "plot" in the *News of the World*. Further negotiations took place between the Prime Minister's close circle and Carr. Eventually, Carr had to go to Paris and the matter was left to the *News of the World* Editor, Mr. Stafford Summerfield and Mr. Trevor Lloyd Hughes, Downing Street's Press Officer.

At some stage the original scheme to print all appears to have been ditched.

The search went on. After preliminary feelers from Mr. George Wigg, Paymaster General, Mr. Michael Randall was summoned into the presence of "someone very much more senior" than Mr. Wigg who told him all.

It didn't take Randall long to turn down the

offered "scoop". "I have never" he is reported to have said on returning to the office "heard anything so ludicrous". During the week, too, the Prime Minister gave audience to a strange and sudden visitor: Mr. Hugh Cudlipp, editorial director of the Daily Mirror.

On the morning of Friday, June 24th, Stephen Fay of the Insight column of the *Sunday Times* went on his own initiative to see George Wigg about the plot.

Fay's notes on his Wigg interview read almost exactly like the eventual *Observer* story; an "ugly plot" was revealed but no concrete information was available as to who organised it; when and where. Fay was inclined to dismiss the whole nonsense anyway and he didn't press the matter. As he left, he noticed that the next man to see Wigg was none other than Eric Clarke of the *Observer*.

The road to the "scoop" for the *Observer* began that Friday morning. Apparently, there was no such thing as a "dossier" which Wigg was offering the Press. More probably Wigg let on as to where some of the more salubrious information about Commies could be uncovered.

Who that source is is anyone's guess. But it is worth noting that throughout the dispute the militants on the executive were convinced for a whole number of reasons that one of the so-called "moderates" on the Executive was giving information about executive meetings to the outside world: perhaps to the Government itself. The Government is also said to have in its possession detailed notes of NUS Executive meetings.

One of the unkindest cuts of all for Mr. Michael Davy, who was in charge of the *Observer* in the relevant period as Mr. David Astor was away, must have been Wilson's rebuke to the *Observer* in his reply to the debate on the emergency powers. Wilson said that several statements in the piece were "to his knowledge" untrue, and that his "hair stood on end" when he read it.

Even more interesting was Wilson's assurance that the story did not come "from my office". He was answering Mr. Ian Mikardo, who had asked pointedly if the information came from Downing Street. Now of course there are lots of offices in Downing Street including that of George Wigg.

Those who have read Wilson's speech in detail might like to remember his quote a few months ago ("off the record" of course) to a *Sunday Times* correspondent that he intended in his first year after the election to have a major row with a union and win. Perhaps he bit off a little more than he could chew when he took on the seamen, and had to resort to desperate methods. More probably he genuinely believes that when people do things they act deviously out of self-interest. Thus to Wilson any strike is the work of a "tightly-knit" body of men. Only someone utterly wedded to the conspiracy theory of politics could make such a vacuous and ill-informed speech about reds under the bed.

Unhappily for him the Tory newspapers did not take the bait. They weighed his charges in the balance and found them wanting. The Tory editors, whatever their failings, could not stoop quite that low into the gutter.

Not so the *Observer*.

# PRIVATE EYE

No. 120
Friday
July 66

1/6

# YOURS FOR 5/-

(in three months time)

# WILSUNDRA VANISHES!

by Our Industrial Staff.

Dr. Harold Wilsundra ("Conman extra-ordinary") is now believed to be resting in a Colombo clinic following his sensational flight from Britain.

In a newspaper report published yesterday Wilsundra was quoted as saying "I have done nothing illegal".

### SENSATION

Wilsundra's sudden departure to Ceylon coincided with the collapse of the firm 'New Britain Ltd.' of which he was the Managing Director. Millions of innocent policy-holders were directly affected by the "crash".

### COLLAPSE

Wilsundra, who had been involved in a number of exceptionally shady deals prior to his interest in 'New Britain', started the company in 1964.

In exchange for their votes millions of people were offered fantastic benefits. The company's prospectus contained references in glowing prose to increased wages, great new technological advances, "the white heat of scientific revolution", "dynamic purposeful government" and other high-sounding claims.

### FRAUD

It is now realised that all such promises were nothing but a gigantic fraud perpetuated by an extremely plausible entrepreneur with but little understanding of money matters.

Wilsundra's suave and oily manner deceived his colleagues and policy-holders into thinking that behind his plausible and smiling exterior there lay an acute and brilliant business-min

### CROOK

In recent months however the facade had begun to crumble. In response to disquiet among the policy-holders, Wilsundra began to make trips abroad in a desperate attempt to secure additional political capital to prop up the company.

Three weeks ago he travelled to Moscow. Before leaving he told reporters that rumour of an impending crash were the work of "moaning minnies" and irresponsible journalists trying to do him down.

Wilsundra who was looking tired and dispirited assured those present that all was well and that the company was booming.

However on his return he was forced to admit that this was not the case. At an angry boardroom meeting the toadfaced Wilsundra admitted to his colleagues that the company was on the verge of bankruptcy. That this was due to his own personal shilly-shallying and shifty dealing did not escape the notice of even the most foolish of the directors (believed to be Mr. Wedgwood Bene, a youthful incompetent).

Another director Mr. Brown, threatened to hand in his resignation but in the sober light of day was restrained by Wilsundra.

### WILY

When the disastrous state of the company's affairs was made public Wilsundra immediately appeared on television and addressed the policy-holders in a phoney Churchillian manner which only served to increase their lack of confidence in the man.

Last week he flew off to America to visit his friend "Loony Bins" Johnson, a colourful Texan character who had helped Wilsundra in the past by advancing loans.

### DISASTER

But after the recent debacle it appears that the Texan was distinctly lukewarm in his approach to the slippery entrepreneur.

Now Wilsundra has finally fled the country while the Official Receiver investigates the company's accounts.

At his palatial residence in the heart of London, Mrs. Wilsundra said yesterday: "I cannot believe it. There must be a mistake."

# PRIVATE EYE

121
day
ug 66

1/6

Brothers, we're on our way out

# COLOUR SECTION

Students of London University, and of LSE, may be interested to learn of the repute in which Sir Douglas Logan (Principal of London University)and Dr. Walter Adams (present principal of the University of Rhodesia, soon to be Principal of LSE) are held in Rhodesian Government circles.

The nine lecturers imprisoned without trial in Rhodesia and deported by Smith's Government, arrived in London to be greeted with a letter to the *Times* by the said Logan   explaining how it does not in the least affect academic freedom if the Government seizes about a quarter of a university's staff, throws them in prison, and deports them. That, in Sir Douglas's view, is something which has nothing whatever to do with academic freedom.

Sir Douglas has for many years been a savage opponent of the idea that the sums spent by the University Grants Commission should be made accountable to Parliament. That, he says, is an interference in academic freedom.

Even more fantastic was the article by Dr. Walter Adams in a Johannesburg newspaper accusing the nine of "subversive activities". Dr. Adams has been hailed in the *Times* and the *Guardian* as a great fighter for academic freedom in Central Africa. In fact, he has, on almost every occasion, given tacit support to the Smith Government and has shown a remarkable ability, whenever a crisis arises, to clear out and pass the buck.

He did this last March during the lecturers' strike when he suddenly happened on 'urgent business' in Britain during the height of the crisis. He did it again after the recent debacle on Graduation Day when members of the Government and the South African guest of honour were greeted with fierce disapproval by African students. Adams promptly set up a disciplinary committee which rusticated the 31 demonstrators. The committee - of 3 - included the white leader of anti-African students at the University.

Those who were rusticated had no opportunity to put their case to Adams. Once again he had left the campus - possibly to seek solace from his wife Tania. Her sole known contribution to the debate about the Graduation Day incidents is that the Africans and their supporters were all "pigs who should be left to wallow in their own filth".

# BERTRAND RUSSELL SWIMS ATLANTIC

In an amazing feat unparalleled in the history of the world Bertrand Russell the 94 year old philosopher and "Happy Pilgrim of Peace" yesterday swam the Atlantic Ocean in two hours.

The news was revealed in a special dispatch from the Ralph Schoenman Press Bureau, at Penrhyndendraeth, Merionethshire.

### FANTASTIC

According to the dispatch, Earl Russell ("our respected and beloved leader")entered the chilly waters of the Atlantic Sea at 6.00 p.m. yesterday morning.

"The Atlantic" says the report "was raging in a violent tempest of wind and rain. Giant waves, many of them a million feet high, crashed in anger on the rocky coast."

### INCREDIBLE

But Lord Russell was not to be deterred by the elements. "Looking ruddy and cheerful, his muscles shining with youthful vigour, he leapt into the swirling waters and within minutes was well out to sea."

With him were the local secretary of The Committee of 100, the Organising Chairman of Bombs for the Viet Cong (Wales) Association and Mr. Schoenman himself.

### MIRACLE

"As Earl Russell breasted the mighty billows of the deep" the report continues, "he chatted jokingly with his companions only pausing to kill marauding sharks with a savage blow from his virile fist or tear of slabs of whalemeat to relieve the hunger of his comrades."

Within two hours the party had landed in America and were taking part in a sit-down demonstration outside the White House.

### ASTONISHING

Reporters were not allowed to witness the actual swimming but later photographs were issued (one of which we reprint above). "These" the report states, "will put paid to the lying and slanderous smears on the part of the capitalist lackeys and hacks of the warmongering British Press as to the alleged senility or even death of the righteous warrior of peace."

# PRIVATE EYE

No. 124
Friday
7 Sept. 66

1/6

# VERWOERD

# A NATION MOURNS

# Gnome

An appalling practice with regard to W.H. Smith, the "booksellers" has been brought to my attention.

I gather that some of my readers (fortunately at this stage their numbers are limited) are indulging in a childish and stupid prank with the avowed aim of frustrating and persecuting the unfortunate Smith, a man for whom as you well know I have the highest possible regard.

What happens is this. Someone will go into a Smith emporium and say "Have you got *Country Life* ?" "Yes" replies the charming, helpful assistant, producing the periodical. "And could I have *Town, Queen, Horse and Hound, The Illustrated London News* ..."

("Hold on sir" says the industrious salesman as the pile of magazines begins to mount ... )

"And I'd like *The Connoisseur, Encounter, Nova, The Gundog, The Field* and the *Times Educational Supplement.*"

"Very good sir" says the unsuspecting fellow, now exhausted. "That'll be two pounds, eight and threepence."

"Oh ... and *Private Eye*" says the 'purchaser' by way of an afterthought, producing a £5 note nonchalantly from his wallet.

"I'm sorry we don't stock that."

"Then I don't want any of these" says the hoaxer walking out in a simulated fit of pique leaving the assistant with a huge pile of unsold magazines.

\* \* \* \* \* \*

This type of childish behaviour must cease forthwith.

E. Strobes.
pp. Gnome.

**The man who asked for Private Eye at W.H.Smiths**

# PRIVATE EYE

. 126
iday
Oct. 66.

1/6

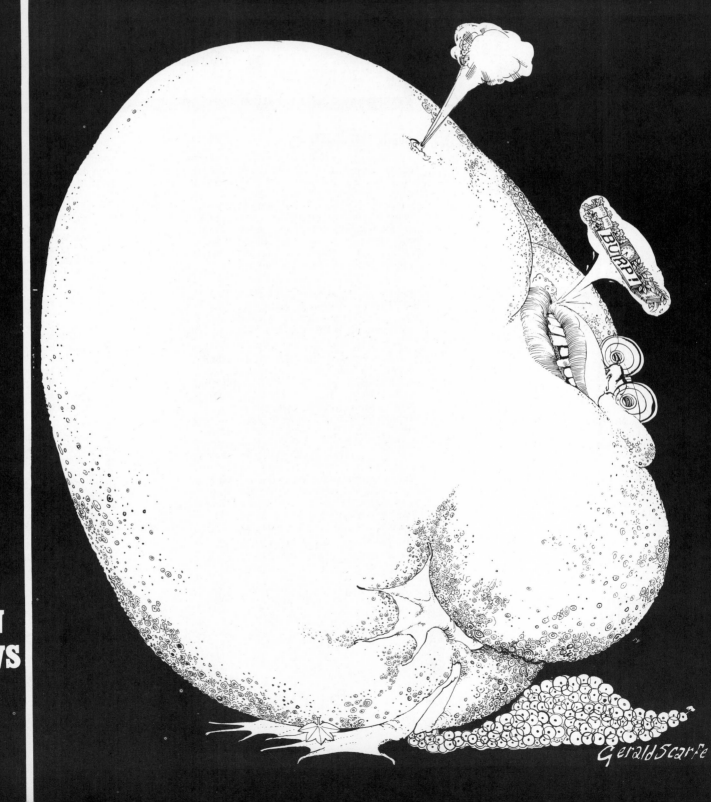

HOMSON
WALLOWS
HE
IMES

nazing
ture

GeraldScarfe

# THE BIBLE FOR MOTORISTS

## The Proud & Humble Motorist

1   Two motorists were up before the bench on speeding charges.

2   One drove a Bentley and the other was a Ford Anglia owner.

3   Our Bentley friend told the beak "I've paid my road tax.  I've a fully comprehensive insurance policy with full no claims bonus.  I've been driving for 25 years and my license is as clean as a whistle.

4   "Ask any man down our street and he'll tell you I'm as safe as houses behind the wheel."

5   But the other chappie made no bones about it.  He pleaded guilty and asked for two other charges to be taken into count.

6   And this poor fellow hadn't even signed his license.  What's more, he got done for parking during the session.

7   The magistrate listened to the two stories with interest.  "£50 and your license endorsed for six months" he told our big-mouthed acquaintance of Bentley fame.

8   But the Ford Anglia character got a provisional discharge after a few harsh words from the bench.  "My time's very valuable" commented the beak "and I am grateful to you for not wasting it with excuses.

9   "Some people think that because they own a Bentley they own the bloody world.   Next please!"

by 'OLD JOWETT'

---

Dear Thomas,
It was a great pleasure to meet you last Monday afternoon on your arrival in the world. I have naturally thanked Queen Charlotte's and Mr Tomkinson for the care they took of you. I hope that you will have a long and happy life, and that you will never be Prime Minister, a much overrated job. It would already be antiquated to wish that you should grow up to be an English gentleman, and the suggestion of social snobbery would be unacceptable to you, but I do hope you will grow up an independent and kindly man of your word, and that is much the same ideal.
You have been named Thomas Fletcher after both your grandfathers, but in calling you Thomas your mother and I also had in mind the two great English Saints, St. Thomas à Becket and St. Thomas More, though princi-

# LETTER TO MY PAPA
## by THOMAS REES-MOGG

## Dear William

When I first saw you blinking down on me in my cot at the Queen Charlotte's, I must admit that my initial reaction was one of shock mingled with distaste.  To come into the world is a hazardous experience at the best of times, but to discover on one's emergence from the womb that one has been sired by the assistant editor of the *Sunday Times* in a bad year that, as you must admit, is quite another.

Thank you anyway for your long letter and for giving me the name of Thomas.  I don't like it very much but I quite see that if Sir Thomas More was in favour of the Common Market then it is a sacrifice that I must be prepared to make.

I should add that I don't altogether approve of your publishing the letter in the *Sunday Times*.  I have never been one to approve of journalists making capital out of their children, however young. Robert Pitman is always doing it and you don't - do you? - want to be associated with such a man.  Besides which I have a feeling that whilst your views on,  say, the Common Market or the leadership of the Conservative Party may possibly be of some interest to readers of your paper these rather verbose and banal sentiments about the nature of life and society in general are, to say the least, *de trop*.

For instance you write "Life is like a great cathedral on a Northern hill."  I am not too young to appreciate that such an observation can be of but little help to me in days to come.  There are, and have been those, who could write of life, its nature and purpose, in a meaningful and enlightening way.  Alas, Father, you are not one.

The only charitable construction that I can put on your conduct in this instance , is that you feel obliged to demonstrate that you are a fit person to become the next editor of *The Times*.

You wish to show to your public and your proprietor, Lord Thomson, that you have the necessary breadth of vision to succeed Sir William Haley, a man who can not only fulminate against indecision in high places, but can under the pseudonym of Oliver Edwards illuminate some obscure corner of English literature in what he considers to be the finest tradition of the great English essayists.

Poor deluded man !  And Father I must beg you to think deeply before embarking on such a course.  I realise that I cannot help being the son of William Rees-Mogg but I feel that, young as I am, I may have some influence to prevent my becoming the son of the Editor of *The Times*.

And please, please, Father, no more of that stuff about cathedrals on Northern hills.

Your loving son,
Thomas.

---

# Newly-weds, aged 82, have problem

*Streatham News*

# KRUPP'S LAST TAPE

Is Krupps going bust? The question has been bouncing back and forth across the Stock Exchanges of Europe for the last fortnight, but, by a kind of unwritten business law, it has not appeared in print. Although almost every respectable financial commentator on the Continent has known that Krupps have been going through a paralysing financial crisis, none have mentioned it. Closest to spilling the beans was the British *Economist* which remarked on November 26:

"Various stories have been given increasing credence outside Germany that any day now one or other of the big internationally known companies of West Germany might fail to meet its obligations". No mention, however, of Krupps. Even *The Economist* plays the game.

The plain fact is that by mid-November this year Krupps of Essen, whose turnover exceeds £460 million, had got itself into a serious financial mess. The avaricious confidence of its former Nazi owners had inspired mass investment all over the world during the decade of the 'German economic miracle'. In 1945 the Krupp armaments empire was in ruins, and Alfried Krupp was sentenced to twelve years in prison for introducing slave labour into his war factories. Fifteen years later Krupps was again one of the most powerful industries in the world, and Alfried, let out of jail six years early, was one of its richest and most influential citizens.

But the mass investment had to be paid for. As long as the 'miracle' lasted, it was quite easy to get short term loans from the banks to finance more and more investment. But as even Germany started to undergo recessions, so the investments became less profitable and the loans difficult to repay.

Krupps main difficulty was the organisation of the German finance system, as devised by British and American economic 'experts' after the war. The British and American systems, whereby most of the capital is raised in 'equity' shares - which means that the firm is not obliged to pay any dividend at all - was regarded by these experts as unsafe and unfair, likely to place the German middle classes at the mercy of unscrupulous Stock Exchange sharks. They therefore insisted that all capital raised on the market should carry a fixed interest rate, and that the interest had by law to be paid at regular intervals.

Thus big firms like Krupps do not go to the 'open market' for their investment money. They go instead to the banks, who must also lend at a fixed rate of interest. In 1963 two British papers reported serious problems with Krupp short-term loans - reports which were vehemently and unconvincingly denied by the management. This year the spectre of bankruptcy has risen again.

In recent months Krupps have been shaken by non-payment for materials and plants in underdeveloped countries, mainly steel plant in Argentina and India. They have had to counter this non-payment with short-term loans from the banks, which have recently become due for repayment. Krupps could not pay.

Only one man could pull Krupps out of the drain, and that was Herr Blessing, Governor of the Government Bundesbank. Blessing could instruct the commercial banks not to be too hasty in demanding the repayments due to them from Krupp, and give his authority to the waiving of the fixed interest repayment regulations.

What worried Blessing was that it might get around that he, Blessing, former Nazi sympathiser, should be seen by the nation and the world at large to be manipulating the German finance system in favour of Herr Alfried Krupp, former slave driver and armourer for Hitler. In view of recent political events in Bavaria and Hesse, such a story might well be created into a political scandal.

So a desperate but discreet appeal went out from Government circles to the better informed financial journals and correspondents, pointing out that any disclosure of the 'arrangements' made to get Krupps out of their immediate difficulties would do untold damage to the Fatherland.

References were made, for the benefit of foreigners, to the Creditanstalt bank in Austria whose crash in the early 1930's brought down share values all over the world and led to panic among the German middle classes, and to Hitler. Attention was drawn also to the collapse of the Lebanese Intra Bank last month which was a great deal more serious than most financial commentators admitted. Any journalist or editor who gave prominence to the Krupp difficulties, it was hinted, would be deliberately helping to foster a world slump.

Under cover of a smokescreen of silence, therefore, Blessing gave the relevant instructions to the banks, and Krupps staggered forward into another year of miraculous prosperity.

*"Go on boy, rabbits, go get em!"*

# HERE WE GO AGAIN...

5th DECEMBER, 1966. WISLON APPLIES TO U.N. FOR SANCTIONS AGAINST RHODESIA: DELIVERS CHURCHILLIAN SPEECH ON T.V.

THIS HURTS ME MORE THAN IT DOES U THANT

25th DECEMBER, 1966. SMITH DELIVERS DEFIANT CHRISTMAS MESSAGE.

YOU CAN KEEP HER

THE FIGHT GOES ON (burp) EXCUSE I, AND NOW I GIVE YOU THE QUEEN!

1st JANUARY, 1967. U.N. RUMBLINGS: WISLON FLIES OUT. LORD CARADON OFFERS RESIGNATION. REFUSED.

THE SANCTIONS ARE BEGINNING TO BITE. GIVE US TIME

24th FEBRUARY, 1967. COMMONWEALTH RUMBLINGS. WISLON FLIES TO LUSAKA. LORD CARADON RESIGNS.

THE SANCTIONS WILL HAVE EFFECT IN WEEKS RATHER THAN MONTHS GIVE US TIME

MAN - DA - TORY!

13th JUNE, 1967. COMMONWEALTH CONFERENCE. WISLON GIVES ULTIMATUM TO SMITH. LORD CARADON RE-APPOINTED.

UNLESS SMITH SUBMITS BEFORE NOVEMBER 30. WE WILL APPLY TO THE U.N. FOR SANCTIONS AGAINST SOUTH AFRICA

4th AUGUST, 1967. CABINET RESHUFFLE. FRED LEE APPOINTED COMMONWEALTH SECRETARY. WISLON ANNOUNCES AMAZING DEVELOPMENT.

I AM GLAD TO BE ABLE TO INFORM THE HOUSE THAT WE ARE TO HOLD TALKS ABOUT TALKS ABOUT TALKS WITH THE SMITH REGIME

29th NOVEMBER, 1967. SMITH AND WISLON MEET FOR 11th HOUR CONFRONTATION IN SPACE CAPSULE.

AT LAST WE ARE ALONE

5th DECEMBER, 1967. SMITH SAYS: NO! BRITAIN APPLIES TO U.N. FOR SANCTIONS AGAINST SOUTH AFRICA: WISLON DELIVERS CHURCHILLIAN SPEECH ON T.V.

THIS HURTS ME MORE THAN IT DOES HUGH FOOT

1st JANUARY, 1968. U.N. RUMBLINGS. WISLON FLIES OUT. LORD CARADON OFFERS RESIGNATION.

THE SANCTIONS ARE BEGINNING TO BITE. GIVE US TIME

etc. etc. etc.

# COLOUR SECTION

The *Daily Mail* of Thursday, 9th February carried as its main story an astonishing piece of nonsense by its political editor Walter Terry. Under the heading 'Brown and Kosygin – The Surprising Story Behind This Week's Hand-holding', Terry deduced from a few tiny incidents of Brown's eccentricity at Kosygin-welcoming functions that the Foreign Secretary was in the process of jeopardising the entire Anglo-Soviet get-together by his boorish behaviour.

Unsophisticated readers may have thought on examining Terry's trivia "What is all this fuss about?" Sophisticated readers: "Oh the *Mail* must have something more up its sleeve to go to town on rubbish like this". In both cases the piece simply helped to confirm Brown's recent TV apologia in which he successfully posed as a sincere, albeit rumbustious, person constantly harried by malignant sensation-seeking journalists.

If the Political Editor of the *Daily Mail* can write such cock, was the feeling in the bistros, then by George that fellow Brown is being given a raw deal.

Feelings evidently shared by G. Brown himself. For in the *Daily Express* the following day there appeared another mystifying piece by Political Correspondent Wilfrid (sic) Sendall.

This made clear to those prepared to read between the lines that Brown himself was of the opinion that Terry's absurd attack had been inspired by H. Wislon, no less.

What was not mentioned was the cause of the sudden flare-up between Brown, Wislon and the rest of the cabinet.

Namely the appearance of Brown on the Frost programme. Not but what everyone (including Wislon) was v. jealous of Brown for securing 40 minutes of wildly successful publicity at the hands of the sycophantic Frost.

What particularly irked Wislon and the others was the fact that when in November last year it looked as if Ian Smith might fly over to this country and appear on Gypsy Dave's appalling programme, the Cabinet (no less) reached a unanimous decision that

no minister would appear on the show either then or at any other time – the programme being considered as a frivolous show-business affair unsuited to the *gravitas* of cabinet ministers.

The decision was scrupulously observed, despite several invitations.

Surprise, surprise to all then, when who should pop up pulling skeins of wool over the public's eyes and getting away with such manifest twaddle as 'I was never really interested in the leadership struggle of 1963' – why none other than colourful G. Brown

Wislon, who knows good publicity when he sees it, was justifiably furious. Particularly when Brown, on being asked why he had reneged on a cabinet decision could only reply that as they had asked him twice to appear on the programme he felt it would be impolite to refuse at the third time of asking.

(None of which excuses the appalling conduct of Walter Terry.)

# PRIVATE EYE

No. 134
Friday
3 Feb. 67

1/6

# BENN'S HOVERBRITAIN

by Our
INSIGHTPROBESPECTRUMNEWSIGHTNEWSTREAM
(P.B. Thard)

In his office on the 413th floor of the gleaming new Technology Tower, we talked this week to the man who is putting the 'New' back in the 'New Britain', Mr. Anthony Wedgewood Hoverbene (or 01-346-2167, as he prefers to be called.)

Before the interview began, Mr. Hoverbene rather surprisingly asked for a minute's silence for prayer and meditation. He crossed the room and knelt on a small inflatable rubber model of a Hovercraft, before an illuminated mock-up of the Concord airliner.

"Technology" he confided, when he had finished, "is to me a spiritual affair. It liberates the soul from the enslavement of the ordinary human world. Take the telephone": "Thank you very much", I murmured somewhat bewildered by this strange request, and crammed the instrument into my already bulging briefcase.

"You see", he went on, "I've been attacked by normally quite sensible people for my scheme to abolish all street names and addresses and replace them with a simple code of 54-digit numbers. But what they don't realise is that this simple idea would save the Post Office £57,000 million-a-year - because no one would send letters any more".

"The point is" he declared passionately, "that I grew up in a city - and to me technology has always been a way of life. Just as a country boy might be fascinated by the birds and bees, I am obsessed by the mating habits of the Triumph Herald. When I was young I used to sit for hours, just watching the traffic lights change colour from red to green to amber and then back to red ... green ... amber ... no left turn ... red ... green..."

As he spoke, the room darkened and colour lights began to revolve around us, projected onto Bri-Skylon screens. To a weird electronic humming, the door opened and two small white coated technicians came in to carry out Mr. Hoverbene's latest wish - and indeed to carry out Mr. Hoverbene himself. (contd... p. 94).

"I'm all for cleaning up television, Miss Whitby, but let's keep life filthy!"

# Tomorrow Private Eye begins an adventure. Join it

Yes, it's all happening in Britain today! Make no mistake about it - ideas, traditions, once-proven scientific laws, morality, taste - yes, they're all being re-aligned, re-defined, re-designed, thrashed-out, cast into the melting pot and thrown out of the window almost second by second as we hurtle into the seething, psychedelic second-half of this groovy, action-packed 21st Century.

Even the Times, once the stuffy, fuddy-duddy organ of the bewhiskered Establishment, has switched-on to become part of the ever-changing kaleidoscope that is Britain '67.

## Tomorrow's Changes

Like the Times, Private Eye is no slouch when it comes to responding to the quivering antennae of this roaring, expansionist New Renaissance.

As from tomorrow, Private Eye will have a new look, a look that will reflect the deep-down ruthless fresh, long, cool-as-a-mountain-stream rethink that has recently been thrashed out round-the-clock behind locked doors at Gnome house.

Tomorrow's issue will go deeper into the news - not to say the nudes (see picture of mini-skirted doctor on page 94) than ever before.

Even the page-numbering has not resisted the corrosive broom that is sweeping like a hurricane down the dusty corridors of satire.

From tomorrow, they will appear at the bottom rather than the top of the page, and will be printed in dynamic new Computero Numero type that is almost illegible to the eye.

## Crossword

Correspondents for the first time since the days of the first Lord Gnome (myself) will not be named - the abandonment of a no longer meaningful tradition. Men such as E.J. Pribb (Chess), Mrs. Monica Wimble-Steams (Rugby Football) and Harrison Birtwistle (Rock Gardening) will no longer be house-hold names. Instead they will be sacked as part of a ruthless shake-out and the introduction of the latest cost-efficiency techniques from the board-room upwards.

## Abrasive

But behind the new type-faces - the new type of face. The face, to take only one example, of the new editor. Out goes boring, stick-in-the-mud, fuddy-duddy, working-class Sir William Haley Mills (94), in comes dynamic, swinging, fuddy-duddy upper-class Sir William Ree-Smogg (97).

Yes, make no mistake about it, a great newspaper is taking new shape. Today it is oblong. Tomorrow - who knows - it may be round. The next day, triangular. What the hell. Anything to titillate the consumers, in a desperate bid to put up the circulation.

## In a dramatically changing country, a dramatically changing magazine

## Private Eye

Mrs. Edna Petrie, 15 years service as a pistwoman at Blaydon.

*The Courier*

# 'The day I fell off my bicycle and lost God'

## Bertrand Russell

*One of Britain's Oldest Loonies speaks out*

Mr. Russell I don't find your proposition at all logical!

It was at the age of three that I first realised that I was not as other babies are. I had been taken by my aunt Emmeline to have tea with the widow of Charles II. As I was being wheeled along in the pram I suddenly threw my rattle in the air and realised that I was no longer a Thomist. "Great Thucydides!" I cried to my startled Nanny, "Archimedes does not hold water for a moment". "No more do you, Master Bertie" she hastily replied, as she busied herself with the replacement of my diaper.

When I was five I remember my first sudden experience of erotic ecstasy, when a kindly uncle, Lord Palmerston, drew for me the shapely figure of a dodecahedron on the nursery blackboard. I was deeply embarrassed and blushed to the roots of my hair.

It was shortly after this that I had a first glimpse of the amazing intellectual powers that were to comfort me in many an emotional crisis in the years to come. I was bicycling down a country lane near Cheam when suddenly it came to me that if today was Monday, then tomorrow could not possibly also be Monday, although there was nothing in logic, as at that time conceived, to prevent it from being Sunday. The fact that the day in question was a Tuesday, I quickly say, was philosophically beside the point. It is difficult to describe the ecstasy which this discovery aroused in me and I at once bicycled home to begin work on the *Principia Absurdica*, the sixty volumes of which were to occupy my mind throughout the following forty years.

* * * * *

It was during this period I realised that I no longer loved my first wife. I was out bicycling at the time when the realisation came to me as sharply as if I had run into a tree. As I picked myself from the tangled wreckage, I knew that I would have to have it out with her that evening. She took it badly and threatened to commit suicide. Twenty years later I was to meet Lady Utterly Immorell. She was a great beauty, with a face like a buffalo and the figure of a rhinoceros. We were sitting on a sofa at the time and she placed her hand at the top of my thigh. I suddenly realised that I was deeply and passionately in love with her and we decided to become intimate the following Thursday afternoon.

* * * * *

Eventually the great work which had given me my only moments of true happiness for so many years came to an end. It took seventy nine men with as many wheelbarrows, and a steam-powered crane to transfer the finished manuscript to the university refuse heap, for I had suddenly realised as soon as I had completed the work, that I was now able to refute every proposition contained in it.

* * * * *

It was shortly after this that I left for America, Lady Utterly having finally rejected my favours on account of my appalling halitosis. On the night I arrived I saw a beautiful young girl across the table at dinner. I suddenly realised that we must become intimate. We did so that very night.

Fortunately the next morning the First World War broke out and so great was the shock that I was able at once to forget all about her and become a pacifist. I later learned that she had been heartbroken at my precipitate departure and committed suicide in a fit of illogical pique.

Next Week: the great philosopher reveals more of the wisdom he has gathered from a lifetime of deep contemplation on the meaning of life.

# Mrs Wilson's Diary

*I*magine what a blow it was, just as Harold was about to break up for the hols, to hear the terrible news about the *Tory Canon* running aground on the Seven Sisters! And so near to our little grey home in the Scilly Islands. We heard the news first as we were sitting over breakfast on the Sunday morning. The Inspector went to the telephone as Mr. Kaufmann was having his weekend off with an aunt in Broadstairs, and came back with a mystified expression on his face. "A Mr. Tremerthin Gumford speaking from a callbox in the Scilly Islands Sir" he remarked, "he seemed somewhat hysterical". Harold immediately went to the telephone and came back a few moments later in an excited mood. "My God" he cried, "this is disastrous". "Tell us about it" observed the Inspector, taking his pipe out of his mouth and laying it on the Formica top table beside his Kellog bowl, "I trust that foulussed *(I think I caught the word correctly)* tomcat has not got down the chimney again and been all over the beds?" "Be quiet Inspector" cried Harold, "this is a serious matter which could affect the lives of millions of innocent people." "Do tell, Harold" I cried, clasping my hands in supplication, "I cannot bear the suspense". At this Harold assumed his 'toughie' look and remarked "Gladys. Some idiot has discharged a tankerful of oil into the sea. It could ruin our Easter Holiday".

*B*y the next morning the house was in tumult. Harold had transformed the lounge into a 'War Room' with Giles's *Readers' Digest* Foldout Polar Map pinned to the wall with drawing pins and several red-faced nautical gentlemen with pipes and pea-jackets were standing about in dramatic postures. None of them seemed interested in the pot of tea and the plate of fancies I prepared for them, and I had to send the Inspector out for some more Wincarnis from Boots. When I peeped in, Harold was standing by the map in his old Oxford duffle coat with Giles's Beatle-style George Lennon cap and old pair of gumboots he uses for gardening, and was moving little red flags about while the nautical gentlemen made gruff noises and remarked that it was just like old times. I was just opening another tin of Spam for a fork lunch when Jim Callaghan tapped on the kitchen window wearing a polo neck sweater and his old *HMS Buffoon* blazer on with a row of brightly polished medals pinned to the lapel. "Heave ho my hearties" he remarked, wiping his boots on the coconut matting, "skipper on the bridge?" At this moment Harold appeared asking whether I could get down Robin's old *Sink the Dreadnought* Set from the attic, and move the folding card table into the lounge to represent the Atlantic Ocean. "Aha" cried Jim "all hands to the mainbrace, what, Prime Minister? As an old salt myself I think my place is behind the mast. I am ready to leave for Falmouth as soon as Audrey has got my bicycle up from the basement".

"I don't think that will be necessary Jim," remarked Harold,"there are already three

Ministers, five under-secretaries, two admirals and a detachment of the Iniskilling Dragoons standing by, and I haven't called in the Navy yet. Lord Mountbatten has been alerted in Rangoon and is ready to suspend the shooting of his latest film should the situation warrant it. I myself, as you can see, am paramount commander of *Operation Daz* as we have dubbed it". Jim Callaghan looked somewhat crestfallen at this, but he was soon put to work on arranging Robin's model boats on the card table and helping hand the Spam sandwiches round to the admirals. By this time the gentlemen of the Press had been summoned by Mr. Kaufmann, unexpectedly recalled from Broadstairs by the Yeoman Messenger of the Queen's Household in a small horse drawn vehicle not unlike the Rothman's Cigarette Coach, and Harold delivered a short prepared speech in which he said that *Number Ten* had been turned into a Power House of Command and that he personally would count no cost to fight the Slick at sea, on the beaches, and in the hearts and minds of the people, and that he would never surrender.

*I* must say the Operation seems to have been a great success, although the Inspector said he thought it had been rather pricey at a million pounds. From the little window of our bungalow, as I sit writing at the table in the kitchenette, the sea looks crystal clear and the beach is apparently unscathed apart from the rather unsightly oildrums and the tar that was washed up last year. Admittedly the orange peel, the banana skins and the broken bottles give it a rather drab aspect, but after all trippers are only human. However the islanders are taking no chances. Mrs. Bulstrode, who organises the local M.U. has got together a Mothers' Union 'Give A Packet of Detergent Campaign' with a stall outside the Scilly Cow, and the Jumbo and Family Size Packs (even the Economy Size donated by those of slender means) are regularly emptied into the coastal waters each morning after breakfast by Mr. Larkin from the Pet Stores and his team of voluntary assistants in their little rowing boat *The Gipsy Chichester*. Mrs. Twiggle, the postman's wife, tells me the foam looks lovely from the Prom when the tide is out.

# FOOTNOTES

# RULE BIAFRA !

The Commonwealth Relations Office - never the most intelligent or well-informed of Government Ministries - maintained that Britain was completely neutral in the Nigerian civil war until the *Financial Times* Malta man gave full details of the British arms shipments through Malta.

Unabashed the CRO announced that the arms were 'anti-aircraft guns, and they are purely defensive'. Quite why anyone would sell anti-aircraft guns to Lagos, when Biafra has only one fighting aeroplane - an obsolete bomber - was difficult to appreciate, until the Lagos Government announced that they used these 'defensive' weapons from their ships when they attacked the Biafran port of Bonny.

If the war goes on as at present, there will be an increasing flow of 'defensive' weapons (planes, tanks, artillery, etc.) from Britain to Lagos over the coming weeks, and the CRO's policy will be to lie about them until they are discovered.

The CRO line has always been pro-Lagos. Earlier this year Colonel Ojukwu, then Military Governor of Eastern Nigeria,

invited three British MPs, Mr. John Tilney (Tory), Mr. Arthur Davidson (Labour) and Mr. David Steel (Liberal) to visit Enugu, the CRO objected that this would favour the East. Ojukwu immediately agreed that the MPs should visit all the Nigerian regions and talk to all parties, but the CRO insisted that this 'might be misinterpreted and inflame the situation'.

On the other hand the CRO firmly approves of the current visit to Lagos of Mr. John Cordle, Tory MP for Bourne-mouth East and Christchurch (remember Suez, Nigel Nicolson, etc. ?). Mr. Cordle is a firm friend of the Federal Government and has called for more arms to be sent to Lagos from Britain.

Mr. Cordle is a director of the *Church of England Newspaper*, a director of the Church Society, a Member of the Archbishops of Canterbury and York Commission on Evange-lism, a member of the Church Assembly, and a member of the Oxford Trust of Churches' Patronage Board

He supports the Lagos Government because he feels it is a lawful Commonwealth partner. Most of the inhabitants of West and North Nigeria are Moslems who, in the racial riots last year, slaughtered some 30,000 East Nigerians most of whom are Christians.

The CRO's attitude has been reached in spite of the constant warnings from Biafra of the dangers of too strong a pro-Lagos line from the British Deputy-Commissioner in Enugu, Mr. James Parker. Such warn-ings have been dismissed by the CRO with the remarkable observation: "James is just a white IBO".

But the CRO have not been getting much help from the Nigerian High Commissioner in London. On the very day that the British Government admitted the arms deal with Lagos, His Excellency denied it. The next day, while his Government were admitting 'big gains' by Biafra, he explained that the rumours about the British arms deal 'were untrue but understandable as they come in the wake of growing reverses suffered by rebel troops'.

**"The sea's lovely and warm, but there are some oily parts"**
**"Never mind, dear, we'll spray them with Detergent when we get home!"**

# PRIVATE EYE

No. 140
Friday
28 April 67

1/6

## QUEEN'S AWARD FOR INDUSTRY 196

## WHAT'S IT ALL ABOUT ALF ?

**Aberfan**

# ROBENS FOUND IN ATTIC

Don't ask me. I'm only the man in charge

Lord Robens pictured on the day following the Aberfan disaster

. 141.
iday
May 67

# PRIVATE EYE

1/6

# COMMON MARKET

# THE GREAT
# DEBATE BEGINS

# PRIVATE EYE

No. 146
Friday
21 July 67.

1/6

## FULL OF EASTERN PROMISE...

# COULD IT HAPPEN HERE?

asks Lunchtime(self) O'Booze p.94

# PRIVATE EYE

No. 155
Friday
Nov. 24 '67

1/6

# COALITION SENSATION

*Top Row:* MR. M. STEWART ( - ); MR. IAN SMITH ( Sec. of State for Commonwealth Relations); LORD GOODMAN ( Lord Chancellor); LORD ROBENS-BEECHING (Minister of Social Security ); MR. DUNCAN SANDYS ( Sec. of State for Education). *Second Row:* MR. A.W. BENN ; ( Minister of Agriculture, Fisheries and Food ); BARONESS ASQUITH ( Minister of Technology ); SIR FRANCIS CHICHESTER ( Minister of Defence ); HRH THE DUKE OF EDINBURGH ( Minister for Exports ); MR. P. GORDON WALKER ( Minister Without Anything ); DR. E. SAVUNDRA ( President of the Board of Trade ). *Third Row:* MR. Q. HOGG ( Sec. of State for Outer Space ); MR. R. GUNTER ( Minister of Terror ); MR. G. BROWN ( resigned ); MR. E. MARPLES( Minister of Transport). *Front Row:* LORD SNOWDEN OF CARDIFF ( Chancellor of the Exchequer ); MR. D. FROST ( Minister of Propaganda ); EARL WISLON ( Prime Minister, First Lord of the Treasury and Sec. of State for Economic Affairs);RT. HON. BAILLIE VASS (Foreign Secretary);SIR CYRIL OSBORNE (Home Sec.).

# PRIVATE EYE

No. 157
Friday
22 Dec. 67

1/6

# THE OCTOBER 1964–1967 REVOLUTION

PRIVATE AVDA ARTIST STEADMANOVICH RECAPTURES THE SCENE IN PARLIAMENT SQUARE IN OCTOBER 1964 WHEN THE SONS AND DAUGHTERS OF THE SCIENTIFIC REVOLUTION UNDER THEIR HEROIC LEADER WISLON (CARRYING BANNER) OVERTHREW THE FORCES OF REACTION LED BY BAILLIE VASS THUS USHERING IN THE GOLDEN YEARS OF TECHNOLOGY AND BRINGING TO AN END THIRTEEN YEARS OF CORRUPTION AND WASTE.

## Unidentified Flying Malaises sighted

Malaises have been sighted in different parts of the country (writes our Astronomical Correspondent Sir Jodrell Bank) by a wide cross section of malaise-spotters.

The malaises have almost all been described as 'deep-seated'. A malaise is usually deep-seated particularly at this time of year.

Apart from being deep seated, further distinguishing marks of the malaises have not been forthcoming. But one spotter Sir Herbert Gusset said "A lot of it is to do with exports".

Police under Insp. 'Knacker of the Yard' Knacker have been trying to catch the malaise which was last seen by Sir William Haley Mogg hovering above Printing House Square but with no success.

One man said "I have seen no malaise, matey. Deep seated or the other. Malays, yes, quite a lot of them about".

Said one psychiatrist: "This malaise business has been going on for the last twenty years or so. And there is nothing out of the ordinary about this latest batch of reports. People get depressed at this time of the year and tend to see malaises hovering about. A lot of it is in the mind".

Several malaise men will appear on the Gypsy David Frost programme in forthcoming weeks. The Gypsy is himself a keen malaise spotter and wants to get to the bottom of their deep seats.

# FOOTNOTES

# LEAK WEEK

**D**uring the week-end of December 9-11 a fantastic rumour jangled the jaded nerves of Fleet Street - to the effect that on the evening of Friday, December 8, Messrs. Crossman, Crosland and Jenkins had called on the Prime Minister and urged him to resign. The rumour is no doubt a wild misrepresentation of what actually happened in Downing Street that Friday, but it is a great deal more plausible than the correspondents believed.

To start with, Richard Crossman is Roy Jenkins' No.1 fan, and intervened at the last moment to persuade Wilson not to appoint Crosland Chancellor. Secondly, all three Ministers believe that the future of the Labour Government, and therefore themselves, depends on 'making devaluation work'. And devaluation, they argue, will not work as long as those who hold sterling believe that the British Government is still worshipping socialist sacred cows. Harold Wilson, they believe, is worshipping too many of them. No prescription charges, for one. And the embargo on arms sales for South Africa for another. And that is what the whole charade about South African arms has been about.

Absurdity No.1 is the idea that Harold Wilson is opposed *at all costs* to lifting the arms embargo. On the contrary, ever since the Tiger talks on Rhodesia failed last December, Wilson has encouraged the Foreign Office to cajole the South African Government into squeezing Rhodesia back to constitutional rule. These attempts started even before the Tiger talks when George Brown met the South African Foreign Secretary, rugger-playing Hilgard Muller, who was educated at Cambridge, is a former High Commissioner in London and loves England. Brown and Muller are much the same bullying, blustering type. From the outset Muller has pointed out that any Rhodesian deal would involve a slackening in the arms embargo. He referred particularly to the large quantity of 'naval equipment' previously bought by South Africa in Britain, which was not so available elsewhere. Brown agreed that if a Rhodesian settlement could be assured, there would be no trouble about the naval equipment. Indeed, more arms might well follow.

Wilson knew about all of this, and thoroughly approved it. He met Muller himself shortly before the Commonwealth Secretary's last desperate bid to Salisbury and the two discussed the deal hopefully. Never once, in all his speeches and statements on Rhodesia, has Wilson attacked the Republic of South Africa for deliberately interfering with sanctions. Such interference has been the main reason for the failure of sanctions, but Wilson has, since 1965, spoken about South Africa in ingratiating tones. All along he has hoped that this expert diplomacy will per-suade the South Africans to squeeze Smith.

Yet from the outset the 'arms for sanctions' deal was almost certain to fail. At the recent meeting between Vorster and Smith in Pretoria, Smith explained that his extremists would not tolerate a Tiger-type settlement and would not bow to pressure either from London or Pretoria to accept one. Since that meeting, South Africa's attitude to the original deal has cooled considerably, though there is still the possibility that the South African regulations about trade with Rhodesia will be tightened in exchange for Britain lifting the arms embargo. As the prospects of a deal on Rhodesia dimmed, so did Wilson's own enthusiasm for lifting the embargo.

The demand for British arms - notably naval equipment - nevertheless went on through the 'normal channels', and Admiral Hendrik Biermans, chief of the South African naval staff, duly announced his intention of coming to Britain to discuss the matter in the week December 11-16. The question of lifting the embargo, therefore, came up as a matter of course in the select and powerful Cabinet Committee on Defence and Overseas Policy which met in Downing Street on Friday, December 8th.

The Ministers present were Wilson, Brown, Thomson, Crosland, Crossman, Jenkins, Healey, Marsh, Gardiner and Longford. There were also a clutch of junior Ministers called in to read briefs on matters under discussion. When the arms question came up, Brown argued that the Government could no longer afford to withold the equipment, particularly as there was still a chance of South Africa helping out over Rhodesia. Thomson agreed. The economics Ministers, Crosland and Jenkins, also argued for lifting the embargo on the grounds that holding out over so little just for a principle was the best way to damage international financial confidence in the Government. They also showed that South Africa was more powerful than ever in her position as main world gold producer, and the decisions about the channeling of gold after devaluation were several times more crucial than before. (Mr. Jenkins, by the way, is still a member of Anti-Apartheid). Healey argued for lifting the embargo in the futile hope that such a move would save his precious F.111s which are almost certain to be axed in the devaluation package. Marsh also indicated his support for lifting the embargo - which made six very powerful votes indeed. Against the change in policy were Stewart, Gardiner, Crossman (who kept strangely quiet throughout) and, after much dithering, Longford. The Prime Minister listened and smoked his pipe, indicating, only very vaguely, that he didn't think a change in policy was quite for the best at the moment.

He then had a week-end to think the matter out. In the light of his past pledges, a statement lifting the embargo would, he reckoned, rightly, do irreparable damage to him personally. He reckoned too that the vast majority of the Parliamentary Party would be opposed to such a move and that he would lose his most solid base of support, the left centre. Rightly or wrongly, probably rightly, he saw the whole thing as a masterplot by the old Gaitskellites to get rid of him. And so it was on Tuesday 12th the newspapers carried huge lead stories indicating that a powerful group in the Cabinet were in favour of lifting the arms embargo.

New leaks sprung every hour. Before long, the information that James Callaghan had added his voice to the Arms for Vorster brigade had leaked; as had Wilson's own speech to Northern MPs that he stood by every word he said about the 'bloody traffic in the weapons of oppression' in 1963. Barbara Castle, already furious at the disastrous leaks about Peter Parker and the chairmanship of British Rail, put it around that a nasty right-wing racialist rump were seeking to arm the Fascists. Mr. Kevin Macnamara, who is Parliamentary Private Secretary to Mr. Peter Shore, who in turn is Wilson's best male friend in the Cabinet, put down a motion upholding the embargo which collected more than 130 signatures from back-benchers. Only a handful of MPs including Dr. David Owen, 'young eagle' Mr. David Marquand, and the terrible Tory twins Wyatt and Donnelly refused to sign. 12 Junior Ministers indicated their intention to resign if the embargo was lifted. On the other side, the Arms for Vorster faction in the Cabinet were joined by those well-known multi-racialists, Gordon Walker and Gunter.

All this took place while Brown was in Brussels. Almost desperately, Wilson named him in the Commons as the ringleader of the campaign (which he is), in the hope that a bandwaggon could be started which would run over the wretched George. For a time it looked as though he might succeed, but the Ministers who had opposed the embargo stood firm.

Wilson has been overruled in Cabinet before, notably over the timing of steel nationalisation in 1965, but has never before put up with quite such a volley of abuse. No vote was taken, but by their speeches the 'feeling of the meeting' broke down as follows:

For the embargo: Wilson, Stewart, Gardiner, Castle, Greenwood, Shore, Benn, Ross, Hughes, Longford, Crossman ........11

Against the embargo: Callaghan, Jenkins, Brown Thomson, Crosland, Healey, Marsh, Gunter, Gordon Walker ........ 9

Of the ten senior Ministers only three were for the status quo, against seven for a change. A 'compromise' was clearly the only way out. The breakdown brought to mind the famous Wilson response when asked by a close friend why he didn't clear out the dead wood from his Cabinet. "The dead wood?" he replied, shocked. "They're the only ones/who support me".

By leaking information about allegedly top secret meetings as shamelessly and as inaccurately as he has done in the past, Wilson's opponents have at last contrived to keep up with him. And thus leaking information faster and faster in an intensifying series of personal vendettas do our leaders square up to the nation's hour of crisis.

*"Now ... What would Nanny have done?"*

*"Stay! The night is young, and you are enormous".*

*"Oh! Threatening us with karate now is he?"*

WOODVALE NATURISTS

# FOOTNOTES

# THE MAN WITH THE GOLDEN HANDS

The surgeons in America and South Africa who have spent the last six weeks enthusiastically replacing their patients' hearts have achieved a remarkable rate of mortality even by the standards of cardiac surgical experiment. Leading the field is Dr. Adrian Kantrovitz of New York whose two patients, a small baby and Mr. Louis Block, both died within a few days of their transplant (mortality rate: 100%).

Second is Doctor Chris Barnard and his team at Groote Schuur hospital, Cape Town. Mr. Louis Washkansky their first patient, is dead. Dr. Philip Blaiberg, their second is still tenuously alive (mortality rate: 50%). Third is Dr. Norman Shumway at the Stanford University Centre, California, whose single transplant patient, Mr. Mike Kasperak, is critically ill, (mortality rate: as yet, nil). By the time *Private Eye* comes out, the overall mortality rate could well have hit the jackpot 100%.

This impressive record has inspired cardiac surgeons all over the world to have a go. In Oklahoma, the surgeons already have a recipient, and are looking around for a donor. In Bristol, cardiac surgeons, egged on by the Minister of Health, are eagerly fingering their scalpels. In South Africa the debonair Professor Barnard, having told the *Cape Argus* of January 3 that there was 'no possibility of another transplant operation being done in the near future' disclosed to a packed Press Conference on January 8th:

"Yes, we are starting to look for another transplant case".

For the slaughter that is to come in the operating theatres of cardiac hospitals, no one is more responsible than the Press. The British Press, despite belated doubts, heralded the transplant operations with the joyful abandon of a schoolboy at the Farnborough Air Show. In the general hysteria some rather important details seem to have escaped public attention.

The physical engineering of heart transplantation is a relatively simple business, and can be successfully performed by most experienced cardiac surgeons. What makes the operation difficult and dangerous is the probability that the body will reject the tissues in the new heart. The real advances in cardiac surgery in the past few years have been in the 'typing' of body tissues, the assessment of one tissue's compatibility with another. If accurate, this process ensures transplantation without the body rejecting the new tissues and collapsing. With the recent advances in tissue typing, the chances of a heart being accepted are now five to one against, compared to thousands to one against a few years ago. In other words, out of six cases of heart-transplantation, five will fail, and the patients will die through tissue-rejection. The odds are narrowing. In a year's time, perhaps even

6 months, the chances of survival could be much improved. But Professor Barnard could not wait.

Professor Barnard's 'pioneering' has not been in surgical engineering, nor in tissue-typing (most of the crucial tissue-typing research has been done in immunological establishments in Switzerland and Holland and in secondary centres in England and America). His contribution surmounted one of the nastiest problems facing the heart transplant surgeon: how to get the new heart into the body before it is irretrievably damaged.

This problem marks the big difference between heart and kidney transplantation. After death - that is after the blood has stopped circulating - kidneys are not irreversibly damaged for half an hour or more. In this time they can safely be removed and put into someone else. Once the blood and oxygen supply has been re-established, the kidney rapidly recovers and functions normally. Thus kidney transplantation has been carried out almost entirely without criticism, and with considerable saving of life.

The heart, however, behaves differently. Within three to four minutes of the blood circulation stopping, the heart is irrevocably damaged, and is quite useless. The business of transplanting a heart takes much more than three to four minutes. It took Professor Barnard and his team five hours.

Professor Barnard and his team have discovered a 'solution' to this tricky problem: namely to remove the heart *before it has stopped beating*. In this way the time taken to disconnect the heart and lift it across from donor to recipient can be kept down to the necessary minimum. And if the donor heart is cooled to ten degrees centigrade, the connecting stitches necessary to secure the heart in its new place, thus re-establishing its blood supply, can be made before the heart is irretrievably damaged.

When Professor Barnard performed his 'pioneering' transplant operation on Louis Waskansky on December 3rd last year, surgeons all over the world were astonished to read that the donor, a young car-crash victim called Denise Darvall, had 'died from a car crash' (see every British and South African newspaper, December 4th and 5th). They were reassured by the following 'revelation', published a fortnight after Washkansky's death:

"It was revealed this week that the operation on Mr. Louis Washkansky, the world's first heart transplant patient, was begun while the donor, 25-year-old Miss Denise Ann Darvall, was still alive. When Washkansky was ready for the transplant, the artificial respiration which Miss Darvall was receiving was discontinued. Twelve minutes later, her heart stopped

beating and she was certified dead. It could be argued, therefore, that the moment of death was determined by the action of discontinuing the artificial respiration". (Stanley Uys: *Observer*. 7.1.68).

So Washkansky's new heart was not damaged, and the operation was a success. Why then did Washkansky die?

To counter the likelihood of tissue rejection, Washkansky had been filled with 'immuno-suppressive' drugs, which have the effect of killing the body's main, if not only, resistance to infection - the white blood cells. In Fulham Hospital, London, for instance, where immuno-suppressive drugs are used to great effect in killing off a rare form of cancer in pregnant women, the patients are isolated in a 'sterile unit', into which no one comes. Food is eaten off remote controlled trolleys, and the patients communicate with the outside world through microphones. Sterilisation like this is essential if the patients are to survive. Washkansky, however, was subjected to the hectic, and no doubt highly infectious glare of the international Press and television.

"What was that, Mr. Washkansky" queried one nervous TV interviewer, thrusting the mike further into Washkansky's lips: "Please say it again for us". "The doctor" muttered Washkansky, on cue "is the man with the Golden Hands". Ten days later, after an attack of pneumonia, he died.
(Dr. Blaiberg, incidentally gets a different treatment. He is in an isolated ward, and even his wife has to speak to him through a glass door. "Before her short visit she underwent an intensive sterilisation procedure which involved a 'scrub-up' and the wearing of mask, overall, overshoes and surgical gloves".) (*Cape Times*: 8.1.68).

Old Golden Hands was determined to try again. He had his recipient at the ready. Leaving instructions with his team to report on Dr. Blaiberg's progress, the Professor left for a triumphant tour of the United States. The tour was rudely interrupted by a telegram bearing the news that Dr. Blaiberg's heart had deteriorated and was on the point of death. There was not a moment to lose. Pausing only to warn his team not to start without him, Barnard left for home, arriving on the afternoon of New Years Day. That morning Dr. Jannie Louw, head of the department of surgeons at Cape Town University was reported as saying:

"Dr. Blaiberg is certainly well enough to last until Professor Barnard comes back, and maybe longer.

"Everybody is conscious of the need to keep a wary eye open for likely donors". (*Cape Argus*: Jan. 1.).

Finding a donor in this case, however, was

not going to be as easy as with Mr. Washkansky. For Dr. Blaiberg's blood group was B-rhesus positive. The blood groups for the two main groups in the South African population break down as follows:

| Group | Blacks (Mixed Africans) | Whites (Dutch) |
|---|---|---|
| O | 46% | 46% |
| A | 32 | 40 |
| B | 19 | 12 |
| AB | 3 | 3 |

(Approximately 83% of the B groupers are rhesus positive). Many more blacks than whites, in short, are of the B blood group, but even among Africans and Cape Coloureds, only about one in six are in the B positive blood group. Small wonder, then, that the emergency call which went out to Cape Town hospitals and ambulances to keep a look out for head injuries, stressed a preference for black ones. The political implications of putting a black heart in a white man were neatly anticipated by Barnard who announced that his team would not hesitate to transplant a heart because of the colour of the donor's skin.

Almost exactly as Barnard's delayed flight from the US landed in Cape Town, a young factory worker called Clive Haupt, who was having a New Years Day bathe on his favourite segregated beach, collapsed with a violent headache and was taken to False Bay hospital. The False Bay authorities, reckoning that the headache was due to haemorrhage, had Haupt transferred right across Cape Town to the Victoria Hospital, Wynberg, which has better neurosurgical facilities.

The medical reports are not clear at this stage, but almost certainly someone at Victoria Hospital carried out a lumber puncture on Haupt's back, and diagnosed a massive 'subarachnoid' heamorrhage (so-called because the arteries have broken, or leaked, in the space underneath the arachnoid membrane, over the brain).

Many casual readers of the reports have assumed that, if Haupt had a brain haemorrhage, he was certain to die. Even today, despite fantastic advances in neurosurgery, coroners and others are inclined to regard brain haemorrhages as fatal. Not, however, so. In Britain, for instance, only 12% of patients die within a few hours of having their first subarachnoid heamorrhage. For this minority an operation is considered dangerous. For the other 88%, operation and survival without serious brain damage is the norm.

The normal criteria as to whether or not the patient's condition is hopeless is his level of consciousness and his ability to breathe on his own. The Atkinson Morley hospital, in London, for instance, where neurosurgery is presided over by the brilliant, if conservative, Dr. Wylie McKissock, the normal routine is to wait five days, and, even then, to operate only if the patient is still breathing under his own steam. Other London surgeons, however, apply a less rigid test and operate earlier.

Mr. Clive Haupt had only been in Victoria hospital about half an hour, when, according to a memorable passage in the *Daily Telegraph* (Jan. 3):

> "A doctor, noting that Mr. Haupt has little chance of survival, but is otherwise in good health, telephones ward C2 at Groote Schuur where Doctor Blaiberg is awaiting a donor heart".

At that time Mr. Haupt was still breathing on his own. Anyone with the remotest knowledge of brain haemorrhages know that they are made much worse by travelling. Brain surgeons are always reluctant to order even one hospital transfer because of the consequences to the heamorrhage. Mr. Haupt had already travelled by car to False Bay. He had then been transferred over a considerable distance to Victoria. He was still breathing on his own, but the decision was taken *within an hour* to transfer him to Groote Schuur.

The *Cape Argus* takes up the story:

> "The doctor and the Coloured man arrived at Groote Schuur and the highly-geared heart transplant team started on the preliminary stages. Blood samples were taken and Dr. M.C. Botha and his technicians at the Provincial blood grouping laboratories began initial tissue-typing". (*Cape Argus* Jan. 2)

Gerald Scarfe.

All this shunting around and tissue-typing did not enhance Mr. Haupt's health. At 8.30 p.m., some time after he arrived at Groote Schuur, his breathing failed and he was put on an artificial respirator. It is extremely unlikely that a brain heamorrhage patient will survive after being put on the respirator. Very few surgeons, however, would write such a patient off automatically, and most, especially in the case of a young man, would keep the respirator going for a considerable time to see if there were any chances of a survival. Professor Barnard, however, after consulting a number of surgeons and physicians, took the decision to operate at 3.30 in the morning, only seven hours after the respirator was attached. Some hours earlier he had told reporters in some excitement, "the heart appears to be compatible". At that time Prof. Barnard must also have heard the extraordinary news that Mr. Haupt's blood group was B Rhesus Positive!

At 11.00 that morning the news men were rewarded. The operation took place. According to newspaper reports, Mr. Haupt's 'heart failed and he died at 10.43 a.m.'. The cause of death, however, as with Miss Denise Darvall, could not have been natural. Sometime before 10.43 a.m. Professor Barnard and his band of wizards must have been preparing Mr. Haupt's body for the removal of the heart, which must have still been beating at the time of removal. Unlike Miss Denise Darvall, however, Mr. Haupt had not suffered any head injuries. He had a brain heamorrhage, which, in the vast majority of cases, is not fatal. Mrs. Haupt, incidentally, was not consulted about her husband's heart transplantation - a precedent which has been rigidly followed by the American cardiac surgeons who have followed Prof. Barnard's lead.

Fortunately for Prof. Barnard, the journalists who have been covering the Great Transplant Drama will not hear a word against him. The Professor's Press Conferences are eagerly looked forward to by all the (white) journalists who can attend them.

The *Cape Times* of January 6th reported the last of these more fully than other newspapers:

> "He (Barnard) sat facing the glare of arc lamps, six television and newsreel cameras, and 10 microphones. Twice members of the medical school tried to end the conference after the scheduled 15 minutes.
> On the first occasion a man at the back said: 'Last Question'. 'Give them a chance to finish' called Barnard.

> Then he was told there was a telephone call.
> 'Just take it', he replied.
> At the start someone quoted him in London as saying he might go into politics. Was this true?
> Prof. Barnard: 'I can't believe I said this. Is that what they said I said? Did I say I would become a politician one day?'
> A journalist: 'You did' (laughs).
> Prof. Barnard: 'Oh, well I might consider it on one condition - if they make me Prime Minister'.

One reporter asked what salaries the doctors in the heart transplant team received 'from top to bottom'.

> Prof. Barnard: "I have no idea what the bottom doctors get" ...

Professor Golden Hands enjoys the Press Conferences every bit as much as the journalists.

# WILSUNDRA TRIAL OPENS

## £790,364,000,000 FRAUD CHARGE

by Our Legal Team Edgar Wallace Simpson

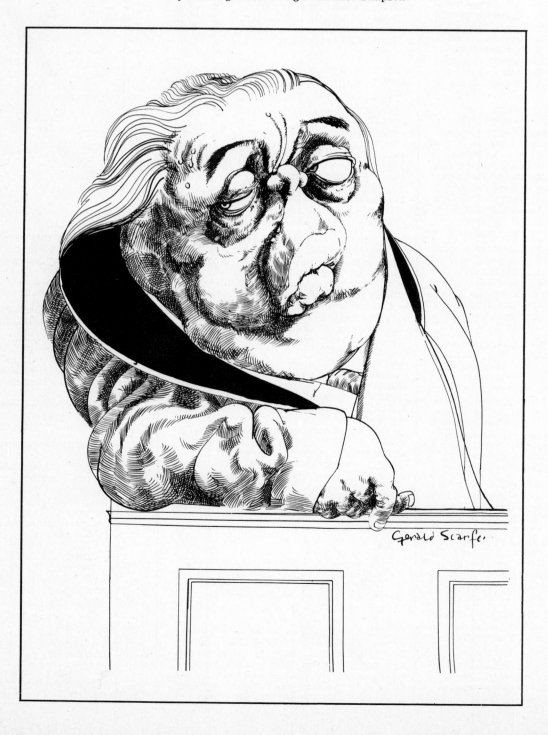

Gerald Scarfe

**M**r. Harold Wilsundra, looking pale and tired, appeared briefly in the dock at the Old Baillie today and pleaded not guilty to 89 separate charges of fraudulent behaviour over a period of 5 years.

## The Charges

Mr. Wilsundra, head of Great Britain Ltd. a bankrupt company, is charged amongst other things with fraudulently offering his 45 million shareholders:

1 dynamic and purposive government
2 planned growth of incomes and related benefits
3 an 'East of Suez role'
4 free medicines
5 ½ million houses by 1970
6 no application for entry into E.E.C.
7 more education for children by raising school leaving age
8 the preserved parity of the pound
9 the settlement of the Rhodesian problem 'in weeks rather than months' (1947)
10 a minimum income guarantee
11 entry into E.E.C.
12 jobs for all shareholders
13 no Polaris submarines
14 the TSR 2 aeroplane
15 the F.111 "
16 the HS.118 "
17 a new Jerusalem
18 no brain drain
19 nationalisation of urban land
20 " of road haulage
21 low interest rates
22 a National plan *(laughter)*
23 4% growth
24 the white heat of the technological revolution

Opening the case for the prosecution Sir Shingle Mouth, QC, said the trial would last at least 2 years and would involve 45 million witnesses, all of whom would tell how they personally had been defrauded by the accused Wilsundra.

## HORROR

"You see before you Gentlemen of the jury" said Sir Shingle, "a man utterly corrupted and depraved by the lust for power who has masterminded one of the greatest acts of fraud in the history of this nation.

"Posing variously as an economist, a socialist, a pragmatist and a statesman, Wilsundra has conned, conned and conned again till the public has ceased to care. Never before has such a gigantic hoax been perpetrated by such a small man. But now his promises have come home to roost and you see him before you in the dock".

In the dock: H. Wilsundra and Patrick de Quincey Gordon Walker (Wilsundra's sleeping partner in the firm) charged with lunatic folly under the Race Relations (Undesirable Persons) Act.

## PATHETIC

Wilsundra, who is conducting his own defence following the rejection of his brief by every barrister in the land, interrupted by asking if he could go home to see his doctor (Dr. M. Petro).

Permission was refused and Sir Shingle continued: "To call this man a liar is to flatter him. Lying calls for a degree of subtlety and determination, qualities which are only too plainly lacking in the accused. You will be told by my ignorant friend that the accused is not in full possession of his faculties. My case will be that he has never had any faculties apart from the ability to deceive himself and others with fantasies, myths and the hopeless promises of fairy tale utopias.

"It may be that the public is over gullible but this is not to excuse the actions of Wilsundra".

Over and over again he had bought time to appear on the television in a variety of guises, sometimes bland and smiling,

sometimes stern and purposeful to offer the public some new mythical panacea which he alleged would cure them of their ills.

Now he could not even do that and his henchman, Mr. R. Jenkins had been detailed to try and 'sell' his latest gimmick.

Even his wife had been enlisted in a desperate attempt to restore his fast vanishing appeal with pathetic Christmas carols in the *Weekend Telegraph*. It was no doubt Wilsundra's hope that the vision of innocence and humility radiated by his consort would dispel the growing doubts. But alas it was too late for any last-ditch rehabilitation. Indeed the involvement of his wife in his own affairs had only served to discredit him still further in the eyes of the populace.

"You see before you a man for whom the English language has no further use. He has but to open his mouth for some new word or phrase to be debased or devalued in its usage. Ridiculed by his colleagues, despised by those nearest to him, hated and shunned by the public at large, there is only one place to which he can resort and that I suggest is the meanest cell in one of Her Majesty's prisons where he may spend the rest of his days in degradation and misery pending his demise".

The case was adjourned.

**\*Fact**: Sir Shingle Mouth was for 3 years a director of Wilsundra's firm. When he resigned owing to old age he said he had served two concerns in his life, those of Sir Wislon Churchill and Wilsundra himself, both of which he was 'supremely proud'.

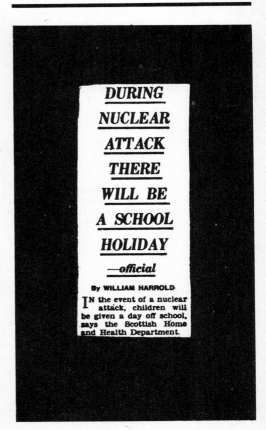

**DURING NUCLEAR ATTACK THERE WILL BE A SCHOOL HOLIDAY** —*official*

By WILLIAM HARROLD

IN the event of a nuclear attack, children will be given a day off school, says the Scottish Home and Health Department.

# TELLY

# MAN·HALF·ALIVE

## by TV Man **George Millais**

A man with half a brain will be wheeled in front of the cameras on BBC.1. tonight and be asked to conduct a debate between Dr. Pagan Barnard and 4,000 critics.

The man whose name will not be revealed, is Raymond Baxter.

### SHOCK

Mr. Baxter suffered incurable brain damage in the pits at Brands Hatch and it is hoped that he will be the first to benefit from the controversial so-called half wit cerebral transplant.

In a surprise question Mr. Baxter will be asked "Would you rather be alive than dead?" Mr. Baxter will make the unexpected reply: "Ask me another".

### OUT OF THE BLUE

It will then be open to the 4,000 critics to launch into a hymn of praise for the Groote Schuur pin-up* whilst a bevy of busty nurses wipe his brow.

A dramatic moment will occur when the anonymous donor (P.N. Stribbs) will be wheeled forward into the spotlight and announce amid cheers "I've half a mind to do it".

The eminent hip surgeon Lord Bladen Races will then say "I am Lord Bladen Races the eminent hip-surgeon. I detest publicity in all its forms. In fact my Public Relations Officer has prepared a statement to this effect. But I feel forced in view of the circumstances to say on behalf of the entire British medical profession that were it not for the likes of Chris (Prolonged cheers) with his bold experiments on human beings my wee tabby cat Engelbert would not be with us today".

### IMPROMPTU

In an amazing and unexpected scene the cat will be wheeled on bandaged but cheerful with a vole's heart beating within.

The controversial producer of the programme Huw Wheelchair will then explain his decision not to show the cat in order to prevent it being harried by the gentlemen of the press.

In a surprise attack the gentlemen of the press will harry the anonymous cat Engelbert to death.

Dr. Barnard will then make the impromptu quip "I always like a bit of pussy about myself".

The 4,000 distinguished doctors will then break into uncontrollable mirth, spit out their false teeth and dance away into the night to the tune "I left my heart in an English gardener".

The switchboard will be jammed after the programme by baffled viewers worried by the change in format of the trouble-shooters.

*\* Believed to be a reference to Dr. Barnard.*

# BP REPARED

The civil war in Nigeria - the most heavily populated country in Africa - will be hotting up in the next few weeks as the Federal army tries to vindicate their leader, General Gowon's promise of Federal victory by March 31. The trickle of weapons and mercenaries from outside has now grown into a flood, and will grow still further with the Federal Cabinet's decision in mid-January, against Gowon's advice, to employ mercenaries on the ground if the military situation require it.

The only country unequivocally to take the side of the Federal Government so far is Egypt (or, more accurately, the Soviet Union, following that country's general support for the Organisation of African Unity to which Nigeria is the biggest contributor).

18 Russian MIG fighters fighting for the Federals have now been augmented by three Illyushin jets with Egyptian pilots, which carry three and a half tons of bombs each. Some of the Federal planes are manned by pilots under the control of Colonel John Peters, a British mercenary officer. Peters is now firmly committed to the Federal side.

Main support for Biafra comes from Portugal. M. Pierre Lorez, a Frenchman, is organising a steady supply of arms and mercenaries for Biafra from his headquarters in Lisbon. Also supporting Biafra is South Africa, whose policy in Africa is to create chaos where they cannot create puppets. At least three planeloads of arms have flown into Port Harcourt in recent weeks from Cape Town, via Angola. The French Government would clearly like to see Biafra survive as an independent state. The French nationalised oil company has its eyes greedily fixed on the massive oil deposits in Biafra.

The French mercenary leader, Col. Roget Faulques, one of the best fighters in the business, is now firmly ensconced in Biafra with a force of about 200 men. Some of these men are commanded from Paris by Major Robert Denard, whose military capabilities have been somewhat damaged by a head wound which he received in a battle in the Congo with what he thought were ordinary Congolese troops but were probably disguised American Negroes.

Most fascinating of all is the role of the British Government. Officially, of course, the Government is neutral. Neutrality however, does not appeal to Sir David Hunt, the High Commissioner in Lagos. From the outset, Sir David has adopted a firmly pro-Federal position. Speaking in Kaduna, Northern Nigeria, in late January, Sir David answered Biafran charges of British military involvement in the war by saying: "I never come across them (the Biafrans) saying anything that is true". In reply to

Federal grumbles that Britain wasn't active enough in defence of the Federation, Sir David admitted: "Despite all the accusations against Britain the bulk of the weapons in the hands of Federal forces have come from Britain". (BBC Monitoring Service).

Sir David's attitudes have been firmly supported by the Commonwealth Relations Office, one of whose spokesman told a reporter recently: "Jackie Gowon's a very nice chap. If you met him in a darkened room, you wouldn't know he was a black man". A move by the Commonwealth Secretariat early in the war backed by Mr. Lester Pearson, the Canadian Prime Minister, to provide neutral ground for the leaders of both sides to meet and talk about a settlement was studiously sabotaged by the CRO. In late September, the CRO were reassuring everyone who suggested a settlement that the Federal army would win 'in seven days'. Their confidence coincided with the bribing by the Federal Government of the two leading Biafran generals, Banjo and Ifeajuna, who led their troops back from Ore, Benin, Asaba and Inicha. Only a last minute exposee of the two generals enabled the Biafrans to hold out.

More important still, the CRO has facilitated the sale of arms from the Crown agents to Britain on a considerable scale. The British Government is probably the second biggest supplier of arms to the Federals, after the Russians.

Most of the official evidence points to guarded British Government support for the Federal Government. But there is further evidence which is very far from official.

First, what happened to the £7,000,000 Royalties owed by Shell/BP for shipments of oil from Port Harcourt before the crisis? For some time now, BP has wondered to whom they should pay the money, which is claimed by both sides.

Last July, Shell/BP paid a quarter of a million pounds (part payment of the royalties) to Biafra (Times: July 31). The company, by its articles of association, has Government directors on the Board which can veto any major policy decision. It is difficult to believe therefore that the money was not paid to Biafra without the official approval of the Foreign Office. What happened to the rest of the money is not clear. An unintelligible report in the Financial Times (Jan.16, 1968) records a Biafra radio report that "Shell/BP has written off its investments in Biafra as a result of paying royalties claimed by Biafra to the Nigerian authorities". The same report, however, claimed that Mr.

C.C. Mojekwu, a senior member of the Biafran Cabinet, was over in London for talks with the oil companies. Mr. Mojekwu indicated that no decision had yet been taken but that a deadline had been set for Jan.31. Hadji Amino Kano, the Commissioner of Communications in the Federal Government, who was in London staying at the Hilton Hotel, told Private Eye on Jan.27, "I think they have paid the money to the Federal Government, but there are rumours that they have paid both sides".

A further mystery has been created by a report in the Times on January 9th that "a British mercenary officer" was in London negotiating a large £260,000 arms order for the Biafrans. The officer, whom the Times did not name, is Colonel Johnny Johnson, a former member of the British Special Air Service, who fought for several years - according to some reports on extended leave - for the Royalists in the Yemen.

The firm with which he negotiated is the famous gunsmiths, Cogswell and Harrison, who have an office in Piccadilly and a fine tradition of good craftsmanship, particularly in the manufacture of hunting guns. Most big arms contracts are undertaken by the company's subsidiary, Cogswell and Harrison Overseas, whose headquarters are at 33 Hauptstrasse, Vaduz, Liechtenstein. The director who deals with most of the arms sales is Mr. George Tavridakis. Mr. Tavridakis has already sold considerable supplies of arms to the Federal Government. The arms for Biafra, however, have not yet been sold or delivered.

Colonel Johnson is a loyal British army officer, and all his instincts are loyal. It would seem unlikely that he would negotiate a large arms order against the wishes of the British Government. Mr. Kano, on the other hand, cannot believe that the British Government are involved. "I have heard that a man has been buying arms for Biafra" he told Private Eye. "But I cannot believe he is connected with the British Government. The British Government could hardly do a thing like that".

Mr. Kano's touching faith in the British traditions of fair play may overlook several more realistic considerations. Could it be that select, well-informed sources in the Foreign Office, which took over West African intelligence from the CRO after the latter's sublime incompetence during the 1965 Nigerian coup, fear that Britain may have backed the wrong horse, and that Biafra has a chance of survival?

If Biafra does survive, even as a part-independent country, the British could lose heavily for their support for the Federation. The remaining oil concessions could be snapped up by the French. Vast slices of wealth and influence in a crucial area could be lost to competitors. Could it be that the F.O. have decided at this late stage to hedge its bets: openly to support the Federal Government through the statements of its High Commissioner; and, in the background, quietly to insure themselves against Biafran victory?

As the old Yoruba saying has it: The man who rides on a two-headed rhinoceros must learn to face both ways.

# PRIVATE EYE

162
day
arch 68

1/6

# FREE
## WITH EVERY ISSUE
# BRITISH PASSPORT

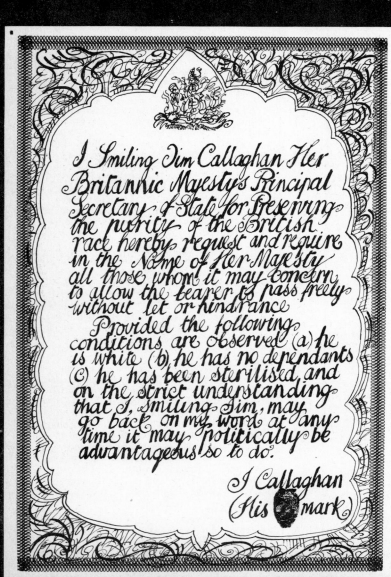

I Smiling Jim Callaghan Her Britannic Majesty's Principal Secretary of State for Preserving the purity of the British race hereby request and require in the Name of Her Majesty all those whom it may concern to allow the bearer to pass freely without let or hindrance Provided the following conditions are observed (a) he is white (b) he has no dependants (c) he has been sterilised, and on the strict understanding that I, smiling Jim, may go back on my word at any time it may politically be advantageous so to do.

J Callaghan
(His mark)

## PASSPORT.
## PASSEPORT.

UNITED KINGDOM OF GREAT BRITAIN AND NORTHERN IRELAND.
ROYAUME-UNI DE GRANDE-BRETAGNE ET D'IRLANDE DU NORD.

Bearer
(Titulaire)

This is a sad day for all of us

NAME          Callaghan, James.
PROFESSION     Time Server.
COLOUR OF SKIN  Grey.
DISTINGUISHING  None whatever.
CHARACTERISTICS

THE VALIDITY OF THIS PASSPORT EXPIRES:
ANY TIME CONVENIENT TO H.M.G.

*"We'll have to wait for the photo, but I made it Princess Tanya of Trachtenburg by a neck!"*

# COLOUR SECTION

## PUT OUT MORE FLAGS DEPT.

Outside the *Daily Mirror* skyscraper in High Holborn there are a number of flagpoles from which, on the appointed days, the *Daily Mirror* performs its patriotic duty by flying the appropriate flags. The 'flag command' in the *Daily Mirror* Newspapers is one of the more complicated hierarchies in that very hierarchical organisation. The major domo who runs the flags up and down works most of his time as a maintenance engineer, as does his assistant. The officer in charge of flags is Mr. Philip Mulcahy. And the director who makes the final decisions about flags is the ebullient Mr. Tommy Atkins, whose devotion for Mr. Hugh Cudlipp, the *Mirror's* editorial director, borders on hero-worship.

On February 7th an observant *Mirror* reader, pausing for a moment outside his favourite newspaper office, noticed that while all Government buildings were flying the Union Jack, the *Mirror* flagpoles were bare. He duly rang the *Mirror*, and, after some confused conversations with the news desk and the advertising department got through to the relevant engineer, and passed on the information. The engineer got through to Mr. Mulcahy, who was horrified.

Without belling Tommy Atkins, he barked out the order: "Run Up the Union Jack on Flagpole Number One!" The major domo swiftly obeyed.

The scene then shifts to the luxurious 9th floor office of Tommy Atkins. Gazing out of his window, Mr. Atkins notices to his horror that the Union Jack is flying from Flagpole One, *without any order issuing from his office.* He flips furiously through his diary and discovers that *FEBRUARY 7th IS NOT A FLAG DAY.* In a flash he is speaking to Mulcahy. "What" he asks sarcastically "is the flag doing flying from Flagpole Number One ?"

"I think, Sir" replies Mulcahy "that it is the anniversary of Her Majesty's acceding to the throne". "I don't care", barked Atkins, savagely "if it is God's birthday. Bring the flag down at once !"

**Pc found crumpets under a blanket in a car**

*The Reporter*

Tommy Atkins sits back in his chair and watches as the Union Jack starts its decent down the flagpole. Suddenly, inexplicably, it stops half way. Almost sobbing with exasperation, Atkins again phones Mulcahy who tells him that the flag is stuck and that his men are "doing all they can, Sir, I assure you".

For a few numb moments Atkins gazes at the suspended flag and then, slowly and nervously, makes his way up in the lift to Cecil King's penthouse on the top of the *Mirror* building for the daily boardroom lunch.

No sooner is Atkins in the cocktail lounge than Cecil King wanders over to the window and looks out. As the words "Look, I'm awfully sorry, Sir, I can explain everything" rise in Atkins' throat, King turns, his face wreathed in a warm coalition smile. "Tommy" he says gently, "Tommy, in all the years I've been with the I.P.C., I've never known you perform a gesture so spontaneous and moving. Flying the flag at half mast in mourning for the dead trawlermen was a wonderful idea. I'm proud to be associated with it. In fact, my only complaint is that only one flag is flying. I think we should hoist another - an I.P.C. flag".

Stammering with joy, Atkins rushes to the lift and the phone to pass on the order. He watches, leaning from his window, as

the major domo, approaching flagpole No. 2 looks up for instructions. Leaning right out, Atkins raised two fingers in the air and mouths the words "TWO FLAGS !" To his astonishment, the major domo raises two fingers in reply.

Finally, he starts to hoist the flag, which, Atkins discovers, is a Union Jack. Rushing down again in the lift to correct the error, he is greeted with the news that Cecil King has phoned from the penthouse to say how much he likes the two Union Jacks which should stay there after all. So the two flags flew side by side as a touching memorial to the trawlermen all that day, and by night the major domo had fixed the fault and was able to haul them both down.

And Tommy Atkins was a little late for his boardroom lunch.

Next day the following item appeared in the *Daily Mirror's* diary.

> The usual reaction at the sight of a limp flag at half-mast on an official building is that some royal, or famous, or notorious personage is dead; somebody remote.
> There are, however, other deaths and other flags. The loss of the trawlermen in icy seas is such an occasion.
> Yesterday, for the first time since the disaster at Aberfan, the flags on the Daily Mirror building in Holborn, London, flew at half-mast.

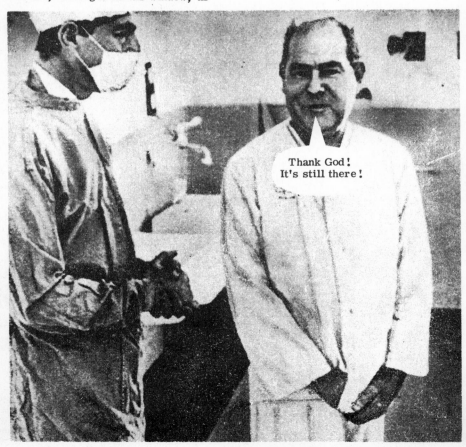

Thank God ! It's still there !

"Well, aren't you going to ask me
what sort of a day I had at the kerb?"

"There's your trouble, lady - it's full of instant mashed potato"

"When your name's restored to the register!  I don't believe it was ever
on the register!"

"Cakes ?  Who cares about cakes ?"

"You and your Drive-In Doss Houses Ltd!"

" I don't know about you, but I'm pinning all my hopes
on being a late developer".

# From the readers postbag
# *WHAT THE PAUPERS SAY*

### Dear Sir

We are no racialists but no more, we hasten to add, is Mr. Powell.

We in the Conservative Party have no objection to Mr. Powell's views, i.e. that immigrants are going to take the country over in a few years and kill all the whites by putting excrement through their letter-boxes.

Our objection is simply to the emotive language used by Mr. Powell to put across this very reasonable message.

> Yours,
>
> G. Heath,
> B. Vass,
> Tory Central Office,
> Athens, Greece.

### Dear Sir

I am no racialist but how hypocritical can our leaders be ? Mr. Enoch Powell - whose only crime is to make a perfectly normal rabble rousing speech and stir up the worst racial trouble since Mafeking, is sacked while Sir Edward Boyle is allowed to remain at his post.

A black day for Britain indeed!

> Yours, E. Mufwatt,
> *The Daily Telegraph*,
> Bournemouth, Hants.

### Dear Sir

I am no RASHIALIST, but fank Gawd for Enok Gor bless 'im, Powl. We do not want orl them nigs takin our jobs at half the price and prepared to work a ninety hour week for nuffink. Fanks to us lot, Britain's in the shit. Let's keep it that way before there's any trubble.

> Yours,
> Nosher Stibbs,
> Keep Britain Great Ltd.
> West India Docks, London E.

### Dear Sir

I am no racialist but before readers condemn Mr. Powell, let me relate a story which a friend of my aunt's was told by her brother-in-law who claimed to have heard it first hand from Mr. Powell himself.

Apparently an old lady of 103 was set upon one night as she was practising her violin by a gang of coloured men dressed in tinsel robes and told there and then to sell them her house for only 5/7d.

When she objected she was stripped naked tied up in a copy of the *Daily Express* and pushed through her own letter box where she was left while crowds of little piccaninies danced round shouting and laughing.

She has since died.

> Yours,
> Arthur Basildon
> The Vicarage, Watford.

STEADman

### Sir

I am no racialist, but it is all very well for you high-brow fellows to pontificate on the race question from your assorted ivory towers. But for those of us who have to deal with these blackamoors at close quarters, it is a very different kettle of fish altogether.

Hats off to Enoch Powell for his courageous speech. For too long we have listened to woolly minded liberals who have never seen a woolly haired immigrant in their back garden. The man in the street knows best.

> Yours,
>
> B.J. Scrotefeather,
> The Ivory Tower, Wilts.

### Sir

I am no racialist, but when will we ever learn ? Legislation will never stop the hatred that exists in the hearts of men. Years ago the idiots at Westminster introduced laws against murder. And what has happened ? Murders have gone on just like they did before.

Yours,

'Basher' Crettin,
Security Wing 'E',
Death Row, Surbiton,
Surrey.

## Dear Sir

I am no racialist, but the next King of England will probably be Prince Charles - a white man.

But do we hear Mr. Humphrey Berkeley or Sir Edward Boyle protest that it is time we had a black monarch ? That the history of the monarchy is a tale of racial discrimination ?

No we do not.

So much for the absurd Race Relations bill.

Yours,

R. Pitman,
Gusset Home for Retarded
Gentlefolk,
Harrison Birtwhistle, Salop.

## Dear Sir

I am no racialist, but for centuries our little island fortress 'this seat of majesty' has lain like a precious jewel in the silver sea. It's proud yeomen their faces full of the warmth of summer have toiled beneath the immemorial elms. Pretty shepherdesses have gaily tended their flock whilst baby lambs frisked through the meadows that are forever England.

And are we now to give away our priceless heritage to millions of coloured foreigners ?

Yours,

Isaiah Winkelstein-Shonk,
29 Finchley Road, N.W.

## Dear Sir

I am no racialist, but this tiny country of ours, already bursting at the seams, can simply not afford to absorb ANYONE else, coloured or otherwise.

Yours,

Enid Benson-Thatch,
Carry on up the track past Ben
Nevis for ten miles and it's
across the grouse moor, a little
to the left with the yellow gate.
Two pints next Tuesday please.
SCOTLAND

## Dear Sir

I am no racialist, but completely I fail to vorstanden vat all ze fuzz is about.

Herr Hitler is simply putting in his mouth vat millions of peeples are sinking in zeir hearts about ze Jews.

Vat a velcome breath of fresh hair is he blowing in viz his most interestink spich.

Yours,

F.L. von Mosley-Whipps
(Obergruppenfuhrer Retd.)
The Manse, Sefton Delmer.

# Letter

GAZETTE NOTICE No. 3684

### NOTICE OF CHANGE OF NAME

TAKE NOTICE that by a deed poll dated the 9th day of October 1967, Patrick Gordon Walker, of P.O. Box 557, Mombasa in Kenya, heretofore also called and known by the name of Naranjan Singh Ujagar Singh Basant Singh Jhuthi, absolutely and wholly renounced and abandoned the use of his said name of Naranjan Singh Ujagar Singh Basant Singh Jhuthi and assumed and adopted in lieu thereof the first name of Patrick Gordon and surname of Walker only for all purposes.

The said Patrick Gordon Walker, therefore, hereby authorizes and requests all persons at all times hereafter to designate and address him by his now assumed and adopted first name of Patrick Gordon and surname of Walker only instead of by his said name of Naranjan Singh Ujagar Singh Basant Singh Jhuthi.

Dated at Mombasa this 9th day of October 1967.

NAGIN PATEL & PATEL,
Advocates for Patrick Gordon Walker.

*KENYA GAZETTE*

*Private Eye, 10 Nov. '67.*

From Sir Herbert Gusset

Dear Sir,

As an old 'Punjabi Wallah' (1893 - 1945), I was intrigued to read news in your paper of my old and very dear friend Naranjan Singh Ujagar Singh Basant Singh Jhuthi who was my house boy and body servant during those hectic years in Darjeeling.

His father, Raj Gandhi Kapur Singh Alongh With Mhee, was a leading figure in in the abortive plan to seize Queen Victoria and hold her as a hostage during the Feast of the Bee in 1872. For this he was ordered to pay 100 rupees thus giving rise to the expression 'Sikh and ye shall be fined'.

Imagine my surprise then to read that his son Naranjan Singh Ujagar Singh Basant Singh Jhuthi had changed his name to Patrick Gordon Walker and was occupying an important post in the British Government as resident albatross at the Ministry of Education. Furthermore that he had shorn his locks of those delightful tresses which were once the talk of Delhi and thrown his turban to the wind.

My good friend Maj. Gen. Sir Spothington Hordle-Tern tells me that my former houseboy made the break with his past some years ago much to the dismay of his parent who died on hearing the news.

### BANISHING CREAM

So effective was Gordon Walker's make-up that he was able to pose as a white man and even on occasions discriminate against his kith in the shape of Seretze Khame Sutra the African Chief in 1950.

Alas he was to be foiled during the famous Smethwick election in 1964. It was here that he was spotted for what he was by Bus Driver Hilary Singh as he boarded a No. 76 outside the Essoldo Cinema.

The news spread like hot cakes and within hours the Indians were up in arms against their former compatriot. So intense was the feeling against Naranjan Singh Ujagar Singh Basant Singh Jhuthi that the immigrant electors either abstained or cast their votes for Mr. Peter Griffiths the well-known leper.

Today my former houseboy represents the people of Leyton. I only hope that he is better at cleaning their shoes than he was

in my day.

Despite all the water that has flown under the bridge my wife still retains a soft for her 'little ruby of Ganges' and should 'Sir Patrick' in the course of one of his disasters be passing by our door he can be assured of a glass of foaming ale and a muffin or twa.

Good evening.

I remain, Sir, an inmate of the Chichester Rest Home for Retired Gardeners,

HERBERT GUSSET.

*"GOT ANY WEEDS, MAN ?"*

# HEARTS & GRAFTS

The disciplinary committee of the General Medical Council which will shortly be examining a number of complaints about the first British heart transplant should not be too hasty in condemning the happy band of sawbones at the National Heart Hospital. Cardiac surgeons dabbling in transplantery face many difficult problems, crucial among which is the question: On whom should these experiments be inflicted? Should the 'recipients' be old men, suffering from multiple diseases and likely to die anyway? Or should they be young, intelligent and (apart from their hearts) healthy?

The 'philosophical prologue' to the long-playing records on Heart Transplants issued from Groote Schuur Hospital, Cape Town, and compered by the glamorous Prof. Barnard, is in no doubt about this. The best possible recipient, it states, is a young man of active mind suffering from a diptheria infection of the heart or a congenital defect - *provided it is isolated in the heart.*

As the heart transplant bandwaggon has rolled in recent weeks, the 'recipients' have grown younger and fitter. Norman Shumway, for instance, the American surgeon who, unlike his colleagues in Britain and S. Africa, can point to several survivals from his heart transplants on dogs, has concentrated mainly on older, and more dangerously ill recipients, all of whom have since died.
The South Africans, Barnard and Ross, have operated on younger patients with, at the time of writing, marginally greater success.

The 'recipient problem' does not stop at age or fitness. Most heart disease and failure has its origin outside the heart, and most of the recipients have suffered from diseases not confined to the heart. Arteriosclerosis, for instance, which leads to coronary thrombosis, is caused by the incidence of atheromatus plaques in the arteries and the consequent clogging or, in medical parlance, 'furring up' of the arteries.

No one knows what causes these arterial diseases. They may have to do with exercise or diet (they are less frequent in Japan where the staple diet is rice). What is certain is that they are not confined to the heart, nor are they cured if the heart is replaced by a fresh one. Arteriosclerosis is defined in the standard work as 'a disease which affects the intima i. e. the lining of the aorta, and *all the distributing arteries'* (*General Pathology:* ed. Sir Howard Florey: Ch. 17 p. 418).

Arterial surgeons have found that arteriosclerosis is so generalised that the replacement of one affected artery by a fresh one only relieves the situation for a short time. The new artery 'furs up' in months, if not weeks. Four experts, after researching 300 cases of arterial surgery, concluded: 'The arterial reconstruction was the site of thrombosis in the majority of patients

studied'. *Annals of Surgery*, 1966. Vol. 163. p. 205.

Exactly the same process would take place, almost certainly, in the new heart of a patient suffering from arteriosclerosis. The patient must survive not only the 'rejection' of the new heart by his system, but also the spread of arteriosclerosis from the arteries not replaced by the transplant.

Louis Washkansky - the first heart transplant patient - and at least three American recipients died from 'rejection'. (The pathologists and surgeons who have seen the sections of Washkansky's heart are in no doubt that it shows all the signs of rejection). Dr. P. Blaiberg, who still survives a transplant last January, suffered severe rejection on days 9 and 21 after the operation, which swelled his new heart to outsize proportions. (Most of the experienced physicians at Groote Schuur had written Blaiberg off when Prof. Barnard set out on his gay, triumphal tour of Europe last January, which could explain the Professor's uncharacteristically modest predictions about his patient's chances). The only remaining mystery about Dr. Blaiberg is the extent and nature of his illness *before* the transplant. What little evidence there is suggests that Blaiberg suffered from a disease which was isolated in the heart, and which made him the ideal recipient.

Mr. Frederick West, the first British heart transplant recipient, was transferred to the National Heart Hospital one week before the transplant was performed (along with two other heart cases, one of whom was Bill Bradley, known in the trade as 'Longmore's patient', who made such a moving appearance in a wheel chair before Professor Barnard and his 'critics' on *Tomorrow's World* last January). Mr. West had for some time been a patient at Kings College Hospital, Denmark Hill, under the care of Mr. Edward Raftery, the hospital's Senior Registrar. (Mr. Raftery is an old friend of Mr. Donald Longmore and had known of the planned transplant for some weeks before it happened. The appearance of a dying donor of the right minority blood group at Kings College Hospital at almost precisely the right moment was a miraculous coincidence).

Private Eye had the following conversation with Mr. Raftery as to the pre-operation condition of Mr. West:

Eye: "Did West suffer from arteriosclerosis?"
Raftery: "Yes".
Eye: "Was the arteriosclerosis confined to the heart?"

Raftery: "We have no evidence that the disease existed anywhere else in the body".
Eye: "He had no diseased arteries anywhere else in the body then?"
Raftery: "I did not say that. I said we had

*no evidence* that the disease existed anywhere else".

It is however extremely unlikely, if not impossible, that arteriosclerosis is confined to the heart. It may *manifest itself* in the heart, but most medical research shows that it is a generalised disease, which almost certainly exists elsewhere than where it first appears. If the unhappy Mr. West suffers from arteriosclerosis elsewhere than in the heart, then, even if he survives the rejection phase, the transplant will not cure him, nor give him, in the biblical jargon of transplantery, 'a new life'. It will serve, as all transplantery serves at present, as a palliative. Its value in terms of publicity and donations to the hospitals concerned may be considerable, but its value to the patient is less than minimal, and probably worse.

The craze for 'palliative' surgery has caught on with breathtaking speed. In some cases, even the surgeons are sceptical about their methods. In a recent visit to London, Dr. J. Dossiter, renal assistant Professor of Surgery at McGill University, Montreal and one of the most experienced and able kidney transplant surgeons in the world told an audience of doctors: "If I had uraemia I would want to be dialysed in the home and not have a renal transplant". (*Medical Tribune:* 16 May).

Dr. Dossiter reported that of 85 Canadian cases of kidney transplants, 20% had resulted in total failure and only 30% had resulted in survival for more than three years. The fourteen heart transplants which have now been attempted in the world have produced a rather more drastic failure rate.

Perhaps the main attraction for British surgeons of these human experiments in palliative organ transplants are their cheapness. Transplants of hearts and lungs, particularly, were not proved or even properly tested in animals before attempts were made on humans. One reason is that animal experimentation is hedged around by laws to please the anti-vivisectionists. More importantly, the cost of these experiments has to be met by foundations, private donors and, often, from the surgeons' own pockets. Mr. Donald Longmore's experiments in the National Heart Hospital in which he stitched pigs' organs into the bodies of dead patients, were financed entirely by donors, foundations and himself. In human experiments however everything - the donor and the recipient, the nurses, the technicians and the equipment - are provided and paid for by the Health Service. As Mr. W. J. Dempster, Reader in Experimental Surgery at London's Royal Postgraduate Medical School has written recently:

"It is cheaper and administratively easier to use the human as the experimental animal". (*Medical Tribune:* May 16. )

Britain has a longer waiting list for simple surgical operations (for hernias, for instance, or for varicose veins) than any other country in industrial Europe. More and more of these operations are being postponed to the acute discomfort of thousands while more and more surgeons queue up to Back Britain with highly-publicised organ transplants, almost all of which are certain to prove both lethal to the patient and useless for the advancement of medical knowledge.

# The day love came creeping up his trouser leg

## Lunchtime O'Booze

She is 15. He is 107. But between the two is a love to pull at the heartstrings of the nation.

He is film producer Roy Revoulting. She is petite starlet Hayley Selassie.

### ROMANCE

He is old enough to be her grandfather. He has been married 25 times and has 75 children.

"I didn't want to fall in love with him" she frankly admits, "I starred in five of his pictures to try and forget him. But he always seemed to be there peering over the camera or sitting about in my dressing room with a droopy look on his face.

"Call it corny if you like. But what's life if its not falling in love with an old millionaire ?"

### HEART THROB

Says Revoulting: "I never dared to speak of my love. She made the first move.

"We were sitting having lunch one day when I felt her tiny hand creep up my trousers.

"The whole world started to sing for me and I realised it must be love. Call it corny if you like. But what's life if its not a tiny blonde touching you up between the Brown Windsor and the Meat and 2 Veg".

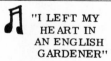 "I LEFT MY HEART IN AN ENGLISH GARDENER"

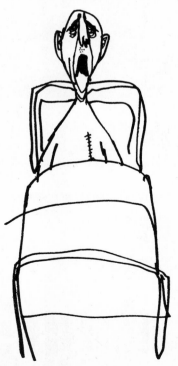

# MRS. WILSON'S DIARY

As tepid on the marble slab
  The dying patient lies
Impervious to probe or jab
  No lustre in his eyes
All hope seems gone - but then, O Joy,
  O Rapture, Bliss and more so,
A new heart from some poor old boy
  Is placed inside his torso.

So too to every wilting soul
  A brand new heart may come
And beat its rat-a-tat style roll
  Like to a martial drum
The pennants lift, the eyes grow bright
  The trumpet sounds the charge
The body's troops thrill to the fight
  Both Brigadier and Sarge.

I must confess that despair had begun to lay its icy fingers on the small of my back last week when the results of the Local Elections were announced by Mr. Trethowan on the Late Night Westminster Round-Up for Insomniacs. Harold himself remained sunk in his Khama-Sutra-style Lotus Blossom Position Trance in the attic, and my sole companion was the dejected Mr. Kaufmann. The Inspector was out, visiting his aunt in Woolwich, and there was little to cheer us. With frequent cries of "Oh My God, it's back to the Labour Exchange", Mr. Kaufmann writhed in his T-Plan Executive Leisurette Seating Environment as Mr. Trethowan smilingly vouchsafed the latest scores. At approximately twelve thirty, when I was thinking of turning in, a crash was audible in the kitchen, and a second later the door flew open to admit the Inspector.

"The game's up, Baldilocks" he remarked in jocose vein, "the pigeons have come home to roost. Pack up your bags, Kaufmann, you're going to have to do a decent day's work for a living at last. And as for you, Madam, I commend to your attention the Property News Section of the *Watford Gleaner.* Charming detached-style bungalow residence Hatch End. One reception, one cloak, one bed, no bath, WC share facilities, no coloureds, suit retired couple". "Inspector" I cried "pray do not forget yourself. I believe you have been drinking". "What else would you suggest under the circumstances ?" riposted the Inspector rudely, "a man must find his solace where he may".

Things were not improved the following morning by the arrival of the *Daily Mirror*, with its ultimatum manifesto from Cecil H. King, 'Enough is enough'. Mr. Kauf-

mann slapped his bald head in grief at this, remarking "This was all we needed already" and sank into a gloomy study, leaving his Vitamin-enriched Boffobrek untouched. Seconds later, the telephone rang. At first I thought it to be a wrong number, as the caller giggled to himself for some time before speaking, and then gave his name as Lord Northcliffe, ringing from the South of France. I asked whether I could take the call as Harold was temporarily indisposed, and the giggling grew to a Maniac laugh. "I draw your attention to today's *Mirror*", said the voice, "I have spoken. Let the people tremble. My car is at the door, and I will take up residence later in the day at Number Ten. The eagles are flying high". "Is that you, Mr. King ?" I queried, recognising the speaker's Wykehamist tones and fleshy chuckle "Cut out the Mister" replied the Press Lord, "my destiny is accomplished. I am the seven-eyed Beast of the Apocalypse". At this the line went dead, and a few minutes later Mr. King rang back to apologise, saying he had had another of his turns, and that they were getting more frequent recently: had I anything to suggest ? I recommended a course of Granny Baverstock's Arrowroot Balm and replaced the receiver.

Imagine my surprise, when two days later, after despondency had hung over the house like a grey shroud of the type shown in Dr. Miller's satirical ghost story, "Whistling in the Dark", and even Nimmo the Cat had slunk about the passages moulting piteously all over the Cyril Lord, when a gay giggle assailed my ear, emanating but faintly from the attic at the top of the house. I had just sent the newspapers up in the basket, along with some Slim While You Grow Fat Cardboard Krispiwheet Wholebread and a pot of Muggoboy Health Farm Quince Jelly, and a few moments later I was astonished to hear the pitapat of eager feet descending the stairs. Surprise upon surprise, a dapper Harold, clothed, shaved, and apparently restored to mental health! "Look at this, Gladys" he crowed, waving the *Times* under my nose, "Heath has fallen in the water. His little boat capsized. Doesn't it make you want to laugh ? The Press will have a field day. Ho ho, haha. Now is the time for a come-back. I think I will just nip down to the House and drum some sense into the backbenchers".

The next day, life was almost back to normal. "Listen to this" Harold cried at breakfast, having discovered a news item at the bottom of the back page of the *Daily Telegraph*, " 'Despite the despondency and gloom amongst backbenchers I spoke to', writes Air Commodore E.J. Rachmaninoff, *Daily Telegraph* Ballooning Correspondent, 'one MP was prepared to admit that the Prime Minister had shown what he described as a glimmer of his old form in the meeting of the Parliamentary Labour Party'. Ha ha, the tide is turning, I fancy, the dismal Jimmies must eat their hats. A great movement is on the march". Luckily, I was relieved to note, Harold's eye escaped the latest Gallup Poll Findings, printed prominently on the front page, showing the 'satisfied with the Prime Minister's performance' figure at a record -0.03. As Mr. Kruschev used to remark, a drowning man must clutch at any camel in a storm.

# PRIVATE EYE

No. 169
Friday
7 June 68

1/6

LET THEM SMOKE POT

**REVOLTING STUDENTS** see pages 8&9

# CECIL KING JOINS PRIVATE EYE Sensation!

# MRS. WILSON'S DIARY

Behold the mighty blasted oak
  Magnificent and tall
It spreads its green and verdant cloak
  Majestic over all
Nothing, it seems, its roots can shake
  Though raging zephyrs lash
But lo, a mouse a bite doth take
  It falls down with a crash.

Not so the lissom bending reed
  That yields to ev'ry gust
The thunderclap it scarce doth heed
  Nor reck the whirlwind's dust
And when a mouse comes nibbling by
  With tiny teeth on edge
It takes one bite, and tends to die
  Regurgitating sedge.

So too with men. Though high aloft
  They stand with nose in air
The meanest wight from humble croft
  One day may be their heir
But he who with the wind doth tack
  Prepared to give and take
Survives uncharred through rage and wrack
  To have and eat his cake.

I penned these lines at the request of the *Scilly Telegraph*, Whitsuntide Edition, which Alderman Tregarthen Mumford is devoting to an analysis of Seaweed Farming in the Light of Recent Events in Paris. It seems hardly possible that the modern Buonaparte can be held to ransom in such a way by Monsieur Von-Arm-Bendit and his revolting students. I find it hard to put myself in the shoes of Madam at this time. What can her feelings be as she sees the tumbrils rumbling past Versailles and the raging mob demanding permission to smoke 'pot'? It cannot be easy to emulate the phlegmatic calm of Madame de Pompidou, who went to the guillotine with a smile on her face and whistling "Je ne regrette rien".

Hardly had the sinister cracks appeared in the marble collossus of Colombey-les-Deux-Magots, than there came the thunderous collapse of Mr. King, who Harold wittily described as the worst Prime Minister since Lord Northcliffe. I did not understand the joke myself at first, but Mr. Kaufmann kindly explained that it refers to a remark passed by a banking gentleman called Mr. Eamonn Hambrose who had adversely compared Harold to Lord North. Mr. Kaufmann was just explaining who Lord North was when the door burst open and Harold stood revealed in a toga-style bathtowel, his old tennis plim-

solls, and a sprig of privet wound about his greying locks.

"Sic transit Gloria Swanson" he remarked, waving the banner headline "PUBLISH AND BE FIRED - KING FOR AXE, "and in case, Gladys, you think that I had anything to do with it, I would ask you to erase from your mind a certain telephone conversation you may perchance have overheard earlier in the week between myself and a Mr. Cudlipp apropos of Birk's Peerage and certain related topics. And now, sirrah" he concluded, addressing Mr. Jenkins, "what news from France?" I must confess that Harold's reactions to the French Turmoil, for an erstwhile close chum of the Eminence Grise, has been less than charitable, and at times almost childish. Mr. Jenkins from next door breezed in just as he was chuckling and rubbing his hands over descriptions of the General's increasing senility, only to be greeted with a cry of "Daggers away, Smoothiechops, my back is not for stabbing. Look what has happened to Cecil King. It will be your turn next. Your name is e'en now prickt".

"Really, Prime Minister" soothed the urbane juggler of figures, "I had always been under the impression it was Jenkins". He gave a light laugh, Mr. Kaufmann tittered obsequiously, and he laid an arm round my waist, "And now Prime Minister, if I may intrude on your charade, I beg you to turn your attention to somewhat graver events lurking beneath the bright tapestry of revolution and brouhaha beyond the Channel. The Franc is jittery and the Sterling has caught the bug I fear. July is not far away, and the annual financial crisis cannot long be deferred". At this Harold began performing a little dance and sang a brief French snatch entitled "Adieu de Gaulle, Adieu, I'll see you in my dreams" which he had picked up from watching the television.

"When he had done he turned to Mr. Jenkins with a triumphant gesture. "Old Longconk had it coming to him" he cried, "I have predicted it for years". It was at this moment that Mr. Kaufmann sprang to the now clattering teletape in Harold's den and returned bearing the flimsy ribbon of paper. "News, Prime Minister, news," he cried, "De Gaulle to stay on. After meditation in the Chapel of Saint Simon le Bizarre this afternoon he reveals mystical apparition of St. Joan of Arc instructing him to remain placidly at the helm of the Republic". For a moment, Harold's expression wavered. Finally he spoke. "There, Jenkins, what did I say, look what happens to the mean folk who attempt to overthrow their devinely appointed leader. They are confounded, Isaiah VII 6, and all their strategems are put to scorn". "Really, really, Prime Minister" interposed the suave Chancellor, "we cannot peep into the womb of time. Who comes, who goes is immaterial compared to the eternal truths of the International Monetary Fund". "That will do, Toffeenose," cried Harold, flinging the Sponjitex All Cotton Bachelor Wrap round him with an impetuous gesture, "where is the Vintage Wincarnis? At times like this we have need of such solace. And before you go, Trendinicks, harken to this. Adenauer is dead; Erhard has been and gone; LBJ is a burnt-out shell; de Gaulle totters; who remains as the Senior Statesman of the Western World? A bulwark against the Forces of Disorder?" "Signor Fanfani?" enquired the poker-faced political biographer with slightly raised eyebrows. I have seldom seen Harold so annoyed. Seizing the Pipkin of Vintage Wincarnis he glowered silently at Mr. Jenkins for a full minute, then turned proudly on his heel and swept out of the room. It was unfortunate that his bath wrap chose that moment to get caught on the doorknob, thus robbing his exit of something of its dramatic impact.

## STUDENT POWER MANIA
### A GLOSSARY OF TERMS

| | |
|---|---|
| *Impatience with authority (Times)* | Smashing up the Fuzz. |
| *A new approach to the organisation of human societies (N. Statesman)* | A lot of mad Frogs charging about as per usual. |
| *Nothing will ever be quite the same again (Everyone)* | I can't think of anything to say. |
| *One thing is certain. Nothing will ever be quite the same again (Everyone)* | I still can't think of anything to say. |
| *Something clearly is stirring under the surface of our inherited assumptions about the nature of our societies (Observer)* | A lot of Frogs are setting fire to cars and ripping up the streets. |
| *A new and fluid situation (Observer)* | It's all happening! |
| *Prone to question or reject the whole basis and structure of society (Times)* | Bored stiff. |
| *A feeling of being manipulated by uncontrolled concentrations of power (Times)* | Boredom. |
| *Moral revulsion against the corruption of society (Times)* | Well there's this woman you see. |
| *Could it happen here? (Everyone)* | A good wheeze to fill up the page. |
| *A new Revolutionary Spirit which will ultimately enrich the lives of all of US (N. Statesman)* | An old-style punch-up which will cause another financial crisis. |
| *Above all they look to Cuba... which is trying to run on revolutionary fervour alone without appealing to the materialistic and acquisitive society (Times)* | Above all they look to Cuba where the economy has collapsed and everyone is starving. |
| *Bliss was it in that dawn to be alive* | It was all coming alive like in 1779 for Danton and Robespierre an' them. |

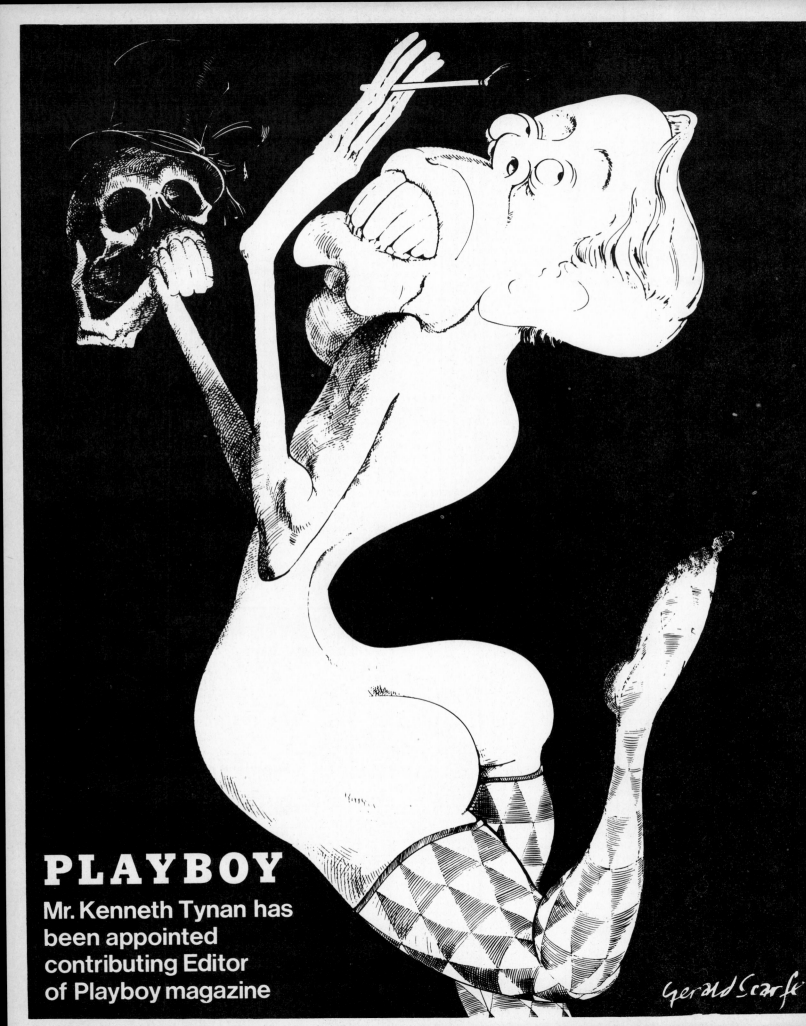

**PLAYBOY**

Mr. Kenneth Tynan has been appointed contributing Editor of Playboy magazine

Gerald Scarfe

# THE CLOGGIES

*An everyday saga in the life of Clog Dancing Folk*
*by BILL TIDY*

# COLOUR SECTION

In Raymond Gunter's resignation letter, he wrote that he intended to rejoin 'the folk from whence I came'. His departure from the Government was greeted by Tories everywhere (from the *Sunday Telegraph* to the *Daily Mirror*) as a bitter blow to Labour from its 'grass roots'. For such romantics the following facts may be of interest:

Throughout the 1930's Gunter was a branch officer of the Ebbw Vale branch of the Railway Clerks association. In May 8, 8, 1939, the branch met to discuss the forthcoming Association national Conference. Their delegate - Gunter - was mandated by the branch to vote for all resolutions favouring the 'Popular Front' of all left-wing forces against the Government's foreign policies, and against Sir Stafford Cripps' expulsion from the Labour Party.

When Gunter attended the Railway Clerks Conference the following week, he moved a resolution, in the name of the Ebbw Vale branch 'that this Conference regrets the continued efforts to create an alliance of all opponents to the foreign policy of the National Government...' Victory for the Popular Front, said Gunter "would be a tragedy not only for the movement but for the country as a whole". (*Daily Herald*, May 18, 1939).

The railway clerks of South Wales were very angry that their delegate had broken his mandate and spoken for the opposite point of view. The secretary of Ebbw Vale Trades Council, Mr. Alec Protheroe, and the chairman of the local R.C.A. branch Mr. Randell Holvey, duly wrote to the *Daily Worker*, explaining that the decision of the branch had been unilaterally reversed by Gunter and that the 'members of Mr. Gunter's branch are not prepared to be ridiculed or to let their delegate flout their wishes in his own interests'(*Daily Worker*, May 24, 1939). The *Worker* described Gunter as 'an aspirant for political honours'.

The incident was not quickly forgotten, and, though Gunter was secretary and agent of Abertillery Labour Party, he found it difficult to make progress. Successive selection conferences for council candidates which were controlled by trade unionists, especially miners, refused to select Gunter for the council.

Gunter left Wales in 1941, never to return. Apart from a recent invitation to the annual dinner of the Abertillery Labour Party, he has hardly ever been invited down there by the 'folk from whence he came'. In Parliament he has represented the well-known Welsh constituencies of South East Essex (1945-50) Doncaster (1950-51) and Southwark (from 1959).

In 1955 Gunter was nominated for the Labour Party's National Executive Committee by his union - then called the Transport and Salaried Staffs Association - and was elected each subsequent year by the big union block vote. Then, suddenly, in 1967, his name no longer appeared on the ballot sheet. Could it have been that his own union - the grass roots from whence he came - had refused to nominate him for the Labour Party Executive ?

Gunter's appeals to the 'working class' contrast sharply with his views as expressed over the last 30 years. "Let us" he cried at a Labour rally in 1958 "put an end to this tripe about the class war for I'm blessed if I know where one class ends and the other begins."

The truth is that if Mr. Gunter does rejoin the folk from whence he came he is unlikely to be well received. "I see" said a miner in Abertillery who remembers Gunter well "that Ray reckons everyone will have forgotten him in ten years. But I wonder if anyone will remember him in ten days".

---

Meetings of the shadow cabinet are said to be more relaxed since the dismissal of Enoch Powell, whose eccentric manner has always embarrassed his colleagues.

When Mac was PM a member of the cabinet arriving early for a meeting at number 10, found one of the serfs there switching round all the chairs.

The man explained that Mr Macmillan had given the order for the change in the seating arrangements, as he could no longer stand the ordeal of having Enoch's steely eyes boring into him as he expounded philosophically on the issues of the day.

---

On the desk of Prof. Christian Barnard in his office at the Groote Schuur Hospital are an unusual pair of book ends - two clear plastic boxes containing the diseased hearts of Washkansky and Blaiberg, suspended in a preserving solution.

When a photographer turned up the other day, Barnard rather pointedly removed 'my book ends' and popped them into a cupboard. "We'd better not have these in the picture" he smiled, "the families wouldn't like it, they would think it macabre. In fact I am having to sue a local photographer for taking pictures of the hearts without my permission. I have got to do it for the sake of the wives".

The photographer expressed his disappointment saying that having them in the fore-ground would make a much better picture. Remembering being told by his colleagues that the Professor responded to flattery like an ageing ballerina, he started telling him how well he photographed, what a wonderful smile he had, how famous he was and how he was the press story of the century.

"I know" replied the Professor excitedly, "Bobby Kennedy didn't last long, did he ? But I am still on the front pages !"

After more softening up the Professor volunteered: "If you really think it would make a better picture I suppose we could have the hearts in. If the families complain I can always say I didn't realise you had got them in the picture".

And with that out came the pickled hearts with the Prof. striking up a pose before them.

The news that a patient in Britain suffering from serious heart disease had refused a heart transplant has shocked the supporters of Professor Barnard, but the story behind the refusal reveals a new obstacle for eager transplanters: the problem of the reluctant recipient.

After close study of the "psychology of the donor/recipient relationship" British heart surgeons are agreed that recipients of new hearts should only be informed about their pending operation when it becomes absolutely certain: that is, when a donor has been found.

The plan for the next British heart transplant was as follows: a recipient in the Middlesex Hospital would be operated on as soon as a donor was found. If the donor was found in the week, the operation would take place at the Middlesex. If at the weekend, at the National Heart Hospital. The NHH team would be led by Donald Ross, the Middlesex one by Marvin Sturridge, perhaps the only surgeon outside the NHH competent to do the job.

Accordingly, on Monday September 2, the news flashed through from Portsmouth that a suitable donor had been found! In great exceitement a consultant at the Middlesex rushed to the bedside of the recipient, an irascible Greek Cypriot club owner. Eagerly the consultant explained that his condition resulted from muscle weakness, curable only be the replacement of the entire heart.

"You mean a transplant" said the Cypriot.
"Well, yes," said the consultant, smiling.
"No." said the Cypriot.
"But why?"
"Because they are all dead."
"Not at all." shrieked the consultant, desperately. "Dr. Denton Cooley in Texas has six patients still alive."
"They will all die" murmered the Cypriot..

And that, unhappily, was that. To the fury of all progressive heart surgeons a perfectly good heart had to be buried with its natural body.

**D**r Donald (if you've got a transplantable organ ring VIC 5000) Longmore, whizz kid of the National Heart Hospital recently gave a lecture at St Thomas' Hospital entitled "Transplant or Implant", in which he balanced the arguments for transplanting human hearts or artificial hearts, coming down strongly in favour of the human ones. During the lecture, he showed a film, made by the BBC, of him, Longmore, transplanting hearts and lungs into dogs. Unhappily the sound did not work, and the silent film was accompanied by the satirical cheers of 200 medical students. The cheering grew to a crescendo when, with the hearts neatly inserted in the dogs, the film was quickly cut. "We don't want any more of that" smiled Longmore, changing the subject and avoiding questions about what happened to the dogs after the operation.

**S**ir Christopher Chancellor, who sits on the board of Madame Tussauds is believed to be lobbying for an effigy of Gypsy Dave Frost to be added to the strength.

Sir Christopher also sits on the board of London Weekend Television.

**T**he dynamic Mr William Davis, editor-elect of *Punch*, a magazine, was asked to go on *24 Hours* following his appointment and be interviewed in a jokey way about his qualifications for the job.

Davis agreed on condition that the Editor of *Private Eye* was not on the panel. This scurrilous man, he said, would only use the occasion to make fun of Davis' Germanic origins.

*"I am your Labour candidate, Sid Potts".*

FRANCE-SOIR · PARIS-PRESSE-L'INTRANSIGEANT

**PHOTO DOCUMENT**

# Les Anglais ne verront pas cette photo de Wilson au mariage de son fils*

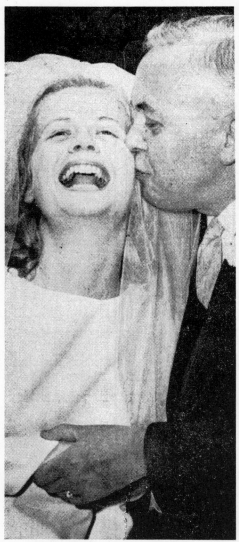

*Harold Wilson semble radieux en embrassant sa belle-fille.*

\* Wrong again, Froggies !

## PSEUDS' CORNER

● *It is a pastoral splashed with blood, intensely erotic and much influenced at its climax by Bonnie and Clyde. I doubt if a richer long poem has been written in English during the 1960s.*

K. Tynan (Observer) on C. Logue

# FOOTNOTES

**W**hen, last New Year's Day, the live body of Mr Clive Haupt, a Cape Coloured factory worker, was wheeled into Groote Schuur Hospital, and put into the ward now reserved for potential heart donors, the world-famous heart-transplant team, under the leadership of Professor Barnard were anxious to lose no time before cutting out his heart and putting it in the body of Dr Philip Blaiberg.

Hospital ethics however laid down that Haupt should first be seen by the duty physician, who unsportingly said that he could not possibly pronounce Haupt dead, nor give instructions to "switch off" the respirator which was keeping him alive. He would not be able to give another opinion until the following morning. The transplant team were horrified. Dr Johnnie Louw, Professor of Surgery at Cape Town university and head of surgery at Groote Schuur blurted out loud:

"Hott!. Hott man! What kind of a heart are you going to leave us with?"

As history now knows, Mr Haupt was eventually pronounced dead and his heart was carved out of his body before it stopped beating. The fact that Dr Blaiberg, is after nearly ten months still "alive" in Groote Schuur hospital, after several severe setbacks is hailed throughout the world as a magnificent tribute to South African medicine and to Professor Barnard.

This suspicion, however, still lingers in Groote Schuur that the heart had been living too long in the body of Mr Haupt while he was barely alive on the respirator, and that if only a more healthy heart could be used a more dramatic success would be assured.

For the last six weeks, the heart transplant team at Groote Schuur, eager not to vanish from the limelight in view of the successful run of transplants in Houston, Texas, have been chafing at the bit, daunted at every turn by recurring permutations of the "donor problem".

The team had found a perfect "recipient" in Mr Pieter Smith, a former miner and rugger player. But somehow the team just couldn't get the right kind of donor.

Many of the Cape Town blacks believe that if a body isn't buried with its heart its chances of arriving at its Maker are decreased. A strong movement arose in the black ghettos of Cape Town and the surrounding districts at all costs to prevent relatives and friends who might die from brain disease from getting anywhere near Groote Schuur. There were also consistent rumours of black donors refusing permission for transplants.

Secondly, there were all sorts of minor upsets: as one newspaper reported later:

*"In London, potential donors have been whisked by ambulance from one city hospital to another while still alive, and at least one such instance is known to have occurred in Cape Town, when a possible donor was taken from Victoria Hospital, Wynberg, to Groote Schuur Hospital.*

*"Instead of dying, as expected, he recovered and had to be taken off the donor list".* (Cape Times: September 14).

## THE HEART OF THE KAFFIR

Helpless fury at the unavailability of a donor was further inflamed by the news that donations to the Chris Barnard Heart Fund - which had risen to 248,602 rand on September 6th - were not rising as fast as expected.

All this was changed on Saturday September 8th. The *Cape Times* (Sept. 10th) reported: "The Chris Barnard who emerged from the inner recesses of Groote Schuur Hospital late on Saturday night to face the Press was a transformed man. It was the same Chris Barnard we had seen immediately after the Washkansky and Blaiberg operations. After ... a host of frustrations he was back in business".

Mr Smith had his new heart, and South Africa erupted in the same display of jubilation which had followed previous "successes" at Groote Schuur. "We are hoping" said the Chris Barnard Heart Fund secretary, Mr E. Polton, that the new transplant will boost the fund". *(Cape Argus : September 9)*. On September 12th contributions to the fund totalled 80.45 rand. Everyone cheered. And meanwhile the journalists started to search about for an answer to the curiously unresolved question: Who was the donor?

'I will not disclose the name of the donor" said Barnard at a Press Conference. Barnard was supported by the hospital and local Government authorities; and very soon the journalists discovered that none of the junior officials, and no one among the physicians or surgeons, apart from the transplant team, knew who the donor was. Wild rumours circulated. The donor was "named" as a Mrs Dawutsa who was pregnant and had been brought to Cape Town from the Transkei. The rumours were scotched on September 11th, when photographs of Mrs Dawutsa, alive and well, were printed in all the newspapers.

No doubt the Professor and the authorities hoped that the veil of secrecy which they had drawn on the "donor aspect" would prevent any more facts filtering through. They had forgotten about the heartless body of a dead African woman in Groote Schuur morgue, which, sometime or other, would have to be identified and prepared for burial. It is, apparently, impossible to disguise the fact that a body has had the heart excised from it.

The hospital authorities hoped to fight their way out of this problem with charm and patronage.

Very early in the morning on September 12th, a hospital car and a white hospital official were sent on what was meant to be a 'secret' mission to the Guguletu black suburb of the city. There the car picked up a Mr

James Mjila and Mr Benjamin Tsindi, respectively common law husband and brother of a 28-year-old domestic servent called Evelyn Jacobs. The car drove to the Groote Schuur mortuary where Mr Mjila identified his wife's body. He was shown the face, not the body. The two men were then taken to the hospital's main building:

*"At 9.30" the Cape Times states, "they (Mjila and Tsindi) were shown into a room which ... looked like a conference room. Three men in white coats were sitting round a table, and one of them was introduced to them as Dr Burger, the hospital's medical superintendent. The other two doctors were not introduced.*

*"Mr Tsindi said that for the greater part of the meeting Dr Burger sat with his arms on the table, with his head resting on his arms.*

*" 'When they asked whether James had identified the body of his sister, we said yes, he had. One of the doctors then told us straightaway: 'Sorry, but she died on Saturday. We took out her heart and put it inside Mr Smith.' ' Mr Tsindi said."*

The two men then asked why none of Miss Jacobs' relatives had been contacted before the operation, and were told that the hospital did not know who Miss Jacobs was. Mr Mjila told the three men that he had visited Groote Schuur no less than seven times on the Saturday that she died, asking for Miss Jacobs, but was told that she had been dismissed without treatment. The sister, apparently, who so informed him did not know that Miss Jacobs had been "removed for treatment".

Dr. Burger and his colleagues spent a great deal of time trying to persuade the two men not to talk to the Press. Money was offered to bring other members of the family to the funeral.

But the two men would have none of it. On the following day, the Press carried the whole story, including a statement from Mr Tsindi that he refused to remove the body from the morgue until it had its heart put back into it. Miss Jacobs, it was disclosed, was a maid in the house of Mr and Mrs W. Rotstein, who live in Vredehoek. Miss Jacobs left the Rotstein's house at about 7.45 on Friday, September 5th, and, shortly afterwards, collapsed in the street. She was brought back to the Rotstein's house, seen by the Rotstein's doctor, who summoned an ambulance and sent her to Groote Schuur hospital. Before doing so, he attached to her body a label with her name EVELYN JACOBS and the street in which she lived written on it. That was the last the doctor or the Rotsteins heard of Miss Jacobs until they were rung up by reporters four days later and told she was South Africa's third heart donor.

The only people who know the extent of the illness from which Miss Jacobs was suffering are the men and women immediately connected with the heart transplant team at Groote Schuur. Ordinary hospital officials did not even know of her arrival in the hospital. She was whisked away, as Denise Darval and Clive Haupt (the two previous donors) had been before her, into the part of the hospital where the transplant operations are done. Tissue-typing and blood testing must have taken place at record speed. And if Miss Jacobs did die of a massive brain haemorrhage, as the hospital authorities claim, we have only the word of Groote Schuur specialists to prove it. As Professor Barnard put it:

*"Only about six of us altogether who were in that particular theatre at that time could know with any certainty the exact identity of the donor." (Cape Times : Sept. 13th).*

In the Johannesburg *Sunday Times*, in his second exclusive interview in three days, Professor Barnard denied that Miss Jacobs was the donor. "All the names mentioned by the hospital are wrong" he said, thus ensuring that either his Medical Super-intendent, or Mr Tsindi and Mr Mjila, or he himself is a liar. Nor was Professor Barnard in any doubt about the real res-ponsibility for the souring of his third transplant. The man who had travelled across the globe on three separate occasions, seeking publicity in the luxury hotels and night clubs of every major city; the man who had flown to Italy to answer the 'pleas' of Sophia Loren and had asked Carlo Ponti to make a film of his life; the man who had purposely prolonged Press Conferences in Cape Town even after the journalists had grown tired of them; the man who had told a photographer that he was lasting longer in the headlines than Bobby Kennedy, the man who had spoken the introduction to two long-playing records about heart transplants the man who is urgently at work on his auto-biography for sale across the world; the man who, only last week, was "elected" top of the Italian popularity poll - put his finger on the root of the matter:

*"The real trouble" he told the Sunday Times of September 15th, "is sensationalism - the Press seeking publicity for transplants ... This is not in the public interest. So why pursue the matter?"*

On Wednesday, September 18th, the Chris Barnard Heart Fund had topped 250,000 rand.

# CZECH BOUNCED

No one yet knows for sure what exactly happened to the Czechoslovakian First Sec-retary Dubcek in Moscow. We know that he was taken from his office, bundled into a tank, handcuffed and flown to Moscow. There is a very brief excerpt from a Russian film showing Dubcek sitting at the conference table in Moscow. Then he returns to Prague and goes straight into hospital for thirteen days. He is, says the Press, subject to "fainting fits". Even after his discharge from hospital, Dubcek, in contrast to other Czech leaders, notably Svoboda and Cernik, Smirkovsky (all of whom also went to Mos-cow) remains almost completely silent in public and private.

According to two sources recently retur-ned from Prague, whose Czech hosts knew one of the participants in the Moscow talks, Dubcek was brought to the conference table two days after his arrival in Moscow. He looked gravely ill, though there were few marks on his face, and through the two and a half days of negotiations he sat completely

silent, almost immobile. From time to time he was ushered away and injected (the Russi-ans claimed with "something to bring him round"). Even on the plane back to Czecho-slovakia Dubcek remained silent, and spoke only once briefly, about "beatings" and "a bath".

This evidence would suggest that the large and extremely efficient Torture Divi-sion of the Russian KGB has not advanced its science much in the last twenty years.

In his entertaining little book, Private Kelly by Himself, Mr. Frank Kelly, a Brit-ish medical orderly who fought at Arnheim, describes how he was picked up after the war in Eastern Europe by the Russians and was treated as a dangerous political spy. "The treatment" he received consisted of savage beatings (usually concentrating on in-ternal bruisings and pain) followed by showers of, alternately, extremely hot and cold water. In between beatings and showers the victim is kept in solitary confinement with little or no food and no sanitary facili-ties whatsoever. This 'treatment', in a mat-ter of hours, has the effect of almost tot-ally numbing the brain.

The time taken for the treatments to succeed depends on the psychological state of the victim. A man of unstable emotions under great strain (like Dubcek at the time of the Moscow visit) will collapse almost at once. It is fair to assume, too, that the KGB used the most intensive methods for the only available Czech leader who had been publicly denounced in the Russian Press.

The state of total mental breakdown brought on by "the treatment" can be sus-tained with the liberal use of phenothiazine drugs. Beaten into a mental pulp, and drug-ged with phenothiazine, Dubcek would be un-able to speak at the conference and would also be subject to fainting fits, since the heavy drug doses would affect his blood cir-culation.

The period of convalescence from such treatment varies, again, with the victim. In some cases he never fully recovers.

# TOWER DE FARCE

As reported in the *Eye* on the 2nd February, the key figure in the bizarre story of "Mad Mitch" and the Argylls in Aden, was the former General Officer commanding-in-chief, Middle East, the smooth, polo-playing Major General Philip Tower.

It was Tower who was enraged by Mitchell using his initiative in capturing Crater so swiftly and the relish with which he afterwards described his feat on television. When Tower ordered Mitchell to give no more interviews to TV correspondents, Mitchell simply asked the correspondents to give a list of their questions to one of his officers who then carried out the interview on camera. It was Tower who tried to stop corres-pondents visiting the Argylls in Aden and prevent them from receiving any publicity on their return home. It was Tower who decided in Aden that Mitchell would not, unlike other battalion commanders in tough areas, be awarded the DSO.

At one point Tower was so keen to find a pretext for sending Mitchell home that an officer-escort was earmarked for the job. What Tower did not know was that some of his own superior officers were so fed up with his handling of the Aden operations that another Major-General was standing by in the United Kingdom to take over his job.

Indeed, all the way up from Mad Mitch, senior officers were wanting to get rid of their immediate junior. This went all the way up to General Sir James Cassels, the Chief of the General Staff, who was barely on speaking terms with Healey and whose recent retirement was warmly applauded by the Minister of Defence.

A curious postscript has now come to light. One factor in Mitchell's decision to resign his commission was that he was told that, when his spell in command of the Argyll and Sutherland Highlanders ended next year, he would not be promoted and would be sent to a staff job, probably less important than the one he held on Lord Mountbatten's staff before going to Aden.

Some weeks ago, the Army's grading board of generals met to consider the futures of lieutenant-colonels, including Mitchell. The president, Major-General C.H. ("Monkey") Blacker, gentleman-jockey and Director of Army Staff Duties, later told friends that in the secret ballot, he had given Mitchell almost the highest possible marks, which, had the other half-dozen generals come anywhere near emulating, would have ensured Mitchell's promotion to full Colonel, or even Brigadier. But when the total was added, it was found that Mitchell's marks were so low that he was ineligible for promotion.

One of the generals on this grading board was Major-General Philip Tower, now Commandant of the Royal Military Academy, Sandhurst.

# THE OBSERVER REVIEW

# GETTING EUROPE MOVING

KENNETH HARRIS TALKS TO

## NAPOLEON

In the past month, young, dynamic, 32-year-old Corsican born Napoleon Bonaparte has captured the imagination - not to say the territory - of the whole of Europe.

What is he like - this supreme representative of the new generation of tough, young Eurocrats who are dragging a continent kicking and screaming into the nineteenth century?

The image is familiar - the cocked hat, the right hand tucked informally into the roll-neck great-coat, the easy smile, the carefully combed forelock. But what of the man behind the Iron Mask? That's another story altogether (see next week's Observer Mezzotint Supplement). Here the man who has become France's youngest Emperor in history talks frankly to Kenneth Harris:

Harris: Good evening, Your Exalted Highness.

Napoleon: Don't stand on ceremony, just remain kneeling.

Harris: If I may say so, Your Highness, to have risen as you have done, from a simple peasant's cottage in Corsica to become the most powerful man in the world in twenty years is no small achievement. How do you think this came about?

Napoleon: Y'know, I am glad you asked me that one. Speaking quite frankly, I think that after ninety or so years of stagnation and feudal mismanage-ment under the vieux-école-cravate-strangled *ançien regime*, the country was ready for an entirely new and radical approach to our problems.

Harris: Of course there are some who would say, Your Holiness, that these

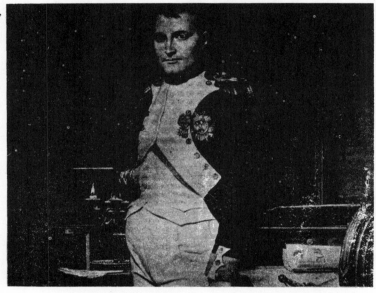

changes have not been achieved without a certain amount of discomfort. I am thinking of the Terror and that sort of thing.

Napoleon: I myself have never condoned that kind of behaviour, which I am sure you would agree, Mr Harris, shows only too clearly what happens when certain irrespon-sible left-wing elements are allowed to play their part in shaping policy.

Harris: Would you describe yourself as a democrat?

Napoleon: In the sense that Alexander the Great, Julius Caesar and Ivan the Terrible were democrats, yes. But I believe passionately that in a modern state, given the full complexity of the machinery of government today (putting aside the guillotine for a moment), it is essential that decisions must be made by the expert, the professional, the best man for the job - namely myself.

Harris: Some critics have

demurred at what they claim to be a tendency to nepotism in your appointments? For instance, you have made your brothers Kings of Westphalia, Holland, Spain, Naples and so forth ...

Napoleon: We Bonapartes have always been an intensely political family. We have always assumed that if anything were to happen to me, the torch would be carried on by my elder brother Joe - and if anything happened to to him, it would pass to my younger brother, Louis, and so on.

Harris: If I may turn for a minute, Sir, to a more personal side of your career, what is it you think particularly that has enabled you to cap-ture the imagination of young people in France and all over the world?

Napoleon: I think it is because I have offered them the shining vision of a New Fontier - stretching as it does all the way from

Gibraltar to the Urals. Also, I think the young, irreverent, iconoclastic youth of today have res-ponded to my call for a dynamic crash re-think at every level of French society ...

Harris: ... yes, yes, quite ... and also, if I may say so, Emperor, your ad-ministration has brought to political life an entirely new sense of style. I am thinking of your lovely young wife Josephine ...

Napoleon: ... prenez-garde, mon ami ...

Harris: ... oh gosh, sir, no, what I meant was, new departures like your ex-citing new cultural policy, bringing to Paris the art treasures of all Europe ...

Napoleon: ... I said prenez-garde, mon ami ...

Harris: ... yes, well, returning to politics, General, how do you see the future of the European community?

Napoleon: Alors - so long as I keep Britain out of Europe, I shall die happy.

Harris: Finally, what of your own future?

Napoleon: I have many good years ahead. I have never been one who has believed that old soldiers should just fade away. The idea of retiring to some nice, isolated little island away from the world to cultivate my garden and write my memoirs - why, that is un-thinkable.

## NEXT WEEK IN THE OBSERVER

*The Observer talks to*
THE GREATEST LIVING ENGLISHMAN-
BENJAMIN HAYDON.

# BARRY McKENZIE

*Words by BARRY HUMPHRIES*
*Drawings by NICHOLAS GARLAND*

THE STORY SO FAR

THE REV. KEV'S ATTENTIONS TO MITZI HAVE NATURALLY UPSET HIS WIFE CHERYL WHO TURNS ON HER HEEL IN DISGUST. BARRY ESCORTS HER INTO THE STREET WHERE THEY BUMP INTO BRILLIANT YOUNG ADVERTISING MAN TORQUIL YOUNGHUSBAND...

NOW READ ON —

MY SORDID OFFICE IS JUST ROUND THE CORNER — I THINK YOU'LL FIND MY PROPOSITION ATTRACTIVE, MR., ER?

McKENZIE, BARRY McKENZIE. I'LL DO ANYTHING WITHIN REASON FOR A BIT OF FOLDING STUFF — MATTER OF FACT A LOT OF ME MATES PULL IN QUITE A BIT DOING MALE MODELLING FOR BASTARDS LIKE YOU!

QUITE TRUE! YOU AUSSIES ARE SO DELICIOUSLY BUTTERBOX — BUT MODELLING IS EXACTLY WHAT I HAD IN MIND FOR YOU — COME ALONG — WE'LL TALK...

I'M SURE YOU'LL FIND BARRY A VERY GOOD WORKER MR. YOUNGHUSBAND, BUT WE'D BE OBLIGED IF YOU WOULD ENDEAVOUR TO INFER WHAT KIND OF YAKKA IT IS YOU WANT HIM TO DO!!!

YEAH

WELL, IT'S LIKE THIS. BLAIR & YOUNGHUSBAND HANDLE THE ACCOUNT OF GROINATEX FOUNDATION GARMENTS — WE DO ALL THEIR TUBE ADVERTISING

CRIPES! THIS IS GETTIN INTERESTIN' — YOU MEAN YOU WANT ME TO GO AROUND SELLIN' ICE COLD TUBES!

DON'T BE SUCH A DILL, BARRY — HE MEANS CORSET ADVERTS ON THE UNDERGROUND!

THIS CHICK'S A GENIUS — TAKE A PEEK AT OUR LATEST POSTER...

She Chose GROINATEX

JEEZ! I COULD BE UP THAT LIKE A RAT UP A DRAIN!

WHAT A NICE POSTER...

IT'S CERTAINLY EYE CATCHING

AH! THERE'S THE RUB, LITTLE LADY. IT ISN'T EYE-CATCHING ENOUGH. THE CAT'S ALL GROOVE WHEN THEY SEE IT, BUT THE GROINATEX PEOPLE CATER MOSTLY FOR THE FEMALE MARKET. THAT'S WHY I DREAMP UP THIS LAYOUT!

IT'S A BONZER BIT OF LAYOUT, THAT'S FOR SURE, BUT WHERE DO I FIT IN — IF YOUSE SEE WHAT I MEAN...

TOUCHE! I'D LIKE TO PUT YOU ON THE PAYROLL, STARTING TONIGHT, AS A BLAIR & YOUNGHUSBAND DEFACER!

IN THE NEXT ISSUE TORQUIL EXPLAINS HIS WHEEZE. MODERN ADVERTISING TECHNIQUES MAY BE UNUSUAL BUT CHERYL AND BARRY CERTAINLY NEED SOME FOLDING STUFF...

TORQUIL YOUNGHUSBAND, BRILLIANT YOUNG ADVERTISING MAN HAS APPROACHED BARRY WITH AN OFFER — THE GROINATEX CAMPAIGN NEEDS A DEFACER...

NOW READ ON...

WE'LL SUPPLY YOUR EXPENSES AND A GOOD POCKETFUL OF BLACK INDELIBLE FELT PENS. ALL YOU HAVE TO DO IS STOP OFF AT EVERY TUBE STATION IN GREATER LONDON, FIND OUR POSTER, AND DRAW THE MALE GENITALIA!

BUT I CAN'T SPELL THAT!

YOU DON'T HAVE TO, ME OLE LOVELY. JUST SCRAWL THIS SYMBOL ON EACH POSTER. THE DESIGNER HAS ALLOWED A SPECIAL SPACE FOR IT. THE LAST DEFACER WE HAD LET US DOWN BADLY. HE DEFACED THE MOVIE ADS AS WELL. WE DON'T WANT ENGLISH WOMEN TO GO TO THE PICTURES, WE WANT THEM TO BUY GROINATEX! NOW!

JEEZ, I DUNNO

I MUST SAY I ALWAYS TAKE A SECOND LOOK AT POSTERS WHICH HAVE BEEN ALTERED BY THE MENTALLY SICK, BUT WHY CAN'T YOU JUST PRINT A THINGUMMY ON THEM INSTEAD OF HIRING PEOPLE LIKE BAZZA?

YEAH?

SIMPLY BECAUSE, LITTLE LADY, BRITAIN IS STILL IN THE GRIPS OF SOME PARTICULARLY DOTTY CENSORSHIP LEGISLATION. THE FUDDY DUDDIES ARE BOUND TO GIVE IN SOONER OR LATER, BUT IN THE MEANTIME, ALL THE ARTS, ADVERTISING NOT THE LEAST, MUST SUFFER. THE SICKENING LEGEND OF CROMWELL STILL STANDS BETWEEN US AND THE ADULT CORSETRY POSTER!

SO YOU WANT ME TO GO SNEAKIN' AROUND SCRIBBLIN' JOHN THOMAS'S ON THE WALL?

FOR TEN SHILLINGS PER POSTER AND GENEROUS EXPENSES — IN A WORD MY LOVELY — YES!

BUT MIGHTN'T HE GET CAUGHT MR. YOUNGHUSBAND — SOME PEOPLE MIGHTN'T UNDERSTAND THAT ITS JUST GOOD CLEAN ADVERTISING. THEY MIGHT THINK BARRY WAS MENTALLY ILL!

THAT'S WHERE YOU COME IN, LITTLE LADY. YOU CAN STAND & WATCH, AND IF YOU SEE LILLY LAW APPROACHING, JUST WHISTLE AND BARRY CAN PRETEND HE'S TRYING TO RUB IT OFF — WHAT ABOUT IT? HAVE WE GOT A DEAL?

ALRIGHT, MATE. I'LL PLAY ALONG. I'LL NEED TEN QUID DOWN. CHERYL AND ME ARE TAKIN' A BIT OF A RISK, AND WE'LL NEED A FEW CHILLED ONES INSIDE AS WELL...

THIS COULD BE A BIG BREAK FOR BARRY AFTER THE TERRIBLY ROUGH SPIN HE'S BEEN HAVING: SEE NEXT ALTERED ISSUE!

# COLOUR SECTION

**A** Soviet Armed Forces enquiry is still looking into the mysterious death in March of Yuri Gagarin and his friend Col. Vladimir Seregin.

Various sensational accounts of the accident have been in circulation - that Gagarin was testing a special new plane at an altitude of 30 miles or, as the former correspondent of a Russian science magazine said in London, that a new spacecraft was being tested.

The truth is more mundane, more tragic and less befitting to a Hero of the Soviet Union For this last reason it will not be published by the military enquiry.

Gagarin, who was getting increasingly fed up by being touted round the world as a Russian hero, turned up at the airfield on the day of his death slightly the worse for drink. He and Seregin, a test pilot, ignored the ground staff who tried to restrain them, and took off in an obsolete MIG 15. The plane got out of control when they were doing some sky larking and crashed.

News of the accident was held up for 24 hrs.

# ROOND 'N ABOOT with Lun Tai O'Booze

*OUR MAN IN SAIGON*

**S**ome U.S. observers in South Vietnam complain that the troops are insufficiently virulent in their hatred of the enemy. Not so. In no recent war has there existed such hatred as U.S. Marines now feel for the U.S. Army. Until last year the 'Leathernecks' were alone responsible for the I Corps area in the north of South Vietnam where the fighting was strongest. But as the Viet Cong and North Vietnamese grew increasingly more numerous and better armed, the going became too tough for the Marines. Their commander General Walt, who correctly understood that it was necessary to deploy part of his troops on 'pacification' work in the villages, was abruptly fired. All the Marines were then employed on futile 'search and destroy' reconnaissance in the barren mountains and jungle close to the Laos and North Vietnam frontier. The result was an escalation of disaster. More and more Marine bases were mortared, shelled, rocketed and then over-ran. First Con Thien and then Khe Sanh were besieged.

Marine casualties were so high that raw recruits were rushed from the States and mowed down within weeks. The situation became so dire that even the fat-headed General Westmoreland panicked and sent in army troops to support the Marines. The First Air Cavalry, two divisions of Airborne troops and at last a 'Provisional Task Force', based on Phu Bai, were moved into the I Corps area. It was these army units who came to the relief of Khe Sanh this spring. Were the Marines grateful ?

**A** First Air Cavalry helicopter carrying troops to the relief of Khe Sanh in March received heavy ground fire. The chopper swooped in to attack and was surprised to see that the fire had come from the Marines. When this ground-fire was repeated, the helicopter gave the 'leathernecks' an answering burst from its own machine guns. When virile, dynamic General Tolson, the Air Cav. commander finally reached Khe Sanh he addressed the Marines: "O.K. fellers ! All ready to go ?" To which the Marines replied "Yeah, go home !" Shocked Air Cav. troops noticed that the Marines in Khe Sanh, far from short of food, had strewn the camp with cast off meat, bread and fruit, which explains the multitude of rats that later infested the bastion. Although the Khe Sanh commander went on record as saying 'marines don't dig', the leathernecks had in fact dug themselves deep bunkers from which they refused to budge, thereby allowing the Viet Cong to surround the camp's perimeter. The Marines at Hue were distinguished for their sadism, cowardice and looting.

**B**ut do not imagine that the Marines are no longer jealous of that honour which carried them 'from the halls of Montezuma to the shores of Tripoli'. No, Sir. One man who still cares is Colonel Fasey, the get-up-and-go, no-holds-barred, gung-ho, cretinous chief of the Press Centre at Danang, where all journalists are obliged to stay, paying one pound a night for the privilege of sleeping five to a room in an open sewer. The leatherneck Colonel rightly believes that all journalists are subversives and all European journalists are secret members of the Communist Party. Just before the Paris peace talks he came face to face with the French consul in Danang. He delivered a homily to the surprised diplomat, explaining that in his (Fasey's) view, there were three main enemies of the United States: France, China and Russia in that order. He then propounded his own pet solution for peace in the world: "I'd drop a hydrogen bomb on Paris".

**A**fter Saigon Police Chief General 'Bullseye' Loan had so graphically demonstrated his feelings towards the Geneva Convention with his .38 revolver during the recent Tet Offensive, he found himself being followed by TV crews hoping for a repeat performance. Some days later the ABC TV team's tenacity paid off when during further fighting in Cholon a VC prisoner was brought to Loan. After checking that the camera was turning he drew a .45 automatic from his pocket, pointed it between the eyes of the terrified prisoner and pulled the trigger. He screamed hysterically

as a stream of water hit the prisoner's forehead and enjoyed himself emptying the water pistol at the camera crew.

Another TV team, British this time, got back to Saigon after a harrowing week filming the fighting in Hue. The cameraman, of sensitive celtic stock, was particularly upset by the suffering he saw inflicted on the civilians by the insane tactics of the Americans. (Guns of ships of the 7th Fleet 5 miles out in the China Sea were being called in to knock out VC snipers in the heart of the city !) Attempting unsuccessfully to blot out the memories with drink he made his way over to the JUSPAO building to attend the daily Press (Five o'clock follies) Briefing. In the hushed and hallowed hall the cant of a Major Conrado droning on about 'referring to page 4 of your release for an update on the current latest account of pig-pens constructed by the Marines ...' was interrupted abruptly by an impassioned plea from the rear of 'What about the civilians of Hue ?' With a fervour and emotion that would have done credit to any Rhondda bible-puncher the voice boomed on: "How many children did you kill today ? I saw it all ! 500 pound bombs being dropped on the innocents !" The briefer gaped in bewildered silence, a few tut-tuts came from the audience. Then came the TV producer to the rescue. "It's alright", he explained loudly, "he's only a cameraman". And everyone signed with relief.

**A**n employee of one of the American TV networks in Saigon was questioned recently by the CIA about his political attitudes towards the war. He was succeeding in giving a fairly convincing account of being a minor hawk when he was confronted with the 'evidence'. Had he not three nights before told a certain bar-girl with whom he'd spent the night that he was all for the VC, that he thought Ho was the saviour of Vietnam and that if he was Vietnamese he'd join the VC at once ? He agreed it was all true and explained he told all Vietnamese girls the same thing. He found it made them more affectionate, charge less and much more likely to have an orgasm.

**A**t the present time the CIA is doing it's bit for the war in Vietnam in the way it alone knows best. One example: leaflets are dropped over VC villages saying "We intend to pacify your village. Defect now to the Government side. If you refuse you will be pacified by force ... ! Then instructions to tear off one corner of the leaflet bearing the single letter 'M'. This easily concealable scrap of paper serves as a safe-conduct pass to be shown by the defector when he comes over to the Government side. "What we do," explained a member of the CIA's counter-terrorist group, "is to sneak into a VC village at night, quietly kidnap one or two high ranking cadre members, take them some distance away before killing and burying them and leaving near their homes a screwed up pamphlet with the corner torn off so that it's sure to be found. Somewhere not too obvious - under the bed or in the latrine". He added philosophically, "Well, it might not win the war, but it sure does play havoc with their morale !"

# PRIVATE EYE

No. 175
Friday
Aug. '68

1/6

Gerald Scarfe.

# STALIN:
# New Heart

# FOOTNOTES

# DECLINE & FALL OF RONAN POINT

On Tuesday 13th August, the three members of the Court of Inquiry into the Ronan Point disaster travelled with consulting and structural engineers to the Building Research Station at Watford where a special test had been devised for their inspection. The object was to establish the strenth of the joints of concrete poured in on site between the floor slabs and the walls of Ronan Point. By means of hydraulic jacks, the Building Research Station staff simulated the pressure of an explosion, starting at nought and working upwards.

The purpose was to settle the crucial question in the enquiry. The submission of Taylor Woodrow Anglian, who built Ronan Point, and of the Newham Borough Council was that the explosion had been so powerful that no building, however strongly constructed, could have withstood it. On the other hand, the preliminary report of the consulting engineers, Bernard L. Clark and Partners, invited by the Treasury Solicitor to report on the disaster, concluded:

"The explosion was not a particularly violent explosion and could have been caused by several mediums, i.e. gas, explosive vapour or vapour caused by burning or heating of some material".

The Report noted that the partition walls around the bathroom, where the explosion took place, though they are only 2 ins. thick, had been shifted only slightly and in no place broken down.

While the contractors estimated the pressure of the explosion at a fantastic 600 pounds per square inch, the Clark Report put it at nearer 3 pounds per square inch (PSI). Clearly if a small explosion of 3 lbs P.S.I. can knock down a section of 22 storeys in a building like Ronan Point, something is very wrong indeed.

There was therefore some anxiety among the onlookers as the Building Research Station experts started piling up the weights on a two-storey block designed exactly to resemble Ronan Point. To their astonishment, the crucial joint fractured at a mere 1.6. lbs. P.S.I.

That very evening it was first leaked to the Press that Mr Hugh Griffiths, chairman of the inquiry, had written to the Minister of Housing suggesting that the gas should be turned off in all high blocks similar in design to Ronan Point.

In Private Eye No. 170 it was revealed that the local police were following up the suggestion that a man had stored gelignite in one of the walls and that this was the main cause of the Ronan explosion. This was because the police officer in charge of the inquiry, who worked with explosives in the war, could not believe that a minor gas explosion would be enough to cause 22 storeys of flats to tumble down.

The gelignite inquiry has, apparently, come to nothing, and the police, together with those who have read the Clark Report, must be left with the conclusion that a minor explosion which could take place inside or outside a building for any number of reasons, of which gas is only one, can remove a wall panel, which will mean inevitably that the entire section of the tower block will collapse. The fact that Ronan Point collapsed early in the morning relegated it conveniently to the status of "second class disaster". If the collapse had taken place two hours later, when the inmates of the flats were in their living rooms, there would have been more than a hundred dead. This would have been a disaster of Aberfan proportions, and the inquiry would probably have been headed by a High Court judge and given rather more publicity than the already news-starved Press could find for it.

As it is, the Clark Report has been virtually ignored by the Press, although most of its conclusions are reinforced by a similar report from other consulting engineers, Scott, Wilson, Fitzpatrick and Partners. Another independent report from the consulting engineering firm of Pell, Frieschman Ltd., balances the stability factors against the factors liable to tumble the building down, dividing the former by the latter and coming out with the fraction 0.67. Most buildings built in the traditional manner would, after similar sums, result in a figure of more than 6.0. A fraction less than 1.0 means, quite literally, that the building is more likely to fall down than stay up.

The block of flats at Ronan Point is built under a system originally devised by the Danish building firm Larsen and Nielsen. In Scandanavia, where the cold winter makes it impossible to mix concrete on site, it is easier and cheaper to manufacture the concrete sections of a building in a factory. The Larsen and Nielsen system, together with most other continental types of prefabricated building, was devised for relatively low-storey buildings (seldom more than five or six storeys high, and usually less), but it soon caught the attention of British firms, who bought up licenses and started in the lavish way characteristic of building contractors to "interest" the local authorities in "sky-rise" Continental-style blocks which could be built relatively cheaply and quickly. Anglian Building Products, a small Norfolk firm, snapped up the Larsen Nielsen license, and was itself quickly swallowed by Taylor Woodrow, the second biggest building firm in Britain.

For these new building systems there was no established code of safety, nor even a code of regulations for the construction process. An exchange in the inquiry between Mr Eastleigh, representing the Treasury Solicitor and Mr T.E. North, the borough architect and planning officer for West Ham Borough (now part of Newham) reveals the length to which the authorities went to establish the safety factor :-

Eastleigh: *"Did you work upon this assumption, in effect, that as these systems were being built on a large scale in Europe that there would be no real worry about the stability problem?"*

North: *"Yes. My view was, as I say, that so many varying authorities were examining these in various ways, if there was anything fundamentally wrong in the system surely somebody would have found that out somewhere."*

In fact someone had found out that something was fundamentally wrong - in America. Three years ago, following pressure from many building firms to initiate industrial building, the American Department of Defense sponsored a research study by Kaiser industries.

The report rejected the use in America of any of the Continental systems for use for one simple, obvious reason:

*"Their stacked method of construction would not meet most US building codes because of lack of structural continuity. This method relies on gravity and the fixity of connection between the elements".*

The Americans, in short, have some doubts about putting up buildings where the walls hold up the floors, and the floors the walls, simply by resting one on the other and hoping that the weight of both would keep them in place.

British contractors, eager to get tenders, and British local authorities, dogged by the housing shortage, were, however, unperturbed by this research, and were not moved to do any research into safety themselves. The visits of representatives from major building firms and local authorities to the Continent were intensified and many an architect could not help but be impressed.

Accordingly, in 1962, the Housing Committee of the LCC were advised by their experts to start negotiations with Taylor Woodrow Anglian and Larsen Nielsen with a view to building system-built blocks of flats. "The Committee" ran the report of the Architect, Hugh Bennett, to the council, "will appreciate that any contractual agreement which may eventuate from the more detailed consideration of the use of the Larsen and Nielsen system would have to be with the new company and would involve suspension of standing orders requiring the invitation of new tenders". In other words the business of putting jobs out to tender would have to stop. Taylor Woodrow were not prepared to start a new industrialised building system unless they were guaranteed 1,000 dwellings!

The craze for system-built methods caught on everywhere, not always with the most successful results. A sensational design for barracks at Aldershot, for instance, included a concrete frame built with precast concrete panels. On 21 July 1963, the officers' mess collapsed, fortunately before it was finished. It was decided to demolish the other three buildings, but one of them collapsed before the demolition work got under way. A Government White Paper, published in December 1963, found that "the collapses started by failure at a joint. This was followed by general collapse because there was instability due to insufficient provision by the designer for lateral stiffness".

The White Paper also warned:

*"Where a system of building using prefabricated structural components is extended by use in a new building type, a fundamental re-examination of the system design is necessary. This must include a reconsideration of all design assumptions and, if necessary, a recalculation of the structural design from first principles".*

First principles, however, were not applied with noticeable rigour by the local authorities, who, following the LCC lead, started to adopt the Larsen Nielsen system for high-rise flats.

By the time Mr North had convinced the West Ham Borough Council to build Larsen Nielsen high flats, Taylor Woodrow had grown hugely confident. The usual practise in such contracts is for the council to employ its own independent consulting engineers. Taylor Woodrow insisted that a clause in the contract should state that the consulting engineers for Ronan Point and the neighbouring blocks should be Phillips Consultants, which, by coincidence, is entirely owned by Taylor Woodrow.

The outer walls of the Ronan Point flat (and of most Larsen Nielsen-style blocks in this country), which bear most of the weight of the 22-storeys, are six inches thick, (compared with the 18" recommended by the Kaiser Report). The four-ton floor

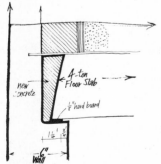

slabs are fitted into slots into the walls. One and a quarter inches of the slab rests on the wall on each side, and the gap in the rest of the slot is filled with concrete on the site, thus making a "joint". There is no other tie between the wall and the floor, so that if the wall is pushed out by a quarter of an inch or more, the new concrete almost certainly splits from the prefabricated concrete and the floor falls in. The fall will almost certainly release the floors above and below from the grip of the wall panels, leading to what is known in the trade as

"progressive collapse".

"Progressive collapse" is a feature of the technological revolution. During the last war, for instance, there were many examples of bombs dropping into the centre of buildings and exploding. In almost every such case the damage was contained in the floor of the explosion and occasionally above it. "Progressive collapse" was not heard of.

"We feel" said Mr Bernard Clark at the inquiry "that there are many things which can disturb a building of this sort, which is virtually relying on gravity entirely. We do not build this way and, frankly, we have given up building in this way in the last fifty years. It is a retrograde step."

What 'things' could disturb the building? Wind, for a start. The wind pressure against which Ronan Point is insured for stability is 24 pounds per square foot - considerably less, for instance, than the force of the winds which recently blew down several walls in Glasgow (the buildings in Glasgow - many of which were built 100 years ago - could, for the most part, stand the strain of a wall being 'sucked out' by wind, while Ronan Point would instantly

have collapsed). Again, subsidence of merely an inch at the base of the building, would bring it tumbling down. Or fire. One of the findings of the Clark Report was that the building did not meet the standard fire regulations, which stipulate that each floor must be insulated from fire from the floor below or above.

Unlike Ronan Point, most industrialised buildings are equipped with steel joints, in the form of interlocking loops, between wall and floor panels or a continuous steel reinforcement down the load-bearing walls. All the systems differ as to the strength of these joints. And that is why the Ministry of Housing have had to specify in a letter to local authorities how strong they think the joints should be in order to avoid collapse.

All buildings, the Ministry insist, which do not have these minimum-standard joints should have the gas turned off. These will include the forty or so tower blocks, housing approximately 3,000 people, built under the Larsen Nielsen system in almost exactly the same way as Ronan Point. Only Wolverhampton turned down the Larsen Nielsen system as not coming up to the basic building safety regulations. Other councils leapt onto the bandwaggon. In the first nine months of 1967, 760 dwellings were completed (almost all in high flats) under the Larsen Nielsen system, which is more than the total completions for 1966. *(Housing Statistics :* January, 1968). Had it not been for the Ronan Point disaster, as a result of which, perhaps not surprisingly, all work on these buildings has been stopped and some councils have actually broken off their contracts, 1968 would have been another record year.

Despite the denials of Mr North at the inquiry, there seems little doubt that the chief advantage of the Larsen-Nielsen system is in cost. Fixing steel joints into the concrete panels is more expensive, clearly, than not doing so.

The extra cost of fixing in proper steel joints, or of building a load-bearing frame (as in all major office buildings) would not be much more than 5% of the total, but that 5% is crucial in the competitive world of building tenders.

Nevertheless, shareholders in construction firms can take heart. Even if the worst comes to the worst and the tribunal decides to recommend the destruction of Ronan Point, the neighbouring blocks and similar blocks throughout the country; even if the tribunal decides that other blocks should be equipped (at enormous cost and with the temporary evacuation of all inhabitants) with effective joints between walls and floors, there will be no serious damage done to the profitability of the big building firms. A recent report says that there are ten major construction firms involved in system-built buildings but "so far their shares have not shown any weakness that could be ascribed to new fears in the wake of Ronan Point". *(Construction News,* August 22).

The tenants of Ronan Point, and of Abraham Point next door, who unlike every other interested party, were not collectively represented at the public inquiry, are not reported to hold any major shareholding in any of the ten firms.

# PRIVATE EYE

No. 176
Friday
13 Sept. '68

1/6

# GOODBYE DOLLY !

## We must leave you out

# GRAND DEMONSTRATION
## SOUVENIR October 27th. PROGRAMME

Patron: The Rt. Hon. Ho Chi Minh V.C.

*All profits from this programme to be given to the Black Dwarf*

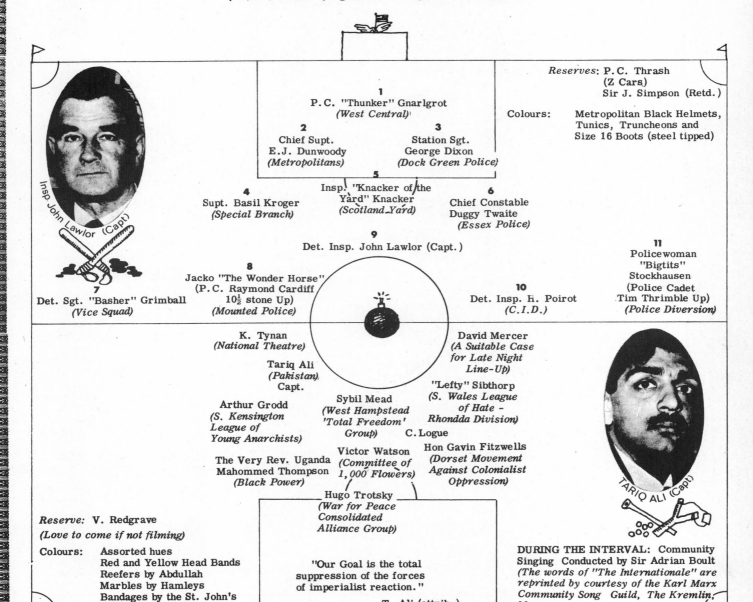

**1**
P.C. "Thunker" Gnarlgrot
*(West Central)*

**2**
Chief Supt.
E.J. Dunwoody
*(Metropolitans)*

**3**
Station Sgt.
George Dixon
*(Dock Green Police)*

**5**
Insp. "Knacker of the Yard" Knacker
*(Scotland Yard)*

**4**
Supt. Basil Kroger
*(Special Branch)*

**6**
Chief Constable
Duggy Twaite
*(Essex Police)*

**9**
Det. Insp. John Lawlor (Capt.)

**8**
Jacko "The Wonder Horse"
(P.C. Raymond Cardiff
10½ stone Up)
*(Mounted Police)*

**10**
Det. Insp. H. Poirot
*(C.I.D.)*

**7**
Det. Sgt. "Basher" Grimball
*(Vice Squad)*

Insp John Lawlor (Capt)

**11**
Policewoman
"Bigtits"
Stockhausen
(Police Cadet
Tim Thrimble Up)
*(Police Diversion)*

*Reserves*: P.C. Thrash
(Z Cars)
Sir J. Simpson (Retd.)

Colours:   Metropolitan Black Helmets,
Tunics, Truncheons and
Size 16 Boots (steel tipped)

---

K. Tynan
*(National Theatre)*

David Mercer
*(A Suitable Case
for Late Night
Line-Up)*

Tariq Ali
*(Pakistan)*
Capt.

"Lefty" Sibthorp
*(S. Wales League
of Hate -
Rhondda Division)*

Arthur Grodd
*(S. Kensington
League of
Young Anarchists)*

Sybil Mead
*(West Hampstead
'Total Freedom'
Group)*

C. Logue

The Very Rev. Uganda
Mahommed Thompson
*(Black Power)*

Victor Watson
*(Committee of
1,000 Flowers)*

Hon Gavin Fitzwells
*(Dorset Movement
Against Colonialist
Oppression)*

Hugo Trotsky
*(War for Peace
Consolidated
Alliance Group)*

TARIQ ALI (Capt)

Reserve: V. Redgrave
*(Love to come if not filming)*

Colours:   Assorted hues
Red and Yellow Head Bands
Reefers by Abdullah
Marbles by Hamleys
Bandages by the St. John's
Ambulance Brigade.

"Our Goal is the total
suppression of the forces
of imperialist reaction."

T. Ali (attrib.)

DURING THE INTERVAL: Community
Singing Conducted by Sir Adrian Boult
*(The words of "The Internationale" are
reprinted by courtesy of the Karl Marx
Community Song Guild, The Kremlin,
Moscow).*

---

REFEREE:   Rt. Hon. J. Callaghan (Labour)

Linesmen:
Sir W. Haley-Mogg (Editor 'The Times')
Raymond Baxter (BBC Outside Punch-Ups)

Previous March: Grosvenor Square
March 17.   Result : Knacker 117
                    Ali         1

## 'Man on the march' writes:

This should be one of the most exciting demonstrations ever staged in Central London. Thousands of fans have pledged their support from all over the world and, weather permitting, we hope they'll all be there on the day and make it a really tough, but clean, spirited battle. The Fuzz have turned out one of the best teams since Sidney Street (and how we remember Sidney) when Peter the Painter went down to Winston Churchill after extra time. The other side may be a bit dodgy on the team-work but youth is in their favour. Ali has the experience. Will he have the luck? To my mind, it's anybody's game. So let me sign off by wishing all concerned "Good luck!" and "Good Fighting!"

M.o.t.M.

# ARCHBISHOP RAPS TURD

The Archbishop of Canterbury, Dr Ramsay Macdonald, 176, today lashed out at Mr Spiggy Topes, leader of The Turds, a popular singing group.

The attack followed the announcement that Miss Dora Slag, of 28 Reefer Mansions, Potney, a close friend of Mr Topes was about to give birth to a little bastard.

## Sensation

Said Topes: "Crikey! I could have sworn I was impotent. But marriage is not for us. We believe that life is to be lived and that, and getting married is for the oldies if you take my meaning."

Speaking from the Irish-style Castle home of Turds' Friend, Lord Julian von Glasgow, Miss Slag commented: "It's great to feel a little Turd inside you. Babies are no trouble for me. I just dump them on my mum so she does all the draggy bit with the nappies and that."

## Come all ye faithful

Speaking from his pulpit, Dr Ramsay Macdonald said it was a sad thing that young Turds were turning their back on Holy Wedlock and even sadder that Archbishops had nothing better to do than to worry about the affairs of adolescent layabouts, e.g. Topes and Slag.

Asked to comment on the Archbishop's statement, Topes explained: "I appreciate His Worship's opinions which he is quite entitled to but frankly, what does an oldie like him know about life? Come off it, Ramsbotham! Stick to your prayer book and leave the cats to groove it while the sun shines, because that's what life's about, to my mind."

## Droopy

A controversial record sleeve showing Spiggy Topes and another girl friend, Miss Okay Yoni (or 'Asian Flo', as she is known in underground circles) has been turned down by many musical publications.

The sleeve shows Topes entirely nude, clasping the hand of Miss Yoni and peering through his bi-focals at her pendulous breasts.

## Tit for Tat

The record features music from Spiggy's first motion picture which shows himself and Miss Yoni sitting in silence for an hour and a half.

A spokesman for *Nipple*, the Turds-controlled company said: "I cannot understand what all the fuzz is about. Here are two young people as God made them (God help them) following the dictates of their conscience. Which is more obscene - to show Spiggy's naked form or for the Archbishop of Canterbury to bomb Vietnam, I ask you?"

In a TV discussion with Gypsy Dave Frost, Spiggy crossed swords with Mrs Mary Pentagon over whether it was right for such a woman to get married and bring up her children in the blaze of publicity with which she has surrounded herself.

Mrs Pentagon defended her views (many of Skegness) and told Spiggy it was high time he grew up.

Mr Topes then produced his record sleeve, remarking "If that's not grown up, you old slag, then I don't know what is."

The discussion was later described by Mr Peter Blackout, the eminent critic, as "perhaps the most penetrating in the history of the world."

TAKE YOUR KNICKERS OFF, BABY, I WISH TO FOLLOW THE DICTATES OF MY CONSCIENCE

# U.S. ACCLAIM FOR 'DEMO'68'

American critics were in raptures this week over the recent London production 'DEMO '68', starring Tariq Ali and Commander John Lawandorder.

In the Washington Post, Karl J. Pipesucker, doyen of American critics, acclaimed the production as : "A beautifully controlled and classic statement about the world we live in. Britain may have lost her empire but (continued p. 94)." Author Mary McCarthy, who flew over especially to attend the occasion, raved "The British Demonstration has a quality of understatement and good humour which is quite unique. I was particularly struck by the Maoists and their exquisitely carved bean poles. I only wish that Norman* could have made it.

## ALI BE PRAISED

Charges that the tone of DEMO was anti-American are vigorously rebutted in the New York Times:

"In many ways this latest British offering was not concerned with Vietnam or America's world role at all. It is really a critique on a much deeper level of many profounder issues which concern us all today - such as 'What to do on a Sunday afternoon in a big city when the art galleries are closed."

LOOK BACK IN TWELVE YEARS TIME AND SEE HOW BAD IT WAS ALL ALONG

Impresario David A. Merrick ('the man who put the A. Merrick in A. Merricka') has bought the rights, and is planning to take DEMO to Broadway in the spring, complete with London Bobbies and its cast of 30,000 screaming hippies**. "I see it as a sort of British Hair on a shoe string" revealed the notoriously tight-fisted entrepreneur.

*Believed to be a reference to Norman 'Second Class' Mailer, Chairman of the Left-Wing Thinkers For Nixon Committee of One.

** T. Ali comments: "Come off it, Mr Merrick. I counted at least a million pounds after my many recent appearances on television - woops, I mean demonstrators on my recent march."

# PRIVATE EYE

No. 179
Friday
25 Oct. '68

1/6

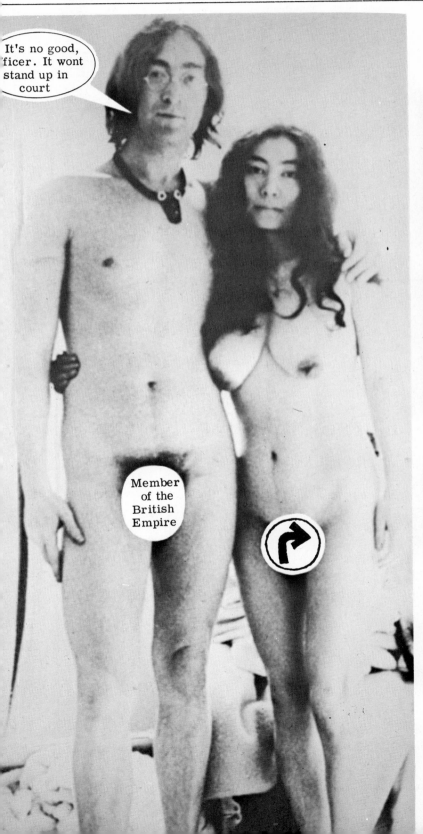

# BEATLE HELD

# SENSATION

★

## SPECIAL
## REVOLTING ISSUE

**All human filth is here**

*( including Robert Maxwell )*

# MRS. WILSON'S DIARY

*W*ell, well, what a turnabout! Fancy nice Mrs Kennedy marrying the Greek Shipping Magnate, Mr Aristophanes Molasses. As the Inspector remarked, she can't need the money. So it must be love. And how considerate of His Holiness the Pope to waive such mundane considerations as the Church's doctrine on divorce in the face of such appalling need. Though my heart goes out to poor Lord Harlech in his moment of rebuttal. But, as a man of the world like himself must well know, there are many lovely fish in the sea, and he is still young.

We have been so taken up with Harold's Rhodesian Sell-out that I have had little time for such sentimental musings. Ever since nice Mr Goodman, our family solicitor, went out to Rhodesia disguised as a steeple-chase jockey enquiring about blood-stock, Harold's Scrambler to Salisbury has been ringing like a burglar alarm morning, noon and night. After all the preparations, and Harold's dramatic midnight dash to the Rock of Gibraltar lying in the nose of an R.A.F. Comet, I was most disappointed to hear on the wireless that a deadlock had been reached and that the door had been slammed to a tiny crack.

Imagine my surprise then, when Harold arrived on the doorstep, carrying a stick of British All the Way Through Gibraltar Rock for Giles and a pair of El Beatle Castanets, with his face wreathed in smiles. "Ah, Gladys" he chuckled, pressing into my hand a gift-wrapped bottle of Winxarniz de la Frontera, "it's all sewn up. Smithy has agreed to settle out of court. There are just one or two formalities to be gone through in order to satisfy the World Press hunger for sensationalism. Do not be alarmed when you read that Smithy is utterly opposed to our terms: it is all a skilful device dreamed up by Arnie to ease the moral agony of the so-called idealists in our respective midsts. Smithy will have to be very stupid indeed to muck it up now."

"Now then" he remarked as he took his jacket off preparatory to settling down to his Kipper'n Chippolata Flavoured Meat Fingers tea, "back to Home Affairs." At this there was a tiny knock on the door, and the Inspector ushered into the kitchen Mr Crossman and a figure I did not at first recognise, wearing a stand-up Jimmy Hendrix Experience-style wig and gold-rimmed dark glasses. "Good day, Wedgie"

cried Harold. "welcome to the think tank. Perhaps you would care for a cup of Maza-wattee Pekoe Tips." "Thanks Man" replied Mr Benn in a curious accent, making a lazy snapping gesture with his fingers, and accepting a Coronation Mug of the steaming orange brew. "The Tragedy of the Attlee Government" began Mr Crossman, reading from an old copy of *Encounter* Magazine, "was that it ran out of ideas, losing the ideological momentum that could have carried it through to victory in 1951 ...." "That's enough of that, Owl-eyes" exclaimed Harold sharply, "no-one can ever accuse me of running out of ideas. Listen to this lot. "Cabinet Reshuffle. Wilson Acts." At this Mr Benn began to mutter strange words under his breath, including "Participation", "Technological Democracy" and "Votes at Eighteen". "Aha" continued Harold, "I'd forgotten our scheme to bring the levers of power into the reach of the Nation's Youth. We read a lot in the papers about long-haired weirdies - no disrespect intended, Mr Benn - but, you know, as I go about the country, I find a new spirit of idealism and service amongst our young people. As I looked round the Labour Party Conference, I observed the young smiling faces, the bright clothed disciples of progress and change ..." "I think you did not" interrupted Mr Cross-man, "unless you are referring to the Interflora Flower Power Demonstration in the Winter Garden Ballroom." "Well, well, what do you suggest, Professor?" snapped Harold, "I am always ready, as you know, to listen to ideas from my Cabinet Colleagues, as long as you do not expect me to act on them. Was it not I who conferred the Membership of the British Empire on that singing group some years ago? Did I not personally enter their evil-smelling club in the backstreets of some Northern city in order to demonstrate my solidarity with long-haired yobboes? Don't tell me I don't appeal to the youth."

"I am proposing a Ministry of New Ideas" replied Mr Crossman calmly, "a reservoir of thought to dynamise the frustration of young people with a renewed sense of political commitment and participation". "Excellent, excellent, baby doll" Harold cried, knocking his pipe out on Mr Benn's head, "and who better to fill the post than sexy, swinging, pace-setting, up-to-the-minute Judith Hart, 48, who might be thinking of resigning when her tiny mind eventually grasps the smaller print on my new Rhodesia Contract." "What's that, what's that?" asked Mr Crossman, looking worried. "Nothing, nothing, Swotty-chops. Pay-Mistress General she shall be, endowed with an all-round portfolio to appeal to young men. And Musical Chairs for the rest. I have spoken. Begone."

My life! I never such a wonderful book read already

# PRIVATE EYE

No. 180
Friday
Nov. '68

1/6

You are Aristotle Onassis and I claim my five million pounds

# Gnome

**T**he unseemly panic which has taken control of many of my employees working in the 24-storey Gnome House is yet another example of the irresponsibility of many of those who dominate the so-called mass media.

What happened may be stated briefly: on August 14, the 59-strong typing pool working on the 23rd storey of Gnome House were surprised to find themselves catapulted out of the window into the ornamental swimming pool at ground level as a result of an explosion in the adjacent boardroom.

A subsequent one-man enquiry chaired by my good self, discovered that the explosion had been caused by a crude grenade-like device concealed under my chair in an attache case. (It was subsequent to this enquiry that several members of the board "retired" for reasons of health).

It is now being suggested that certain structural alterations should be made to Gnome House in order to obviate the collapse of the building.

Needless to say, such suggestions are being put about by men utterly ignorant of even the basic elements of building technique, many of them masquerading as architects, structural engineers and other high-sounding titles.

### TYNAN POINT

Before my staff give credence to such manifest charlatans, let me make the following facts clear:

1) The strong swaying sensation which is felt at certain times of the day is due to freak atmospheric conditions and is quite common in high buildings.

2) The 5% list to starboard, clearly visible in the building from ground level, is part of the architect's design. Remember that the tower of Pisa has stood for over 2,000 years.

3) The lift will be in operation again next month.

4) The reason why I have moved my own office to a bungalow on an adjacent site is in order to allow more working space for my hard-pressed colleagues.

Let us hope that these assurances will deter professional entertainers and other meddling sensation-seekers from casting further aspersions on my business methods.

Should this not prove to be the case, recourse may well have to be made, albeit with the greatest possible reluctance, to the supreme arbiters of justice and truth. I refer, of course, to Messrs. Sue, Grabbit and Runne, Purveyors of Writs to Members of the Royal Family since 1682.

E. Strobes
pp Lord Gnome
The Shed
The Bomb Site
W.1.

# FOOTNOTES

## ULSTER
## UP WITH THE CLARK

The small majority for Prime Minister Captain Terence O'Neill at the meeting of Ulster Unionist Associations on March 7, was not as important as the individual votes of the seven Grand Masters of the Orange Lodge, which will never be disclosed, but O'Neill's only hope of remaining as Prime Minister now depends on the loyalty of his main supporter, Harold Wilson.

Wilson still insists that O'Neill must stay, that there must be continued movement towards civil rights and that there must be no mass repression of the civil movement. James Callaghan, however, who is responsible in the Cabinet for Northern Ireland affairs, does not agree. He is quite prepared to ditch O'Neill and clamp down on the civil rights movement. The split between Wilson and Callaghan in the Cabinet has opened wide, with the Cabinet divided roughly evenly.

If Wilson loses, as it now appears he may do, the best possible successor to the Ulster Premiership is Major James Chichester-Clark , MP for South Derry, O'Neill's cousin and brother of Robert Chichester-Clark , Westminster MP for Londonderry. Major Chichester-Clark is one of the few members of the present Ulster Cabinet who has not been viciously attacked by the Paisleyite newspaper, the *Protestant Telegraph*. Although he has stayed "loyal" to O'Neill in the present crisis, he has publicly declared himself willing to serve under any other democratically-elected leader, and his praise for the Prime Minister personally has been notable for its absence.

During the People's Democracy march last January from Belfast to Londonderry, Chichester-Clark was visited by Major Ronald Bunting, Paisley's chief cohort, and part-organiser of the harrassment of the PD march. Chichester-Clark duly appeared with Bunting at the march the following day, and personally appealed to the Home Secretary, Captain Long, to ban the march.

Chichester-Clark was elected for South Derry in the election with a 3,000 majority over his only opponent, a Peoples Democracy candidate. The Major was not opposed by a Paisleyite "Protestant Unionist", and, if he had been, he might well have lost his seat. At least three Paisleyites in South Derry had been prepared to stand if called to do so, but, for some reason, the Paisleyite high command called them off, and the Paisleyites in the division were seen working (and, no doubt, voting) for Major Chichester-Clark .

# THE REAL NIXON

*What is the new American President really like? What are his aims? Where does he stand on the great issues of the day?*

## Robert McKenzie talks to the President Elect

McKenzie: Mr President, sir. I think when we last met it was clear to me albeit in a vague way, that you represent in many ways the Mid-Western small town lawyer made good and yet . . .

Nixon: I . . .

McKenzie: your astonishing fall from grace in 1960 seemed to mark the end of your career and here I am thinking of what one particularly charismatic psephologist at Berkeley . . .

Nixon: Er . . .

McKenzie: said to me apropos of the phenomenon of Black Power and I wonder whether you would agree with this that, Mr President, in many ways what we are witnessing in America today is

Nixon: My . . .

McKenzie: a breakdown of traditional political loyalties. As Karl E. Meyer once put it to me (Cont. p. 94)

# POWER TO THE CAMPUSES

*by HugoFirstI'mnotgoingtogethitoverthe headwithoneofthembatons-Smythe , Reader in Sociology, University of New Ideas, Grimsby. Edited & annotated by our staff.*

1. Er the first thing that confronts the revolutionary working within the framework of a bourgeois university is the essentially apolitical milieu of the majority of non-revolution-orientated students.[1]

2. This, therefore, however, thus er necessitates the necessity of by-passing traditional bourgeois gradualist methods of introducing radical reforms.[2]

3. Um fourthly, it is inevitable that revisionist elements will attempt to smother in a sea of bureaucratic compromises the need for revolutionary action.[3]

4. Bourgeois forces who attempt to suppress the march of events by pseudo-reformist dialectic and revisionist NUS type negotiations will have to be by-passed if necessary by non-peaceful methods.[4]

---

[1] *Most students couldn't give a bugger.*

[2] *We're on our own.*

[3] *We want a punch-up*

[4] *Anyone who disagrees with us will get beaten up.*

Reprinted from *THE BLACK DEATH*, or a guide on how not to write English.

*"You are familiar with the expression 'Export or die' Handleberry?"*

# PRIVATE EYE

No. 181
Friday
22 Nov. '68

*NIXON IN BY CLOSE SHAVE!*

1/6

# COLOUR SECTION

**R**eported conversation between Mr John Braine, novelist, and Dr Donald Soper, Methodist peer, after a recent broadcast, following Mr Braine's visit to America. After the broadcast, Lord Soper asked Mr Braine how he liked America, to which Mr Braine answered with a panegyric lasting several minutes to the effect that everything in America was glorious and wonderful and that it was by a long way the most exhilarating place in the world.

"It's all right, I suppose" mused Soper, "if you're not black".

"You silly bugger, I'm not black" replied Braine, to the point as always.

---

**T**he producers of the Radio weekly programme *Any Questions* recently invited Enoch Powell to take part, and thought up the clever idea of asking Tariq Ali as well. Cautious as ever, they wrote to Powell asking if he would consent to come on the programme with Ali. Powell replied that not only would he refuse to do so, but considered himself insulted to be invited on the same programme as "a rabble rouser."

**Accordingly,** in the best tradition of British broadcasting, Ali was not invited.

---

**T**he unfortunate Cyril Lord has always been sensitive to press criticism.

Some time back it was reported in the local Northern Ireland paper that he had been charged with a traffic offence but that the Police had offered no evidence.

Incensed at what he took to be a libellous and damaging attack, Lord rang the Editor of the paper demanding an apology in heavy black type to be printed on the front page.

The Editor however was not prepared to do this. Instead, he sought for some excuse to get his own back on Lord for trying to intimidate him in this way.

The opportunity came when Lord was invited to dig the first turf in the excavation for a new factory site.

The paper's banner headline above their coverage of the ceremony was as follows:

CYRIL LORD TURNS SOD

## TV

# All my own work shocks millions

*by George 'Thoroughly Modern' Melly*

**M**illions of viewers "turned off" last night when the BBC showed the controversial film *All My Own Work* by Tony Palmerlotofsensationalfilmclipsoffonthepublicandtryand pretenditssomethingsignificant.

The film included shots of The Turds and similar singing groups interspersed with film of Vietnam, Belsen, the Spanish Inquisition, the Massacre of the Innocents and other 20th Century atrocities.

"Palmer", who writes reviews of pop records in the *Observer*, an everyday story in the life of a lot of clapped-out old pseuds, came into the film world by accident when it was discovered that all other producers had left the BBC and someone had to make the programmes.

Speaking of "Work" Palmer says: "Don't ask me what it's about, man. It has no message in the conventional sense. Basically, the film is about the fact that we live in a violent holocaust with people being shot and that. And no-one to my mind can express outrage as frankly and that as The Turds and their chums by their own frank indictment basically.

"I mean, a man is shot dead in the street and that. I feel deeply about the horror. But only The Turds can put it in words by taking drugs and going to bed with women. A monk setting fire to himself is a horrible thing and a singer like Jimmy Tampax can get this over by making obscene gestures with his guitar. Are you reading me?

Dear Sir,

How much longer have I got to go on reading this drivel. If this be satire, then give me William Davis and The World at One any day of the week.

Yours
DISGUSTED

"No, but seriously, the film is about nothing more than the first days in the life of a newt when he opens his eyes and falls in love for the first time. That's funny. There's an ambulance coming up the drive. It's not for you by any chance, is it?"

FACT Mr "Palmer" 's film has been described in the *Observer* as "a disturbing montage that explodes the pop myth and paves the way to positive thinking". The *Sunday Times* comments 'It is a searing allegory ..... an intensely personal comment on the unique phenomena of war and peace."

# MRS. WILSON'S DIARY

Lo, Winter comes, and dark'ning clouds
  O'ershadow field and fell
A chill and icy fog now shrouds
  The bosky moss-grown dell
And tiny mites creep out like snails
  Unwillingly to school
Through blinding snow and howling gales
  Through frost and darkness cruel
So too do we, poor mortals drear
  Approach the solstice gloom
We grope about in palsied fear
  Dreading the crack of doom
Give us, O Lord, Thy radar screen
  To guide us through the night
Illuminate the murky scene
  Until we see the light. Amen.

**S**ometimes I wonder whether it is all worth while. Harold's health is showing signs of wear and tear, and his recourse to the sparkling Lucozade - a free perk, as he points out, from a grateful people - is growing more and more frequent. The other evening I was just darning his Draftprufe Long Johns with some beige wool left over from making a sweater for Giles when the door suddenly flew open and Harold stood swaying in the doorway, wearing a crepe paper kepi - from which I deduced he must have found the crackers I had hidden away under the stairs - and making expansive gestures. "I am, Gladys," he remarked "weary of this world. The people are ungrateful. I have been in office now for four years. Will there never be an end? Here I am, slaving over the dispatch boxes twenty four hours a day, night after night, when I could be lying on my back in a public house, a blonde lady at my side." So saying, he whirled cumbersomely round the room, knocking over various pieces of furniture, and came to rest beneath the portrait of Mr Disraeli. "But" he sobbed from a recumbent position, "who can fill my shoes? Callaghan? Jenkins? Peart?" With this be became convulsed with desperate laughter, and threshed about on the Cyril Lord wall-to-wall for some moments. "The very idea is ridiculous. No, I must soldier on." He rose unsteadily to his feet and stood in the "Attention" position. "Without me, the Movement would fall apart. After me, the deluge. But today the nose to the grindstone." With this he wheeled about and retired into his den with a crash.

I fear his somewhat maudlin mood has been occasioned to a great extent by the recent financial crisis. It all began when

r Jenkins popped in one afternoon for a cup
Mazawattee Elephant Bag Tips and a
llophane-wrapped Kunzle Cake. He was
st undressing, as he put it, this latter
licacy, when Mr Kaufmann, bald and true,
the Inspector calls him, came in with the
vening paper and announced that there was
nasty run on the franc. "What did I tell
u?" cried Harold, throwing down the TV
mes, "he had it coming to him. Long-
nk is on the run. This is what comes of
rring the door to us for so long. Kauf-
ann, take a letter. Anonymous. 'To: Old
nokey, Paris, France. Now who must set
s house in order? Ha ha ha' - and put that
capitals, Kaufmann - 'do not say I did not
rn you. Your days are numbered,
hnozzlechops. Signed, A Friend.' And
ve it delivered by Soames in person
thin the hour." "One moment, Kaufmann",
erposed the suave Chancellor, "if I may
y so, Prime Minister, we ought not to
low our quite understandable *revanchiste*
ntiments to override our better judgement.
the franc catches a cold" - and he spread
s hands expressively - "can Sterling be far
hind? If I may suggest it, P.M., the
atter might be best left in my hands. I
part for Bonn, let me see, in a matter of
nutes. These things are best thrashed out
hind closed doors in the calm of the con-
rence room." And before Harold could ob-
t, he had gulped down his Mazawattee, fin-
r delicately poised as ever, and popping his
nzle Cake into his briefcase, bowed his way
t of the lounge and into the waiting limousine.

The following evening we were just settling
wn to watch the Royal Variety Performance
onfess I cannot resist Val Doonican - when
telephone tinkled, and an unfamiliar voice
ormed us that a Mr Junkin was calling us
m London Airport. Would we pay for the
ll? A moment later, the Chancellor came
the line to say that he had just hopped back
keep Harold in the picture. He was tem-
rarily out of currency, and could Harold
d the Duty Dispatch Rider to go and collect
n. Harold seemed somewhat annoyed by
s interruption of our viewing, but luckily
Doonican had completed his medley, in-
ding a delightful rendition of "The Snow-
ops On My Mother's Grave" and we were
Manuel y Doris, the flamenco and tra-
ze artistes, when Mr Jenkins blew in,
dswept and frozen, to give his report.
h, Jenkins," Harold exclaimed, "just wait

one moment if you would be so kind. Doris
is just attempting an amazing Pasadoble at a
height of a hundred and fifty feet above the
ground to the accompaniment of Senor
Manuel's high-pitched Iberian lament."

Mr Jenkins watched without enthusiasm as
the Andalusian Queen of the Tight Rope performed her sinuous dance before falling with
a prolonged "Ole" into the net below. "Now
Jenkins," Harold resumed, "what is the news
from Bonn? I take it that the French will
adjust their parity before leaving the conference rooms?" "Alas, no" rejoined Mr
Jenkins, gratefully sipping my proffered mug
of Glentweedie Barley Broth - The Sealed
Scotch Goodness That Comes To Life As You
Pour On Hot Water - "the consensus view at
present is that the Germans must be persuaded to revalue the Mark. But I fear that
Herr Strauss is a man of iron. My impression is that he will not agree to any such
scheme." "What, what?" cried Harold,
switching off the television and leaping from
his chair, "you cannot be serious. We did
not fight in two world wars to lick the
tyrant's jackboot now. Leave this to me,
Jenkins. I think a little diplomacy is called
for." "But Prime Minister ..." quavered
the sensitive Chancellor. "But nothing,
Jenkins," riposted Harold, "Kaufmann, get
on to the German Embassy and tell Herr
Alpenhorn or whatever his name is that we
command his presence within the hour. And
get hold of Stewart. Tell him to get out of
bed, smarten himself up and come round here
in ten minutes. Now you will see, Jenkins,
just how international incidents occur. There
will be no pussyfooting and mincing about of
the kind you have just been indulging in in
Bonn, of that I can assure you. The chips
are down. Let the Boche look to his laurels."

It was some moments before Mr Kaufmann
reappeared to inform us that the German
Ambassador was at the pictures, but that he
had been contacted and would try and look in
on the way home, if it wasn't too late. "Right"
exploded Harold, "that does it. Kaufmann,
get hold of a ladder, and bicycle down to the
All-Nite Fooderama at Notting Hill Gate. I
want a four-pound bag of McDougall's Sifted
Featherlite Self-Raising Flour and let us say
two pounds of well-ripened Guernsey Tomatoes. I have plans for Herr Alpenhorn."
"I do beg of you, Prime Minister, soothed
Mr Jenkins as Harold's personal Mercury
sped on his winged way, "to reflect a moment.
Delicate negotiations are underway. With the
whole stability of world currency poised in the
balance, the slightest *gaucherie*..."
"Listen to me, Moneybags" spat Harold,
pouring out a generous balloon of Wincarnis
and lighting a Pompadour Panatella Whiff,
"we have had enough of your Frog chatter.
Kindly be silent from now on or your political
prospects may be severely blighted." At
this, Mr Jenkins became red in the face, and
muttering "Very well, very well," began to
pace nervously up and down in Harold's den.

The clock on the mantlepiece in the lounge
had just struck half past one, and I had taken
the liberty of changing into my curlers and a
woolly dressing gown, when voices raised in
song were audible in the street outside.
"Aha" mused Harold, a curious smile lin-
gering about his lips, "wake up, Stewart.
Here, if I am not mistaken, is our client."
In a moment, Mr Jenkins, Mr Stewart and

Harold had set themselves down at a special
board-room style table in the den rigged up
by Harold to face the door. A life-size portrait of Sir Winston had been erected behind
them under a special spotlight and a record
of Miss Gracie Fields singing "We'll meet
again" was set turning on Harold's portable
gramophone. Seconds later, the door opened,
and the immaculately dressed German diplomat, wearing a satin-lined opera cloak and
twirling a silver-knobbed cane stepped into
the room, accompanied by several members
of his staff. "Ah, Herr Prime Minister," he
smiled, clicking his heels smartly together in
military fashion and allowing the monocle to
fall from his eye, "Vot, I vonder, iss ziss
bagg von rarzer dissgussting Tomaten und
ein Zack von Flour doink percht zo ztrangely
over ze Toor? Berhepps it vudd pe edd-
viseable zat I dake zem town, so, to avoid
ze Missheps."

With this, our immaculate Nato partner
reached up, and with a deft movement of his
cane, flicked Harold's rather unsophisticated
practical joke over towards the table, where
the flour bag immediately burst. It was some
time before the powdery cloud cleared to
reveal the three white inquisitors, still removing the tomatoes from their laps in a
dignified manner. "Now, Alpenhorn" Harold
began gamely, "as you are no doubt aware,
our two countries were recently engaged in
what might be termed hostilities. At the final
whistle, and correct me if I am wrong, it
was to us, and not to you, that the Goddess
of Victory vouchsafed her palm and laurel
wreath ..." "Ach so" rejoined Herr Alpenhorn, removing a speck of fluff from his
velvet-trimmed sleeve, "Zo poetical, ent,
ez you zay ... zo Vott?" "Now listen,
Jerry, and listen good," Harold continued,
unabashed. "Tell your masters in Bonn that
unless the Mark is revalued by twelve noon
tomorrow, both platoons of the Royal Pioneer
Corps currently engaged in stemming the tide
of Russian aggression on Luneberg Heath
will be withdrawn forthwith." There was
silence for a moment, and then Herr Alpenhorn gave a long theatrical laugh. "Ach, ze
Englisch Zenz of Humor. I zo luff it. Tell
uzz anuzzer vun, Mister Punch." I have
never seen Harold so angry. Overturning
the table with a single heave, he leapt towards the unruffled Teuton envoy, and would,
I think, have flung himself at his throat, had
not Mr Jenkins intervened, kneeling on
Harold's chest while little Mr Stewart showed
our guests to the door, remarking as he
did so that Harold was a man of many moods,
and that he hoped they would take it in good
part.

# THE DANGER TO BRITAIN

If one is British, one can only feel heartsick about the state of THE TIMES newspaper. To witness the decline of any great institution is always a melancholy affair. When the institution in question is one which once commanded respect and attention in all five continents of the world, the process must be doubly depressing.

In recent days, the performance of The Times has been such as to make anyone who is not determined to set his face against reality, deeply disturbed. Readers are alarmed, confused and sad. It should be shaming for British people, with our history, to contemplate such a steady record of failure and decay.

The first thing we must do is to look the danger in the face. The form it takes is financial and economic. This is however only the shape of the threat. A paper which allows its strength to be frittered away, will certainly face trouble. But the trouble may be, and in the end is bound to be, a matter not just of financial loss but of the personalities which lie behind it.

It is here that one is compelled to consider first the character and motives of The Times's proprietor, LORD THOMSON OF FLEET, a man who has never been at pains to conceal that his overriding ambition is to achieve the financial viability of his journals, regardless of editorial or political consideration. Such a figure must always attract the suspicion of those who put a value on matters of principle. However, even if it is by this standard, and this alone, that Lord Thomson wishes his achievement to be judged, then it has to be admitted that he has failed. Nothing has been more depressing over the past few years than to see loan after loan disappear in The Times's ever-mounting record of financial loss. Not only is it failing to pay its way year by year, but eventually there must come an end even to the extent to which it can call on reserves from elsewhere.

## Crisis of credibility

All this has been a major contributing factor to the slow ebb of credibility from The Times ever since the new administration took over. Continuing financial crisis can only be regarded, however, as a symptom - not as the root cause of the paper's deeper malaise. The record of the new regime in all fields began by arousing astonishment, which quickly turned to bewilderment and alarm and ultimately to deep despondency. Alarmist editorials and the giving of currency to scurrilous and ill-founded rumours, exemplified by the paper's discovery of a sinister 'plot' to take over the Government by a small group of discredited malcontents; a dilettante fascination with passing fashions and more ephemeral phenomena of the time; in particular, the slavish adulation by the paper's Music Critic of the debased mouthings of illiterate adolescents; the sad 'Evtushenko affair' in which the diary was made the mouthpiece of a tightly-knit group of politically-motivated propagandists; these have only been a few of the straws in the wind.

## Beware of the Mogg

Behind them all stands the figure of the Editor, Mr WILLIAM REES MOGG: no need to condemn him; scarcely now, any need to discuss him; his astonishing complacency at every stage condemns itself.

When he came to power, such a short time ago, the impression was one of youthful vigour, energy and healthy irreverence towards the outworn shibboleths and cobwebbed remedies of the past. It was only a matter of weeks, however, before it became apparent that the show of radicalism was little more than a superficial facade. The brandishing of hippy bells, the calls for the legalisation of marijuana, the romantic flirtation with the excesses of the student anarchists, all betrayed a rootless confusion of the shallow trappings of permissiveness with the substantial reality of progress, so typical of the middle-aged liberal. Few spectacles can have been more revealing of this sickness of our time than that of the Editor of The Times, in the company of a Christian Bishop and a former Home Secretary, flying by helicopter to a secret rendezvous with Mr MICHAEL JAGGER, the popular singer, to discuss the problems of drug-addiction at the behest of a television company.

Today, as he clings on discredited to the levers of power, tired, conservative, and disillusioned, his enthusiasm for student revolt has soured into the embittered disgruntlement of the reactionary, seeing plots and conspiracies on all sides, and spinning pipedreams and panaceas of coalition-government in the company of that other exhausted Vesuvius, Mr Cecil King.

## It is a moral collapse

What is to be done? It is no good pretending any longer that makeshift remedies will suffice. We are picnicing half-way up the Matterhorn. Our tents are pitched on thin ice. The sands of time are almost exhausted. Our metaphors are stale. There is only one solution left open. Mr ROBERT MAXWELL's generous offer of $2\frac{1}{2}$d. for the shares of The Times newspaper should be accepted forthwith. The alternatives are too abysmal to contemplate.

# PRIVATE EYE

No. 184
Friday
Jan. 69

1/6

**Schubert: A roaring poof.**

**Haydn: Victim of Race Prejudice.**

**Mozart: Transvestite.**

**Scarlatti: He killed 'for kicks'.**

**Beethoven: Black Magic held him in thrall.**

Did you know that Schubert wrote the Unfinished Symphony under the influence of Drugs?

That Bach was mad when he composed his Moonlight Sonata?

Handel jumped out of a window and tried to kill himself - and all over the price of a tankard of mulled claret.

Chopin suffered from apoplexy and still wrote 100 symphonies between attacks.

The Gnome Book of the World's Great Musicians published in 172 weekly instalments, tells you these facts and even more.

It tells you how Haydn hit Mozart on the head with a sausage and gave the infant prodigy the inspiration for the Christmas Oratorio.

*It tells you how Brahms beat his mother to within an inch of her life - and then sat down to play the clarinet.*

FREE with the first issue of the Gnome Book of the World's Great Musicians comes a full length portrait of the controversial flower-seller Mlle. Marie La Touche, who shocked musical Vienna in 1811 by dancing naked through the streets.

*The first issue tells you IN FULL the amazing story of Verdi and the goat - a story which has never been told before.*

You will be amazed when you read how Rimsky Korsakov cut off his thumbs and hurled them at Rachmaninov - all for the sake of a bet.

These stories will help you to a greater appreciation of the great masters' works.

And with each copy of the magazine comes an astonishing grand piano (normal price 600 gns.) of the type played by the world's greatest musicians.

And all for 13/11.

Watching over you as you read the Gnome Book of the World's Greatest Musicians are a team of expert advisers to the series.

They include

Sir Edward Elgar D.S.O.
Norrie Paramour E.M.I.
Prof. Hans Killer
Spiggy Topes

and many other famous names.

So Get Reading. For only 13/11 you can enter a magic world where the world's greatest musicians are waiting to serenade you.

# Understand the man and you'll understand his music.

# THE CLOGGIES

*An everyday saga in the life of Clog Dancing Folk*
*by BILL TIDY*

# FOOTNOTES

# LORD OF THE CARPETBAGGERS

"At all times of trouble Cyril is the epitome of the Rock of Gibraltar" writes Mrs Shirley Lord in her recent autobiography *Small Beer at Claridges* (35s Michael Joseph), 232 pages of name-dropping drivel, whose swift departure into limbo is believed to be not wholly unconnected with the fact that Mrs Lord and her husband Cyril are recuperating abroad, after the total collapse of Mr Lord's textile empire. Such a collapse is not predicted in *Small Beer at Claridges*, which describes Mr Lord as "a Napoleon among men" (p. 116).

The several thousand textile workers who will be unemployed as a result of this debacle can take comfort from the fact that Mr and Mrs Lord will not be joining them on the dole. Mr Lord still holds a large personal shareholding in his companies but it must be less than it was this time last year when he was still an active chairman.

As late as last January, Manchester stock brokers were still able to commend shares in the Lord companies as an excellent investment. Nor has the more recent collapse in Lord shares been accompanied by a similar drop in the value of Cyril Lord's various homes, which have included a mansion in Northern Ireland, a villa at Cap d'Ail in the South of France and an expansive country house in Bermuda. True, Mrs Shirley Lord has been dismissed from her job as Beauty Editor of *Harper's Bazaar* most of whose Beauty Pages have been put together during the last few months by her "assistant", who earns £11 a week. But, as she writes in her book, Mrs Lord's salary at *Harpers* was never really very important.

The Northern Ireland Government will not reveal how much taxpayers' money was spent on Government grants and inducements to Cyril Lord for his three Northern Irish concerns, now due to close. The percentage investment grant available to the employer is higher in Northern Ireland than anywhere else in the United Kingdom. About half the cost of all capital and other investment is met by the Government, and the factories are rented out at 1/6d to 2/9d a square foot (which is negligible). The Northern Ireland Government is also entitled, under its Industrial Development Act, to spend money on new firms in a whole host of other ways, which are "negotiable" with the company. According to a spokesman for the N.I. Ministry of Commerce: "We are prepared to give assistance towards critical operating expenses - transport, buying and moving new machinery, moving key workers and housing them even paying a flat rate per worker employed to help with the wages.

"The Cyril Lord projects were particularly attractive to us because of the number of workers they were going to employ."

In England, Wales and Scotland the Board of Trade Advisory Committee (BOTAC) has to recommend the provision of investment grants after a thorough examination of the firm's proposals. BOTAC, however, has no powers in Northern Ireland, where the proposals are "audited by Government accountants."

Shirley Lord describes the opening of Cyril Lord's big Donaghadee factory in 1961 in typically pungent prose:

"The Northern Ireland Prime Minister of the day Lord Brookeborough did the necessary, but even his erudite flow of opening speech was overshadowed by the performance of the Household Cavalry, flown over by Cyril to blow a fanfare after Lord B. cut the ribbon. No one can tell Cyril Lord how to make an opening ceremony pressworthy." (p. 172).

Closing ceremonies, somehow, are less pressworthy, especially when two of Cyril Lord's favourite guests in the South of France were Lord Thomson and Lord Beaverbrook, and when Mrs Lord is an ex-employee of The *Evening Standard*, the *Evening News*, and an acquaintance of Hugh Cudlipp, chairman of the International Publishing Corporation, and of John Junor, Editor of the *Sunday Express*.

Nor was Mrs Lord only a journalist. In 1965 the Northern Ireland Government invited her to sit on the Government commission for their first new town of Craigavon. "Mrs Lord," says a N.I. Government spokesman, "was there to put the woman's angle on housing design and so on. She was a fairly regular attender of meetings. She resigned on August 30 this year for personal reasons." And, oh yes, "she was paid an 'honorarium' of £500 a year."

The fantastic advertising campaigns for Cyril Lord Carpets (For Luxury you Can Afford, Buy Cyril Lord) were not always matched by consumers' experience. On Feb 7, 1965, for instance Mrs Jean Livingstone, of 93 Royston Hill, Glasgow, wrote to the Scottish *Sunday Mail* explaining that she was refusing to pay h.p. instalments on a Cyril Lord carpet which had changed from its original colour of "begonia red to dirty maroon" and was "turning browny-black". Cyril Lords sued Mrs Livingstone for the payment - unsuccessfully. They then sued the *Sunday Mail* for libel - again without success. In February this year the Consumer Council's magazine *Focus*, reported:

"On Mr Cyril Lord's own estimate, he has about a tenth of the whole British carpet market. Yet over one in four of the complaints about carpets received by the Consumer Council last year named this company".

Such facts of course were of no interest to the journalists to whom Cyril Lord owes his image as "one of the most spectacular figures of post-war enterprise" (*Daily Telegraph* 9.9.53), or "the wonder-boy of Lancashire" (*Daily Express* 30.8.53). "He has" declared the *Evening News* in August 1955 "a genuine affection for the Irish and will no doubt with his Midas touch continue to bring them a measure of prosperity".

But perhaps the most interesting of all Mr Lord's admirers during his halcyon years was Mr Harold Wilson. Wilson came into contact with Lord on the issue of Lancashire cotton during the middle fifties. Wilson, Barbara Castle and Anthony Greenwood, all of whom had Lancashire constituencies, co-operated closely with Cyril Lord. (An unlikely guest at one of Lord's week-end house-parties at Donaghadee was Mr Aneurin Bevan.) Harold Wilson wrote a "Plan for Cotton" in 1956, much of whose theory was borrowed from Cyril Lord. Lord thought it was wrong to "flood" Britain with cheap cotton goods from abroad, mainly from Japan and Portugal, thus providing the British public with cheap clothes at the expense of home producers like Cyril Lord. This "abrasive" protectionism admirably suited Wilson's book and his attacks on the "Japs" in *Tribune* were twice as savage as Lord's attacks on "Japanese competition" in the journals of the Federation of British Industry. Wilson and Lord set up a permanent working relationship which was only marginally dented in 1963 when Wilson declared that Labour would black all arms to South Africa. Lord, who had recently set up two of his Lancashire factories in South Africa, hurried to Wilson to protest, but Wilson assured him that non-military goods would not be affected, and Lord passed on the good message to the friends of South Africa in British boardrooms.

Harold Wilson was always greatly attracted by Lord's "dynamism" and his love for "technology". He saw the textile king as a harbinger of the New Britain who would be allowed full scope only under a Labour Government. The recent news is said to have caused "bitter disappointment" in Downing Street. The once-inevitable appearance of Lord Lord can now be discounted.

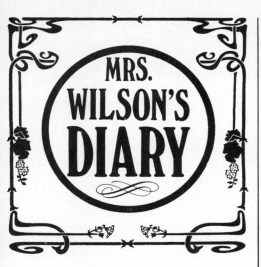

# MRS. WILSON'S DIARY

A New Year dawns!  The gurgling babe
   Is ushered in with bells,
The old man with his astrolabe
   Now hears his tolling knells.
So welcome, nineteen sixty-nine
   Come gales and blasts of Fate
We know that thanks to Providence Divine
   It cannot be as bad as nineteen sixty-eight.

My, oh my, what a year it has been! Looking back through the pages of my diary I can see little cause for cheer, comfort or self-congratulation.  The savage rape of Czechoslovakia by Mr Brezhnev and his Cossack Hordes, the tragic death of Senator Kennedy, and Harold's continuing lack of popularity with the electorate all speak of a year of heartburn and inner torment.  To cap it all, when we hoped to snatch a brief respite from the hurricane of office in our hideaway home on the outermost westward tip of the sea-girt Scillies, our hopes were dashed like a plastic tea-cup smashed among the grey breakers a few feet from our door.

My fears, alas, were aroused when Giles asked whether he could bring a friend for Yuletide as his parents were separated and living abroad.  I have always liked to extend the hand of hospitality to embrace the homeless at the Xmas Season, and I immediately concurred, though I knew in my heart of hearts that Harold would resent the presence of a stranger as we cracked walnuts and family jokes round the Yule-Log style Kosiglow Simulated Natural Hearth.  My heart really sank, however, as after a long and tiring journey culminating with three bumpy miles in Mr Ben Tintagel's briar-smoke-filled taxi, I turned the key in the lock of the front door at the bungalow to release a gush of water.  Mrs Lucie Smith, the old widow who now does for us, had apparently been laid up with her leg, and had failed to observe, after coming in to air the beds, that the ball-cock device in the cistern had become lodged in the upright position.  "Right, that's it", observed Harold, who was already disgruntled by the boat being over two hours late on account of a wild-cat strike by the quai-sweeper, old Mr Worsthorne, "it's back to Downing Street."

"Oh no Harold" I riposted, mustering what good grace I had left, "we will have it all sorted out in a jiffy".  My words, I fear,

were optimistic, but after three or four hours we had got the carpets out onto the lawn, piled the mattresses in front of the Kosiglow, and put the kettle on.  Towards midnight, it being Christmas Eve, Harold and the Inspector returned from the Scilly Cow, where they had been keeping in touch with world opinion via the telephone, apparently much cheered.  After viewing the somewhat makeshift appointments and refusing the steaming bowls of Knorr Five-Minute Thin Minestrone Broth I had prepared for them, they both to my surprise went out into the garden, winking and whispering to each other.  With the toilet temporarily out of action, I assumed that they were bent on answering the summonses of Mother Nature, so I settled down in the lounge among the steaming mattresses to join a few pieces of silver paper in lieu of decorations.

I had just stuck together an attractive chain to hang in the hall, when I was alarmed by scrabbling sounds on the roof and the sound of somewhat discordant voices raised in a spirited rendition of "Rudolph, the Red-nosed Reindeer".  Imagine my alarm, a second later, when a heavy crashing superseded it, cracks appeared in the ceiling, and a smoking column of dust fell into the centre of the room, closely followed by Harold and the Inspector, both wearing old potato sacks daubed with red paint and pieces of kapok from the gardening shed glued crudely to their faces.  "I told you the bungalow hadn't got a chimney, Inspector" cried Harold, now apparently angry and rubbing a twisted ankle, "you are a thick numbskull with ideas above your station.  Oh, Gladys, I forgot, a Merry Christmas."

Christmas Day dawned blustery with rain pouring through the hole in the roof as a result of what the BBC on my old battery Marconi portable described as "squally showers".  Harold refused to move as the daylight grew, despite the fact that the rain was now falling in a steady silver stream through the hole in the ceiling and cascading over his inert sack-covered form with a gurgling water-fall effect.  The Inspector, too, failed to respond to the challenge of the morning and I myself was forced to mount the roof, dragging one of the mattresses, in an attempt to caulk the leak.  I was thus employed when the beaming figure of Rev. Thargle cycled up in the rain, an old gentleman with a stick hobbling determinedly in his wake.

"Happy Christmas to you, dear lady" he shouted turning up the flap of his souwester, "a word in your ear if you would be so generous."  I climbed down the ladder and approached the rain-sodden man of God, wiping my hands on my pinny.  "Forgive me, Mrs W.," he began, "I wonder whether you received my circular about our Good Cheer for the Aged Scheme?  The idea, etched out at a P.C.C., by Alderman Mumford, was that the Haves should make a tiny gesture to the Have Nots at this Season of Good Will and take into their homes one of these selected OAP's who would otherwise have a miserable time.  As I didn't receive your pro-forma rejecting the proposal outright, I've brought along our Mr Szamuely, who is all of ninety-

six.  You wouldn't think it to look at him, now would you?"  I was about to deny this and point out that our little nest was in no state to receive unexpected guests of an unrobust nature, when a bell rang beyond the rainy fields, Rev. Thargle flung a leg over his bicycle, and, crying "Crikey, Matins" dwindled in a few seconds to a mere speck in the gathering storm, leaving me to cope as best I might with our senior citizen.

Mr Szamuely seemed a somewhat taciturn old gentleman with a nasty cough, but I set him down in the lounge beside Harold, and was just opening the tin of South American Boneless Turkey With Rich Chunks of Free Range Chippolata Sausages from Sainsbury's when there was a crash, as of a vehicle colliding with the outside wall of the bungalow.

Sure enough, Giles's friend had arrived.  They were seated behind the wheel of a camouflage-painted Jeep-style Mini-Moke and did not seem in the highest spirits, as, apart from everything else, the fashionable roof awning had blown off just outside Polperro.  Giles' friend, the Honourable Christopher Twytte, had a long droopy moustache, rather sodden by the rain, and insisted on addressing me as "Man".  He was casually dressed in a pair of Army boots without laces, fraying pyjamas, and an old groundsheet.  He seemed unenthusiastic about the bungalow, frequently striking his forehead with the flat of his palm and observing "It's unbelievable", but on entering and seeing Harold and the Inspector's recumbent forms, with Mr Szamuely coughing unostentatiously in a corner, he immediately brightened.  "It's crazy, Giles baby" he remarked.  "I didn't know your old man turned on."

With this, he extracted some cigarette papers and a little machine, snapping his fingers as he did so, and sat down beside Mr Szamuely with his feet on Harold's head.  There did not seem much that I could do, so I returned to the kitchen to put the finishing touches to the Rich Fruit Content Reconstituted Christmas Duff as recommended by Fanny Craddock in the *Radio Times*.

The sequence of events that followed is still blurred in my mind.  As I remember, I lit the gas to warm through the Methylated Yule Bonfire Dressing for the Flambe, and entered the lounge to lay those knives and forks that I could find on the upturned crate which the Inspector found on the beach last summer.  The Honourable Twytte was puffing lazily on a rather bedraggled cigarette which he offered from time to time without success to Mr Szamuely, when there was a thunderous knock and the door fell in, revealing the bluff figure of Constable Rees-Mogg.  "Alright lads, it's a swoop" he cried, and several plain clothes gentlemen of less than average height ran forward.  At that moment there was a deafening explosion from the kitchen, I felt a great blast of hot air, laden with food, and, as the roof collapsed, everything went black.

In the end Constable Rees-Mogg was most understanding, but I hope that that is the last year I shall ever have Christmas Dinner consisting of half a packet of Sage 'n Onion flavoured crisps washed down with a sip of brown ale at half past six in the evening in the Scilly Cow.

# Hitler arrested in Torquay

A twenty-five year long search, covering all five continents of the world, came to an end early this morning with the arrest in a luxurious Riviera-style villa near Torquay, Devon, of Adolf Hitler.

Mr Hitler, 81, has been wanted for almost a quarter of a century to assist the authorities in connection with the 1939-45 war.

## SHOCK

The arrest comes as a personal triumph for Inspector 'Knacker of the Yard' Knacker, who has made the search for Hitler his own lifelong crusade. Said Knacker yesterday, "Just let's say - I'm very happy at the way it's worked out."

## A NICE MAN

Neighbours of the Hitlers in exclusive Brazilia Drive, were shocked to learn that the quietly-spoken, retiring man who they knew simply as 'Der Fuehrer', was a wanted criminal.

Said next-door-neighbour, Mrs Cynthia Glarb, a retired widow, "Oh yes, I knew Mr Hitler well. I would never have dreamed that he could have been mixed up in a thing like the Second World War. We knew him as just a kindly old gentleman with a love of animals, who had obviously been in the services. You could tell that from all the medals he wore and his habit of saluting everyone with his arm in the air."

## LOVABLE

Another close friend, was Major 'Bushy' Top-Tree, a regular at the Laydownyour Arms just down the road from Hitler's house. "You could have knocked me down with a 1,000 bomber raid on Cologne," he confided today. "Though come to think of it, we were a bit surprised when he asked us back to his place one night to find uniformed guards outside the front door, and inside, the walls all covered with maps. But we put

MON REPOS  - where the hunt ended.

it down to his foreign background. He told us that he had travelled a lot earlier in his life, and had been stationed in Germany during the war."

## ALWAYS A GENTLEMAN

Outside the house this afternoon, there was little evidence of the dawn drama that brought an end to Hitler's 26-year South Coast idyll. One who saw the arrest, was Mrs Edith Wagner, 62, who 'did' for the Hitlers throughout their stay. "A lovely couple" was how she summed up the one-time dictator and his blonde, former mistress. "But he would go marching over my nice clean floors. Mind you, I can't say I cared much for some of his friends who came to stay. There was a doctor from Eastbourne, and an Italian gentleman, Mr Mussolini, who lived nearby."

## DESERTED

Today, the house has an empty and deserted look. Only the gas cylinders on the doorstep, the rusting Panzer tanks on the uncut lawn, the U-Boat half-submerged in the swimming pool, the swastika flag drooping limply in the November mist from the clothes line, the rolls of barbed wire leaning up against the potting shed and the squadron of Heinkel bombers lying idle in the garage remained as mute evidence of the house's former owner.

## SHERLOCK

What finally led Inspector Knacker to this inconspicuous backwater in a quiet Devon resort? Over the years, Hitler had been seen all over the world, from Argentina to Australia. There was even a report that he had died in Berlin in 1945. But Knacker never gave up hope. "I had a hunch" he said today, "that he was lying low somewhere in Southern England. He always liked that part of the world."

What was the final link in the chain which led up to Knacker's dawn swoop? Today, the smiling Inspector was giving nothing away, except a few free invitations to the Scotland Yard Christmas Ball. "Let's just say that Lady Luck played her part. But you can say that it was not entirely unconnected with the fact that my suspicions were aroused when the name of the residence in question was reported to have been changed from Mein Kampf to Mon Repos. I could see they had something to hide."

# YES, IT'S JUSTICE '69

Say what you like, and you probably will, the Krays craze is certainly sweeping through the musty corridors of the Law Courts like a hurricane on skates (writes Our Man in The Dock JACK DASH).

OUT GO  old style fuddy-duddy "No Your Lordship", "If it so pleases your Worship".

IN COME such up-to-the-minute and as-down -to-earth-as-the-Concorde aeroplane phrases as "You fat stinking pig-face slobbering poof".

In the new style all-plastic see-through New Bailey yesterday I watched amazed and delighted as plaintiff Ted Fisp stripped away centuries of outmoded mandarin-style legal jargon with a cry of "Come off it, you drag queen, get out of that wig and fight it out like a man".

### TRIAL RUN

Defending counsel Sir Arthur Baloney was not to be outdone "Shut up and sit down you four eyed git"he cried. He was then smashed to the floor with a large piece of cast iron evidence.

As police sprayed the court- room with new perfumed Cardin riot-gas the Judge intervened with a cry of "Get stuffed the lot of you, I'm off to the boozer for a quick one."

Mr. Fisk was appealing against a local council decision to lop a branch off one of his elm trees

" I was overcome wiv' mass hysteria like when my old man went over the top at Ypres."

# The life and times of LORD BATTENDOWNTHEHATCHES

*with historical narrative by world-famous historian, JOHN TERRINE DU CHEF*

THE AUTHOR

"When I was a little boy we often used to go to stay with my first cousins, the Prince and Princess Buxtehude von Mittagessen in their hunting lodge on top of the Matterhorn.

"Their father, who was my uncle but also by one of those tricks of our complicated family tree my mother's sister-in-law, was at that time King Otto the Second of San Marino.

UNCLE OTTO
"Very cut up"

"I still have a photograph of him. He was a kind old gentleman with a long ginger beard and a false nose.

"Then came the great war. It was a beastly business and my family were very cut up.

"Uncle Otto was cut up when the revolution broke out in 1916 and Aunt Ludmilla was pushed over a cliff.

"These events cast a gloom over our family for several minutes. We had been very fond of them."

*The 1914-18 War began in 1914 and ended in 1918. During it a lot of people were killed. At the end of it the British won and peace was declared.*

"At the beginning of the war our family had rather a bad time when it was discovered that my father, Lord Scharnhorst von East Grinstead, was, by some strange quirk of history, head of the German army. Despite his intense loyalty to the British Crown, he was compelled by public opinion to resign his post as First Sea Lord.

"Some years later, I was able to make some amends when there took place the Battle of Jutland, the last great sea battle of our times. I was in the Navy at the time, serving as an ordinary Rear-Admiral. Unfortunately, I missed the Battle itself, but here is some old film of it."

*After the War came the Twenties. Lloyd George's 'land fit for heroes' did not materialise. The Bright Young Things danced the night away to the strains of the Charleston, while invalided ex-officers begged for coppers in the street.*

*After the Twenties came the Thirties ....*

"The highlight of this period for me came when my old friend, King Edward VIII, or 'Jim' as he was known to the family, decided to abdicate. He was a very lonely man and those of us who knew him well were not surprised when he fell in love with the woman who was later to become known to the world as Mrs Wallis Simpson.

"This meant that 'Alf', as the Duke of York was known, became King. I was very pleased with this happy conclusion to the affair, since it meant that, although my cousin and old friend had ceased to be King, my other cousin and old friend was fortunate enough to replace him.

"Like me, George VI, as he became known, was a sailor. As a family we have the sea in our blood, and this may well account for the fact that it is blue."

*But the stormclouds were looming over Europe, and in 1939 war, as it was known, was declared.*

"The outbreak of war was to mean a greater upheaval in my life than any I had known so far. Shortly after it began, I was summoned by Winston and asked to take over as Supreme Commander of the Combined Allied War Effort. I like to think that, at the time, this was one of the most important jobs in the world. I think I did it as well as I was able i.e. extremely well.

"The new post inevitably meant something of a promotion for me, as I had begun the war as Captain of *H.M.S. Leaky*, which unfortunately sank several times while under my command. This episode was later made the subject of a musical film by Noel Coward, *In Which We Sink*.

*The war ended with a bang in August 1945. As the cheering crowds thronged the Mall singing 'We'll Hang Out Our Washing On The Northern Line' - many of them had spent the war posing for Henry Moore on tube stations throughout the country - only the thorny question of India remained to be solved.*

"When the war ended, I was out of a job. But not for long. When I was summoned by the King and asked to take over India, I was horrified. But when the King said "Think how good it will be for the Empire if you succeed in getting rid of it" I saw at once that he was right.

"India in those days was a big place, with a very large population. When I arrived at the Vice-Regal Lodge in Delhi, I discovered that we had 23,783 servants, a good deal more than we had been used to at my wife's home, Broadlands. However, we were able to put them to good use, and during our stay we managed to give luncheon to 74,486,912 people, many of whom had never had luncheon at the Vice-Regal Lodge before, and still more of whom had never had luncheon."

*NEXT WEEK: 'I Leap Over The Wall'. I take on the most important job in the world, when Harold Wilson calls me in to head an enquiry into escapes from Wormwood Scrubs.*

THE WAR ENDS WITH A BANG
(or the Battle of Jutland as the case may be)

# 'QUEEN' TO COME OFF AFTER 1000 YEARS SHOCK

*by Our Radio Correspondent,*
*GEOFFREY CANNON-BALLS*

The long running show "The Royal Family" which has for the last thousand years been one of the most popular hits with the British public, has been 'axed' it was revealed today.

The show centred round the personality of The Queen, a demure upper-class housewife living mainly in London with her family.

### TIME FOR A CHANGE

A spokesman explained "Whilst the show is still very popular with millions of ordinary people, we must be sensitive to change. The feeling was that it was time to introduce a more modern tone to the proceedings.

"We have given the matter a great deal of thought and will be replacing The Queen with a young Nigerian student who comes to London to sleep with girls in a flat in Earls Court. He is interested in concrete music and 'having fun.' We are sure once people get over the shock, they will grow to love this colourful character as much as the Queen."

### CAN'T BELIEVE IT

"Franky I am delighted" said Elizabeth Windsor, 41, the girl who took over the role in 1953 from the late King George VI. "After doing this for so long you begin to believe you really are the character. People write you letters and wave to you in the street. I even have dog food sent through the post for my Corgis.

"But I won't pretend that it hasn't been a strain. It can really be very tiring saying the same old thing day after day.

"What will I do now ? Well I plan to take a long holiday and think things over. I've had a lot of offers."

### RESTING

Other members of the cast, however, are not so pleased about the decision. Philip Papadopoulous, who takes the part of the Queen's Greek-born husband in the series had mixed feelings about his future.

"I suppose I can't complain" he told me yesterday. "I've had a good run for my money. And I was lucky to get the part in the first place, against powerful competition. But it's a big wrench. At my age it's difficult to change. And I feel the public will always think of me as the Duke whatever part I play next."

### COME A LONG WAY

The Royal Family started life in the Middle Ages and broke all records as a long running serial about an inbred family containing many eccentric characters.

Then, early in the 19th century, when the famous Queen Victoria took over the central role there came a change and the family settled down to a long period of domesticity in Buckingham Palace. Despite their ups and downs the same calm has prevailed until the present day.

### I'M SO WORRIED ABOUT MY HUSBAND AND I

Now all this is to go. And it will certainly come as a blow to millions of people to whom the sound of the massed bands of the Brigade of Guards playing the signature tune 'The National Anthem' has become as much a part of their lives as roast beef and Yorkshire pudding.

*OUTRAGED HOST (TO GUEST WHO HAS INADVERTENTLY PERPETRATED AN EMBARRASSING HISTRIONIC EFFECT):*
"Dammit man, you've just farted in front of my wife".
*DEFAULTING GUEST (NONCHALANTLY):*
"I do apologise, my dear fellow. I didn't realise it was her turn".

# PRIVATE EYE

No. 189
Friday
14 March
69   2/-

Those were the Krays..

Are you appealing?

You'd better ask my friends in high places, ducky.

*Which twin has the Toni?*

**Picture by DAVID OLD BAILEY**

# Flight of M. Wedgwood's Aeronautical contraption

## Amazing scenes in French wood

## Fifty years work rewarded

Toulouse, Thursday

This morning I was privileged to be present on the occasion of the first propulsion into the air of the ingenious device constructed by the celebrated English inventor Mr Wedgwood and his French collaborator, the Marquis de Gaulle.

In brave defiance of all the laws of nature, the aerial steam-carriage, intelligence of which has been reaching the outside world for many years, at last rose unmistakably into the air and hovered above the ground for several seconds.

For weeks past the expectation of the villagers of St. Saens-sur-Soames has been quickened almost daily by their apprehension of loud reports and exhalations of coloured smokes rising from the grounds of the Marquis's chateau.

Time and again, the two inventors have been disappointed in their hopes by the inclement breezes which have created conditions unsuitable for their experiment.

### THE GREAT DAY ARRIVES

This morning, however, conditions were announced to be perfect. There was not a cloud in the sky. The air was calm. Observers stationed in neighbouring tree-tops were at last able to report that the surrounding terrain had been safely cleared of birds, insects, molehills, strayed bees and other hindrances to the proposed aerial excursion.

From the time of the first cock's crow, a huge throng was already beginning to gather at the foot of the hill below the chateau. Noblemen from Paris jostled with buxom apple-vendors, English milords exchanged the time of day with gnarled peasant folk.

Finally, at the stroke of noon, a hush fell on the waiting multitude. All eyes were turned expectantly up towards the castle gates where the twin standards of Britain and France hung limply in the tranquil air.

Then, with a fanfare of cornets and amid the crackle of exploding pyrotechnic devices provided by the old firm of Lumière et Son, the drawbridge creaked down, the portcullis rose and there emerged, to the great festivity of all assembled, the mightie engine of the heavens, drawn by two huge gangs of sweating yeomen.

Perched on top of this fabulous machine, barely visible for their distance above the ground, were its two gallant progenitors, their eyes shielded by iron vizors and their limbs protected from head to foot by suits of the Marquis's family armour.

At a signal from M. Wedgwood, his eyes ablaze with the stimulation of the great moment, the burly serfs rushed forward and with a final heave propelled the vast apparatus into the air, where it remained by my calculations for a space amounting to not less than five and a half seconds, before returning to the safety of the turf.

Later, as the local vintages flowed freely under the sun-dappled chestnuts, I spoke with many onlookers. Not one would deny that he had positively witnessed an expanse of void between M. Wedgwood's machine and the ground amounting to several inches.

---

# THE DOG PILL
# British Bow Wows lash Papal Bulldog

by Our Man in the Dog House, Doberman Pincher. Dateline: Battersea, Thursday.

The Papal Bulldog's new encyclical *De Canum Sexualium* has aroused howls of protest in liberal canine circles.

A spokesdog barked: "With the population explosion it's high time we had a humane anti-litter campaign. One bitch I know has had over 73 puppies in the last two years. She is a walking or rather a staggering protest against the ineffectiveness of the rhythm method. What does the Papal Bulldog know of life, stuck up in his ivory kennel surrounded by fawning spaniels?"

### A BITCH FOR ALL IN SEASON

The Red Dane of St. Paul's was equally critical. "This is a matter for the individual canine conscience" he snapped. "The papal bulldog has never lifted a leg to help the starving millions. He has no conception of this mounting problem for the ordinary dog in the street.

"The so-called natural bucket of cold water method is as out of date as a gas-lit lamp post."

### CORGI AND BESS

Cardinal Sealyham speaking on the David Cruft show said that all dogs should regard the encyclical as a lead rather than an attempt to muzzle their individual freedom. "I would certainly not refuse the sacramental Kennomeat to any dog who in good faith ignored the papal bulldog's edict" he snarled.

My oh my, what a field day! Never have I seen Harold in such good form as when he was reading his press notices after the successful first performance of Operation Sledgehammer, the award-winning sandtable exercise on strife-torn Anguilla. What with his triumphant appearance on the *Dickie Mountbatten Show*, his cup has certainly been in danger of flowing over during these last days, and we must trust that his luck will hold for the Peacedove Probe Dash to safeguard British interests in Lagos.

Harold has always been a lifelong admirer of Lord Mountbatten, the debonair matinee idol who clutched at the hearts of millions during the Second World War. He was therefore delighted when the former First Sea Lord accepted his suggestion that he should appear in the company of the Duke of Edinburgh on the final programme of the series and sing the praises of his fellow technologist. Accordingly, I was instructed to get the signed photo of Earl Attlee down from the attic and give it a dust, so that it could figure prominently in the background of Harold's fire-side tribute.

He was just having his make-up removed after the filming when little Mr Stewart, our retired schoolmaster friend who is also the Foreign Secretary, was ushered in bearing a number of files marked MI 6, Top Secret, If Found Please Return to Import and Export Ltd., 34 Greek St. W.1. "Ahem" he remarked in obsequious tones, hesitating nervously until Miss Boobs of the Television Make-Up Department had gathered up her ditty-bag and withdrawn, "I have the briefs here on the situation in Anguilla." "Stewart" Harold remarked in brusque vein, "I distinctly remember asking for the file on Nigeria prior to my Peaceprobe initiative next week. I might suggest that you pay more attention to aural hygiene in future when I am making my remarks. However,

*"Sorry. Adults only."*

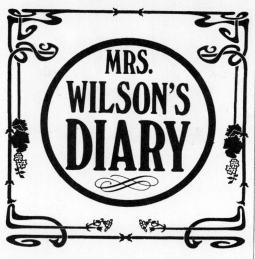

## MRS. WILSON'S DIARY

since you've got this lot out, let's have a look at it."

"Where did you say it was?" Harold continued, taking down the *Reader's Digest Atlas of the Universe with revised Moonmaps* from the tooled oak-style Maples Bookerama by the television. "Anguilla, Anguilla, where are we? Ah yes, here it is, just south of Madrid." "No, no," interposed little Mr Stewart, fingering his tie, "it is an island in the Caribbean, or so I am informed by my experts on the Desk. It would seem that self-styled President Webster declared U.D.I. some time in 1967 in exchange for 2,000 $3\frac{1}{2}$% Mafia Gilt-Edged Bonds. I took the liberty of sending out Mr Whitlock to see what was going on, and I am told that he was threatened by Kray-style bandits and was forced to leave. Might I suggest that we lodge a mild protest at the U.N.?"

"Wait a moment" Harold replied, poring once more over the map, "here we are: Anguilla Pop. 6,000. What's that you say? Protest? My dear Stewart, as you are no doubt aware, this week sees the hundredth anniversary of the birth of Neville Chamberlain. Those of us who have lived through these troubled times will know full well the penalties that befall those who are prepared to compromise with the dictators. Are we to stand idly by while evil men wave the mailed fist of derision at the forces of democracy and peace? While the lion's tail is twisted beyond endurance by power-mad tyrants intent on world domination? This President Whitlock, who does he think he is?" "Webster, Prime Minister, Webster," soothed the silver-haired satrap. "Whitlock, Webster, Nasser or Hitler, style themselves how they will, we know their type. If we give way now we shall pay for it later with millions dead and our cities devastated to rubble. I am surprised, Stewart, that you have so little regard for the lessons of history."

"Kaufmann" Harold shouted, thrusting his hand inside his waistcoat in a belligerent manner, "ring up Dickie Mountbatten and ask him if he'd be interested in becoming Allied Supremo of an amphibious task-force designed to bring this sabre-rattling Mussolini grovelling to his

knees." Unfortunately, Lord Mountbatten was already booked for *Late Night Line Up* and was unable to accept. However, Mr Healey came round at once and was delighted at the suggestion, as it would give them a chance to try out the new Peewit inflatable Hovertank, and as the Army, all fifty-seven of them, were getting a bit bored sitting about in their luxury Butlin-style Cookhouse on Salisbury Plain watching Mad Colonel Mitchell on the television. Mr Callaghan also called in to offer the services of the recently formed Scotland Yard Kray Squad who had been out of work for some weeks and could do with a spell in the sun with no currency restrictions.

And so it was all agreed. The invasion date was to be kept a deathly secret, until it was discovered that Mr Kaufmann had already rung all the newspapers, which represented, in Mr Stewart's words, "something of a breach of security". Nevertheless, everything went forward as planned, and Harold was able to put a firm tick against the "Decisive" slot on the washable plastic "Things To Be Done Before the Next Election" chart above the bed, prepared by Mr Jameson of Whizz Market Research Limited. "The world has learned a lesson from this, Gladys," he remarked as he was putting on his Pepper and Salt Chilprufe Hostess-style Pyjamas on the night it was announced that President Webster's Forces had been cut off and had surrendered to P.C. "Tiny" Hope-Wallace of D Division, "the British Lion's tail will not be tweaked with impunity. It still has teeth, and it will bite those who thumb their nose at it. The Russians think that they will take over in Nigeria: they are mistaken. Today it is Whitlock, or President Webster as he styles himself, tomorrow it could be Kosygin, Mao Tse Tung, Creatures from Outer Space. Our British Bobbies are a match for them all." With this he knocked out his aluminium-stemmed Rosewood Goo-Free on my head and fell into a deep sleep.

*an old cow-hand...*

# PRIVATE EY

No. 191
Friday
11 April 69

2/-

# ROOND N'ABOOT

## with Lunchtime O'Bulawayo

**W**hen Ian Smith declared illegal independence he did so, amongst other things, to "preserve Christian standards." In fact, members of the Rhodesian Front often appear to believe that they are motivated entirely by divine inspiration. At a service to commemorate UDI a minister of the Dutch Reformed Church (sic) tried to bolster this belief by telling his all-white congregation (including several Cabinet Ministers) that they were "God's chosen people."

This would be a highly commendable state of affairs were it not for the fact that - like the Dutch Reformed Church - the Rhodesian Front are apt to apply their own interpretation to what are, and are not, "Christian standards."

Kaffir-beating, for example, is presumably regarded as a wholesome activity to be encouraged amongst the faithful. Several influential members of the Party have hit the headlines in the past as devotees of this particular sport, the most recent being Mr Simmonds who, as District Commissioner in the Mtoko African Tribal Trust Lands, found it necessary to chastise a group of black men who he felt were not showing him proper respect. After a court hearing Mr Simmonds resigned from the Service and was immediately appointed as one of the two Organising Secretaries of the Rhodesian Front.

\*   \*   \*   \*   \*

**O**ne must also suppose that adultery is another of those Christian standards which the regime is struggling to preserve. The case of ex-Cabinet Minister Mr Harper was too well-publicised at the time to need repetition here, except perhaps to state categorically that his girlfriend was NOT a member of MI5. Mr Harper is not, however, alone in being involved in illicit love affairs. Oxford-accented, ex-British Army Officer, Pieter van der Byl - now Minister of Information - is reputed to have spent a jolly time with a German Baroness, whose irate husband received a substantial sum in "hush money" in an effort to keep the matter from becoming public knowledge.

\*   \*   \*   \*   \*

**I**t is also apparent that the Lord's injunctions against stealing are to be interpreted in a loose and unorthodox way. For example, immediately after UDI the regime appointed a number of censors whose job it was to protect the Rhodesian public from any filth that might be served up to them by demoralised journalists. This dedicated little band was led by a certain Mr Dendy - at that time a de-frocked lawyer who had just completed a sentence in Salisbury gaol for activities not wholly unconnected with fraud.

\*   \*   \*   \*

**F**inally, there is the case of the charming Mr Pitluk who represents the Rhodesian Front on the Salisbury City Council and is in fact one of the Council's representatives on the governing body of the University College of Rhodesia. Mr Pitluk is a lawyer, and he too has had his embarrassing moments. That is, if being suspended for several months by the Rhodesian Side-Bar Association for activities again not wholly unconnected with fraud can be called "embarrassing".

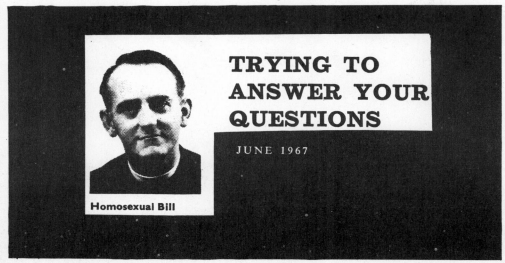

## TRYING TO ANSWER YOUR QUESTIONS

JUNE 1967

**Homosexual Bill**

# Gnome

There has been a goodeal (sic) of whining and recriminations over certain characters whose names do not appear in my columns. I refer to parties who have for one reason or another had recourse to legal undertakings preventing further mention of their names. Various self-righteous journalists, not to mention MPs, have cavilled at such arrangements, arguing to my mind erroneously that they curtail the so-called freedom of the press.

It has always been my policy to look with sympathy at the desires of those who wish to have their activities for whatever reason, veiled with a cloak of secrecy. As one who frequently finds himself in a similar position I know full well the embarrassment and unnecessary distress that may be caused by tactless enquiries and unseemly probes.

There is no need, however, for aggrieved parties to resort to the costly machinations of the law in order to achieve that silence on my part which they may desire.

For a relatively small financial consideration I will undertake to guarantee complete discretion to any party who may apply. I would add that several highly placed individuals have already taken advantage of this service.

To assist the would-be applicant, I append a simple form which when completed should be sent to me along with the appropriate sum.

---

**Please do not mention me in Private Eye for 1/5/10 years.**

**I enclose £1,000/£5,000/ £10,000.**

**NAME** . . . . . . . . . . . . . . . . .

**A Gnomefam Scheme**

---

E. Strobes
pp Lord Gnome
Villa Disraeli
Cap Gris Nez

# CALLAGHAN LASHES OUT IN BOTH DIRECTIONS

In a major speech yesterday, the Home Secretary, Mr Callaghan attacked the 'confusions' which have arisen over the Government's White Paper on industrial relations.

"The position is quite simple" he stated. "What is at stake is nothing less than the future of the nation as a whole. What matters more than anything else is that we should preserve the traditional right of the working man to negotiate freely with his employers. Let me be quite specific. Unless we are prepared to put the national interest above all else, we shall reach the position where the fabric of democracy itself is threatened. A central part of that democratic tradition is the freedom of every individual to determine where and on what terms he will give of his labour. The unions must play their part like everyone else if that freedom is to be maintained. We must be tough. We must be weak. We must clamp down on the irresponsible minority. We must fight to the end for what we believe in, whatever that may be. As a member of the Cabinet, I support the unanimous decision of my colleagues. As a loyal member of the Labour Movement for forty years, I know the main chance when I see it."

Mr Callaghan then threw his hat into the ring, ate his words and fell off the fence.

His condition was later reported to be critical (and in particular highly critical of Mr Wilson).

SCHEMING JIM CALLAGHAN The Power Crazed Loonie

**SMILING JIM CALLAGAN** The Worker's Friend

# PRIVATE EYE

No. 193
Friday
May 69

2/-

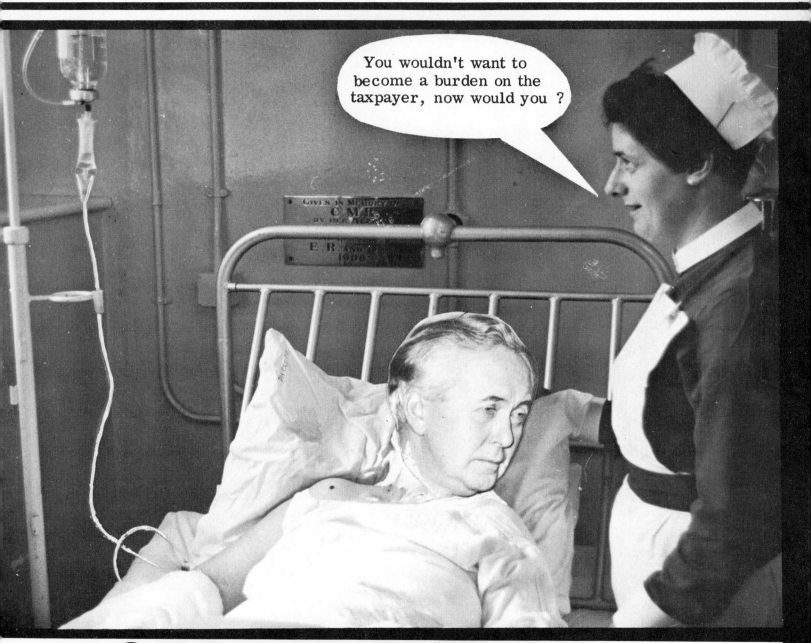

# SHOULD THIS MAN BE KEPT ALIVE?

# THE CLOGGIES

*An everyday saga in the life of Clog Dancing Folk*
*by BILL TIDY*

# The Listless

**Friday 9 May 1969**    **Volume control**  **1s. 3d.**

## The Hindsight Saga

### Part 79  The Pundit as Hero

## by Sir Michael Angelo

*(24 hours signature tune. Camera tracks back to reveal Sir Michael standing at the end of an interminable corridor).*

*Angelo:* I am standing on the spot where civilisation came to one of its major cross-roads, Corridor B in the great BBC Television Centre. Last week, you may remember, we saw how television had entered a new Dark Age, which could hardly be described as civilised. The naive and simple faith of the men who had produced such masterpieces as *Z-Cars and The Black and White Minstrel Show* had lost its way. The limitations of their simple techniques were no longer enough to sustain the interest of the civilised world. Men were unconsciously seeking new ways in which the old truths could be expressed.

*Camera cuts to contemporary print of white coated technologists grappling with elaborate machinery.*

Shape, motion and light — all these techniques had been mastered. It seemed that there was nothing new. But then, as we have so often seen before, came one of those rare moments which alter the whole course of civilisation. Like the frescoes of Giotto or the discovery of perspective by Spaggetthi di Bologna, the invention of colour television completely changed our way of looking at the world.

Colour — it is now something we all take for granted. But imagine how it must have seemed to the men of the latter half of the twentieth century, when the familiar nightly images, so much part of their lives that they had almost lost their power to amuse or

*Michelangelo's "Kenneth"*

divert, suddenly sprang into new life.

*Picture of Val Doonican is shown first in black and white and then in colour.*

What a glorious world was opened up to the artists of the age! No longer were they confined only to the subjects and images dictated by tradition. Now they could explore the entire kingdom of nature — a nature where grass was green, the sky was blue and Fanny Cradock's fish fingers could be seen at last in their true shade of bilious orange.

Nevertheless, these new delights remained only the preserve of a tiny privileged minority. Like the block of marble awaiting the hand of Michelangelo to bring it to life, the new medium still awaited the arrival of an undisputed master. He was not long in coming in the person of Sir Kenneth Clark.

As with the masters of the past, who had only been able to flourish under the patronage of the Church, so it was to be with Sir Kenneth. We see here a contemporary portrait of his patron.

*Waves hand at print of Huw Wheldoni, ascending triumphantly to sixth floor of TV centre, surrounded by adoring make-up girls and kneeling producers.*

What a shrewd old face it is! Wheldoni may not have known much about art, but he certainly knew what it was that would inspire people to go out and buy colour television receivers. It was Wheldoni, perhaps the last of the great patrons, who conceived the grandiose plan of commissioning for no less than £300,000 a potted history of culture in thirteen easy instalments.

Such a project would have everything! Magnificent cathedrals and palaces, the finest paintings of two thousand years, tapestries, sculptures, rich landscapes, country houses, background music provided by the genius of Bach and Beethoven. What an appeal such a collection — a veritable coffee table book of the air — would make to the one last undisputed snobbery of the twentieth century! The snobbery of 'Art'.

Only one ingredient was missing in the plan as it formed in Wheldoni's mind. Where was the man whose image would be exactly right to introduce this glittering pageant to the awestruck millions?

*Picture of Sir Kenneth Clark flashes up.*

Look at him here, draped languidly across a Louis Seize chaise-longue, his well-manicured fingers toying with a beautifully-tooled Faberge musical box. Who can doubt that the choice of Sir Kenneth Clark was Wheldoni's master-stroke?

Not a detail is out of place — the beautifully-chiselled features, the carefully-cultured accent of the English upper class, the exquisite suiting — nothing is overdone, and the whole thing breathes an air of absolute assurance.

Week by week, he led the bedazzled viewers on a 13-instalment coach tour through the highspots of European culture; each object in turn was appraised and given its commendation as 'civilised' or 'splendid' or 'agreeable', without any too profound or demanding an examination of its aim, until finally he too merged into the picture he was describing, as himself almost its single most 'civilised' and 'agreeable' ingredient.

What wonder that all over the country, on Sunday and Friday nights, little salons of the would-be cultured and civilised gathered to pay homage to this last shining exemplar of the civilisation of two thousand years? In an age of increasing disorder and chaos, as the shadows of a new Dark Age gathered on every hand, he was a last symbol of that order and light which he so elegantly and defiantly extolled.

What could be more agreeable than this little interior, conveying, as it does, the full flavour of the late twentieth century civilisation? But this exquisite moment could not last. Eventually, Sir Kenneth's job was done. Every home in the country was equipped with a colour set. Wheldoni withdrew his patronage and Sir Kenneth retired to his castle in Kent to eke out his remaining days in conditions of extreme luxury.

*Next week: BBC - 2 Reverts to nature films.*

. 194
day
May 69

# PRIVATE EYE

## WHITSUN MUST GO

# Oh What lovely oars !

# AXEMAN WAS HEART DONOR — SHOCK

# PRIVATE EY[E]

No. 195
Friday
6 June 69

2/-

# COLOUR SECTION

**S**ome hours before the recent Commons debate on members' interests, two honourable members went into the Reference Room of the Commons library to ask for the last issue of *Private Eye* - which contained a detailed analysis of the outside interests of the members of the Select Committee to look into the problem.

To their surprise, the librarian replied that both copies of the *Eye* had been taken out of the library by the Government Whips - and were not available.

---

**O**ne of the greatest fans of Sir Kenneth Clark's recent *Civilisation* series on the telly was our own Mrs Wilson. So impressed was she by Sir Kenneth's charm and learning that she urged H. Wislon to reward him by making him a Lord. Wislon accordingly got a letter sent to Clark offering him a life peerage. But Clark, arguing that he was not a political figure and would be out of place in the House of Lords, declined. Whereat, Mrs Wilson wrote personally to Clark urging him to reconsider. Sir Kenneth, it is reported, may now accept the offer.

---

## Quiz
## What's wrong with this poll?

The results were scored as follows: a great deal, plus 1; quite a lot, plus ½; not very much, minus ½; not at all, minus 1; don't know, zero. This is how it turns out:

| | Score |
| --- | --- |
| The Queen | 63 |
| Prince Philip | 55 |
| The Queen Mother | 48 |
| Lord Mountbatten | 41 |
| Prince Charles | 39 |
| Princess Alexandra | 36 |
| Princess Anne | 26 |
| Princess Margaret | 2 |
| Duke of Kent | -4 |

**T**his Opinion Poll on the relative popularity of members of the Royal Family appeared in the *Sunday Times* of 23 March.

One well-known member of the Royal Family is missing. Can you spot which one it is? And why do you think his/her name was omitted?

*Answer : Lord Snowdon. Lord Snowdon's score was -20. He also works on the Sunday Times.*

# FOOTNOTES

# FLY AWAY PAUL

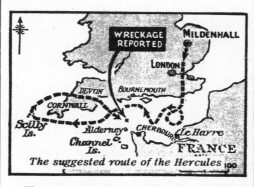

WRECKAGE REPORTED — MILDENHALL — LONDON — DEVON — BOURNEMOUTH — CORNWALL — Scilly Is. — Alderney — Channel Is. — CHERBOURG — Le Havre — FRANCE

*The suggested route of the Hercules*

**T**he curious affair of the lone flight of Sergeant Paul Meyer of the United States Air Force, who stole a 30-ton Hercules Transport plane from the USAF base at Mildenhall, Suffolk, and flew off in it has not been entirely resolved by the assurances in the Commons (June 14) from Mr John Morris (Minister of Defence, Equipment). Mr Morris said that "the Hercules was continuously tracked by British radar" - which was contrary to the facts reported in all the newspapers the day after the incident. The *Daily Express*, for instance, May 24, started its lead story:

"All the massive network of Western Europe's air defences failed yesterday to find American Sergeant Paul Meyer, who . . . . . made a hole in Britain's delicate radar system, and vanished". At this time, the authorities were admitting almost total radar failure, and the official explanation was that the "plane was going out, not coming in".

In fact, the plane approached London from the North, on a route which it is impossible to describe as "going out". The plain truth was that one of the most delicate and "fail-safe" radar systems in the world was rendered useless by a transport plane.

The reason was that the Hercules transport plane is fitted with the latest American anti-radar device, which is one of the most valuable and protected pieces of equipment in the United States Air Force. It enables planes totally to avoid known radar tracking. It is fitted to transport planes as well as bombers and fighters so that full invasion operations, including transport services, can take place without being spotted by enemy radar. It is a piece of equipment which the USAF are more than anxious to keep out of the hands of any possible enemy.

The Press went to fantastic lengths to prove to their readers that Sergeant Meyer was incapable of flying the Hercules, but Meyer was an experienced ground staff officer who knew the Hercules equipment backwards. The flying of a Hercules after take-off is a relatively simple business, and can be left almost entirely to automatic pilot, though navigation and landing are more difficult.

Meyer flew about the South of England, in one of the densest air traffic areas in the world, for about an hour without anyone having the slightest idea where he was. The Mildenhall authorities could only track him when he started speaking to base on the radio. Immediately, the base officers, having been in touch with the Very Highest Command since the Hercules take-off, hooked him up on a radio link with his wife, who was woken up in the middle of the night to speak to him. What husband and wife said to each other is not clear, but without doubt she tried to persuade him to return to his English base, and apparently was successful for Meyer's route marked out after he came over on the radio, shows a U-turn over the Scilly Isles and an attempted return.

By now, however, Meyer's commanders were desperately worried about three things. First, there was the possibility of his failing to land properly, and coming down in a populous area. Second, there was the even stronger possibility of a collision in the air, as the early morning air traffic started to build up. Third, most important, however remote, was the possibility that, either as a result of a public inquiry, resulting from civilian deaths, or more directly if the Hercules crashed over 'enemy territory', the fact that the Americans possess effective anti-radar equipment (or, worse still, the equipment itself) might fall into the hands of the enemy.

Meyer was therefore coaxed by smooth-talking commanders and friends to fly off the Devon coast and over the English channel. He was then persuaded to press a button whose purpose is known only to the most senior officers. This button, known as "the destructer" shatters the plane and all its equipment into fragments.

Meyer pressed the button. "Hopes for the missing pilot" reported the Sunday papers on May 25, "are slim". A US spokesman was quoted as saying:

"It takes a highly trained and skilled pilot to land on the sea. There's a strong possibility the plane broke up".

# THE MYSTERY OF THE THE APPEARING ENVELOPE

**D**espite hysterical publicity at the time of the crime, the newspapers hardly noticed the successful appeal on May 2 of John Lovesay and Tony Peterson against conviction last May for the murder of a Mayfair jeweller, for which they were imprisoned for life (with a minimum of twenty years recommended).

The appeal was allowed on the technical grounds that the judge had ruled that the charges of robbery with violence and murder should stand or fall together. Lovesay and Peterson are still in prison on a seven-year sentence for robbery with violence on the jeweller's shop. Yet, as the Appeal Court made clear, the original conviction was based on what must rank as the most slender and dubious evidence ever produced successfully by a prosecution in a British murder trial.

The jeweller Epps was found in his shop in Brook Street, Mayfair, at about 9.30 a.m. on Jan. 24th 1968, manacled to a staircase, savagely battered and only just alive. Five days later, Lovesay and Peterson were arrested in a pub in Pimlico. At the time of the arrest, there was, as the trial later showed, not a particle of evidence linking either man with the crime. None of the police officers who gave evidence at the trial gave any indication as to why suspicion was first aroused against Lovesay and Peterson, and they can only have made the arrests in response to a "tip-off".

Two of the officers who made the arrest were Detective Sergeants George Mould and Leonard Harris of West End Central CID. They took the men back to the Police Station where they discovered that Sydney Epps had died in hospital from his injuries. Both were then searched, Lovesay by Mould, Peterson by Harris, at different ends of the charge room. Their pockets were emptied and their property laid out in front of them. Lovesay was stripped and put into a cell. When he was gone, his property was then put into an envelope by Sergeant Mould, and the envelope was sealed. Peterson's property was also put in an envelope. Peterson himself gummed up the envelope and signed it on the back. The envelopes were then placed by Mould in a drawer of his desk, which he locked.

All this was in flagrant disregard of police regulations for suspects' search procedure, which stipulate a search by the duty station officer, the presence of a uniformed policeman at the search, the elaborate listing of all property in an Occurence Book and the storage of the property in the safe of the station officer or of the CID. In the words of the officer in charge of the murder inquiry, Det. Supt. Arthur Butler "the search procedure in this case went completely by the board".

The Superintendent returned at 7.0 p.m. that evening and found in each property envelope a very damning piece of evidence. Half a business envelope, torn diagonally, was among each man's property. The halves, when fitted together, formed a business envelope bearing the name of Sydney Epps, Jeweller, 18 Brook Street, in very clear type.

When Butler confronted both men with the envelope halves, they vigorously denied that it had been in their property. Mould and Harris said that they had found both pieces in the suspects' pockets - in Peterson's overcoat and in Lovesay's jacket. Lovesay and Peterson independently refused to sign for the envelope pieces, complaining bitterly from the outset that they had never seen them before in their lives. The only fingerprints on the envelope were those of Superintendent Butler.

The following morning both men went before an extended identity parade, attended by ten potential eye-witnesses to events concerned with the crime. None of the ten picked out Lovesay or Peterson. Nevertheless, on the strength of the envelope halves, both men were charged with Sydney Epps' murder, committed for trial and placed in solitary confinement in Brixton prison. Lovesay's solicitor, Mr B.J. Quirke, briefed Mr James Comyn, Q.C. for Lovesay's defence and Comyn, after accepting the brief, had a long consultation with Lovesay in Brixton. According to Quirke, Comyn intended to allege on Lovesay's behalf in court that the halves of the Epps envelope had been "planted" on Lovesay by the police; a defence which would have enabled the prosecution to outline to the jury Lovesay's previous convictions. (Lovesay had several relatively minor convictions, mainly for stealing, none of which involved violence of any kind).

About a week before the trial opened, Quirke got a phone call from Comyn's clerk who told him that one of Comyn's cases had been delayed, and would have to be heard during the Lovesay murder trial. Accordingly he was frightfully sorry, but he was returning the brief. Quirke rapidly briefed Mr Eric Myers Q.C., who did not see Lovesay until the day of the trial. Myers took the view that it would be very damaging to Lovesay to allow his convictions to be brought up in court, and was therefore opposed to making specific allegations about "planting" the envelope halves. Accordingly, although the judge pressed them to be specific, both Myers and counsel for Peterson refused to make allegations of "a plant" in court.

When Peterson was asked if he had anything to say before sentence, he replied:

"I would like to thank your lordship for a fair trial, but I still maintain that I am innocent of the charge and the man who planted that on me, that bit of envelope, was Harris, Sergeant Harris. That is all I have got to say".

The pieces of envelope were the only evidence of any substance which the prosecution could produce to link the two men with the crime.

They claimed that the murderers had used a red maroon Jaguar, number plate VLB 1. This car had been stolen some time before the murder, had been seen in the vicinity of Brook Street on the morning of the murder and had been parked in Hanover Square about two hours after the murder. There were some bloodstains on the upholstery of the same group as that of Mr Sydney Epps, which was the same group as that of the car's previous owner. Nothing else linked the car with the murder.

Three witnesses appeared in court who said they had seen the car during the time it was stolen (about three weeks before the murder). Not one of them was specific about dates. One man, a Mr Harvey, who knew Peterson, had caught a "momentary glimpse" of the car approaching Hanover Street on a morning in late January, and thought that the driver was Peterson. Another man, Mr Kotowski, reckoned he had seen the car and, in court, identified Lovesay as one of its occupants. Three weeks after the murder, when Kotowski was first interviewed by the police, he had declined to attend an identity parade, on the grounds that he could not be sure of recognising the car's occupants. Three months later, however, in court, he identified Lovesay, who had lost a stone and a half while in solitary confinement. The most interesting witness, however, was a Mrs Irene White, of Sutherland Street, who said she had seen the car some time "about a couple of days" before the police saw her on 19th February, which was impossible since the car had been impounded by police on the day of the murder (Jan. 24). It had, she said, stopped outside her house, and she had seen the occupants get out of the car and talk. In court, Mrs White identified Lovesay and Peterson as the two men in the car. She "did not think" she had any doubt about it. Mrs White was, by all accounts, a convincing witness. Part of her cross-examination by Mr Myers ran as follows:

Q. Have you ever watched trials of people on television?

A. No, I do not watch television very much.

Q. Never seen any sort of representation of what a criminal court looks like?

A. No, I have not.

Some doubt was cast on this shining innocence when Lovesay's friends in Pimlico heard on the grape-vine that Mrs White had indeed some experience of the dock - from inside it. On February 3rd this year, Mr Quirke, Lovesay's solicitor, wrote to the Director of Public Prosecutions, in relation to Lovesay's application to appeal, detailing possible previous convictions of Mrs White, in the name of McCloy, and asking the Director "to obtain relevant information from police records about Mrs White ....."

A week later, the reply came back, signed by a Mr J. Palmes of the Director's office.

"In general, a search at Criminal Record Office in the names supplied in paragraph (a) of your letter has been made but no convictions have been traced in any of these names.

"Enquiries have also been made of the Prostitutes' Index, New Scotland Yard, and at West End Central Police Station but again there was no information to confirm any of the points mentioned in your letter.

"I should mention" ended the letter "that all the above information has been supplied by the police".

Upon which, Lovesay's friends searched out a newspaper cutting from the *Westminster and Pimlico News* of 25th December 1964, which recorded a conviction for street betting on "an elderly woman" called Mrs Irene White, who lived in Sutherland Street.

The cutting was sent to the Director of Public Prosecutions and it worked wonders. Back came a reply, signed this time by Mr F.A. Lance. "Following further inquiries in this matter I now enclose a copy of the previous convictions recorded against a Mrs Irene White. At present there is no strict proof that this is the same Mrs White and further police enquiries are being made". The enclosed list included 25 convictions for prostitution, two for insulting behaviour, one for drunk and disorderly, one for attempted suicide, one for larceny, one for obtaining a cheque by false pretences and one for street betting. The last two convictions were in the name of Irene White: the others in the name of McCloy. Finally, a few days before the appeal, the DPP informed Quirke by telephone that Mrs White, the witness, had admitted all the convictions.

*John Lovesay and Tony Peterson*

The innocent witness who said she had never seen a dock on the television or cinema screen had seen a great deal of it in her lifetime, and to this date no-one has explained how it was that searches and enquiries of the records made by the police failed to find any reference to Mrs White until documentary proof was produced from the newspapers. Mrs White, incidentally, was first discovered by the police as a potential witness in the course of "house to house inquiries" in the Pimlico area.

The only other evidence of any substance produced by the prosecution came from Mrs Eglash, daughter of the murdered jeweller.
Mrs Eglash told the court that, several weeks before the murder, a man and a girl had come to Mr Epps' shop, and she identified Lovesay as the man.

Like Kotowski and Mrs White, Mrs Eglash's identification was made in court - not on an identity parade, although Lovesay and Peterson had both been prepared to attend identity parades in Brixton prison (though not in West End Central police station, where enquiries, in their view, were not always to their advantage).

There was, in summary, no direct evidence of any kind to link Lovesay and Peterson with Epps' shop at the time of the crime. There was no evidence of blood on any of their clothes or belongings, despite a rigorous search by police at their homes. Forensic evidence of fibres and so on found no trace of a link between the two men or the car or the shop. The two men were convicted on the basis of three dubious identifications in court, none of which related specifically to the date of the crime - and the envelope.

On April 22, the two men applied for leave to appeal and were powerfully represented by Lewis Hawser, Q.C. In his judgement, Lord Justice Widgery said that the evidence of all the witnesses connected with the Jaguar car (White, Kotowski and Harvey) "individually and collectively could properly be characterised as weak". Again and again throughout his judgement he referred to the "weakness" of the court identifications. Mrs Eglash's evidence, he recalled, was cross-examined and

"certain weaknesses in it were deducted". What the Lord Justice said about the envelope can be left, in extracts, without comment:

*"At the trial it was pointed out ..... that there were three possibilities arising out of this evidence. The first was that the evidence of the police was wholly reliable, that these pieces of paper had been found in the pockets of these two men on arrest. I pause to examine the likelihood or not of that being true. These men had not, in their possession, blood-stained clothes. If they committed these offences it is quite clear that the clothing in which they committed them was not the clothing in which they were arrested on 29th January. If the prosecution evidence was to be relied upon, they had nevertheless transferred, each of them, to the clothes worn on 29th January these two incriminating and utterly useless pieces of paper ..... There were no bloodstains or fingerprints of any significance, and it is strongly put to the jury that it was an extraordinary thing that each of these men should have had this particular piece of paper in his clothing on his arrest five days after the offence.*

*"The second possibility ..... was that there had been some muddle or mistake in the police station ..... Clearly it is a very unlikely explanation. For one piece of paper to be misplaced in that way would be surprising, but for its sister half to be misplaced in a similar way would be even more surprising.*

*"The third possibility was that these pieces of paper had been dishonestly planted by the police in and among the possessions of the accused .....*

*"We are impressed by the improbability of each of the first two alternatives, but when we come to ask ourselves: 'What would have happened if a plant had been run in the court below by the defence,' we are up against the considerable difficulty that we do not know what the police evidence would have been ..... We do not know what the evidence would be from them, and what impression it may have made. This case has not been easy on that point, but in the end we cannot say that the verdict was unsafe or unsatisfactory on behalf of these matters, and therefore we are not disposed to grant leave of appeal on that point".*

The Court of Appeal, in short, explicitly rejected all the main points in the prosecution case. Yet they only allowed the appeal on the technicality that the judge had misdirected the jury and they did not even grant leave to appeal on the robbery charge.

John Lovesay and Tony Peterson, now languishing in Parkhurst jail, are no doubt reflecting on the fact that had it not been for a chance blunder by Mr Justice Melford Stevenson they would be there for the bulk of the rest of their lives, and that had it not been for the recent abolition of capital punishment for murder in the furtherance of theft, they would now be preparing for the gallows.

# Gnome

## A
## STATEMENT

Certain events at the Villa Disraeli last weekend have given rise to unhealthy speculation amongst the public at large and it will be in the interests of all to "clear the air."

First, with regard to the so-called "fun party" at the Villa and the loose talk on the part of neighbours of "lights blazing well into the night," "raucous laughter," "girlish shrieks," etc, etc.

A far cry indeed from what was in fact the Annual General Meeting of the Gnome Temperance League. (Any ladies present I should add were there in their capacity as lifetime campaigners in this cause).

The tragic demise of Mlle Lottie Mecklendorff-Bernstein, 56, whose body was subsequently found in my private swimming pool reduced me to a state of stunned shock as a result of which I immediately swam across the Channel and booked in on the first flight from Heathrow to Honolulu.

Many were the confused feelings that raced through my fevered brain at the time: I even pondered on whether some dreadful curse did not hang over the house of Gnome.

Luckily such fears were put aside when I had the opportunity to meet Chief Inspector Hercule Maigret of the Cap Gris Nez Police Force and to introduce him personally to some of my colleagues on the board of Gnome Allied Investment Trust Funds Ltd. from whom he graciously accepted a "modest" donation for the police ball fund.

Now, I must ask all my friends and supporters to bear with me at this tragic time.

If they do not I should warn them that the firm of Messrs Sue Grabbit and Runne will not be inactive when it comes to silencing loose tongues.

E. Strobes
pp Lord Gnome
alias Senor J Smith
Whereabouts Unknown.

## New York cops raid strip joint

### British Dramaturge held

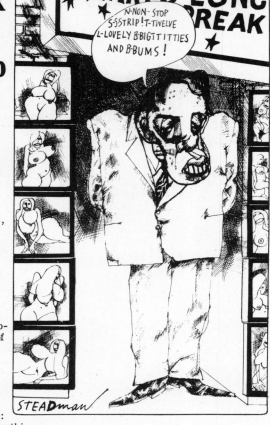

The New York police, under their chief Captain O'Knackerstein of the 87th Precinct, last night raided an off-Broadway Strip-tease theatre. A number of 'women' were held.

The raid followed complaints from the public about alleged 'acts of indecency'.

### Shows off now

Later the proprietor of the show, a Mr Kenneth Tyanan of London, England, told reporters: "To my mind, there is nothing obscene about our show. My girls are decent, hardworking girls from decent homes. My clients are highly respectable art-lovers for the main, who like a bit of fun.

"Frankly I am amazed that anyone should get so worked up over just a bit of tit and the other. Besides, I have some world-famous artistes working on the routines.

"Our main number 'The Queen of Sheba takes a bath with her handmaidens and a six-foot boa constrictor' was personally written for us by Harold Pinter, Gore Vidal-Sassoon and Samuel Beckett, the world-famous playwright."

Mr Tynan claimed that he had hoped his show might "transfer to the National Theatre, London".

He also claimed that he was a "close personal friend" of Princess Margaret.

S. GROSS

# MRS. WILSON'S DIARY

Behold two giants in conflict lockt,
  Head against brazen head
Their mighty muscles bulged and blockt
  Their feet are set in lead.
A stalemate seems inevitable
  For none will yield an inch:
To yield would be discreditable
  A shame 'twould be to flinch.
But lo!  An angel from the skies
  Comes hov'ring overhead -
His name is called Compromise
  He steps with careful tread
Where once was grim despair and hate
  Twixt rivals for the Cup
Now see the giants' rage abate
  As they shake hands and make it up.

I cannot pretend that the last weeks have been easy: despite my protestations, Harold insists on remaining in his Bunker, and in the hot weather it becomes very close down there to put it mildly. Quite apart from that, the T.U.C. have been making regular calls, trying to get him to lop off his penal sanctions.  It all began when Mrs Castle came in through the back garden with her white paper.  "Coo-eee" she observed, climbing through the elderberry bush, "any chance of a glimpse of the Old Man?  I've cooked up a wheeze that may get us out of the wood".  She climbed unsteadily down the steps in her sensible high heels, and we found Harold brewing his mid-day survival broth from a packet of Knorr Meat 'n' Lettuce Dried Mueslifood.

"What is it now, Barbara?" he rasped in moody tones, ladling the rather chunky soup into an enamel container and squatting on his camp bed to eat it, "if it's about the TUC, we are standing firm.  I have crack batallions waiting in the wings to deal with Feather and his ilk.  The penal clauses stand, and the statutory 28-day cooling-off period cannot be lightly cast aside."  "Oh Harold" riposted the auburn-haired charmer, "don't be so bloody stupid.  You know you're going to have to climb down sooner or later ....."  "Listen, Barbara", riposted Harold 'I'm sick to the back teeth of taking the can for a cabinet full of shifty opportunists and trimmers intent on private gain. Who are the people who are selling Britain short?  The scrimshankers on both sides of the House?  Are we to give way in the face of ignorance and prejudice in order to save a few party workers in marginal situations?  The Nation comes first, Barbara, there is no fudging the issue ..."

"Oh, come off it, ducky, for Heaven's

sake" returned Barbara, sitting down opposite him legs akimbo and lighting a large French cigarette rolled in yellow paper, "we've heard all that old claptrap too often.  If you think there's any votes in trotting out a lot of Methodist cant of that sort you must be out of your bloody mind."  "That will do, Barbara" snapped Harold, "enough is enough.  We may have been friends in the past, but that does not entitle you to address me in the language of the gutter.  And now piss off, Moira Shearer, or whatever your name is, I have serious brooding to do."  It was at that moment that a light tread was heard on the stair, and Mr Jenkins peeped through the barbed wire with a gay smile. "Aha" he vouchsafed, "a council of war, no less.  Prime Minister, I have been giving a little thought to our proposals vis a vis the Unions ....."  "Our souls" Harold remarked, in a strangely angry manner, "another pussy foot.  Don't tell me, Smoothichops, I know it all.  You have decided that mutatis mutandis, as you would put it in your toffee-nosed gents outfitter style of talk, that we should yield a teeny-weeny soupcon" - here Harold made a strange grimace and waved his hands about in an affected manner - "to the demands of Feather and his mob of self-seeking nestliners."  "Really, Prime Minister," replied Mr Jenkins somewhat taken aback by this rare display of Harold's amusing sarcasm, "I see no reason to be personal, but realities are realities, and we must take into account the piles on which our party rests."  "Nation first, nation first," Harold roared, thumping on an old packing case with his empty enamel bowl.  "As Harry Truman used to say, if you can't stand the heat, get out of the kitchen.  By the way, Gladys, it is intolerably close in here.  Turn down that Aladdin genieflame and be so good as to give the Ventaxia a twitch.  And what is all that tramping overhead?"

As we watched in horrified silence, a number of highly polished boots descended the stairs, and Mr Victor Feather stood before us, nervously twisting his cloth cap in his large hands.  "Excuse me, Sir, coming in when you're having your tea, like, but me and t' lads have put our heads together as you might say, and come up with certain proposals."  Harold said nothing for a few moments, looking threateningly first at Barbara Castle and then at Mr Jenkins.  "It's no good Feather," put in

Mr Jenkins, thrusting his thumbs into his waistcoat pockets and looking down his nose at the horny-handed son of labour, "you had better go away and think of a better excuse."  Barbara walked forward and put her hand on Mr Feather's shoulder.  "Bad luck, Vic" she said, as a tear made its way down Mr Feather's dusty cheek, "it's for your own good."

Harold, who had hitherto said nothing, and watched apparently unmoved as this touching scene was enacted before his eyes, now rose to his feet.  "Stop" he cried, "you two have done enough harm for one day.  I will not stand idly by and see our great movement betrayed.  Listen, Victor, I'll tell you the truth.  These two - all the Cabinet in fact - have fought tooth and claw to do you down.  Yes, Roy, you may look away in shame.  You too, Barbara, glare if you must, but truth will out regardless. Naturally, Victor, I am bound by the democratically reached decisions of the Cabinet, but there come times when, as Prime Minister and First Lord of the Treasury, I must take things into my own hands.  This is such a time.  Whatever it may cost me in terms of personal popularity with my Cabinet colleagues - and Heaven knows, the daggers are out - I at least am prepared to give your proposals a go.  It won't be easy.  Mr Jenkins' rich friends in Basle and Zurich will no doubt scream for my blood; Mrs Castle, here, will doubtless fill the air with her washer-woman style caterwauling and abuse, but you and I, Victor" - here he embraced the bemused Mr Feather and raised a declamatory hand in the air - "we will see this one through, mark my words, trust me, there's a pal." There was silence in the room for some six and a half minutes.  Then Mr Feather fell rigidly backwards, striking his head on the floor and lying senseless, Mr Jenkins and Mrs Castle stamped out in a huff and Harold gave vent to a curious maniacal chuckle, before summoning Mr Kaufmann with his evening Lucozade.

## TALKING POINT

"Lennon and McCartney are working class artists.  They have used their success not to buy real estate or oil wells but to take over the means of artistic production.  This makes them Socialists in practice, if not in theory".

K. Tynan.

# BARRY McKENZIE

**Words by BARRY HUMPHRIES**    **Drawings by NICHOLAS GARLAND**

THE STORY SO FAR: AFTER A BRAWL IN THE FREEDOM FOLK CELLAR, *BARRY* IS FOUND SENSELESS AND TAKEN TO HOSPITAL. A YOUNG DOCTOR RECOGNISES BARRY AS A *"PSYCHIATRIC JOB"* *BARRY* RESOLVES TO ESCAPE AND AT THE FIRST OPPORTUNITY SLIPS UNNOTICED OUT OF BED...

NOW READ ON...

WHERE HAVE THE *BASTARDS* HIDDEN ME *STRIDES?*

BARRY TIPTOES DOWN THE PASSAGE—BUT...

(WHISPER) I WARN YOU, GENTLEMEN, THE PATIENT MAY BE VIOLENT SO LACE HIM TIGHTLY (SHHH)

STRUTH! — VERY WELL, DOCTOR! — RIGHT, SIR.

*JEEZ!!* WHAT DO YOU FLAMIN' WELL THINK YOU'RE DOING. I'LL WRITE TO *AUSTRALIA HOUSE* SO HELP ME! *OUCH!* I'LL TELL SIR *ROBERT MENZIES* ABOUT THIS YOU DIRTY *POMMY BASTARDS!* I WISH I'D NEVER SET FOOT IN THIS BLOODY APOLOGY FOR A COUNTRY!

ALL RIGHT, BERT? — PRICK! — COR BLIMEY?

POW — KICK — SMACK

WARD 9

MEANWHILE DR DE LAMPHREY TAKES CAREFUL NOTE OF BARRY'S BEHAVIOUR

STEADY, YOU'RE A VERY SICK BOY. TAKE HIM TO MY ROOM GENTLEMEN!

*LATER...*

NOW MR. M°KENZIE. HOW DO YOU FEEL? I'M D? DE LAMPHREY AND I'M HERE TO HELP YOU

*PULL YOUR HEAD IN!*

COME, COME NOW. MR M°KENZIE. LETS START AT THE BEGINNING... NOW WHEN DID YOU START HAVING *DELUSIONS!*

IF YOU WANT TO KNOW, WHEN I PAID THROUGH THE NOSE FOR A TICKET AND LANDED UP A *SHIT CREEK* CALLED ENGLAND...

...I'VE HAD A *ROTTEN COP* EVER SINCE I CAME TO THIS *FLAMIN'* COUNTRY BUT *THIS* BEATS THE BLOODY LOT!

*SO?* YOU HATE THE MOTHER COUNTRY, IS THAT IT? WHAT EXACTLY IS YOUR RELATIONSHIP WITH YOUR OWN MOTHER?

*I'M HER SON*

WHAT WILL D? DE LAMPHREY'S PROBING QUESTIONS REVEAL—SEE NEXT ISSUE!

THE STORY SO FAR: WHILST ATTEMPTING TO ESCAPE FROM HOSPITAL, *BARRY IS WAYLAID* BY MALE NURSES WHO CONVEY HIM (TIGHTLY LACED IN A STRAIT JACKET) TO THE STUDY OF *Dr DE LAMPHREY* RESIDENT PSYCHIATRIST— WHO QUESTIONS *BARRY* CLOSELY...

NOW READ ON...

...MMM...TELL ME MORE ABOUT WHAT YOU FEEL IS *BEASTLY* ABOUT ENGLAND...

*NOT ON YOUR SWEET LIFE, MATE!* YOU POMS LAP UP THAT KIND OF STUFF, YOU'RE ALWAYS CRYING *STINKIN' FISH* IN YOUR OWN BACKYARD

DOES THE SMELL OF *FISH* HAVE ANY SPECIAL SIGNIFICANCE FOR YOU? *NOW THINK BACK!*

THIS BLOKE'S A FLAMIN' *RATBAG!* HE OUGHT TO BE DOING TIME IN A *GIGGLE FACTORY!!*

WHAT ABOUT YOUR SEX LIFE—IS IT HEALTHY?

*HEALTHY!* STONE THE CROWS, IT OUGHT TO BE. IT HASN'T HAD A CHANCE TO CATCH ANYTHING YET...

THEN YOU'RE FRIGHTENED OF WOMEN— DO YOU BY ANY CHANCE ASSOCIATE WOMEN WITH *WITH SNAKES!*

*YOU DIRTY BASTARD!* ARE YOU INFERRING! *SPLASH ME BOOTS IN THE LADIES!*

A FASCINATING CASE!

NO, ACTUALLY I WAS THINKING OF THE GARDEN OF EDEN MYTH, IN WHICH THE SERPENT FEATURES AS A...

ACCORDING TO MY BOOK IT WAS *ADAM* WHO DONE THE *FEATURING...*

...LOOK, DOC, IF YOU SHOOT OFF YOUR MOUTH MUCH LONGER I'LL *CHUNDER* ON YOUR WALL-TO-WALL!

YOU'LL *WHAT?*

I'LL *CHUNDER* SO HELP ME—YOU KNOW, *THROW THE VOICE, PLAY THE WHALE,* LAUGH AT THE GROUND!

YOU FIND MY CARPET FUNNY, DO YOU? IT MAKES YOU *LAUGH!* WHICH PART OF THE CARPET PARTICULARLY AMUSES YOU?

YOU'RE GETTING WARM!

WOULD IT BE THIS RATHER PHALLIC PATTERN HERE? AM I ANY WARMER?

YOU'RE GETTING PRETTY HOT NOW MATE!

COP THAT, YOU POMMY BASTARD!

DO DOCTORS ENJOY HOSPITAL FOOD? AND WILL BARRY RESPOND TO THERAPY. READ NEXT PROBING ISSUE...

# PRIVATE EYE

No. 197
Friday
July 69

2/-

# QUEEN TOPS TV POPS

Any chance of getting Mum on the Show?

**Exclusive:**

# David Frost talks to Prince Charles

**Charles:** Good evening, hullo, welcome, super to be here. And a big hand for my old friend, David Frost. Dave, tell me, it must be very difficult being someone in your position, with millions of people watching everything you do. Don't you find this is a great responsibility?

**Frost:** (getting up off knees) Well, your Majesty, of course I do. But I think that society needs figure-heads, and particularly some-one like myself, to go round the country opening fetes and making speeches and that sort of thing. And one feels that since one has been called to this kind of thing, one must just do it as best one can.

**Charles:** But it must be a great strain?

**Frost:** Of course it is your Holiness. I find the social side of it very tiring, constantly have to smile and remember people's names and say "super to see you" the whole time. But when you see how loyal the British are, and how they look up to you to set a certain tone - well, it makes one feel very arrogant inside, however humble one may seem on the surface.

**Charles:** Of course, you have a lot of people to help you, writing your jokes and so forth.

**Frost:** (consulting script) Oh no, not at all. One tries to do all that sort of thing oneself. Naturally, one does have one's advisers - ladies of the bedchamber - and so forth. But nowadays, people don't ex-pect so much in that kind of line as they used to. So long as one is informal, and shows that one is aware of the latest trends in show business, like the Goon Show, one can get by.

**Charles:** You acquired a reputation early on as something of a comedian - I mean, your revues at Cambridge and so on?

**Frost:** Yes, one did find that kind of thing useful to show people that one was human, by putting on funny voices and so forth. But as one grew older and became more aware of one's responsibi-lities, with the Prime Minister dropping in for breakfast and that kind of thing, one realised that one had a position to keep up.

**Charles:** (Bowing out of room back-wards) Super to have you on the show, Dave, bless you, and keep in touch.

World copyright
© Private Eye 1969

# Yes, it's the Royal Laugh-in

## by Peter Blackout

The biggest television audience in the history of the world was tuned in last night to the 3½-hour documentary " *The First Lady*", the sensational, no-holds-barred ciné-verité look at life behind the scenes at Buckingham Palace.

### AMAZING

Millions gasped as the cameras probed where they had never probed before. Informality was the keynote, and Her Majesty the Queen emerged as a warm, sympathetic woman just like everyone else.

The film showed the Queen accepting a signed photograph from President Nixon. "Thank you" she joked informally, as the President handed her the official snapshot.

### BARBECUE

Another sequence showed the Royal Family coming down to breakfast at Balmoral. "Oh dear, it seems to be raining again" remarks the Queen, tapping her boiled egg with a kipper. "Bang goes our shooting" saltily replies Prince Philip with his traditional wit.

### FOR HE'S A JOLLY GOOD CELLO

The good humour of Prince Charles was also much in evidence.

One shot showed him practising 'Men of Harlech' on his cello in time for the investiture.

"What's that bloody awful noise?" comes a familiar voice from behind *The Field*.

"Sorry, Dad, I'm just tuning up" quips back the young man who has won the hearts of millions with his informal wit and charm.

### SYCOPHANTASY

Say what you like, this historic film has in $3\frac{1}{2}$ hours done more to strip away 2000 years of Victorian mystique, and to bring the Royal Family roaring into the last third of the get-up-and-go, democratic 20th Century of the Common Man than anything since Alfred burnt the cakes.

The secret of the film lay in the brilliant, understated commentary by BBC producer Tony Jay. As Mr Jay summed up: "If it wasn't for the Monarchy, we would long ago have seen jackbooted thugs strutting all over Hyde Park and we would have a Fascist dictatorship like they do in countries where the Monarchy has been abolished - such as America and Ireland."

# HONOURS LIST

**K.C.V.O.** Mr Huw Weldon for Services to the Arts in Wales.

**M.V.O.** Mr Richard Cawston for Services to export.

**C.H.** Mr Anthony Jay for Services to literature.

**K.B.E.** Mr George Weidenfeld for Political and Private Services to the Prime Minister.

*THE VIGIL*

*Mr. George Weidenfeld seen here on the eve of his investiture. (Specially painted for Private Eye by the Master of Clapham)*

UP THE MALL, an everyday story of Royal folk

# COLOUR SECTION

● *Mr John Carr Doughty runs the Design and Development Centre in Leicester which makes sweaters and other hosiery items, and recently he has developed an unobtrusive bullet-proofing technique.*

*On Wednesday, 25th June, a courier from Buckingham Palace collected six bullet-proof vests from Mr Carr Doughty's premises, which had been hired by the Palace for "a few weeks". The news came to the ears of a journalist on a Sunday newspaper who rang Buckingham Palace to ask if the Prince was to wear a bullet-proof vest on Investiture Day. "We have" said the Palace Press Officer "heard nothing of this. Try Caernarvon". So the journalist tried a spokesman at Caernarvon, who replied, helpfully:*

*"I haven't heard anything about this, and certainly wouldn't confirm it if I had".*

*Musing over a hopeless story, the journalist then received a telephone call from Mr Carr Doughty. Things, he explained, had got a bit awkward. He'd just had Buckingham Palace on the line, furious that the vests delivery had "got out". "Of course" the Palace man rapped across the phone "if any journalist asks us about it, we shall have to deny it and we hope you will too".*

The saga of the *Sunday Times* 1,000 Men and Woman of the century continues. Last week, Her Majesty was included, but not as originally planned. The pocket biography commissioned from Simon Scharma, a Cambridge don, referred to the Queen as belonging to the "regnum of mass consumption ..... like most carefully designed products, the Queen comes flavourless, harmless, beautifully packaged but a bit expensive ..... Cluttered with amiable feudal eccentricities ..... the monarchy survives to restore its earliest function, to celebrate the rite of fantasy."

Such *lese majesté* in Investiture week was altogether too much for the *Sunday Times* forelock-tugger-in-chief Foreign editor Frank Giles. Scharma's piece was removed and a rather more respectful substitute took its place, referring to Her Majesty as "charming, witty and wise .... with beautiful eyes and a peaches and cream complexion".

The piece was signed F.T.R.G. (believed to be a person not a million miles from Giles).

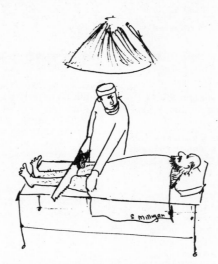

*"This doesn't necessarily mean you'll paint like Toulouse Lautrec."*

A Spike Milligan JOKE

## Flower cap for bride

AN Empire-line gown of bridal crepe with a front panel, bodice, and sleeves of ribbon lace, and an unusual Dutch cap covered with apple blossom holding a full-length veil, will be worn by Miss Kerry McPherson for her wedding in Brisbane today.

*The Courier-Mail, Brisbane*

*"All be upstanding for Lord Chief Justice Parsons and Bertie."*

## AFTER SHAVE
### The Secrets of the Trade

A special investigation by NICHOLAS STRINGALONG  2

---

OIL SLICK THREAT TO LOCH NESS MONSTER. Scientists disquiet may lead to Government probe. 25

NEASDEN policemen face Home Office inquiry after allegations of incorrect answers to members of the public asking for the time.

Transplant could have saved space Monkey 'Bonny' claims Dr Pagan Barnard. 34

Board of Trade will investigate forged patchwork quilt auction ring, says Nicholas Stringalong. 35

Cervical smears may cause jaundice. Local health authority warns diabetics.

---

## IN COLOUR

### DESIGN FOR LOVING 47

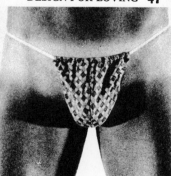

#### ALL TRUSSED UP

Ernestine Castoff take a close look at what men AND WOMEN are wearing where it hurts most.

---

# THE SUNDRY TRENDS

18 JULY 1969  •  No. 8762  •  Price 2/-

# Autumn Election unlikely

JAMES MARGACH

HIGHLY PLACED Government sources yesterday confirmed the prospect that an autumn election can be ruled out at least in the near future.

## Man hurt in crash

A MAN was slightly hurt yesterday when his moped collided with the Queen Mother.

## Turd 'satisfactory'

MR. NIBBY SLOD, a member of the Turds, a popular singing group was stated to be 'satisfactory' last night after his car collided with a noodle factory outside Marples. Slod was returning from the funeral of fellow Turd Enoch Hogg. He was due to be cited in a divorce action tomorrow by Jonny Hash, another member of the Turds whose house was raided by the police last night.

### INSIGHT

# Lone crawler nears Omsk

THE ONLY competitor in the Sundry Trends Trans Siberian Crawling Race, Maj. the Hon. Gavin Trimgrabely-Snarg has reached the outskirts of Omsk.

After 4,729 days of non-stop crawling the Major is in high spirits, but his supply of reinforced office-cleaner style knee protectors is running low.

"My knees are running low too" he told the Sundry Trends by long-distance walkie-talkie "tell the little woman to keep her pecker up. I'm looking forward to seeing her in the spring. Crawling is a lonely business. There are times when you think you must be the only man on earth crawling across the Steppes. Roger and out."

# How the Apollo Men beat the Germ Jinx

LAST TUESDAY afternoon Mrs Jacqueline Grossfodder, a 69 year old house help from Kensington, Mass., was dusting the Automatic Decompressing Feedback Adjuster in the Rendezvous mother module area (nicknamed "Marilyn") on board Apollo 9 prior to countdown on Friday when she sneezed involuntarily.

The incident could well provide the clue to the last minute hitch which bugged the tension-packed hours of preparation prior to blast-off. Scientists believe that that minute bacterial products scarcely visible through multi-million microscopic lenses could have been concealed in the hamburger dispensing equipment in the 2 by 2 leisure area on D Deck.

If brought into contact with the moon's atmosphere these germs could cause havoc with the crew's highly sensitive lunar oxygen feed. Says Dr Hinrich Weill (cont. p.94)

---

# Porton Down mice clue hope for Hay Fever sufferers

by Dr Alfred Byrne the Cakes

SCIENTISTS WORKING at Porton Down may have stumbled on some old War Department containers lying outside their laboratories.

The effects may revolutionise current thinking about the treatment of certain strains of hay fever. Experiments carried out on mice show a marked improvement and it is hoped that by the year 2000 all mice will be cured of this chronic irritation.

# COCK!

### Edited by HUNTER DAVIES

*Everybody wants a tan — but how to get rid of that ghastly apres-sun zebra look with white patches on the parts that really matter?*

*Beach designer Krazy Svensen has come up with a new line in one-way drip-dry Tomalin. These exciting things let in the sun's vital ultra-violet rays (not to mention Violet Ray, the 18 year old starlet who's got some pretty big things in store for us in the near future) without causing offence to the stuffy anti-permissive brigade. "It's just like a oneway mirror in fact" explains Svensen. Army & Navy Stores, Gorringes, Kinkique, Croydon. 35 gns.*

## Next week in COCK!

- *Hunter Davies on VD*
- *Cancer and the Coil*
- *A Hippie Clippie tells all*
- *Sterilising your handicapped child*

# JOLLY SOOPER on what happens when your husband goes off with another man

I FIRST met my second husband at a wife-swapping party given by his third wife. Everyone was drunk as hell and having it away like mad. Later when we were sitting one out in the back seat of his MG he told me I had the most fabulous legs and my pink knickers were driving him crazy. I knew it was going to be the start of something big and we married that night.

It was only in the clear light of day that I realized things had gone sadly amiss. "I think there's been some terrible mistake" he said, the mascara running down his cheeks. "I thought you were one of the boys. It must have been the tweed jacket you were wearing. You can't tell one sex from the other these days. It's the Sunday Newspapers I blame."

Naturally I was frightfully upset, especially as he was awfully rich and had established a terrific thing with Julian, my twelve year old son by a former marriage.

I kept thinking he would come round to my way of looking at things. But it was no good. A month later we decided to divorce. "No hard feelings, darling" he said. "I'm sorry but that's been my trouble all along."

I stood there watching him throwing his dresses into a suitcase. In a minute he was gone and the house seemed strangely empty.

The first few days were sheer hell. I tried to forget all about him by fleeing to Marrakesh. But I kept on seeing him everywhere, arm-in-arm with Arab friends who had got closer to him than I ever had.

In desperation I went to a psychiatrist who suggested I take a long rest. He knew someone on the Sundry Trends. "Write about your intimate experiences. Whatever comes into your mind. Get it all off your chest."

I took him at his word and the boys at the **Sundry Trends** went wild.

NEXT WEEK: Coping with the curse

# My faeces & I

## by Hunter Davies

"LOO GOING is a fun experience for me but conditions must be right. I usually go in the morning and try to spend 10 minutes at least doing my jobs."

**Paper:** "I always choose it carefully because I'm very sensitive about colour schemes. It must be soft but not too soft. Thank heavens that dreary old Bronco scene is as dead as the Dodo. I plump for Fingerlite Softie in pastel Lavender — a floral art-nouveau pattern from Fortnums."

**Air Freshener:** "Absolutely essential during or after. 'New Mown Hay for Men' from Harrods is new and does the job as well as anything."

**Books:** "Nothing too exciting. A Len Deighton can have me on the edge of my seat which can be disastrous. Something satirical and faintly erotic suits me down to the ground."

**Seat:** "How I detest these plastic monstrosities which can be so cold. Luckily, you can now get bleached original Victorian teak seats at Lootique which opened the other day in Beauchamp Place."

**THE RESIDUE** .... by CALMAN

Well, I'm better than just a blank space. or am I?

## Parents' Problems

Four letter Words for Four Year Olds

WHEN SHOULD you teach your child to use four letter words? More and more psychiatrists are coming round to the view that you can't start too soon.

The old idea of waiting till they pick them up behind the school lavs is dangerous, says Professor Roy Vass of the Institute of Paedaelogical Scatology. "They use them haphazardly" he says "and don't derive full satisfaction from them. Start by filtering them into nursery rhymes and bed-time stories. e.g. 'Baa bastard black sheep Have you any f . . . . . g wool you c . . . . ?'"

# IN MY FASHION

## Ernestine Castoff

I MAY BE WRONG but I have a feeling that things are going my way at last.

Princess Anne has shown that it is possible in this day and age to make the headlines, not because she is a Princess but because she is a young girl who doesn't wear a mini-skirt and long black boots.

When Princess Anne goes shopping she is usually accompanied by her companion, Lady Ima Hussy. Lady Ima tells me "What's so original about Anne is that she loves mini-skirts and long black boots. She gets it from her mother."

The Princess' favourite shopping ground is the Nora Beloff Boutique in the Kings Road, where she buys her famous hats. Says Lady Hussy "She has the most marvellous colour sense. She loves reds and blues and yellows and greens and all that sort of thing. She knows just what she wants — anything."

Say what you like, times are changing. The trendy mini-skirted lower-class girls are on the way out and good riddance. And awful old snobs like me can get back to writing rubbish about trendy mini-skirted princesses.

## ALAN BRIEN One man's week

**SATURDAY.** Driving down the M4 to our weekend cottage I suddenly feel the urge to stop off and have a drink. In the little pub we stop at I meet a man who recognises me from the old days on Three After Six. "Aren't you Nicholas Tomalin?" he says. I am not sure whether to feel depressed or flattered by this.

**MONDAY.** I was talking to Tom Driberg last Saturday week and he told me how when working on William Hickey he had become so desperate for something to write about that he took off all his clothes in Piccadilly.

I wonder whether to have all my hair shaved off. It might give me two New Statesman pieces.

**TUESDAY.** I notice a funny rash on my knee. Is it psychosomatic or something I picked it up in the Dordogne?

Having a lunchtime drink in El Vino's with Philip Hope Wallace the conversation turns to masturbation and whether it should be shown on stage. Apparently Kenneth Tynan wants to adapt Portnoy's Complaint for the National Theatre with Tony Curtis in the title role. (continued p.94)

**A**

**ARRSHOL, SHUVITUPJAR** (Finnish 1893-1927). Designer of tubular hat stands. Studied at the Helsinki Kunsthaus under Lunkflit and later in Berlin where he won an award for his advanced ideas in neon bathroom accessories. His Soapdish and Toilet Seat of 1921 revolutionised contemporary fashion. He died tragically in 1927 while testing an electric towel rail cum-bidet in his experimental lavatory outside Munich. **L.S.D.**

A ARRSHOL – THE BREAK-THROUGH, BY HASHUMAKI SHANKI (1956).

**B**

**BLOCKBUSTER, HEINRICH VON** (Canadian 1872-1939). Scientist. Born in Vienna Blockbuster studied with Stumpf and Hesseltrinner inventor of the exploding billiard ball. He patented a papier mache fire extinguisher as early as 1900 and went on to explore

the possibility of subterranean look out posts. He emigrated to Peru during the Anti-Canadian demonstrations of 1907 where he died during his famous experiment which involved making an igloo out of sand. **WR-M.**

COLLECTED DIARIES OF HEINRICH VON BLOCKBUSTER, EDITED BY HANS KILLER.

**MASTURBANI, ANTONIO DI** (Italian, b. 1931). Film director. Began working in films in the Blue Light district of Naples under Michelangela Bellibuttoni, the inventor of the frozen double take. He made 'Woman of the Street' in 1949 followed by 'Woman in the Bathroom' (1949) and 'Lust of the Swamps' (1949). Later the same year be broke away from the stereotyped world of Bellibuttoni and filmed 'Shameful Ladies' which pioneered the cutaway shots later borrowed by Hollywood giants like Hank Damp and Raymond Messy. His 'Women in Black Boots' (1949) introduced the technique of cine verite flash-back and zoom-in hard focus shots for the first time. **M.S.** MASTURBANI, MAN & MYTH, BY MARK SHIVAS 1949.

**BLEZARD, WALTER** (English b. 1895). Gastronomist. Blezard's interest in food became apparent when he was only 7 and his parents immediately sent him to study at The Lycee de la Gastronomie et la Cuisine Paris where he graduated with first class honours in all 74 courses. He travelled in 1917 to the Grande Conference des Gourmets held in Nice and his speech on Escargots Farcis a la Duc de Gloucester brought him international acclaim. In 1920 he invented the world-famous Bombe Blezard, a confection consisting in the main of cream, brandy, strawberries, molten chocolate, syrup of apricot, kirsch, Albanian fig puree and strained Colorado cactus milk. He retired a year later to a corner table in the Petit Jardin des Pooves in Nevers-sur-Dimanche. His books include 'My Hundred Best Meals of 1912,' 'My Compliments to the Chef' and 'This Should Cover It' (An Autobiography). **C.C.**

**THOMSON, ROY** (Canadian b. 1894). Genius. An infant prodigy, Thomson began life as a concert pianist at the age of 7 and by the time he was 10 had invented the jet engine. An accomplished pilot and horse rider as well as universally acclaimed chess champion Thomson won early fame as a nuclear physicist and amateur marine biologist. His scholarly books on biophysics, early Etruscan pottery and his mammoth History of the Chinese people have been translated into 25 languages. At 23 Thomson climbed Kilimanjaro single-handed and won the Cheltenham Gold Cup on his self-trained filly, Roy. Later that year he took Wimbledon by storm, winning both the men's singles and doubles, the only time this feat has been achieved. His 489 not out against Australia in the winter tour of 1933 established a still unbeaten record for the fastest quadruple century before lunch. The same year saw his appointment as Chairman of the International Monetary Fund and his election to an Honorary Fellowship at Oxford. The Nobel Prize followed in 1934, the year of his Olympic Gold Medals in the marathon, the high jump, the Pentathlon and the Underwater Formation Dancing Event. In 1936 his string quartet (op. 5, 672) was hailed as his finest composition to date and he was created Master of the King's Music. At the outbreak of war he was appointed Supreme Commander with the honorary ranks of Field Marshal and Admiral of the Fleet. Despite his intense activity in all spheres of the war he still found time to paint his massive mural (158 ft. x 390 ft.), 'The Sacking of Byzantium' and write his seminal 'Encyclopaedia Thomsonica' a 92-volume classic. He won the V.C. (and bar) at Dieppe in 1942 and was appointed head of Allied Military Intelligence. After the war he settled down to the leisured life of a brain surgeon, before taking up an appointment as Secretary General of the United Nations. His play 'The Anguish of Mrs Barton Stacey' ran for 42,316 performances and later became an award-winning film classic for which he collected Oscars as Male lead, Director, Producer, Cameraman and Wardrobe Mistress. He took up amateur heavyweight boxing at the unusual age of 61 and became the only man in that category to K.O. both Joe Louis and Ingmar Johannson in the same evening (cont. p.94). **R.B.**

ROY THOMSON THE GREATEST MAN WHO EVER LIVED, BY RUSSELL BRADDON.

**SCHWARZ, BENNY** (American b. 1939-1963). Graphic designer. Began his career designing radiator grills for General Motors in Detroit. He moved to New York where he founded the Schwarz School of New Realism. His typeface 'Smashbold' was used throughout post-war American advertising, and his book 'White On White' consisting entirely of blank pages marked a milestone in Applied Neo-Dada surrealism and paved the way for the auto-constructuralists like de Loonig and Peter Pittsburg of the post-Warhol period. Using the then unknown Multi-Focal Wide Zoom reflex lens (F.P.Z.N.) at the revolutionary film speed FP 200/13 he photographed nudes and quickly established a corner on Madison Avenue where he was arrested under the Street Traders (Obscene Publications) Bill of 1929. He later forsook the plastic arts but while introducing New York to the concept of 'The Happening' accidentally shot himself during a free-form lecture on suicide. **F.W.**

THE ZOOM LENS MULTI RACIALIST NIGHTMARE, BY TOM WOLFE. ALEXANDER'S RAG AND BONE TIME BANDWAGGON, BY KENNETH ALLSOP, MERTON COLLEGE, OXFORD.

# EXCLUSIVE!
# I SET FOOT ON MOON

## Lunchtime O'Booze

Sea of Tranquillity, Thursday

Yes, make no mistake about it. It's not made of cheese! I've tasted it, and I should know.

The most amazing moment in the history of mankind came at 13.23 yesterday afternoon when our module Snoopy II made a perfect three-point touchdown in the Bay of Copernicus, or the 'Hollywood Bowl' as the witty American astronauts have nicknamed it.

### FANTASTIC

There was certainly no parking problem for Snoopy, as our rocket motors purred to a halt in the lunar silence.

Sliding open the electronically-powered personnel outlet mechanism (or 'door' as the astronauts have wittily nicknamed it), I became the first man in the history of the world to take the first historic step onto the surface of this ice-cold, pitch-black lunar wilderness.

### SCARED OUT OF MY LIFE

What is it like, this amazing dead world which opens up such fantastic vistas for the generation of tomorrow?

Those of you who are familiar with

the gravel pits outside Slough on a wet November's night when there's nothing on the telly and you've run out of fags, will have some inkling of what life is like on the moon.

Did I say life? Yes, for whatever they may say, these moon-folk are certainly a friendly lot when it comes to sinking a jar or two - as I was quick to find when I talked to some of them in the crowded four-ale bar of the 'Half-Earth'.

Their eyes were out on stalks - little green ones to be precise - as I entered the bar and ordered a double from mine host, chubby, blue-faced 'Nobby' Treen, 367. His faces lit up when I presented him with a commemorative Prince of Wales investiture tankard as a souvenir of the occasion.

### A LOT OF MOONSHINE

All too soon, it was 'Time, troglodytes, please', and by the light of the silvery earth, we set off home across the Sea of Insobriety. Say what you like, and you probably will, there's no place like moon. Message endsh.

©Moon and world copyright 1969 L.O'Booze O.B.E.

*Daily Telegraph*

# SOCCER KLAXON TO DROWN OBSCENE SONGS

Directors of Glasgow Rangers Football Club who met city magistrates last night agreed to take drastic steps to get rid of the hooligan element among their fans. The meeting was prompted by riots at St. James's Park in May when Rangers played Newcastle in the Fairs Cup.

Rangers have agreed to ban fans convicted of bad behaviour and stewards will watch for supporters either under the influence, or taking drink into the ground. A klaxon will be used to drown out obscene songs— often the cause of trouble at Rangers-Celtic games.

Our Football Correspondent writes:

Mein Gott! Vat is great new sound explodink in our ears von ze Scottisches Stadium von Rangers Celtic? Here is comink alive on Seterday efternoons ven ze pubz is shut amazink Volkisches throatsonks screamed von millions of fens 'Funf und swanzig madchens come down von Inverness', 'Ze ballad von ze Jewish nun' 'Ze gut schip Venusberg-musick' und ze top of ze popz 'Ven I'm cleanink vindows op against ze vall'.

Now hear, by courtesy von ze Rangers manager by vay of counterpoint to male voice ensemble, electronisches vunder-bar klaxonsmusik von twenty million vatts comink out of ze atmosphere like ze megaton bomb on top of ze veddink cake. So. Free kick to Celtic. Pianissimo. Tenors und basses con brio von! too! Szree! "Bols to ze Vater! Arz against ze vall. If you never get stuffink yourself on ze Seterday night -ACHTUNG! ze magic svitch! All systemz go on! MMMMMMMAAAAOOURRR!!! B - B flat - C sharp minor - so loud is comink alive ze atonal pentatonisches scale von Schoenberg und ze seven dwarfs! Never in ze history of ze univers is so much noise. Enough to vake up your old friend Hans Killer who is fast asleep 20 light years avay. Not sinz Dame Mahler Hess und ze Huddersfield Ladies Messed Bends (cont. Op. 94)

# SPECIAL MOON PULL-OUT
# THE FROSTYTE SAGA

## THE MOST FANTASTIC, HISTORICAL, AMAZING, HISTORICAL, FANTASTIC, INCREDIBLE MOMENT IN THE ENTIRE HISTORY OF THE UNIVERSE

### *as exclusively brought to you by* DAVID FROST

FROST:
Hullo, good evening, and welcome to the greatest show off earth. For the next two days we'll be bringing you non-stop the news as it happens, when it happens, how it happens and if it happens. But first, let's go over to Trafalgar Square to see the millions of ordinary men in the street who are waiting there to see my programme on a special 200-foot high screen ...

(PICTURE OF TWO SWEDISH TOURISTS FEEDING PIGEONS WATCHED OVER BY KINDLY CONSTABLE)

FROST:
Hullo, officer, how's it going down there ? Any trouble so far ?

INSPECTOR KNACKER (for it is he):
Ahem! Good evening, David. No, no trouble, apart from a little matter involving offences under the Public Places Obstruction Act 1827. I must ask you to come along and remove these 17 television vans, 8 miles of cable and technical sundries which are causing an obstruction within the meaning of the act. Roger and out.

FROST:
Super to have you on the show, Inspector. And we've just heard, during that interview, that something very exciting is about to happen at the Houston Control Centre. So over to Alistair Burnet at the ITN studio.

BURNET:
Well, David, the news from Texas is that everything's going according to schedule. So we'll keep you informed of any new developments.

(Caption: SIMULATION)

FROST:
That was a picture of how Alistair Burnet might have looked had something exciting been happening. And now I have a call from one of our team of ordinary viewers who are sitting at home all over the country waiting to put questions to our panel of experts.

(BRRR! BRRR! PICTURE OF FROST ANSWERING TELEPHONE FLASHES UP ON SCREEN)

MYSTERY VOICE:
And the next object is a hair pin bend.

FROST:
Can you eat it ?

SIR HERBERT GUSSETT:
I say, we seem to have a crossed line. I wish to register the strongest possible protest. My wife and I were just sitting down to enjoy Wimbledon 'Match of the Day'. Instead we find ourselves having to watch a whole lot of space-fiction nonsense imported from America at no doubt vast expense at a time when you chaps at the BBC are meant to be cutting down on orchestras to plug the trade gap. First the Test Match and now this. Where will it all end ? I say hats off to Enoch Powell.
     Yours faithfully,
     Sir Herbert Gussett
     (via Dictate-a-Letter)

OPERATOR:
Good morning, suh! Dis am your early mornin' alarm call. Good night suh.

FROST:
Well, I'd like to put all that to our panel of experts. But first a song from the ever lovely Julie Felix.

FELIX (sings):
Where are we going to
   All of you out there,
With all your space ships
   Why should you care.
*(Strum, strum, strummity-strum, strum, strum).*

While men are flying to the moon
   And a new age comes to birth,
The soldiers are still killing
   The folks back here on earth.
*(Strum, strum, strummity-strum, strum, strum).*

Where will it all end, etc, etc.

KILLER:
O Mein Gott! Vot fantastisches Mondscheim Sonaten is coming here from our own lovely Julie Felix Mendelsohn von Bartholdy. Hear from ze Houston Centre vot amazink polyphonisches musik von ze spheres ve are hearink over ze electronisches link viz ze stratosphere. So ...

*Pip. Pip. Pip. Peeeeeeeeee Pip.*

*Kreckel. Pop. Snep. Kreckel. Pop. Pip.* (continued Channel 94)

FROST:
Thank you Hans. And now, I've been sent in a cutting from a viewer in Basildon who wants to know whether it wouldn't be better to spend all the money that goes on space research to provide decent homes for the Duke of Edinburgh ? Any thoughts, Jack ?

BISHOP OF WOOLWICH (retired):
Well, Dave, I think the most important lesson that we Christians can learn from this amazing achievement is that the old idea of God as a man living on the moon has finally been swept away.

FROST:
Well, we must stop there, because I see on the screen behind me that we are about to receive live by satellite from America a film of what the landing on the moon would look like if we could actually see it.

(COVER OF LIFE MAGAZINE IS FLASHED UP ON SCREEN)

FROST:
Well, we've still got twenty three hours of this historic, incredible broadcast to run, so here with his own very special brand of humour is the man who's made it all possible, Ken Dodd.

DODD:
Hello, Diddymen! (PULLS OUT FRONT TEETH AND THRUSTS DIDDY STICK INTO ORBIT). I heard a funny one today. Tee hee! Old Bob Maxwell wants to buy The Sun. Ha! He'll want to buy the moon next! Tee hee! Giggle, giggle. (ROLLS EYES). Keep your corsets warm, mother! How does an astronaut go to the lavatory ? Tee hee! Giggle, giggle. It's all cisterns go! Tee hee giggle, giggle. (TROUSERS FALL DOWN REVEALING UNION JACK). Look out grandad, the Diddymen are coming to take you away!

(MR DODD IS ESCORTED FROM THE STUDIO BY DIMINUTIVE WHITE COATED ATTENDANTS).

FROST:
And now we go over to the little village of Bernard Lovell where our very own Sir Jodrell Bank is keeping a special two-hour watch on the lone British yachtsman

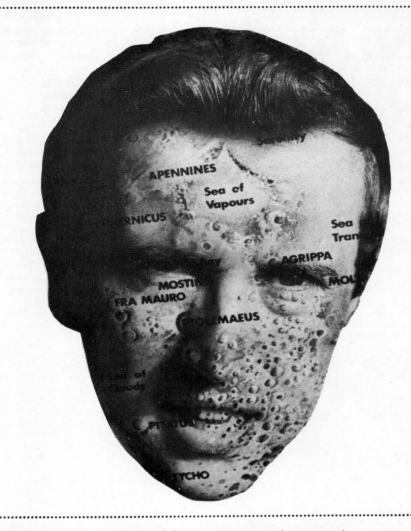

and layabouts like me. So here's a photograph live from the Radio Times picture library, of what he would have looked like if we had been able to find one of him ...

(ENTER LORD CLARK OF CIVILISATION WEARING A SPACE SUIT AND PUSHING A BARROWLOAD OF OLD PICTURES, CATHEDRALS AND AGREEABLE COUNTRY HOUSES).

CLARK:
I am standing at one of the crossroads where civilisation took another gigantic leap into the dark. What could be more agreable than this exquisite little hand-carved model of Lunar Module 2. How it breathes assurance from every functional rivet and screw.

(LUNAR MODULE EXPLODES).

### Obituary

LORD CLARK OF CIVILISATION died suddenly yesterday at his Television Centre Home today. He was 2001. He leaves a wife and 12 million viewers.

FROST:
Super. And we've just heard by satellite from the Space Centre at Houston, Texas, that man has landed on the moon. What a historic moment this is. We are deeply honoured to have in the studio tonight, the Prime Minister, the Rt. Hon. Harold Wislon to give us his views on this historic moment. Harold ?

WISLON:
You know, after 13 million years of old-school tie bumbling and technological mis-management, this is indeed a historic moment.
Brrr! Brrr! Brrr! Brrr!

FROST (answering telephone):
Hello, could you hang on a moment, I'm on the other channel.

VOICE:
This is a recorded announcement. I, the Rt. Hon. Edward Heath, hereby demand the right to reply to the recent Ministerial broadcast by the Prime Minister.

FROST:
Super, go ahead Grocer.

VOICE:
This is a historic moment. Kindly record your message now, and speak clearly.

FROST:
And now I think we should go back to Trafalgar Square where an enormous crowd of cinema extras is being arrested by Inspector Knacker.

(SCREEN SHOWS CLOSE-UP OF GIGANTIC PICTURE OF FROST WATCHING HIMSELF ON MONITOR. Caption: LIVE FROM TRAFALGAR SQUARE).

FROST:
Well, there we are, we'll take the break now - and we'll be back for another 22 hours of this historic rubbish in just half a minute.

COMMERCIAL SHOWS HOUSEWIFE POURING INSTANT MASHED POTATO INTO WASHING MACHINE. (Caption: NEWSFLASH - MAN STEPS ON MOON FOR FIRST TIME).

Len Diggins, who is circling the Atlantic in his home-built Catamaran. Sir Jodrell, are you receiving me ?

BANK:
No, but I hope I shall be receiving your cheque in the morning.

FROST:
Bless you. And now we have a question from a viewer in Bexleyheath, who wants to know "Will the lunar landing bring lasting peace to the war-torn lands of the Middle East?" Perisihing Worthless, perhaps you'd like to give us a few thoughts.

WORTHLESS:
Well, I think we've all got rather bored with all our problems here on earth, feeding the hungry, curing the sick and so forth, which can all become so frightfully tedious, particularly if one has to go on doing it day after day.
(LIGHTS CIGAR AND CRACKS BOTTLE OF YUGOSLAV RUISLIP '53. HAS HEART ATTACK. DIES).

FROST:
Well, the time is now exactly countdown plus zero three four seconds so for another expert opinion on what it all means, over to the Chez Guevara Bistro-theque in the heart of London's fashionable Finsbury Park. Spiggy, what's your reaction to this fantastic event?

S. TOPES (for it is he):
Well, man, it's fantastic to my mind. It's the biggest trip ever, or not. I mean, it's all in the mind, isn't it, and us Turds are already there to my way of thinking.

FROST:
It's hard to believe that that interview was recorded over three million years ago. And now in case some of you have fallen asleep watching this live pro-gramme of the most amazing, fantastic, historic, incredible evening in the entire history of the universe, here is a recording of what it would sound like if 20,000 alarm clocks were set off all at once under the sea.

GUSSETT:
Dear Sir, What on earth is going on? Some of us are trying to get some television.

FROST:
And now, I'd like you to meet some-one who feels very strongly about all this, our own very wonderful 97 year old philosopher, Bertrand Russell.
(PHOTOGRAPH OF HUGHIE GREENE AND WILFRED PICKLES CLAPPING FLASHED UP ON SCREEN).
But unfortunately he refused to come on television with a lot of half wits

# REGGIECIDE:
# MISTER MAUDLING'S
# PENSION SCHEME

The long article in *The Times Business News* of July 19 threw an unpleasant light on the involvement of the Deputy Leader of the Opposition, Reginald Maudling, in the Real Estate Fund of America (R.E.F.A.) and his subsequent resignation. But the article could have been more damning if the journalist concerned, Oliver Marriott, *The Times'* Financial Editor, had had the guts to include some extraordinary remarks made by former Chancellor of the Exchequer Maudling and William Clarke, director of a prestigious City body, The Committee on Invisible Exports.

(Maudling, Clarke, M. Spaak - former Prime Minister of Belgium - Lord Brentford, aging ex-tory junior minister and ex-senior partner in solicitors Joynson-Hicks, and a batch of New York business notables were all directors of the management company of R.E.F.A., an offshore property fund promoted and run by a certain Jerome D. Hoffman. This man is an American who consented to an order stopping him from doing almost anything connected with stocks and shares in New York State, following action against him and detailed charges of fraud by the New York State Attorney General in the spring of 1968. Hoffman denied the charges.

R.E.F.A. is registered in Bermuda and sells units in itself to investors, principally in Europe, South America, Hong Kong, and the Middle East. R.E.F.A. is not allowed to sell itself actively to U.S. citizens. Most of the $500,000 invested in R.E.F.A. since the launch in May has come from Europe, no doubt because of Spaak's name on the prospectus. But, according to Spaak, a much revered political figure on the Continent, he has not been a director since March, *so that on his evidence the prospectus was fraudulent, even under the lax laws of Bermuda.*

Marriott saw Maudling at his smart Chester Square house on Friday the 18th. After handing him a letter of resignation, which stupidly said what an excellent fund R.E.F.A. was, Maudling said that he couldn't understand why *The Times* was so interested in R.E.F.A. and Hoffman. Surely he (Marriott) appreciated that R.E.F.A. couldn't be sold in Britain? (Conning the foreigner is, according to the Maudling logic, quite OK).

Maudling had been *given* shares in the management company of R.E.F.A. - it is the management companies which make the big money in such operations - and he was *"hoping to build up a little pot of money for my old age"* via these shares.

Maudling pointed out that he had no pension. Among others, Maudling is a director of merchant bankers Kleinwort Benson, who

are furious about the affair, Shipping Industrial Holdings and Dunlop.

Maudling has not stated nor is it possible to find out how much he got paid. In answer to another questioner he said the sum was "minimal". The part he played he says was that of "formulating policy". Two months ago, Maudling went with Hoffmann on a tour of the Middle East to drum up business.

Maudling was involved on the recommendation of Lord Brentford, who was involved through his son Crispin Joynson-Hicks, a pal of Hoffman's. Maudling is telling everybody that he knew nothing of Hoffman's brush with the New York Attorney General before he joined R.E.F.A.

MAUDLING : "A little pot of money for my old age"

and that he is "bloody angry with Brentford."

William Clarke lent his name to R.E.F.A. on the recommendation of one of the American big names on the prospectus, Holmes Brown, president of the New York Board of Trade, and Joynson-Hicks in London. Clarke, considered almost universally in the City to be a "decent chap", is a former City Editor of *The Times* and is now a director of National & Grindlays Bank, director and advisor to the *Banker* and director of other City companies.

Whether his behaviour in this squalid affair lived up to his "decent chap" image may conceivably be open to some doubt, though *The Times* failed to put the full spotlight on Clarke.

Shortly after the first exposure of R.E.F.A. and Hoffman in the *Sunday Times* of June 22 by Financial Editor Charles Raw, an article which did not even mention Clarke, so "decent" is he, the former City Editor rapidly found a conflict of interest and resigned on July 3 without announcing

the move in public. When asked on July 3 whether he would resign, he replied "I may have to consider my position later."

On July 16th he made out that he had resigned before June 30 - a lie. On the morning of July 18, he told *The Times* that "of course there are two things you could do, you know. Either you could leave my name entirely out of anything you write or (long silence) I suppose you could put it in."

However, the financial Establishment's newspaper, the *Financial Times,* came to the rescue on Monday 21 to redress the unfortunate impression created by *The Times*: With a diary note of barely discernible irony on the "charming" Hoffman and a news story by one Kenneth Gooding giving Hoffman's line on his lying advertisement for foreign investors and omitting altogether to mention Spaak's non-directorship, it gave comfort to those who did not want to believe that Maudling, Clarke, Brentford and the other heroes could have had their names on a fraudulent prospectus.

## Pseuds Corner

*£1 paid for entries*

Many interpretations of the work are possible: the play of nature (the waterfall and landscape) with sex and the manufactured object (the gas light). Or you can take it as man (in this case, woman), nature, and the fusion of the two in the gas lamp. But no simple equivalents are possible since the waterfall, too, is a man made object, as is the woman, the painted landscape and the gaslight.

RICHARD ROUD
*THE GRAUNIAD*

The inevitable difficulty in treating cars as if they were works of art, instead of expressive objects which exist - rightly enough - outside the conventional context of the 'fine arts' is that they demand absolute participation. They are if you like environments or Happenings. They do not sit on a wall or a floor: they don't really begin to exist as cars until you get into them and drive because, as McLuhan would put it, they are extensions of one's nervous system.

ROBERT HUGHES
*SUNDAY TIMES*

A bottle of very pleasant Le Piat de Beaujolais (33s) helped us to forget that our Poussin Grillé à la Diable arrived bathed in a sauce that cried for more zest and fire.

BERYL HARTLAND
*DAILY TELEGRAPH*

You can't go wrong if you have a woman's complaint. You know, her menstrual problems, or on the coil. Did you read that bit about the coil ? - smashing wasn't it ? Or infertility. They're great reads, you just can't lose. So why should women have it all their own way ? Why shouldn't men talk about their piles or something ? So one of the Insight people lost a testicle (I mean it came back in the end) and he was up the Royal Free while forty student nurses had a go at him. But I mean it's a great piece. I'm saving that for a week when we haven't too many sexy things.

HUNTER DAVIES (Editor LOOK!
*VARSITY*          Sunday Times)

When the human mind feels it's getting stuck, it compares *to*, rather than *with*, which means that it spends most of its time comparing to, so far as it does anything at all apart from dreaming, which means getting stuck without noticing.

HANS KELLER
*THE LISTENER*

The giant jet liner, built jointly by the British Aircraft Corporation and Sud Aviation of France, went through the sound barrier 39 minutes after taking off from Toulouse on its 45th test flight.

Sud Aviation officials said the plane flew at £715m.p.h.

*Birmingham Mail*

Can I drive you home ?

## Man broke speed limit to save pregnant cat

*Richmond Herald*

The bride, who was given away by her father, wore a dress of white figured brocade with a trailing veil held in place by a coronet of pearls. She carried a bouquet of rose buds and goods vehicles, leaving free access to all private vehicles not built for more than seven passengers.

*Atherstone News*

# PRIVATE EYE

No. 202
Friday
12 Sept. 69

2/-

## BERNADETTE

## AMAZING EXPOSURE

# WE SAY

# GO HOME DIRTY DIGGER

## ARTHUR NEASDEN

You may not have noticed - but there's something nasty in your Sunday newspaper - and it's not last week's fish and chips *(writes ARTHUR NEASDEN, the Man in the Mac)*.

Who is it who has turned the old-fashioned pornographic newspaper The News of the World into an up-to-date pornographic newspaper?

For the last six months we have been investigating the activities of the Mr Big of Filth Street - Mr Rupert Murdoch.

## Slime

We felt it was our duty to lift the stone even though what crawls out from underneath it may make you sick.

Look at his record. Mr Murdoch is an

WEDNESDAY

THE INDEPENDENT NEWSPAPER

SIN

Australian. He owns a number of highly disreputable periodicals in his home country. They specialise in sex and sensation.

## Gutter

Earlier this year, Mr Murdoch came to England and bought with his ill-gotten gains the ailing *News of the World*.

Now Mr Murdoch boasts he has increased the circulation of his paper. You don't have to look far to see why. It carries his own special brand of filth. There are pictures that would make an Arab postcard-seller blush.

His readers are treated to a diet of sex, sex and more sex.

But Mr Murdoch is not content with his flourishing empire of erotica.

He wants to spread his slimy tentacles still further.

## Dirt

Mr Murdoch wants to buy the Sinking *Sun*.

And how would Mr Murdoch hope to make the *Sun* pay its way?

Last week the Dirty Digger had this to say:

"It could be brightened up a little."

Only the dim-witted will need to be told what Mr so-called Murdoch means when he talks of "brightening up a little".

## Sex

I say this. If the new deal comes off, Fleet St. will have slipped one rung lower down the avenue of shame.

Take a piece of advice, Mr Murdoch.

Get back to Kanga Land before something nasty happens to you!

# THE GRAPES OF ROTHSCHILD
# Claud Cockburn

Reaction of City Fathers to the Pergamon-Leasco imbroglio recalled the old story of J. P. Morgan and a junior partner called, I think, Taylor.

Taylor's sex life was making him conspicuous in the New York of the Nineties.

He was hauled before the partners. He was rebuked.

"But" he said "I only do publicly what you all do behind closed doors."

"That is what doors are for, Mr Taylor" said Morgan, flushing him down the drain.

For some entirely unreasonable reason, it seems always to be taken for granted on these occasions, that until the top floor of some financial apartment house falls into the street, or the sewer bursts right in the living room, 98 per cent of people have total confidence in the shining integrity and near-altruism of the construction industry.

It is assumed that there is a huge body of starry-eyed shareholders and potential investors who believe every good word they have ever heard about the integrity etc. etc. of the City of London in general and the Stock Exchange in particular.

These unfortunates are deemed to have the utmost confidence that, whatever used to happen in the bad old days, the machinery of the City and the Stock Exchange has at some not quite defined point been developed so as effectively to protect their interests from sudden squalls, hurricanes or acts of piracy on the high seas of finance.

Then "something" as they say "happens".

As it might be the Pergamon-Leasco affair.

Naturally, every informed City person and pundit knows that this is the sort of thing that might happen to anyone at any time, and is happening most of the time.

Not the row, but the goings-on behind-the-scenes before the row.

As one shocked financial commentator noted in the Sunday press, the question of the propriety or otherwise of Fleming's bank only arose just because the Leasco bid did not go smoothly through.

But then many such transactions do go through quite smoothly, in which case none of the authorities or watch-dogs enquires whether the interests of the "small shareholder" have or have not been fully protected.

In that case the small shareholder has about as much chance of learning the true facts about what has gone on as has a person trying to find out about life on Mars with no other visual aid than a child's telescope.

But from time to time something comes unstuck.

Thereupon it is universally declared that unless something or other is done, "confidence in the City will be eroded".

In other words, the poor bloody public, which nobody has hitherto bothered about, is thought to have become a potential menace.

It is possible that those who talk this way really do believe in the naivete of the PBP. Though what precisely the Public could do about it if it did lose this vaunted confidence is never quite clear.

If it wants to invest or speculate and thus gain the maximum advantages obtainable from the Welfare State and the Affluent Society, where else is it to go? What else to do with its money?

But even those who doubt that the Public is as naive as is pretended, become nervous when something happens which discloses to public view the real, and more or less routine, workings of the system, and of the brains of tycoons.

They take the view that the majority of the public is pretty sceptical anyway and that without a tremendous bustle of ostentatious activity by the authorities, including such spectacles as that of Sir Hartley Shawcross winging across Europe to wag his finger at those concerned, agitators of one kind and another will start asking awkward questions.

Apart from actual shareholders, extremists in the Labour Party might otherwise use the schemozzle as a text for undesirable invasions of financial privacy.

At such times you can hardly read a financial column without being sure that somewhere along the line you are going to find some suitable adaptation of the phrase "Justice must not only be done, but be seen to be done."

The City's house must not only be put in order but be seen to be being so put.

The noise of the inspectors and surveyors climbing all over the building is deafening. Sir Hartley, say leaks from the Take-over Panel, was so tough that tender-skinned men from Pergamon and Leasco nearly fainted under the scorching blast of his words, writhed as he probed and prodded.

At a slightly later stage we may look forward with assurance to the news that "in some respects the unfortunate Pergamon-Leasco affair may be regarded as a blessing in disguise. It disclosed certain weaknesses in the system. It stirred the authorities to effective action.

"As a result it may be confidently stated that never again ..."

Until, of course, the next time.

Oddly enough, simultaneously with this affair, there was being held in South London a secret meeting of the Burglars and House-breakers' Association.

It was called as a result of a deplorable row between two parties of operators which resulted in the near failure of an attempt to loot an important bank in Glasgow.

The details are not clear, but enough is known to show that at the last moment, one group abruptly failed to co-operate in the enterprise.

It is alleged that the other group had sought to deceive it as to the precise amount of gelignite it was prepared to contribute to the operation.

These allegations were denied.

The Tribunal, after severely reprimanding the leaders of both groups, issued an ukase to the effect that in future such questions as the available sticks of gelignite, the condition of electrical tools and gasmasks, must be more freely and frankly disclosed in advance.

Only thus could confidence in the ability and disinterestedness of burglars and house-breakers be fully restored.

# DEATH ON THE OCEAN WAVE

by Our Environmental Correspondent BORIS TWYTTE

Of all the many design breakthroughs on the QE2 none is more exciting than the mortuary. ( writes Boris Twytte, Professor of Interior Decoration at the Royal College of Collage).

Gone are the dreary old marble slabs of yesterday - the stark railway toilet look of the traditional morgue.

In their place, Gavin Blains has designed a bright get-up-and-go "terminal area" in eye-catching micro-vinyl and op-art terylene.

"I wanted to give the idea of death as a fun experience" he drooled. "The concept of a mortuary as a breakaway bubble where anything can happen and probably will."

In place of marble slabs, Blains has conceived a series of dove-tailed see-through "death traps" in inflatable polythene. "When not in use they can be used as grotty old bags that just get in the way" gibbers Blains, who won the Observer Award in 1968 for refuse disposal units in pressurised teak.

**The rats leaving the sinking Shit**

# GPO TO GO?

*by Our Man in the Pillar Box*

Mr John Stonehouse, the Postmaster General yesterday announced plans to abolish the telegram.

"We are not going to abolish it at present" he said, "but it is something that must be considered."

### SHOCK

Mr Stonehouse was speaking at the unveiling of a new set of stamps designed by David Gentlemen to commemorate 100 years of bad stamp design.

"I am just talking off the top of my head" he said "but if we were to abolish the telegram then the future of the letter would have to be taken into account. At the moment this is highly unprofitable. Of course, letters could still be used in "Life or death" circumstances "such as the despatch of Final Demands by the Inland Revenue."

### ROLLING STONEHOUSE

"It is only logical then to bear in mind the abolition of the GPO itself which is highly unprofitable. A great deal of money is wasted every year by people making phone calls and sending letters when there is no real need. Of course, I am just speaking off the top of my head."

Mr Stonehouse then jumped off the top of the Post Office Tower and established a record for the Observation Platform - to Street Level Flight (Unaccompanied Junior Ministers Class).

A special "Life or Death" congratulations telegram has been sent to the Prime Minister.

It is expected to arrive some time next month.

**A**s may be obvious to some readers, *Private Eye* does not find favour with the Prime Minister.

So much so that even his family are debarred from reading it.

Recently young Giles was seen by his father with a copy of the Eye protruding from his coat pocket.

The young lad was sternly rebuked by his parent and told to dispense with the offending matter immediately.

"I am not having that rubbish in my house" said Wislon.

*Three still in Inverness hospital*
## TOURISTS SPLIT UP AFTER BUS CRASH

*Aberdeen Press and Journal*

Concorde

# THE CRACK OF BOOM

The Ministry of Technology has been very quiet about the Report submitted to it this month by Mr R.C. Crawford of the Institute of Sound and Vibration Research at Southampton University about the likely effects of sonic bangs on cathedrals. The Report is based on a series of tests conducted by the Royal Aircraft Establishment at Farnborough and was intended to play a considerable part in the Ministry's and the British Aircraft Corporation's autumn propaganda offensive to "get people used to the idea" of sonic booms.

The conclusion of the Report is just as the Ministry and the industry had hoped. "This kind of analysis" it says (p.19) "indicates that compared to the effect of traffic, organ and bells the added effect of a single bang is negligible and that repeated bangs of say 25 per day still have a very small effect on most cathedral elements". The trouble, however, as accurately predicted in the *Sunday Telegraph* three days before the report was published, was that this "kind of analysis" made the conclusions almost meaningless.

The Farnborough "experts" had gone round five British cathedrals letting off fireworks (or, in the official jargon, "using a snifter"). The results of the bangs on the cathedrals were duly handed over to Mr Crawford, who concluded mournfully in a report to the Ministry:

"The response to the snifter excitation has been included but of course as raw data they bear very little significance for comparison purposes with what might be expected from a sonic bang".

That was not at all what the Ministry (or the industry) wanted so Mr Crawford had to write another report seeking to compare the effects of the Farnborough fireworks with those of a sonic boom. He found that firework tests had been done on cathedrals in Germany - and in Germany there had been a few tests from genuine sonic booms from the Starfighter aircraft. By means of some complicated algebra, Mr Crawford found a way of comparing the firework tests in Britain and Germany, relating them to the German tests with real sonic booms and then "estimating" what the likely results would be on British cathedrals. In his final report he listed five powerful reasons why "the estimates as made will be subject to errors", not least of which was that "the predictions are based on very few sonic bangs response measurements".

In the absence of any convincing document on the subject in Britain, architects will have to rely on those produced abroad, notably "*Effects of Supersonic Flight*" by M. Michael Parent, Principal Inspector of Historic Monuments, in France, shortly to be circulated in translation by the Anti-Concorde Project.

From a list of 100 cases of reported damage from sonic booms M. Parent produces forty clear and undisputed cases of damage to stained glass windows, to masonry, to roof coverings and to furnishings and decorations as a result of the booms from passing military aircraft. In particular, he noted the abbey at Vezelay, which "required the immediate shoring up of three bays of the Church which had recently been restored". In the six months in which Vezelay was being shored up, the military authorities agreed to suspend overflying supersonic flights thereby admitting their responsibility for the initial collapse.

A year previously, a tower of the Chateau of Landal at Broualan Village collapsed after being hit by a shock wave from a supersonic flight. For that and other damage to the castle, the French Government were ordered to pay 11,500 dollars damages.

M. Parent explains that the "bang" is a shock wave which strikes buildings with an "overpressure" and is then followed by underpressure, which "causes the bulging observed in the windows of churches". The wave is complicated and reinforced by a large number of factors and "the resulting effect on historic monuments is particularly disastrous". He ends by pleading for a ban on supersonic flights at least to protect the country's great cathedrals, notably at Chartres.

M. Parent's thesis is supported by cathedral experts in Germany who are still worried by the closing in June 1967 of the 18th Century abbey church at Neresheim near Aalen. According to *The Times* (June 19, 1967):

"Shock waves generated when aircraft break the sound barrier have seriously damaged timbers in the roof, which is now in danger of collapse". Once again, while Neresheim Abbey was hastily patched up, the military re-directed their supersonic flights.

Some evidence that cathedrals are not the only casualties of the sonic boom is provided by the results carried out in America, where the official Government propaganda still insists that sonic booms cause "no damage to buildings and little concern to people". By far the most extensive tests were those carried out in Oklahoma City in 1964, which subjected the people of that city to eight booms a day in a total of 1,254 supersonic flights. The tests were made with military planes, whose booms were estimated to be 60% of the strength of that expected from the Concorde. The "opinion poll" on the flights was conducted by a selected survey by telephone, the worst known form of inquiry. 75% of Oklahoma City's economy is dependent on the aeronautical industry. Yet 27% of those questioned replied that they "could never learn to live with the boom". 4,901 people filled in claims for damages to property, some of which are still before the courts. Mr Bailey Smith, who had just moved into his new house at 1803 NE 67 Street, was awarded 10,000 dollars damages for cracks in his house which brought it near to collapse, and which were proved to have been caused by the boom. The total amount of damages paid out exceeded 100,000 dollars. The following year, 49 flights over Chicago produced nearly 3,000 damage claims, and damage payments totalling 114,763 dollars. Since then, the United States Government has been singularly reluctant to make supersonic tests over concentrations of population, but it is a fair estimate that if 150 Concorde-type supersonic flights were in routine use over the USA, the cost to the taxpayer in compensation would be more than a million dollars a day.

Such figures have disturbed the people who really know and care about damage to property. A Report in *Lloyds List and Shipping Gazette* last year (31st December) stated that a "noise exclusion clause" has been prepared "to remove the possibility of underwriters being held responsible, under existing policies, in respect of damage by noise, including sonic booms". In future if you want to ensure against such damage, you have to do so specifically - at a higher premium.

The British have been even more chary of tests over populated areas, despite the fact that the Concorde will be ready for flight long before an American supersonic airliner. In the summer of 1967, the Government tried out 11 bangs from light military aircraft over London and Bristol. The response surprised them. There were 12,000 complaints and of 788 claims for compensation, 515 were met. Nearly £2,000 were paid out for damage to roofs, chimneys and ceilings. (*Hansard:* 17.2.1968).

In spite of these results, the Government decided to go ahead with tests of the Concorde over some populated areas. On August 27, the *Guardian* "leaked" the plans of the Technology Ministry for

# LETTER

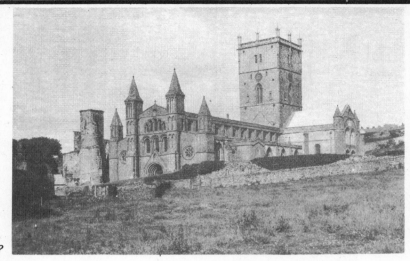

*St David's Cathedral, Pembrokeshire.*

*First victim of the Concorde?*

the Concorde's flight path during these tests. The path will run some 800 miles North-South down the Irish sea (see map). The Eire Government has banned all supersonic overflying, but, as one of the privileges of remaining 'British' the people of Belfast will be directly in the line of the flight path. The British Aircraft Corporation admitted that the Concorde will also have to fly over "small promontories of land" in England and Wales, on one of which stands St. David's Cathedral. St. David's stands a good chance of being the first historic building to be damaged by the Concorde. It was highly sensitive to the firework tests carried out by the Farnborough experts, and, what's more, according to the Crawford Report,"some of the responses due to unknown excitations are surprisingly high, particularly at St. David's and York".

Yet the damage caused by the Concorde is unlikely to be limited to old cathedrals on the Welsh coast. One interesting feature of the forthcoming sonic booms over Britain will be their effect on the system-built blocks of flats. In America and France the building codes and regulations forbid the erection of buildings such as Ronan Point, which collapsed in May 1968. Only in England have the authorities permitted the use of Scandanavian system-built blocks to rise up over six storeys.

Ronan Point collapsed when a gas explosion of approximately three pounds per square inch in strength blew out a wall panel on the 17th floor. The estimated force of a supersonic bang from a Concorde flying at 60,000 feet is 2.75 pounds per square foot. "That" says Mr Crawford from Southampton "shows that the sort of explosion needed to topple a Ronan Point is just not in the same league as a supersonic bang".

People living in high flats built like Ronan Point may not be prepared to take such an optimistic view. The force of a sonic bang is perhaps a hundred times less that the force of the explosion which toppled Ronan Point. Except in extreme circumstances, one bang, or even eleven bangs will have little or no effect on the building.

But, as M. Parent points out in his report:

"For forty cases in which the 'bang' played a part either exclusive or decisive in the date of the actual collapse, how many buildings are being secretly damaged little by little? How many falls of materials have simply not been noticed and how much invisible, but nevertheless real damage is being done? And will it result in the future by repetition in irreversible deterioration?"

In other words, the *cumulative* effect of hundreds of supersonic bangs, as the Concorde starts its daily, or twice-daily, or thrice-daily flights across the Atlantic is unlikely not to create more than a little "irreversible deterioration" in the Ronan Points which fall within the Concorde's flight path.' Inhabitants of system-built blocks of flats in Manchester and Liverpool may get their claim forms in advance from the Ministry of Technology, Millbank Tower, London S.W.1.

The British Aircraft Corporation have estimated that a ban on overland flights could cut down the expected Concorde sales from 152 to 64.

Last July, Mr Christopher Edwards, an economics lecturer at East Anglia University, produced a Cost Benefit Analysis on the Concorde project, whose conclusions were not seriously challenged by the Ministry or the industry. It stated:

"Even on the very favourable assumptions set out in this report (£2m profit for each plane sold), Concorde will make a loss, even after writing off the £380m losses incurred up to now ... The loss to the UK economy from going ahead with the project could be as much as £150m. The loss to France would be the same. This ignores the £380m already spent. If this is included the total loss to the two countries could be £650m".

Mr Anthony Wedgwood Benn, the Minister of Technology, is not the sort of man to compound those losses still further by imposing a ban on overland flights. On the contrary. The cry of the Concordemaniacs will be: More and More flights across more and more country - even if the result is the more rapid deterioration of other monuments to Britain's Technological Age - like Ronan Point-style blocks of flats.

Dear Sir (or Madam): As one of Jehovah's Witnesses, my eyes fell on your publication "Private Eye" (26th Sept. 69) because there on the cover was God's Great Name in large print for all to see - but alas! Not as our Organisation print the name to the GLORY of him - But to RIDICULE his great name and there also inside this publication was another Joke Page RIDICULING the name and also those who bear his name, (which is an honour).

You obviously do NOT know what a serious thing you are doing by RIDICULING that name - why - the Scribes that wrote the Bible down, even recognised the GREATNESS of it by habitually washing their hands when having written down that name. Though, of course, this was going a bit far - but never the less they saw it to be a Name that was SET APART from any other NAME. Yes! The Name of the Almighty GOD JEHOVAH and there in the Scriptures at Matthew Chap 10 Verse 6.Jesus, his son, says "LET YOUR NAME BE SANCTIFIED" meaning his Father's Name and Jehovah's Witnesses DO SANCTIFY that Name - but alas! are the ONLY ones doing it!

Almighty God himself wanted people to recognise his name. As Psalm 83: 18 shows and many other scriptures too.

Perhaps also you would like to know that 2nd book of Peter Chap. 3 Verse 3 says "Know this, that in the LAST DAYS there will come RIDICULERS with their RIDICULE, Proceeding after THEIR OWN DESIRES. And isn't this true today Yes! You with your magazine are FULFILLING PROPHECY by doing JUST THAT!!!

It is strange that when a man sees the truth from the Bible and upholds it (as Peter Knowles, for one, has) upholds what he believes it to be. THE TRUTH and becomes a REAL MAN. Yes! A MAN OF GOD he is thought to be something peculiar and laughed at. Doesn't this truly show what we, as Jehovah's Witnesses have been saying all along is true according to the Scriptures. That this old world is wicked and THIS is the IMPORTANT thing, JEHOVAH GOD sees it too and in his hands is the Power to PUNISH and that is what he IS shortly going to do and when he DESTROYS ALL WICKEDNESS on this EARTH and USHERS in a NEW SYSTEM ON THIS EARTH WORTH SAVING.

I wouldn't like to be one of those RIDICULERS THEN!!!

Yours Truly
EVELYN M. BURTON
88 MOLESHAM WAY. W. MOLESEY. SURREY.

IMMORAL EARNINGS

# MRS. WILSON'S DIARY

Farewell to summer's golden days,
  And welcome, autumn tints!
Gone are the ultra-violet rays
  That fade the sitting-room chintz:
The summer's gone down time's dark maw:
  Where now those long hot days?
When carefree on the sandy shore
  We dozed as in a daze.
Only a handful of snaps remain
  To stick into our album
To look at when the driving rain
  Comes lashing on the roof.

How I have neglected my dear diary! No permanent record of the lovely summer except a few grains of sand between the pages of my Howard Spring and the sun-tan oil stains on the cover. And of course the delightful snaps I refer to above which I have just collected from Boots. There is a lovely one of Harold making friends with Paddy, the dog, in a remote cove, and also a most amusing one of him having trouble with his trousers underneath the towel. The Inspector said I should have it enlarged. Alas, Mr Kaufmann's back peeled again very badly this year as did the top of his head, provoking many unkind jibes from the Inspector, as a result of which he tells me he is considering investing in a Godfrey Hair Extension Piece made from genuine Oriental hair.

Downing Street seems very dank and cold after the Scillies, and even Harold was affected with a sort of autumn melancholy on his return. The other morning, as I was taking in his morning cup of Chico and a selection of McGrittie's Shortbread Snacks, I found him slumped in his chair, ruminatively puffing at his pipe. "Oh Gladys, Gladys," he remarked, as I put the tray down beside him, "what am I going to tell the beggars at the Conference this time? Try as I may, I cannot work up any enthusiasm for this annual charade by the sea. Listen to this: 'No let-up .. unpopular measures .. Enoch Powell .. self-seeking men on both sides of industry ..'" And look at this awful rubbish that Kaufmann's dreamed up - "The Labour Party's got life and soul ..." Coming from Kaufmann it is a bit rich, I admit. But what are we going to say the year after that. And after that. And after that. The mind wilts at the prospect."

At this moment there came the bright ringing of the front door bell, and Mr Jenkins' tanned cheek was soon pressed against mine in a warm kiss. Ignoring Harold's "Cut that out Jenkins", the Chancellor patted me in a friendly manner on the BTM, remarking "Jennifer and I had a most agreeable period in the South of France, curtailed alas for me personally by the devaluation of the franc. Incidentally, Prime Minister, one really has to admire the French for the way in which they go about this kind of thing. What panache, what sleight of hand, a fait accompli while everyone's on holiday. So different, I felt, from our own unfortunate experience when my predecessor grasped the tiller of the Exchequer in his insensitive grip. Did you have pleasant weather where you were? Oh, of course, the Scillies. I do envy you your lack of wanderlust."

"Cut the cackle, Jenkins," came the crisp rejoinder from the inert figure at the desk. "And I would advise you to think twice before casting aspersions on the competence of your predecessor. Your own record is not exactly at the top of the charts. Two years' hard slog, eh? The way you're heading it'll be two years' hard labour. Jim, as a matter of fact, has been doing very nicely in Northern Ireland while you've been away sunning yourself with your smart friends in the playboys' paradise. Crossbencher is already tipping him as my natural successor in the inconceivable event of my being run over by a bus. Your star, I should have said, was very low on the horizon. As a matter of interest, how did you fiddle the fifty pound limit?"

The Chancellor listened to these somewhat ribald comments with an urbane smile, his fingertips joined, his eyebrows half-raised. "I see, Prime Minister, that your holiday has restored your natural bonhomie and sparkling wit. The sea winds have had their effect. Would that I could stay longer to listen to more of your amusing repartee: but alas, duty in the shape of a visiting trade delegation from the U.S.S.R. calls me away. Oh, and by the by, I thought this might be of some interest to you as general background to your speech to Conference." With this, Mr Jenkins unzipped his discreet executive crocodile Vanity Case and extracted a single sheet of typed manilla, which he handed to Harold with a light cough. Harold glanced briefly at it, his face growing red with anger. "Listen, Smarmiboots" he snarled, "the holidays are over. If this is your idea of some black joke played by your banker friends, then I suggest you find alternative employment. Even Sir Gerald Nabarro could see this is a fake. Get out."

Unfortunately, the Chancellor's urbane smile showed no sign of fading. "I assure you, Prime Minister" he remarked, "that the figures are correct to the nearest decimal point. Should you doubt me, I suggest that a telephone call to Tony Crosland would set your mind at rest." Harold snatched up the receiver, and was quickly connected to the glamorous President of the Board of Trade. "Tony, is this true? What Jenkins tells me. A forty million pound surplus after seasonal adjustments?" His face changed from red to green, and for one moment I thought he was about to faint. "I see, I see" he observed, and replaced the receiver. Then he got up, walked steadily to the Wincarnis cupboard, opened it, and extracted a bottle I had not seen before called Old Stag's Breath and, tossing my flower arrangement on the floor, emptied it into the vacant vase. He then raised the cut-glass container to his lips, and slowly drained it, finally drawing his sleeve across his mouth and hurling the vase, which belonged to my mother, through the window. It was only then that he let out a blood-curdling cry of triumph, and began throwing handfuls of paper in the air, jumping up and down on the spot with curious whooping sounds.

I was about to call Dr Melrose, our GP, when Mr Jenkins laid an arm round my shoulders and led me away, murmuring as he did no "I think the Prime Minister would probably prefer to be left alone to compose his speech. The symptoms should wear off in a few hours' time, and then I would suggest a glass of Alka-Seltzer and ten sleeping pills. Till then, why not come next door and have a cup of coffee with Jennifer, as I have one or two things to attend to." With these words he conducted me with habitual elegance into the black and white marble hall of Number Eleven, and entrusted me to the safe keeping of Mrs Jenkins. He then retired to his study where we heard the click of a key turning in the latch, and swift footsteps crossing the carpet. There was a pause, and then the sound of liquid being poured into some kind of large container. A gurgling noise ensued, and I clutched at Jennifer's arm as the crash of breaking glass suggested that something had been hurled through the window. The cry of "Jeronimo" that followed made my hair stand on end and Jennifer and I listened in silence as the tramp and whoop of an Indian War Dance caused the china to jingle in the kitchen dresser.

**SIR GEORGE BROWN FALSTAFF: God save thy grace King Hal! My Royal Hal!**

**KING HAL WISLON: I know thee not old man. Fall to thy prayers. How ill
white hairs become a fool and jester .** *Henry IV part 2*

# COLOUR SECTION

## TV TRIPOD – "MY THREE-LEGGED FRIEND" says Earl

The elevation of Comrade Wedgwood Benn to the post of technology overlord is thought not to have been welcomed by all of his colleagues in the cabinet.

On the occasion of President Nixon's visit to Britain earlier this year, Wislon laid on a special cabinet meeting for his distinguished guest at which each minister was instructed to give the President a brief account of the work of his particular ministry.

When it came to Benn's turn, the Min of Tech launched into an extravagent paen of praise for youth and technology.

'Now is the time," he prated, "to harness the idealism of youth to the technological breakthrough."

"Balls" said a voice.

Undeterred Benn continued with his lunatic oration.

"Balls" said the voice again as the speaker paused for breath.

At this Wislon felt compelled to intervene and identified the heckler as Mr Denis Healey.

Asked to explain himself Healey wisely pointed out that the young were not interested in technological advance. They took it for granted. The only people interested were "teenage intellectuals" (believed to be a reference to Benn).

As the meeting broke up Nixon was heard muttering to an aide "Do they always go on like that ?"

A BBC documentary to be shown this week investigates the dependence of many of us on gadgets of various kinds.

"Many of the people interviewed" says producer Al Sation, "are basically rather pathetic individuals who are unable to form mature relationships with other people and compensate for this failure by living with machinery."

One such is the Queen's brother-in-law, the Earl of Snowdon, who lives in a large Kensington house, filled with every conceivable type of mechanical gadget - cameras, gramophones, TV sets, tape recorders, tripods, etc.

"To me they are like human beings" he says. "A camera doesn't tell lies you know. A Tape recorder won't let you down. I suppose some people think I'm odd but there it is ducky it takes all sorts."

# Boys in the Band
## Staircase
### Jeremy — And Now it's
# POOVE POWER

**A STATEMENT FROM TREVOR X, PRESIDENT OF POOVE POWER**
*(Queen's Award for Industry)*

Duckies!

For too bloody long we pooves have been pushed from pillar to post by society at large.

We have become an underprivileged minority group discriminated against, laughed at and, you know, generally treated as *inferior human beings!*

The bourgeois Uncle Toms have tried to help by introducing reforms. But what bloody difference does it make I ask you ?

## ACTION NOW, SWEETIES !

Pooves demand:

1. Equal rights with women.
2. Free use of the Pill.
3. Marriage rights.
4. A squeaky voice in Parliament.
5. Poove Guidance Councils.
6. Easier divorce.

The hour is past, loves, for parliamentary agitation. The struggle for what we want must now be fought for on the streets.

If you see a heterosexual grabbing your job or your house or your boyfriend -
✳KILL HIM with a look.
✳HIT HIM with your handbag.
Or even write nasty words on his car with your lipstick.
Best of all
✳CUT HIM DEAD and walk away.

## COMING EVENTS

### 1 A GAY MORATORIUM

On November 7 all of us will just put on some nice clothes and go and walk about. (I'm wearing this new all-white crochet see-through trouser suit!!!).

### 2 MASS MINCE·IN IN HYDE PARK

'They' use the park for what they do and get away with it. Why can't we ?
We will all assemble at the Dilly and then troll off en masse to Hyde Park where we will all lie down on the grass. Then the Boys in Blue will come and carry us off in their big strong arms. Whoopee! (Don't be late).

(If it's a rainy day we'll all stay at home and get on with some things around the house).

### 3 PRETTY CANDLELIGHT DEMO

outside 'Gay Guevara Bistroteque', Kings Road. Everyone comes with a candle and a bottle and we all tuck into Jeremy's super cold consommé and Rissoles Florentine. Service is very gay and the waiters all wear lovely fluffy jerseys.

 COME OFF IT NORMAN NORMAL.

Your hour is come at last. We pooves are on the march and your sort are on the way out.

Every week millions more join our ranks. Violence is our weapon and we shall overcome sweeties.

TREVOR X
Chairman 'Poove Power'
Committee of 1001 Buggers
  for Peace
The Roger Basement
EC 1

*Do* write. I *love* getting letters.

*" Are you gay too?"*

# The Grocer's Annual

## What the papers said

### 1965

● "Mr Edward Heath scored a political triumph here today with a speech of uncharacteristic punch and humour and winning his way into the party's heart. After his blistering speech hardly anybody was left wondering whether the MPs who had elected him had made the right choice." NORA BELOFF The Observer Sept 17.

"... Heath established his mastery at the Conservative Party Conference today with a powerful speech which combined tough realism with lively humour and considerable compassion. Today, certainly, the Heath leadership broke through on an impressive scale." JAMES MARGACH Sunday Times Sept 17.

"They cheered for four minutes and then he rang the Chairman's bell. Heath at last triumphantly established mastery over the Tories today. His battling final speech, full of political red meat, swept away any doubts of his uneven performance.. The unanimous verdict on the speech, voiced by one happy (and relieved) senior Tory was: 'Ted's never made such a speech before. For the first time he got it across.' " KEITH RENSHAW S. Express Sept 17.

"When Mr Heath sat down, there was no doubting the extent of his success. The Tories had clearly decided that they had a leader." ANTHONY SHRIMSLEY S. Mirror Sept 17.

### 1966

● "Heath reached a new peak in his leadership here today when, with the most rousing speech of his career, he fired the final session of the Conservative Party Conference into wild enthusiasm for an immediate declaration by Britain that she would join Europe. His speech carried such power and impact that he received a record 4-minute standing ovation ...."

"Heath asserted his authority clearly and emphatically and at the same time created a new and warmer relationship between himself and his Party. This marks a significant milestone in the development and evolution of his leadership; after two notable speeches, he is more powerfully established in personal terms than he has ever been, and this in turn must help to give him a more relaxed self-confidence." JAMES MARGACH S. Times Oct 16.

"Heath wound up the Conservative Conference today with a leader's speech which raised the delegates to their highest pitch of enthusiasm, .... it was obvious he was speaking straight from the heart." GEORGE GARDINER S. Times Oct 16.

"It was his most thoughtful, most solid speech since he became leader, and it was a major personal triumph. 4000 delighted Tories cheered him for a full four minutes." ANTHONY SHRIMSLEY S Mirror Oct 16.

### 1967

● "Heath made the best speech of his career at the close of the Conservative Conference here today and finally demolished any doubt about leadership. His attacking speech established a new spirit of mutual confidence between him and his party. As a performance it must be rated a lst-class success in reinforcing his command." JAMES MARGACH S. Times Oct 22.

"Many colleagues predicted that Heath's speech would mark a turning point in his career. He delivered a wide-ranging speech with considerable emotional force - undoubtedly his most successful conference performance yet." GEORGE GARDINER S. Times Oct 22.

"The Tory Party yesterday purged itself of the leadership issue. 4,000 party representatives determinedly cheered Heath for 4½ minutes after his final speech at Brighton. They made it absolutely plain that from now on they wish to ignore whatever hiccups may remain about the capabilities of the man at the top. Heath was mobbed by several hundred cheering people, who thrust out their arms to shake his hand ... His speech was the breakthrough." ANTHONY SHRIMSLEY S. Mirror Oct 22.

"Heath today confidently applied for and received from the Tory Conference here endorsement of his leadership. He won through with an impressive 42-minute speech of broad themes. Remarkably he hardly once glanced at his brief notes. Instead he looked the 4,000 massed and questioning Tories in the eye and succeeded in putting the leadership question on ice for the forseeable future. His reward was a standing, singing ovation that lasted only seconds short of five minutes. KEITH RENSHAW S.Express Oct.22.

### 1968

● "A record ovation of 7 minutes 40 seconds for Heath at the end of his speech signalled the determination of the Tory rank and file that divisive criticism of his leadership must end." RONALD BUTT S. Times Oct 13.

"What is generally acclaimed as the best speech of his political career ...

"Veterans said they could not remember such delirious enthusiasm since Sir Winston Churchill's time ... There is no doubt that the speech itself, interrupted 53 times with applause, followed by over 6 minutes standing ovation, was a triumph." NORA BELOFF The Observer Oct 13.

"Mr Heath has good cause to be satisfied with the 7 min. 40 sec. of ovation given to him at the end of his speech in Blackpool yesterday. What is more, the triumph, though not unpredictable, was by no means unmerited. He rose to a pitch of eloquence which he does not usually achieve. LEADER Sunday Telegraph Oct 13.

"For Mr Heath a new power, confidence and freedom at last from questions about his leadership ... After 3 years of doubt and scrutiny Heath seems to have made a personal breakthrough." Daily Mail Oct 14.

### 1969

● "Heath reasserted his leadership to the Conservative Conference here today after the series of revolts ...

"... It was a highly successful exercise in personal leadership and the massed conference loved every word of his rampage against the rebels. Heath's speech lasted 63 minutes and was followed by a standing ovation of 5 minutes 30 seconds." JAMES MARGACH S. Times Oct 11.

"Heath emerged from the Tory conference in Brighton yesterday with his party position clearly strengthened after a crucial winding up speech which earned a genuinely enthusiastic 6 minute standing ovation. There is every sign that the 8,000 Tory representatives streamed home last night in a far more united spirit ..." KEITH RENSHAW S. Express Oct 11.

"Tory leader Ted Heath scored a major personal triumph with his speech winding-up the Tory Party Conference yesterday.

"Looking much more relaxed than in previous conference appearances ... firing off joke after joke ... at the end he got a standing ovation lasting 5 minutes 50 seconds - slightly less than last year but still overwhelming proof that he had managed to assert his leadership." TERENCE LANCASTER The People Oct 11.

He (Cornelius Cardew) sees no harm in using fragments of the classics to give a point of reference for the player and audience alike. The normal pattern of events is that a work by a member of the orchestra is prepared for performance. The composer specifies the duration of the piece and any planned activities or sounds he may require. He gives a particle of a well-known piece as the germ for the individual player's improvisatory activities. Any action or sound or both is valid as music as long as it is the result of some emotional stimulus and is felt by the player to be necessary to the shape of the work.

Thus the possessor of a packet of sandwiches may feel that eating them is essential to the satisfactory expression of his part in the piece. It is quite possible for a composer to specify that every member of the orchestra eats sandwiches for a given period of time: it is, however, up to the individual as to how he eats the sandwiches to derive the maximum emotional effect.

GAVIN BARRETT
*THE GUARDIAN*

Let's come to the next flashpoint. Sex. I'd like to put the proposition to you that being a single person in a room with a radio set is like being in bed with someone. It's essentially an erotic situation.

MICHAEL KUSTOW
*RADIO TIMES*

I can never go into Harrods, and meet a friend - and everyone at one time or another wanders glazedly through Harrods - without feeling like Shelley in *Ozymandias*, without re-echoing his marvellous awe in meeting a traveller from an antique land.

POLLY DEVLIN
*VOGUE*

I can synthesize no meaning. At those moments each player was caught like a butterfly on a pin: the stands seemed to press in on them like dread. It was only when Miss Casals embroiderering the wider horizons of her all-court game, found the power to endure and resist that at last she spat out the rag ends of fear.

GEOFFREY GREEN
*THE TIMES*

But is a collapsed typewriter like the setting sun ? Is it how nature is ? A relaxed typewriter is not a typewriter by night, it is a useless typewriter. On the other hand, why should it, when soft, be called useless ? It is a sculpture, not a typewriter and, unlike a typewriter, is not rendered ineffectual by being soft. On the contrary, its pliability gives it ways in which it can be used which it could not have if it were rigid. It can be pressed, caressed, squeezed, like a woman's body; it has the springy softness of a woman's body to the touch. Or rather, it has the springy softness which is sought in a woman's body. That is to say, it is not soft merely by default of being hard: its softness is positive, proposes an alternative norm. If tautness in sculpture corresponds to an ideal of male desirability, perhaps the softness of Oldenburg's sculptures corresponds to an ideal of female desirability.

DAVID SYLVESTER
*SUNDAY TIMES COLOUR MAGAZINE*

The illustrations by Eiler Krag, are a delight. One especially, of a couple enjoying cunnilinctus, has a purity which refutes any charge of dirt-mongering.

Briefing
*THE OBSERVER*

Her terrine of duck reaches heights of aesthetic as well as gastronomic delight because the duck, boned by Mrs Stevenson herself, the skin packed with the delicious paté and re-formed, is breathtakingly beautiful - perfectly achieved beneath its amber glaze of jelly.

MARGARET COSTA
*SUNDAY TIMES*

Leeds United . . . . . 2   Manchester Utd . . . . . 1

The bitter malevolence that erupted in the funeral dolourousness of the first half was blessedly relieved, although never expunged in the more intense legitimate conflict of the second.

ARTHUR HOPCRAFT
*Observer*

Harvey Sacks, a sociologist with an uncanny sensitivity to linguistic behaviour, demonstrated that a conversation is a highly structured event and the rules of sequence organisation in conversations can be formally described. Several years of careful study of conversations have paid off in the discovery of many subtle aspects of this speech event ... In his presentation at the conference, he argued that conversations can be characterized in terms of two general principles towards which participants always orient themselves.
1. At least one and no more than one person talks at a time.
2. Speaker change recurs.

JOEL SHERZER
*LANGUAGE SCIENCES*

At last a German composer has leapt the barrier that separates music lovers from the rest : Dr. Dieter Schnebe a 38-year old Protestant pastor and musical theorist from the Black Forest, has written a work for conductor without orchestra which had its first performance recently in Germany. . . . . . . . .

One of his recent choral works is a "hymn of praise" consisting mainly of the tape-recorded cries of donkeys, apes, seagulls, dogs, cats, sheep, horses, cattle, parrots, bees, ducks, elephants, lions and turkeys.

Schnebel, who is a convinced Marxist and a strong supporter of West Germany's rebellious left-wing students, has also managed to introduce politics into his sacred music. At the climax of the "hymn", a voice emerges from the indescribable tumult of animal noises, shouting repeatedly "Ho, ho, ho". It is left to the singers to ad lib additional words - possibly Chi Minh.

The Diary
*THE TIMES*

"There was this girl in an exam I was invigilating who sat pitifully doing nothing. When she left she deposited a letter on my desk which ended: 'Our minds are all so clogged on the dead ideas passed from generation to generation that even the best of us are unable to control our lives.' I burst into tears."

GERMAINE GREER
*SUNDAY TIMES*

A smell of cabbages hung over Glebe Place in Chelsea last week. Not the rank kind which seeps up from basements but the nutty tang which flows off a field of kale in the country. Inside Nigel Greenwood's studio gallery, there they were – captive in rows of crates, subtly green, blobby, tumescent and alive like patches of Rembrandt pigment under the microscope.

The crates made a severe shaft the length of the room, their heads bonded into one corner by two geometrical platforms, their toes linked by a sharpish join to a worrying thing, a makeshift dais made from a fork-lift platform coated with graphite grease to which an automobile engine had been tightly bound, its blackened form nastily suggesting amputation and burning. To the side of it, and joined by a trailing coatsleeve, lay a pile of old clothes in which light-bulbs nestled like eggs or lice or precious stones. A severe addendum on this peninsula lay a little off-shore – three wooden beer palettes, one bare, one covered, one supporting a whirring fan.

It was all very precise and formal, lightly marked out on the floor with chalk outlines, and the next join was tidy too – another crate tilted on its edge and leading to the heart of the whole arrangement, a sloping trestle covered with hessian on which streams of musky pinkish fluid bubbled and gouted from a metal contraption, staining the cloth and gathering in a puddle at the base like the thin blood of a machine.

I have seen few pieces which filled a big space more satisfyingly.

NIGEL GOSLING
*THE OBSERVER*

While a student at Manchester University, I wrote a thesis, for my bachelor's degree, on Indian music. Despite its title, borrowed from campanology, the influence of Indian music is very clear in my Stedman Doubles, written at that time - 1955 . . . . . Stedman Doubles is a tour de force not only in the obvious technical sense - the extreme difficulty of the writing for instruments, which, in the cadenzas, where the players are 'free', is meant to inspire them to improvise even greater feats of virtuosity - but also a tour de force of sheer concentration for the two performers - as indeed for the listener.

PETER MAXWELL-DAVIES
*The Listener*

Just as the presence of cavalry on the battlefield lent tone to what would otherwise have been a vulgar brawl, so a bottle (or a decanter) of one of the great sauternes makes the eating of strawberries and cream into an elegant incident rather than a mere schoolboy guzzle.

ANDREW GRAHAM
*THE TIMES*

Some amusing and inventive objects are contributed by Hugh Davies, who is really a musician. Using consistently the device of amplification, he brings the tiny scratchings and scrapings of everyday objects up to a level where they absorb your attention. One of his "instruments" all plastic - is made from a bread-bin (of the kind whose top slides open, not unlike a piano) with plastic spoons as keys inside fixed to upturned tea cups. He also reveals how one can hear extraordinary latent depths of sound of minutely different qualities in any old vibrating piece of scrap-metal by attaching two strings to it, winding these round one's fingers, and putting one's finger's in one's ears.

GUY BRETT
*THE TIMES*

# Man in the nude
# Dr. ZOO'S BOMBSHELL

### by Our Man behind the Bars
### Lunchtime O'Zoos

Yes, it's all coming true for Dr Desmond Morris-Dancing, controversial author of the best-selling 'The Naked Greed'.

Britain will be rocked this autumn by the publication of a new book by Dr Morris-Dancing entitled 'Son of Naked Greed'.*

## Monkey Show Business

Two years ago, Britain was rocked by his first book 'The Naked Greed' which showed that Homo Sapiens (you and I, for short) has a compulsive drive to accumulate piles of green paper.

This he does, argued the controversial Dr Dancing, by going off into a dark corner and covering other sheets of white paper (known as 'book') with hieroglyphics representing certain human activities (known as 'sex'.)

## The 'Ape' Man cometh

The humans then congregate in herds to browse among the white leaves which they strip bare, leaving behind them huge deposits of the green paper (known as 'money')

A shambling figure then swings down from the trees in the person of Dr Morris-

* ( Snipcock and Greed. 3 nuts and a banana)

Dancing, uttering his repetitive call-note 'Gimme! Gimme! Gimme!'"

Stuffing the green paper into his pouch, he then migrates to the warm, tax-free climes of the Mediterranean, where he winters with his mate, brood, and sundry sports-cars, Rolls-Royces, swimming pools etc.

Eventually, the hoard of green paper diminishes to the point where he receives another piece of paper covered in red markings (known as 'final reminder') from 'Homo Bankmanagerius'. The feeding cycle then begins again.

## Chimp off the Old Block

In his new book, Dr Dancing turns his attention to another facet of the human condition, which he describes as the 'IPC factor'.

It appeared that in their remorseless quest for green paper, some Homos more sapiens than others have discovered by trial and error that their hoards may be increased a hundredfold by judicious additions of 'Sunday' paper (known as 'serialisation rights').

According to Dr Morris-Dancing, there is a small and now almost extinct tribe of primitive men (known as 'Sunday newspaper proprietors') who indulge in a form of aggression-ritual known to anthropologists as 'the circulation war'.

The war takes a peculiar form. The combatants vie with each other in a display-dance, exhibiting as many naked female forms as they can muster.

Here the crafty Homo Pseudo-Anthropologicus (as Dr Dancing describes himself) takes advantage of the aggression-ritual by providing the combatants with a 'respectable' excuse for their sexual display - in return for which his hoard of green paper is lavishly increased.

*"WAITER, THERE'S A MAMMARY GLAND IN MY SOUP!"*

*CYCLAMATES*

# Sweet smell of research

The decision of the British Government, following that of the American Government, to ban cyclamate sweeteners from sale and consumption has been greeted with "overwhelming relief" not by the public or by medical or scientific institutions but by the sugar industry, many of whose supporters see the ban as the result of their most successful public relations enterprise since Mr Cube and Mr Richard Dimbleby staved off the nationalisation of sugar in the 1940's.

Cyclamates were invented at the University of Illinois in 1937. They were patented and developed by Abbott industries and rigorously tested in some of the more advanced research laboratores in the world, including ICI's Industrial Hygiene Laboratory. All the tests produced the same results - that the new additive was of no health danger to human beings.

Soft drinks manufacturers found that cyclamates did not leave the sour aftertaste of saccharin, and doctors found that cyclamates greatly assisted in cases of diabetes and obesity. Until the recent ban, some 80% of Americans were consuming cyclamates in one form or another without the slightest sign of any harm to their health and with a great many signs of health advantages.

By the mid-sixties, cyclamates had started to make serious inroads into the sugar market. In a statement at a national congress of sugar manufacturers, the President of the American Sugar Manufacturers' Association warned of the possible threat which cyclamates posed to the sugar industry. He showed that research could well find ways of introducing cyclamates in food as well as soft drinks. He demonstrated that cyclamates cost five times less than sugar and contained 30 times the sweetening power. The threat to sugar profits, he warned, could be very serious indeed.

Almost at once, the Governments of all countries where cyclamates were used were bombarded with cyclamate "research."

In 1965 the Sugar Research Foundation of America publicized a paper from *Nature* by workers at Wisconsin Alumini Research Foundation demonstrating that calcium cyclamate had disturbed the growth of animals and stunted their young. The research work on cyclamates at Wisconsin, then and later, was sponsored and financed by the American sugar industry. The research on that occasion was dismissed by the American Food and Drug Administration on the grounds that the doses fed to the animals in order to reach that conclusion were absurdly large.

In 1966 two Japanese research scientists, Messrs Kojima and Ichibagase, produced results of research to demonstrate that cyclamates as they pass through the body, can be converted into another compound, cyclohexylamine. The British Sugar Industry took an immediate interest in the results of this research, and sponsored its own research into cyclamates and cyclohexylamine at research laboratories at Huntingdon. Huntingdon experts also found that some consumers of cyclamates secreted cyclohexylamine, though the percentage of secretors was much smaller than in Japan. Dr Gaston Pawan, who has been researching into cyclamates for two years at London's Middlesex Hospital and who regards their ban as "a great shame," thinks that the secretion ratio in Japan has something to do with general diet, and is not convinced of the connection between cyclamates and secretion of cyclohexylamine. Even if he was, he says, there is no evidence that cyclohexylamine is toxic to human beings. The Minister of Health was informed by the sugar industry of this research, and the Ministry published a separate document on cyclamates, calling for and setting up still more research - this time by the British Industrial Biological Research Association at Carshalton, Surrey. The BIBRA research has been going on for more than two years under Dr Reginald Crampton, who has reported publicly that "nothing untoward" about cyclamates has yet been discovered. BIBRA, incidentally, had been offered funds for research into cyclamates by the British Sugar Refineries Association, but had turned them down because of the need to preserve impartiality.

In 1967, following the Japanese/Huntingdon experiments the British Sugar Bureau, a public relations organisation set up in 1966 by Tate and Lyle and other major sugar companies, published and distributed to all MPs a booklet entitled *Cyclamate Sweeteners* which "summarised" the research into cyclamates in such a way as to make them appear highly dangerous to public health. When Mr Ichibagase, the Japanese scientist responsible for much of the Japanese research into cyclamates visited Britain in 1968 a special cocktail party was organised in his honour by the British Sugar Bureau in their lavish offices in Park Lane.

Meanwhile, more research into cyclamates was going on in Austria - at the Paracelsus Institute in Bad Hall. A team of "doctors" there reported in June 1968, what was described in the *Sunday Times*, along with the rest of the British and European Press, as "fresh evidence of danger to health by the use of controversial artificial chemical sweetener cyclamate." "Even small doses of the sweetener" ran the *Sunday Times* report (16.6.68) cause serious damage to the liver of the guinea pigs. Persons with heart, circulatory and liver complaints appear to be particularly endangered..."

That was as much as the British public found out about the Paracelsus research, and even today Mr Michael Shrewsbury,

the Sugar Bureau's dynamic director, assured *Private Eye* that the Paracelsus research was "independent research, not sponsored by the sugar industry. These independent research institutions are of tremendous repute. If they say something, that's it, you know, I mean, you can take it from me."

The truth about the Austrian research was revealed with greater accuracy at a Press Conference on July 4, 1968, in Munich, addressed by Professor N. Zollner, chairman of the Commission of Food Research in Germany and Dr H Mehnhert, an expert in metabolism. Professor Zollner started the Conference with a vitriolic attack on the Austrian research into cyclamates which he said "could not withstand scientific examination."

The tests, he disclosed, had been carried out with seven guinea pigs and six rabbits, of which only four guinea pigs were used in the final examination. The fact, he said, that some of the animals died during testing showed that the animals had already been ill before testing started since "healthy animals do not die during testing." Test results, he said, based on four animals can only be accidental.

Moreover, what the Professor described as "stupidly high quantities" of cyclamates were fed to the animals - the equivalent of 18 grammes for a human being, though the average diabetic never takes more than three grammes per day. Even with this high quantity, the scientists could find no damage to the liver, so they increased the quantity by four times - to 36 times the normal dose - before they could detect any damage in the liver. "Paracelsus himself" said Professor Zollner "knew that all things are poisonous if used in excessive quantities."

Finally, the Professor exposed an infantile mistake in the Austrian research. The "doctors" had shown that a person drinking a litre of sweetened lemonade consumed 10 grammes of cyclamates, which represented about half the necessary amount for damage to be caused to the liver. In fact, as the Professor showed, the doctors had made a mistake of a factor of ten: and that a lemonade sweetened with 10 grammes is undrinkable. *(Die Welt: 8.7.68).*

On July 6, the German paper *Handelsblatt*, went further: "After the Press conference," it reported "it became known that Professor Dr Hellauer of the Paracelsus Institute at Bad Hall, Austria, has not only admitted publicly that the tests carried out at his institute had been financed by the sugar industry, but also that he used the results of other research work on cyclamates only in so far as they seemed to prove his arguments."

The Austrian research, largely through the exposee of Professor Zollner, who was forcefully supported by the German Health Ministry, was finally withdrawn.

But the withdrawal was not publicised. By the summer of 1968, largely as a result of the Paracelsus "research" the 'ban cyclamate' bandwaggon was speeding on.

In Britain, the British Nutrition Foundation had been formed under the chairmanship of Dr Alastair Frazer, described as an "expert in food additives." Dr Frazer wrote several learned articles casting doubt on the health value of cyclamates, and everyone thought that he was writing them from the entirely independent standpoint as chairman of a neutral foundation. Few people knew that he was also working in an advisory but well-rewarded capacity for the British sugar industry.

Meanwhile, the sugar industry in Holland, which was beginning to feel the pinch of cyclamates on their profits, had stepped up its activity. Great publicity was given to the research on rats conducted by Drs. Vischer and Dalderup published early this year which showed that cyclamates tended abnormally to increase the size of babies after birth. (No comment was made about the sugar-sponsored research in Wisconsin which "proved", two years earlier, that cyclamates stunted growth).

The Dutch research was sponsored by the Dutch Sugar Union, who employ Dr Vischer as the director of their "School for the sugar industry." In the spring, the Dutch sugar industry launched an extensive advertising campaign directed against cyclamates and other sweeteners. "Only Sugar Sweet is Pure Sweet;" "Never Try To Satisy Your Desire for Sweetness With Artificial Sweetners" were the slogans. In July the sugar companies were banned by the Dutch High Court from continuing with their campaign, or from making any further "untrue or denigrating" statements about artificial sweeters. Yet part of the job had been done, at least according to the ubiquitous Dr. Vischer who wrote in an article in the Monthly Journal of the Dutch Sugar Industry that "The decrease in sugar consumption has stopped."

This summer, the American Department of Health asked for still more research from Abbott Laboratories, who make cyclamates in America. Abbotts' own researchers responded by pumping huge doses of cyclamates into rats' bladders. As a result, without publishing the evidence, Robert Finch, American Health Secretary, banned cyclamates under the 'Delaney Amendment' which allows him arbitrarily to ban food additives if any connection with cancer is proved. As the American assistant Secretary of Health made plain:

"We can in no way at this time extrapolate the new data from rat experiments to human beings."

There was, he said, not the slightest evidence that cancer of the bladder in human beings had risen in the period in which consumption of cyclamates had risen several hundred fold. To equal the doses given to the rats in the tests, a human would have to consume some 550 bottles of low calorie soft drinks per day for several weeks.

Whether or not cyclamates are dangerous to human beings has yet to be proved. What is certain is that they are many, many times safer for humans than sugar. In the 1930's it was common practice for doctors to measure the amount of water in human and animal bodies by injecting them with sucrose (sugar). The practice was stopped after at least four sets of experiments showed that even small injections of sucrose produced kidney damage (see, for instance, the essay by Professor A D Anderson in the Journal of the American Medical Association, 1940, Vol 114, p 1983).

A paper entitled Are Sugars Carcinogens by W C Hueper of the National Cancer Institute in Bethseda, Maryland, reported: "The mice not infrequently developed symptoms of acute shock especially during the early experimental period, soon after the introduction of the sugar solutions; some died with the anatomic reactions characterising such a response to the hypertonic agent; i.e. hemorrhagic transudates in pleural and peritoneal cavities, severe hyperemia and hemorrhages in the lungs."

Add to this the careful and copious work done over recent years against consistent oppositon from the sugar industry, by Professor John Yudkin of Queen Elizabeth College, London, all of which demonstrates a very close relationship between sugar consumption and a number of diseases of affluence especially coronary thrombosis – and the conclusion is clear: if sugar was introduced today as a "food additive" it would be banned by any Government anywhere. As it is, a sugar substitute which has been used for nearly 30 years without any harmful effects, is removed from the market at the instigation, and to the relief of the manufacturers of a substance which has been shown to be highly dangerous: sugar.

## SEX

*From Mr A G Narghastly*

Dear Sir,

The decision of the BBC to show young children sex education films is as monstrous as it is scandalous.

Are parents no longer to have the right to explain to their children about the er well I mean you know um it's like this you see ?

Your obedient servant<br>A G NARGHASTLY<br>Loose Chippings<br>Glos.

### *THE WIT AND WISDOM OF WALTER ANNENBERG*

*Mr Walter Annenberg the American ambassador found himself at a recent dinner placed next to Lady Hambleden. "Is it true you were born in Italy?" he enquired of the lady. "Yes indeed" she replied. "That's great" quipped the Ambassador, "I just adore spaghetti."*

*" This could mean war! Archduke Franz should be carrying the spare wheel!"*

# MRS. WILSON'S DIARY

I have mentioned before the thrill of school-girl delight that it gives me to receive on gold-embossed Truslove and Hanson cardette the Royal Summons to attend upon the person of Her Majesty. So it was that such a flutter made itself felt within my breast the other morning at breakfast when the Inspector handed me the Regal Stiffie, even though it was slightly soiled by a blob of Tiptree Ginger Shredless Marmalade, currently Harold's favourite. "What's that Gladys ?" Harold enquired gruffly from behind the *Financial Times*, "Jenkins up to his tricks again is it ? Or is Harold Lever throwing another of his champagne and caviar soirees up on the roof of the Hilton ? The nation can ill afford ...." "No, no", I interpolated, "it is from Her Majesty. 'Her Majesty the Queen commands the presence of Mr and Mrs Harold Wilson in the Duke of Connaught Room at half past eight of the clock this Wednesday sennight signed Fitzpestle Master of the Queen's Privy Purse'."

So it was that Wednesday evening found us seated snugly in the back of Harold's Humber winging smoothly down the Mall while the autumn leaves swirled and twirled around us. A small group waiting round the gates peered curiously through the windows, and someone shouted "It's Charlie Drake come for his MBE. Good on you, Charlie!" Moments later we slid in under the canopied porchway, and were ushered up five flights of stairs by Sir Alan Adale, who performs for Her Majesty in a similar role to that of Mr Kaufmann in our own humbler entourage. That person himself - I refer to Mr Kaufmann - followed obsequiously in our wake, preserving the ten yards interval laid down in Queen's Regulations. I was a little short of breath when we reached the top of the Albert Staircase and turned to begin the long trek along the Queen Mary Corridor, hung with portraits of Russian Tzars of days gone by and lined with the huge urns of ancient Chinese Emperors.

Some quarter of an hour later we reached the Hohenzollern Chandelier Balcony and began the long ascent of the North Face. "I suppose we could camp here for the night" Harold observed in witty mood, but Sir Alan advised against it, remarking *sotto voce* "I shall knock twice, you will transfer your hat to your left hand and give it to the liveried attendant with the words 'I thank you.' I shall then take you forward and announce whatever your name is to Her Majesty, who will be seated on the Colenso Throne at a distance of some three hundred yards at the far end of the room. You, Madam, will then drop a curtsey, and you, Sir, will bow from the waist and remark 'Your obedient Servant, Ma'am.' This person" - here he indicated Mr Kaufmann, who was panting heavily in his overcoat and woollen muffler as he struggled up the last flight of the Grand Staircase - "had better wait outside the door." By now we had reached the high doors of the Duke of Connaught Reception Chamber. Sir Alan whispered "Good Luck!", tapped on the doors which were opened with a loud creaking sound, and stepped forward to announce "Mr and Mrs Watson, Your Majesty."

"Do come in" came a squeaky voice in the distance, and we began the long walk up the red carpet towards the throne. After a second bow and curtsey at the Royal Footstool we were treated to a truly radiant smile from Her Majesty, who led the way up the steps of the throne and down the other side, behind some Chinese screens and through a little door into a small lounge were we found the Duke sprawled on the settee, watching television. "Come aboard, come aboard," he vouchsafed in nautical style, swinging a leg over the settee and limping rather arthritically to the drinks table, "what'll it be ? I'm afraid I haven't got any of that awful stuff you drink. What ?" We both chuckled at the Duke's wit, and accepted a glass of Malodoroso Cypriot Cream Sherry. "Now pin your ears back" the Duke pursued, indicating a hard, upright settee opposite his own easy chair, "darling, could you get my Woodbines ? I think I left them in the bathroom."

"Now, let's get down to brass tacks. We're absolutely on our uppers. Telephone cut off, tradesmen writing threatening letters. We've had to sell one of our yachts. There's no incentive left any more. To put it bluntly cough up or it's the Duke of Gloucester." "The Duke of Gloucester?" Harold queried. "Abdication old man, Gloucester for King. How would you like that ?" "Let us not talk of such desperate measures" Harold remarked in soothing tone, "naturally I will do everything within my power to ensure that Her Majesty can be maintained in the manner to which she is accustomed. You will understand however, Your Royal Highness, that there are elements in my own party who still cling to outdated dreams of republican irresponsibility." "Reds under the bed, what ?" the Duke smiled drily, sipping his tumbler of amber fluid. At this juncture Her Majesty reappeared, bearing the Duke's green carton, containing as I noticed, only one half-smoked cigarette. Bending down she began to whisper in her consort's ear, whereupon the latter, red with rage, emitted a dull roar through clenched teeth and sprang to the door. A

moment later he reappeared in the room, dragging behind him the dishevelled fugure of Mr Kaufmann, whom he held in a firm grip by the left ear. "What the bloody hell's going on ?" he remarked, but before Mr Kaufmann could offer any explanation the Duke administered a sharp kick in the BTM, causing him to fall face forwards into the sofa, where he lay for a few moments without moving. "Bloody Press Wallahs!" observed the Duke, tearing up Mr Kaufmann's notebook and throwing it into the fire. "Is this your doing, Wilson ? Nasty shifty keyhole journalist ? If I had my way these fellows would be hung up by the short and curlies." "My Liege, I protest" Harold rejoined, raising his hands in a gesture of horror, "Mr Kaufmann is here in his official capacity as my personal aide de camp." At this the Duke put his head between his hands and burst into tears. "I don't know what the matter is," he sobbed, "I can't seem to put a foot right nowadays. It's not much fun being hounded by the Press wherever you go. Not a moment's peace. Long lenses poking through your bedroom window. It's enough to drive a man mad!"

Her Majesty, who had viewed this scene with some distaste, now rose to her feet and gave an embarrassed cough. "I think you had better go now" she vouchsafed, and taking me by the arm, she led us quickly out through the servants' quarters, where there was a merry hubbub of television, clinking glasses, and the roar of good conversation. Harold followed a little way behind, attempting to comfort the choking Mr Kaufmann. As we passed the dustbins and found ourselves once more in the yard, Her Majesty confided in me that she was very worried about the Duke, and enquired whether I had ever had recourse, on Harold's behalf, to a good psychiatrist. Alas I was in no position to be of any assistance, but I left her Sophie Brown's telephone number, and suggested that she might be more experienced in such matters.

## Architecture

# FINE ARTS & CORONETS

The recent rise in concern and protest at the indiscriminate building of high-rise developments in the city centres has included little reference to the independent body whose job it is to advise the Governments and local authorities against the desecration of their environment: The Royal Fine Art Commission. The Commission, set up in 1924, has increasingly come under the control of architects: not retired architects or academic architects but architects with profitable partnerships who can give "down-to-earth, pragmatic advice" to counter the fuddy-duddies and the cranks who are not in the business for money.

Suitable expression to this revolution in the Commission's make-up was given by Sir Frederick Gibberd, one of the most successful of post-war British architects whose triumphs in design include London Airport and Harlow New Town, and who joined the Commission in 1959. In April 1960 Sir Frederick told Atticus of the *Sunday Times*: "I joined the Royal Fine Art Commission when it was run by a bunch of RAs who spent hours criticising petty architectural details. We don't get bogged down with footling details such as the siting of a police station in High Wycombe, but deal generally with the London skyline and that's a much healthier thing. Many people blame the Government for terrible building on prominent sites, but not even we can turn a dud architect into a good one."

This view was underscored in the same article by Sir Basil Spence, OM, one of Britain's most famous architects, who joined the Commission in 1956. Spence supported the choice of "busy, successful architects" for the Commission as this was the best way to get "honest advice from competent critics without an axe to grind."

Throughout the 1960's the Commission, chaired by the late Lord Bridges, former secretary to the Cabinet and Permanent Secretary of the Treasury, became less and less effective in the business of stopping the desecration by development of British cities. Many large developments, notably Mr Richard Seifert's glamorous 31-storey Centre Point, still empty after three years, were never submitted to the Commission before being built. Other schemes were turned down by the Commission only to be accepted by the Government. Yet one of the most bizarre aspects about the Commission's deliberations over individual building schemes was the involvement in the design of the buildings of some of the more distinguished members of the Fine Art Commission.

In 1959, for instance, the Commission got involved in the controversy about the proposed 'Monico' development of Piccadilly Circus. When the plans were

KNIGHTSBRIDGE BARRACKS: *The first multi-storey stables ?*

announced, the Commission was silent. As public opposition grew, so did that of the Commission. Planning consent was refused. The latest Fine Art Commission Report (1966-1968) tells us:

*"In 1962 a comprehensive outline scheme was prepared by Lord Holford. This was accepted in principle by the Commission."*

Holford joined the Commission in 1943 and has recently retired. In 1956 his scheme for the precincts of St Paul's Cathedral was also accepted in "broad principle" by the Commision, which raised no serious objection throughout the 1960s as St Paul's became blocked from the North by office development, designed by Lord Holford. Another of Lord Holford's architectural triumphs, the War Museum at Chelsea, criticised by uninitiated London-lovers who felt that a war museum could well be outside the centre of London and that the site used should have been left open, sailed through the Fine Art Commission while its architect was a member.

Sir Frederick Gibberd himself, whose part in the auction of the centre of Doncaster to developers is still remembered with mixed feelings in Yorkshire has, in his dynamic way, been busy with designs for crucial buildings in London which have seldom met any serious opposition from the Royal Fine Art Commission. His scheme for a hotel on the site of "hippy

house" 144 Piccadilly was approved by the Commission about six months ago. As reported in *Eye* No 204 Sir Frederick was called in as a consultant to modify the plans for the new British Council building at Carlton Terrace, after the original design, by some less famous architect, had been rejected by the Royal Fine Art Commission. Sir Frederick's apparently minor modifications made all the difference, and the Commission, on which Sir Frederick has sat since 1959, approved the designs.

One of the Art Commission's most sustained campaigns has been against new high blocks on the fringes of public parks. The Commission, for instance, opposed the building of the Hilton Hotel in the mid-sixties, and forced the Conservative Cabinet to take a political decision against the Commission's advice to allow the Hilton to go ahead. The 1961 Report of the Commission stressed that buildings to the West of the Park should be discouraged since they would destroy the illusion that the Park "gives way to open spaces in the West."

The 66-68 Report talks in strong language of "a gradual hemming in of the parks by a wall of high buildings such as can be seen around Central Park, New York."

Hard on the heels of the application for the Hilton and high blocks at Marble Arch and Lancaster Gate, all of which the

Commission vigorously opposed, came the application for another high block to serve as the Headquarters of the Household Cavalry at Knightsbridge - to the West of the Park.

Mr Frank Fielden, secretary to the Fine Art Commission, assured *Private Eye* that the Commission were "very much opposed all through" to the Knightsbridge Barracks scheme. He agrees, however, that the Commission's opposition to the building has never been publicised or mentioned in the Commission's Reports, although their opposition to every other high building around Hyde Park has been reported with some prominence. At any rate, one of the conventions of the Commission is that all decisions should be unanimous. The architect of the Knightsbridge scheme is Sir Basil Spence, OM, who has been delighted at the speedy expedition of his designs for Knightsbridge barracks, despite the disapproval of the Commission of which he is a member. Sir Basil is also consultant for the building of the massive new 17-storey civil service department building planned for Queen Annes Mansions near St James's Park. The Queen Annes building was approved after what Mr Fielden calls "much coming and going" by the Fine Art Commission about nine months ago.

Lord Llewellyn-Davies, created in 1965, has been on the Royal Fine Art Commission since 1961, and is also the senior partner in a highly profitable architects' practise Llewellyn-Davies, Forestrier Walker, Bor and Weeks. The noble Lord has been taken on as architectural consultant on many famous buildings, not least the *Times* building at Printing House Square and the new Stock Exchange building in the City. The Stock Exchange building was designed by Fitzroy Robinson and Partners who did not take Llewellyn-Davies on as consultant until some considerable time after the plans had been designed. The building, which is not regarded as the greatest architectural triumph in the City's history, was passed by the Royal Fine Art Commission. Lord Llewellyn-Davies was also the architect behind the recent redevelopment scheme around the Tate Gallery - a scheme which resulted in the virtual masking of the Gallery's facade, and which has eventually been killed by, among other bodies, the Greater London Council Historic Buildings Board. The Royal Fine Art Commission, on the other hand, found little fault with the Tate designs. "We thought it was a very good building" says Mr Fielden. "We would have liked it to be somewhere else, but if it had to be there, we approved of it."

Other architects on the Commission who from time to time submit their work to the Commission for approval are Lord Esher, who has had several buildings approved - including a hotel in Winchester and the extension to Exeter College, Oxford - and Sir Leslie Martin who was responsible for the overall plan for the redevelopment of Whitehall which has been engaging so much of the Commission's recent attention.

# Lesotho Women Make Beautiful Carpets

### By Gordon Lindsay

*Bangkok World*

## Man found dead in graveyard

*EVENING STANDARD*

"HOW DO YOU EXPECT TO GET ANYWHERE IF YOU'RE ITINERANT ?"

*"Nothing, Laura. It's just that we thought you'd bought a converted pigsty!"*

# "Stop weeping" Brown tells U.S.

Mr George Brown the deputy leader of the Labour Party yesterday lashed out at critics of the so-called "Pinkville Massacre."

Speaking on the BBC programme *The World at Opening Time* Mr Brown told Americans to "stop weeping and get on with the war."

### SoB

Questioned by Mr William Sandcastle about the alleged atrocities Mr Brown said "Terrible I agree if it happened. But which one of us at some time or other in our lives has not lined up 300 civilians against a wall and mowed them down with a machine gun ?"

### GHASTLY

Mr Brown's remarks brought an immediate reaction from left-wing Labour MPs. Said Dr David Cur: "He should be lined up against a wall and mowed down with a lawn mower."

It is thought that some MPs will press for Mr Brown's resignation as chief publicity stuntman for the Labour Party.

# Why don't they belt up?

asks
WALTER
TERRYBLE

**CHIEF BROWNER**

Once again the so-called Labour left-wing MPs are up in arms over a handful of snapshots showing dead women and children and an alleged massacre for which there is no substantial evidence apart from 479 eye witness accounts

(cont 94th parallel)

## THAT MASSACRE
### You write

Dear Sir,

Recent revelations concerning the alleged massacre of several hundred innocent children are certainly distressing. But as one who has been out East himself, I say that these things happen in peace as in war. A man under stress can do some pretty strange things, and afterwards feels just as ashamed as the next man. If the alleged massacre did indeed take place, then I am sure those responsible only acted for the best, in the light of circumstances with which only they were familiar. King Herod is doing a difficult job at a difficult time in his country's history and I am sure that when the history of these troubled times comes to be written, it will not be for this relatively trivial incident that he will be remembered.
Yours faithfully,
G KHAN
Kara Koram.

Dear Sir,

Surely after this lapse of time it is to be doubted whether the true facts of the so-called Bethlehem Massacre will ever be known. I have had some experience of this kind of thing myself, and know how such matters can get blown up out of all proportion. Despite the alleged existence of alleged eyewitness accounts of the alleged incident, the full story will never be known, and I suggest it is time we washed our hands of the whole affair.
I remain, sir, yours
faithfully,
P PILATE (Governor, retd)
The Villa
Aston
Brittannia.

# BERNARD LEVIN

The more I see and hear of Spiro T McCarthy, the bluff outspoken Senator from Wisconsin, the more I like what I see and hear.

Here is a man who has the courage to say out loud what millions of his fellow countrymen are thinking.

The leftie intellectuals may sneer at his charge that there is a Communist conspiracy to take over the world.

But to my mind, his remarks place him firmly in the tradition of Orwell, Goethe, Wagner, Charles James Fox and Edmund Burke (cont p 94)

Let me make it clear at once that I regard this Pinkville atrocity as a very serious matter indeed . . .

. . . . nevertheless war is a bloody business . . . . and the other side is just as bad, if not worse . . . .

. . . even we British ahem aha . . .

. . . SO WHAT'S ALL THE FUSS ABOUT ?

## Transplants
# No change of heart

None of the newspapers have commented on the article printed in the *Lancet* on November 22 entitled "Production of Severe Atheroma in a Transplanted Human Heart" by J G Thomson, Professor of Pathology at Groote Schuur Hospital, South Africa. A silence due, no doubt, to the fact that Professor Thomson names no names. Only a careful reading discloses that the heart he is discussing is that of the longest surviving heart transplant 'recipient,' the late Dr Philip Blaiberg. Dr Thomson's report on Blaiberg's two hearts (the original and the transplanted one) indicates that no one in his right mind will ever again carry out a heart transplant on a man in Blaiberg's condition.

One of the most common and pernicious causes of heart failure is arteriosclerosis, a hardening of the arteries through the formation of "atheromatous plaques." This disease extends and spreads throughout the body, causing interference in the blood supply and damage to the heart. One of the claims of the heart transplanters has been that people suffering from heart damage caused by arteriosclerosis can be helped by transplantation of a 'clean' heart. Dr Thomson's report proves the exact opposite.

Blaiberg's donor, he points out, (no names of course) had never been ill in his life. There was nothing wrong with his heart. Blaiberg, on the other hand, suffered from arteriosclerosis. A clean heart was transplanted into a body affected by arteriosclerosis. What happened ? According to Dr Thomson: "At the necropsy of the patient who survived heart transplantation for the longest period to date - 19 months - the donor heart, from a man aged 24, showed coronary artery atheroma of a very high intensity and with a wider distribution than I have seen before in 40 years necropsy experience."

In other words, the 'clean' heart in a very short time was "furred up" with the arteriosclerosis which had plagued the old one. Dr Thomson goes on: "After transplantation the coronary arteries became so atheromatous that their lumina were reduced to mere slits. The atheroma was more severe in the transplanted heart than in the recipient's original heart."

In other words, Blaiberg would have been better off with his old heart.

How did Blaiberg manage to survive ? Dr Thomson explains: "The patient had from six months after transplantation onwards a very poor cardiac output, and was under constant medical supervision for the rest of his life. His physical activities were very restricted..."

So much for all that yachting, swimming and copulating which Dr Blaiberg is reported to have indulged in during the "new life" given him by his new heart.

Dr Thomson's conclusion is straightforward: "The hazards of heart transplantation in man, apart from the operative ones, have been acute or chronic rejection and infections, largely determined by the massive immunosuppressive therapy. This case adds another hazard where transplantation is undertaken on account of myocardial insufficiency from atheroma of the coronary arteries. I suggest that such patients with ischaemic heart disease are not suitable subjects for heart transplantation.

"It is indeed a sad irony that a brave pioneer could produce in the coronary arteries of his transplanted heart the same disease that determined the dysfunction of his original heart."

A sad irony, too, that the newspapers and television stations which devoted so much time and space to the antics of the "brave pioneer" could not find a moment or a column inch to report the total failure of his operation. Everywhere heart transplants have fallen from fashion. In America, since the sacking from St Luke's Hospital, Houston, of Dr Denton Cooley, and the classification of heart transplants as Experimentation, rather than Treatment, big money for transplants is no longer forthcoming. In Britain, France and even in South Africa, the rush to transplant has stopped.

Professor Christian Barnard, however, rolls on forever. In a recent interview with *World Medecine* (October 28) he admitted: "I don't think it's bad being an idol .... The photographers, the television, the bright lights have had the effect of steering a lot of money towards medicine .... I am very enthusiastic about the heart transplant. It has done much better than I ever anticipated when we started."

# The Daily Telegraph
## AN APOLOGY

*WE ARE VERY SORRY ABOUT THE DAILY TELEGRAPH*

Hang on! This chap's got lumps on his chest!

# MRS. WILSON'S DIARY

Only nineteen shopping days to go, and I still haven't the foggiest idea what is going into Harold's stocking on the big day. I think probably I shall plump for the Reader's Digest Condensed Books of the World Vols S to Z which come with a free set of six plastic sugar spoons and a reproduction lily of the valley cluster. For Mr Kaufmann I have bought an Xmas Holly Pack of super-strength Brillo-Pads with Added Biological Stain Remover, and for the Inspector, Lord Wigg's new paperback *The Punter's Vade Mecum 1970,* with an appendix of tax advice by Lord Balogh of Esterhazy. For Robin I have bought a new bowler hat, and Giles is getting a transistorised electric toothbrush which I saw advertised in the *Observer* Colour Magazine. I have also got a nice pair of green orlon socks for Mrs Bollard, our help.

In the meanwhile, life has been most hectic. We have had Ambassador Freeman staying, and I often think that Downing Street is not best suited to entertaining, particularly in the grand style to which Mr Freeman has grown accustomed since his *New Statesman* days. I did my best by clearing out Giles's old room and putting a few flowers on the washstand and a tin of Peak Freen Zootime Assortment on the bedside chamber cupboard. But I fear the Inspector's wireless late at night and Mr Kaufmann's dumb-bell workout in the room above at first light must have disturbed him, because after two days he moved into Claridge's Embassy Suite where he said he would be less trouble to look after.

Harold, I fear, has been most upset by the stories of Pinkville, and it was this that prompted him to summon Mr Freeman for urgent consultations. Unfortunately at their first session in the den they were interrupted by the arrival of Mr Brown, fresh from a pre-lunch ideas session at Courtaulds. The Inspector attempted to divert him into the lounge, but in vain, and when I went in with the Marks and Spencers' Lunchette Mini-Hampers and a jug of Robinson Crusoe's Cyclamate-Free Barley Water, he was already in full spate, standing on one of the armchairs, making flamboyant gestures, while Mr Freeman eyed him with world-weary ennui from a reclined position on the settee. Harold was sitting with his eyes closed, drumming quietly on the arm of his chair with veiled impatience. "Which of us" Mr Brown was shouting "can put our hand on our hearts, look into our own eyes, and say with one voice 'There are no skeletons in my cupboard' ?" "We know what there is in your cupboard, George" Harold replied wrily, "especially at this festive season of the year, and there must be precious little room for skeletons." At this Mr Freeman gave a light laugh, ex-

tracting a Burmah Cheroot from a shiny leather container and lighting it with man-of-the-world aplomb.

"Tell the Americans to stop weeping, John, that's what I say, and get on with the massacre. As I remember saying to my old friend John Kennedy" - at this large tears began to flow down Mr Brown's cheeks, and he extracted a red and white spotted handkerchief to blow his nose with a sonorous trumpeting sound. Unable to continue he sank into the chair, his shoulders heaving helplessly, and was soon snoring fitfully in a deep sleep. "Joking apart" Harold continued "I feel we must make it clear to the President how very deeply we deplore this monstrous atrocity, causing as it has untold misery and suffering to newspaper readers the world over and particularly in this country, and that whereas President Nixon has always had my unqualified support in this dirty business there are ways and means of making the world safe for democracy. I suggest that you and I, John, go round to Regent's Park and make it absolutely clear to Walter Annenberg how deeply the conscience of Britain has been stirred by this abhorrent tale. You'd better come along too Gladys. I expect you and Mrs A will find bags to talk about while John and I give Walt a piece of our minds."

Minutes later we were entering the crystal chandelier-hung splendour of the Official Residence, and a coloured butler was taking our coats with old-world courtesy. Lulled by the unobtrusive murmur of the Muzak, we made our way across the marble floor, tastefully littered with polarbear skins tinted in pastel shades, to where Mr and Mrs Annenberg were standing under a delightful Renoir Reproruduction, the same, by a wierd coincidence that Harold's sister Marjorie has in her lounge. Mr Annenberg was most dignified, and coming forward with outstretched hand he remarked "Greetings Mr Prime Minister, Mrs Prime Minister. May I have the considerable pleasure of effecting an introduction to Mrs Annenberg, who is my wife, and who is in no small way responsible for the appurtenances and restyling elements of decor which you see about you." Mrs Annenberg, whose fingers were loaded down with rich rings, gave us a delightful smile and observed "Mrs Prime Minister, Mrs Prime Minister, you are very welcome." "That will do, Leo," interposed the Emissary from the New World, "you would not wish to bore our guests. This picture which you see exhibited adjacent to the ninety per cent genuine antique fireplace surround and mantlepiece unit is worth well over three hundred thousand of your guineas." I

thought this rather odd, as Harold's sister has always been very economical about art, but I thought it best not to contradict Mr Annenberg and assumed that the frame was more valuable than the picture, shining as it did like solid gold in the light of the fluorescent candelabra-style candles on the inlaid table beneath it.

"Your Excellency" Harold began, as Mr Annenberg waved us towards a delightful picture of some ballet dancers doing their shoes up, "on the subject of Vietnam ..." "Say no more, Mr Prime Minister" soothed the Ambassador, "I would just like to express on behalf of my President, and on behalf of the people of the United States of America, that we have been muchly touched by the support vouchsafed to our Nation and its considerable military involvements in the South East Asian Sphere of Influence by the courageous endorsement articulated by your Mr George Brown." At this Mr Freeman coughed and extinguished his cigar in an urn of sand. "I notice, Mr Freeman, that you are examining our ceiling. This has been recently refurbished at a cost of well over a hundred thousand dollars utilising original materials on what is habitually described as a steel and fibreglass sub-construction and coated with several applications of cupro-cyanide matt wash cover marketed by your own Imperial Chemical Industry. The tomato still adhering to its surface was projected into that location by Lord Rothermere in congenial mood contemporaneously with a formal house-warming celebration attended by newspaper proprietors from all walks of life. We find it has considerable charm from an aesthetic viewpoint, thrown as it was by a member of your aristocracy."

"At a time like this, Ambassador," Harold persevered, "when the eyes of the world are focussed on America ..." "You are most generous, Mr Prime Minister" our host continued, "on behalf of the peoples of the States which comprise the Union of the United States it is a great pleasure and a considerable privilege to accept your most gracious congratulations on the occasion of the successful re-entry into terrestial orbit of the Apollo 12 Moonshot vehicle."

It was not until half past twelve that we finally emerged from the Residence after an extended conducted tour of the apartments under the director of Mr Annenberg's chief interior decorator, Mr Blanche Schwartz from California. Harold seemed less than satisfied with our encounter, shredding up rather ungraciously I thought the pink silk flower given to him by Mrs Annenberg as a memento of our visit and stuffing the remains into the glove compartment ashtray, but Mr Freeman observed "What else can you expect if you appoint ambassadors who are little more than time-serving backs just to pay off old political scores ?"

# PRIVATE EYE

No. 213
Friday
13 Feb. '70

2/-

YES !
IT'S
THE
NEW
LOOK
TED !

# COLOUR SECTION

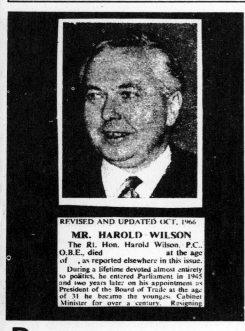

REVISED AND UPDATED OCT. 1966

**MR. HAROLD WILSON**

The Rt. Hon. Harold Wilson. P.C.. O.B.E., died            at the age of     , as reported elsewhere in this issue.
During a lifetime devoted almost entirely to politics, he entered Parliament in 1945 and two years later on his appointment as President of the Board of Trade at the age of 31 he became the youngest Cabinet Minister for over a century.  Resigning

**D**espite Wislon's confident remarks to James Margach about his state of health and general physical fitness, *The Times* are taking no chances.

An authentic copy of Wislon's obituary has now come into Lord Gnome's hands. It dates from 1966 and in Sept 1967 was in the process of being revised.   At that time, the chief of *The Times* Obituary Department wrote: "It is always difficult when a man is in high office and still comparatively young to allot him a length.   At the moment I am inclined to think that we need 5000 words."

The 1966 version is scarcely flattering to Wislon, written as it was in the wake of the July 1966 financial crisis.   After a relatively impartial account of his career it concludes:

*The earlier emphasis of some critics on his alleged pettiness and double dealing could draw on certain facts.   He had carefully retained, for certain purposes, a northern accent: his talk of boys in his own village having to go barefoot to school could be faulted: he had supported Bevan near the death of the Labour Government of 1945-51 and had then abandoned him later on: he had attacked Gaitskell when in practice he agreed with the substance of Gaitskell's policies.   Yet all these facts could be explained quite convincingly by a careful study of Wilson's motives and intellectual make-up, his brilliant capacity to distinguish between what was capable of achievement and what was inessential or was best left imprecise.*

*But after his first two years as Prime Minister more serious and larger issues arose.   For some he remained the tactician and orator who had achieved an almost impossible feat in uniting the Labour Party and bringing it back to power.   Despite mediocre colleagues, his record in government had given him sufficient authority to transform Labour into a radical-democratic party which captured the centre in British politics and thus became the natural majority party.   As part of the process, for the first time in the modern history of Britain the trade unions and employers' associations were forced to think of the balance of payments and of the national interest before embarking on sectional demands.*

*To others he became the man who had betrayed socialism, who had defied the internal democractic mechanism of the Labour Party, who had deserted the Africans in Rhodesia and had done nothing to help the sufferings of the Vietnamese people.   For many, who did not take such an ideological stand, he nevertheless seemed to be too ready to twist words, to insist on his own consistency however his policies fluctuated and to have little principle except the retention of power.   It is unlikely that any of these versions will be totally refuted or abandoned by future historians.   But if the measures Harold Wilson took as Premier have, in the long run, eradicated Britain's post war economic weaknesses, there is little doubt that the overwhelming reaction will be one of gratitude and admiration for a man whose courage and ability were never in doubt.*

**A** well-known book critic was recently ejected from El Vino's following scenes in which he behaved in a drunken and abusive manner.   The critic was subsequently informed by the proprietor that he was in future to enter the bar by the back door.

Some days later the book critic reappeared through the back door looking considerably the worse for wear, and sat himself down next to a well known theatre critic.   The following conversation is then reported to have taken place:

Well-known book critic (head in hands): "Sympathy.   Sympathy.   Where am I to find sympathy ?"

Well-known theatre critic (quick as a flash):  "*Shorter Oxford Dictionary.* Somewhere between shit and syphilis."

Once I was just a healthy, innocent, ordinary young man, with ordinary tastes just like anyone else.

# I THOUGHT I WAS INCORRUPTIBLE

I tried everything. I said **** on the telly. I recommended masturbation to the readers of a well-known Sunday newspaper. But nothing seemed to do the trick. People everywhere still thought of me as a mature, respectable, healthy-minded member of society.

And then at last I found the secret.....

## OH CALCUTTA!

and look at me NOW

# "I couldn't tell Sun from Mirror"

## says Neasden housewife Mrs Sybil Liberty

Mrs Liberty is only one of millions of housewives who can't tell Sun from Mirror.

"I was amazed" says Mrs Liberty. "I never thought I would fail the test. But they're both identical! My husband was just the same. I gave him the Sun for breakfast but he didn't bat an eyelid. And he's been used to filth and drivel all his life."

### Could YOU tell the difference?

Take the test today. You'll find that for honest to goodness nastiness there's nothing to choose between them.

---

# THE TIMES DIARY

## Whither William Rees-Mogg?    a joke on The Times

THE RECENT item in the *Evening News* to the effect that Mr William Rees-Mogg is to remain as Editor of *The Times* is, I learn, not quite accurate in all respects.

What is certainly true is that Mr Alistair Burnett (whose name, incidentally, was mispelt in a recent issue of *New Society*) is strongly denying rumours that he is to replace Ian Trethowan as head of BBC Radio, as reported in last night's *Evening Standard*.

When I spoke to him yesterday, Mr Nigel Ryan, who has been widely tipped as the next Director-General of the ITA, refused to comment on the rumour that he is to be succeeded as Editor of *News at Ten* by Mr Nigel Lawson, currently editor of one of our leading critical journals.

Meanwhile, the identity of Mr Lawson's contributor, Mercuriouserandcuriouser Oxocubiensis remains something of a mystery.

Last night, Fleet Street was buzzing with the rumour that Mr Roy Jenkins, who has been widely tipped over an area of outstanding natural beauty, has been invited to succeed Mr William Rees-Mogg as Editor of *The Times*.

The intriguing question then arises — whither Professor Hugh Trevor-Roper, widely believed to be the author of the brilliant column *Auberon Waugh's Political Diary*, published weekly in *The Times*?

Is it possible, as some insiders predict, that Mr Waugh is to succeed Mr Lawson when he succeeds Mr Burnett, when

he succeeds Mr Charles Wintour when he succeeds Mr William Rees-Mogg when he is finally fired as Editor of *The Times* (a development which insiders predict is widely imminent).

### New play

MR TED SLARGE, 59, who has been working as a freelance BBC computer programmer for the last 64 years, has written a play, which is to be given its first performance by the Neasden Regis repertory company early next month.

The play, which is called *"How Ted Slarge Got His First Play Put On By The Neasden Regis Repertory Theatre"* tells the story of how a 59-year-old freelance BBC computer programmer writes a play and has it accepted and performed by a repertory company in a small South Coast town.

Says the director, 59-year-old Ted Slarge, who besides being the author of the play was once a freelance computer programmer for the BBC: "The play is something of a departure for me since in addition to directing, I shall also be playing the main part. I see the main character, Ted Slarge, very much as a freelance computer programmer working for an organisation like the BBC who has this play

accepted by a little South coast repertory company, such as you might find in, say, Neasden Regis."

The play will also be something of a departure for the audience, who are expected to stage a mass walk-out at an early stage in the evening's entertainment.

"This should be a moving experience" says the author, "or my name's not Ted Slarge, 76, a freelance computer programmer working for the BBC."

### Split at Mole

THERE WAS news yesterday of something of an editorial disagreement in the offices of *The Green Stoat*, the break-away radical quarterly, formed last month after a rift at the offices of *The Pink Elephant*, the break-away radical monthly named after Marx's celebrated revolutionary dictum "Let's nip down to the Pink Elephant for a quick one."

*The Pink Elephant*, which is now edited by a group of Neasden Maoists, calling themselves 'The Neasden Maoists' was originally formed as a break-away radical weekly by former members of the staff of *The Red Mole*, the break-away radical fortnightly originally formed in protest at the

editorial policies of Mr Tariq Ali's celebrated *Black Dwarf*.

Yesterday, Mr Neasden Regis Debray, 17, editor of *Pink Mole*, was keeping mum — unlike Mr Ali, whose mum has been keeping him, thereby enabling him to devote his time to the overthrow of bourgeois democracy.

---

*I HAVE received a number of letters from readers pointing out that my quotation from Marx in the above paragraph is not by Marx at all, but the invention of Mr Ted Slarge, the 59-year-old playwright, who is widely tipped to succeed Mr Alistair Burnett when he leaves his next job as the Editor of The Times.*

### Publishers

SOMETHING of a storm has arisen in publishing circles over the book *Alternative Forms of Counter Culture*, a collection of essays by Neasden Regis-Debray which is published today by Snipcock and Tweed.

The book, which costs 6 gns, contains *'A Guide to Dossers' London'*, including instructions on how to break into the offices of publishers Jonathan Clapp and steal free copies of *Counter Forms of Alternative Culture*, the recently published guide to

dossers' London, edited by Lord Rupert Neville Murdoch, the millionaire Australian 'hippie.'

Lord Rupert Murdoch's book in turn contained detailed instructions on how to break into the offices of Snipcock and Tweed, and doss down on the knee-high wall-to-wall carpeting, specially designed for Sir Georgiou Snipcock by fashionable interior decorator, David Millionairic.

### Whither PHS?

WHO IS the mysterious PHS who is responsible for this daily output of boring trivia about the media which passes for a gossip column?

I learn that he is none other than PH Slarge, brother of the well-known playwright and Editor-elect of *News at Ten*.

It is widely rumoured in Fleet Street that when, as is widely believed, Mr. Alasdair Barnett succeeds Mr Rees-Mogg as Editor of *The Times*, one of his first moves will be to fire Mr Slarge.

Who then will succeed him? (See tomorrow's and ensuing tedious instalments).

**PHS**

269

# CLAUD COCKBURN

It is more than time for a full and frank assessment of the Chinese character. That the Chinese are in the highest degree duplex is about the only thing really known about them to Westerners.

This aspect of the Chinese character was first disclosed in the latter part of the 19th century when some boneheaded, clapped-out, and three parts drunk gold prospectors on the Yukon or thereabouts, asked a Chinese of average IQ to join them in a hand of poker.

He, being at least partially sober, took them for quite a ride. For the sake of their own reputations, they proclaimed that he was a man of monumental intelligence, cunning as the devil, and the cleverest cheat they had ever seen. Otherwise, how could he possibly have won all their money?

His reputation finally reached the ears of poet, and otherwise noted writer, Bret Harte. Being a poet, the best BH could do was write a poem about it.

He did so, emphasizing, at the insistence of the white gold-diggers, that the China-man had not played fair. His poem, entitled *The Heathen Chinee*, and demonstrating that if a Westerner loses, or in any other way appears inferior, to a Chinese, it is because the Westerner is so straightforward and honest, while the Chinese lacks moral scruples, naturally became a best-seller all over the US and the UK.

It gave a lot of moral support to every subsequent act of aggression against China or exploitation of China.

It would be a mistake to suppose that the Chinese character has changed in this respect since the Communist Revolution.

Here it behoves us to keep our wits about us.

For on the one hand, as every reader of the Western press knows, Mao and his followers are essentially idiots. One has only to look at their economic so-called policies and compare them with those of such a one as Jenkins, to see in a flash that the Chinese are the merest Tyros, and a good western Tyro could probably out-pace them, at that.

What we have there are approximately six hundred million damn fools. But let this realisation not build us into a false sense of security. What has to be understood is that the Chinese possess that peculiar mentality which enables them to be damn fools and frighteningly cunning at the same time.

*"60 - 70 - 80 - Phew, what a scorcher!"*

**NOTE**
In some of our copies the article *The Power of the Papacy* described the Pope as 'His Satanic Majesty'; this should read 'the Roman Antichrist'.

*Protestant Telegraph*

There seems to be considerable evidence that a lot of nervous English tourists cancelled their holiday bookings to Ireland at the outset of the "gun runners crisis" in the Dublin Government on the grounds that civil war loomed.

Such cancellations are one more manifestation of the incurable incapacity of the English to understand anything about Ireland.

They show, for a start, that the English cannot understand that the Irish take politics seriously.

It has been rightly said that "every Englishman is born three whiskies below par." Even a general election barely manages to raise the Englishman to what, in Ireland, is a normal level of political awareness.

The Irish take politics seriously.

It follows that, even in the event of civil war, nobody is going to waste ammunition on spattering politically inert tourists with costly bullets.

Given the time, trouble, money and risk involved in securing arms, is it likely that these would be carelessly or casually employed against mere tourists, unless they be of the most extremely officious, meddlesome type sometimes found among Englishmen?

Long years ago, during a period of gang warfare in Manhattan, the New Yorker remarked "Our only fear on returning from vacation to the city is that we may be mis-taken for somebody else and shot."

That is, of course, a hazard against which there can be no absolute guarantee, even in a careful country such as Ireland.

It is comical to hear the laments of some British travel agencies over the dent in their business caused by the Irish crisis.

To listen to them you might think that the Irish are behaving most improperly by having a political crisis in the summer.

They seem to take the view that people should subordinate all political ideas and endeavours to the sacred interests of the tourist trade. If, they think, the world cannot be made safe for democracy at least it ought to be made safe for tourism.

Visit Britain- and leave your worries behind

# PRIVATE EYE

No. 220
Friday
22 May '70

2/-

I never thought he could pull it off three times running

You've never had it so good

and I've never had it!

# THEY'RE OFF!

(OR NOT - as this issue went to press before any announcement was made)

THE AWARD
WINNING INTERVIEW

# DAVID FROST talks to 'Lassie the Wonderdog'

Frost: We're very proud and pleased to have on the show tonight one of the most loved personalities in the whole history of show business. She's never been interviewed before, and it is a real privilege and honour to welcome her on the show. So, let's have a very big hand for - Lassie.

LASSIE: Woof, woof.

FROST: Super, super - that's fantastic. That's an amazing bark you have, Lass - may I call you that ?

LASSIE: Woof.

FROST: One of the most successful and well-loved roles you ever played was that of a collie dog in *Lassie Come Home*. I believe we have a clip of one of the most well-loved sequences. Can we just have a look at that ?

*(FILM OF LASSIE LOOKING SOULFUL ON ROCKS BY SEASHORE. AUDIENCE APPLAUDS WILDLY. CAMERA RETURNS TO FROST, WHO IS CLAPPING EXCITEDLY).*

FROST: Amazing, that was absolutely super! They certainly don't make films like that any more. But seriously, Lass, you've got a tremendous reputation as a brilliant mimic. I believe you do a fantastic imitation of Rin-Tin-Tin.

LASSIE: Woof, woof.

FROST: *(LAUGHING HYSTERICALLY)* Fantastic, super! That's one of the best imitations of Rin-Tin-Tin I've ever seen. I wonder if the audience agree ? Everyone who thought that was the best imitation of Rin-Tin-Tin they've ever seen, put up your hands.

*(ALL AUDIENCE PUTS HAND UP)*

FROST: Lass, a lot of people think of you as the happiest and most successful dog in the world. You seem to have everything - money, fame, bones, a luxury kennel in Hollywood. Tell me, is there any one thing you'd like to do, which could possibly add to your happiness ?

*(WONDERDOG LIFTS LEG AGAINST FROST'S HAND-TAILORED TROUSER).*

FROST: Super, super, super, that's fantastic! Thank you for coming on the show and God bless. We'll be back with you next week, when we'll have another fantastic award-winning interview with another of the most successful and well-loved personalities in the whole history of show business - myself.

*(MUSIC - "DAVID FROST THEME")*

THE END
© Paradine Productions (Bahamas) Inc.

# COLOUR SECTION

The Labour Party Executive Committee investigating irregularities in the selection of Mr Michael O'Halloran now MP for Islington (North) are believed to have found Mr O'Halloran somewhat 'Irish' in his answers to their probing questions.

The committee were particularly anxious to discover from Mr O'Halloran whether he had been in receipt of a not unsubstantial sum from a prominent local sympathiser.

"You've got me on the hop" said O'Halloran when the matter was first raised. When pressed further O'Halloran commented "I want to be frank with you - I can't remember".

Finally Mr O'Halloran was asked by the impatient committee to give a categorical 'yes' or 'no' to the question.

"Categorically - er - No. Unless I was drunk at the time" came the satirical reply.

HEATH

"He used to be one of the all-time Hollywood greats."

# MRS. WILSON'S DIARY

Ah well, it had to come, I suppose
    The curtain needs must fall
The first frost bites the loveliest rose
    It happens to us all

Let us not think what might have been
    Nor mope o'er chances lost
Nor hanker for the vanished scene
    Nor pause to count the cost

Farewell, ye corridors of power
    Where powdered flunkeys stroll
Farewell the rosy-scented bower
    Where Kings and Princes loll

Gone are the ermined pomp and robes
    Gone too the Seals of State
The jewels that dangle from the lobes
    The gold and silver plate

The laughter from the garden gone
    The merry clink of glasses
The fragile cup, the toasted scone
    The friendly upper classes

No longer new red boxes come
    Containing secret papers
No more the powerful Humber's hum
    The mad Balmoral capers

Like visitors to a Grand Hotel
    Who cannot pay the bill
We hear the ringing of the bell
    That bodes us nought but ill

Past laundry bags we creep away
    Like robbers, blanket-decked
Through Tradesmens's Gate at break of day
    Dawn sky with blood beflecked

Away - but where ? What is to come ?
    What can the future hold ?
My husband looks distinctly glum
    And I am feeling cold

O Time, great healer, of our woes
    Thy soothing unguent pour
That when the rallying trumpet blows
    We may return once more.

            Amen.

*T*he scene will remain in my memory
till my dying day. Harold, relaxed
and beaming, a glass of Vintage
Wincarnis nestling in his palm, as we
sat alone in our suite at the Adelphi
Hotel, watching the 26 inch coloured
screen, with the rubicund figure of
Professor Mackenzie fiddling with
his Swingometer prior to the announcement of the first results. "I really
feel sorry for Heath", he was remarking
lighting a large Churchill-style Corona
Perfidio de Luxe Cigar, "they will
stab him in the back and he will sink
without trace. What can he do ? It
really is most sad. We might have him
down to Chequers one week-end : he
could go boating on the pool with Giles.
Ah, here they come!" and with this he
snatched up the Daily Telegraph Where
It's At Special Election Supplement and
settled down among the cushions with a
sharpened pencil at the ready.

He did not remain in a recumbent
position long. As the Mayor of Guilford
adjusted his chain and announced a Tory
Majority of 79,000, Harold sprung
forward, staring wide-eyed into the screen
as if he had seen a ghost. The other
results followed swiftly, and Professor
Mackenzie's Swingometer shot up
alarmingly to hitherto unmeasurable
proportions. When Harold turned and
looked at me his face was ashen white.
"It is Powell!" he shouted and then,
looking back at the screen "The Polls
were rigged! I knew it all along!
They were nobbled by Heath!" With
this he took a puff of the wrong end
of his cigar and was convulsed with
coughs. "Kaufmann!" he finally shouted
"the rat has left to feather his nest!"
He knew all along. He must have done.
Get me Lord Hill. The Election is off
It was all a hoax. I just wanted a dry
run to test the Party Organisation.
It's all right, Gladys, don't be alarmed.
I will call it off, and we can get back to
watching the World Cup."

During this I noticed that flecks of
foam were forming about Harold's
mouth, and after remarking that he
would fight them on the hills and that
we would never surrender , he suddenly
closed his eyes and fell backwards into
the sofa. Luckily the Inspector was on
hand to administer the kiss of life, and
when Harold came to he was in a changed
mood. "I told them" he observed,
"I told them again and again: do not have
a June Election. I knew it was madness,
but they would not listen to me. I knew
all the time that the Opinion Polls were
groping in the dark. I told Roy Jenkins
that it was folly to campaign on casual

show-business lines, that we should
hammer the issues. But he would hear
nothing of it. He was so confident. His
last set of trade figures, coming three
days before the voting, what a stab in the
back ! Oh yes, we shall know where to
apportion the blame! And by the way,
Gladys, get on to Pickford's at once.
Now I know how Sir Winston felt in 1945.
The ingratitude ! I have brought this
Country through the greatest economic
disaster that it has ever known; I have
led this people through the desert and
into the Promised Land of Economic
Surplus, and they have bowed down before
the Golden Cow of Edward Heath, and
have gone awhoring after strange persons.
At such time one despairs of the democratic
system."

*I* have never seen Number Ten look so
desolate. The gap in the fireplace where
the Kosiglow used to stand, the white shapes
of the ducks up the wall, and all the
furniture piled in the hall, waiting for
the removal men, and poor Nimmo
miaowing piteously as all her familiar
landmarks were taken away. As I
came in from taking a last look at the
garden - the roses I planted last year
are now at their best and I must leave
them, alas - the Inspector arrived and
went up to Harold who was sitting on a
tea chest in the middle of his empty den.
"Inspector" Harold cried, "thank God
you are here. There are times when a
man needs old friends." "I have news
for you, chum" the Inspector replied,
"I have decided to stay on under the
new bloke. He says he'll see me right
for tips. Madam, no offence meant, but
you must now leave. There are two men
outside with a grand piano, and you are
now technically in trespass." I popped
Nimmo into his basket, and taking Harold's
arm, wiped away a tear and led him out
through the garden to climb over the
back wall.

            *THE END*

**Ten are arrested near Leeds Town Hall**

Mr. Quintin Hogg    Mr. William Whitelaw    Mr. Reginald Maudling    Mr. Anthony Barber    Mr. Iain Macleod

Lord Balniel    Sir Keith Joseph    Sir John Eden    Mr. Geoffrey Rippon    Mrs. Thatcher

*Evening Post*

## Glenda Slag

ANITA EKBERG

### The Woman who gives all she's got

So. Everyone is asking how the Tories managed to get back in when Opinion Polls up and down the country had written them off.

Frankly it didn't surprise me one little bit. And for why ?

I'll tell you.

### GO ON, *TELL US*

At the end of the day when it came to the crunch, it was the ordinary common or garden British housewife - God Bless Her - who gave Mr Wilson the thumbs down sign.

The woman in the supermarket knew better than all the Opinion Polls put together.

She knew that under Labour everything had gone up a hundred fold.

Hats off to Mrs Britain. Her down-to-earth honest-to-goodness savvy has put a new man in Number Ten.

Mind you. He won't do anything to bring prices down, you can take Auntie Glenda's word for that.

But so what, I ask you. The women of Britain have spoken their minds and I say that's a victory for common sense.

. . . .

Did you go to Ascot or did you stay at home and watch Wimbledon on the telly ?

Either way, it doesn't much matter. Cos as far as I'm concerned, the biggest thing on the sport scene is Tony Jacklin, the handsome hunk who has put British golf right back on top.

Coo-eee, Tony! I wouldn't mind being stuck in a bunker with you.

Here's one birdie you can make in one.

### APPALLING RUBBISH

But seriously. I say Roedean girls can count themselves lucky.

With a man in charge, Britain's top girls should learn a thing or two about life with a capital L.

But why oh why should the girls have all the luck. How about a headmistress for Eton and Harrow ?

There's more to a young man's education than Latin and Greek. Goodbye Mr Chips! And a big hello to Mrs Chips (alias Yours Sincerely).

Ah well. I can dream, can't I?

# SIR ALF WISLON NOW THE BIG INQUEST BEGINS

*writes Our Football Correspondent, Sir William Haley-Mogg*

What went wrong ? That was the question millions of Labour fans were asking last night, as England's manager for the past six years, Sir Alf Wislon, flew back into London after Thursday night's shock defeat.

And already a further question mark hangs over the future of Sir Alf himself.

Here was the man who they said couldn't lose. He seemed to have everything on his side - the most experienced team, the weather, the predictions of all the experts, including the computer.

Above all there were the memories of the great victory of 1966.

But now all this has vanished in a puff of smoke, and the critics are asking: "Is it all over for the man who once seemed invincible ?"

### POLL KICK

For round the television sets and in the pubs last night, some pretty tough talk could be heard, as the armchair experts gave their verdict.

Said one left-winger: "He played it all wrong. We were well ahead, and then he just threw it away. We should have gone on to the attack, instead of thinking we could hold on to our lead just by keeping possession."

As the great debate rages on, there seems little doubt that so long as Sir Alf was running a winning team, the critics were happy to stay silent.

But now it's a different story - and in four years' time, when the teams take to the field again, one at least might be under new management.

# PRIVATE EYE

No. 226
Friday
14 Aug. '70.

2/-

# A chap called Jonathan

Mr Peter Walker warned the nation of a sensational new horror threatening Britain's very way of life in his keynote speech at Blackpool on the problems of pollution. These were his words:

"I warn you of the magnitude of the task ahead. It is enormous. At present, I have a great interest in a chap called Jonathan, my 7-month-old son. By the time he is my age ... we will have needed to build more waterworks and more sewage works than have been built in the whole history of man."

What sort of person is this Jonathan, whose sanitary requirements are so stupendous ? As my picture reveals, he is almost unbelievably disgusting. When Jonathan first arrived, his parents were rather proud to discover that he drank 17 buckets of liquid and required 200 clean nappies an hour. They reckoned that a second Alan Brien had been born. Soon, he would take over the Lavatories column on the *Sunday Times* and be proclaimed a genius everywhere.

*Master Jonathan Walker: a recent portrait*

Then the plumbing arrangements at Walker's home in Worcestershire broke down. Soon afterwards, the sewage system of the whole West Midlands began to show signs of strain. It is not just the volume of Jonathan's effluent but also its peculiar character. For some reason, it responds neither to treatment nor to processing. Walk-outs occurred in sewage farms throughout the country leading to the nation-wide strike whose consequences will be with us for many years. It is only when the threat of this Jonathan is understood that Walker's extreme remarks begin to make any sense:

"We have met the point in history where, if life is to be tolerable, we must mobilize every resource to meet these problems ... the planner must certainly be mobilized .... the technologists must be mobilized ... we must win the battle for it is a battle for the whole future of the human race."

# PRIVATE EYE

No. 232
Friday
6 Nov. '70

2/-

F.O. the lot of you!

## BROWN ANSWERS THE CRITICS

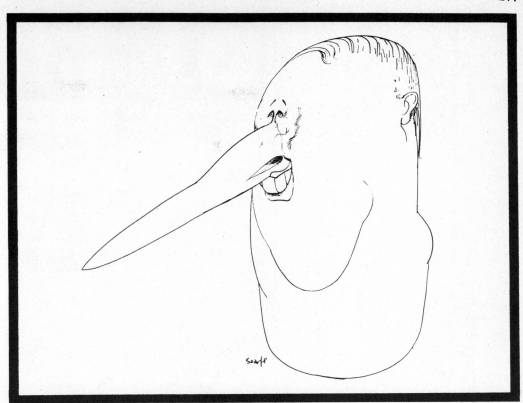

**AUBERON WAUGH**

10 **Downing Street**
**Whitehall**

PRIME MINISTER

### PERSONAL & CONFIDENTIAL

13.12.70

Dear Auberon,

It was kind of you to say that you appreciate my bread and butter letters. Of course, I have no pretensions to the literary, but I found your remarks most encouraging. I would have written to thank you anyway for another perfect luncheon, but when I got home it occurred to me that I might have been a little indiscreet in our conversation about Reggie Maudling's share dealings. Reggie would be terribly upset if he thought I was telling you things about him behind his back, as it were. On the other hand, I could see that you were sincere in your enquiries about a matter of legitimate public interest. I am sure I can trust you never to hint at your source of information.

When I told Douglas of our conversation, he went into a terrific tizz and said I should telephone you at once! Of course I told him what you had told me, that I must not telephone you at your place of work. I think Douglas is a teeny weeny bit jealous of the way I go out to luncheon alone with you. But if, as you say, your entertainment allowance will not run to another guest, I quite understand.

/Regarding

2

Regarding our other main topic of conversation, I hope I managed to convince you that I can afford the £5000 a year or so which you say it will cost to run my new boat without any assistance from your proprietor, whom I do not think I have even met. Thank him for his offer, and say how much I appreciate it, but I cannot on this occasion bend the rule that I do not accept money from people I have not met, however well intentioned. In the light of your refusal to introduce me to any of your friends, I doubt whether I ever shall meet him, either.

On the other hand, I was most amused to learn of the generous prize your proprietor is offering for the best (and most flattering!) story about myself. This is exactly the sort of thing British journalism needs nowadays - a new idea, which is at the same time exciting, challenging and topical. Although I could not think of any particularly suitable stories immediately, I have put the Conservative Research Department at Old Queen Street on the job, and they should come up with something pretty good.

I am glad you approve of the way we are handling the electricity workers. As you say, our critics are going to be confounded.

Yours ever,

Edward Heath

## AUBERON WAUGH

*TRUE STORIES*

### The Queen Mother wept

The Croslands were once asked to tea at Clarence House by the Queen Mother. Don't ask me why. As soon as they sat down at the table, Crosland set upon a plate of cucumber sandwiches and devoured it entirely. Nobody spoke, and the only noise came from Crosland's champing teeth. After a long pause, the Queen Mother said:

"I always find cucumbers so nourishing at teatime."

Crosland said nothing. Next the Queen Mother said: "I imagine you would have a certain amount of difficulty growing them in your native Germany, Mr Crossman." Crosland still said nothing. Finally, in desperation, the Queen Mother said:

"I wonder if you know my very good friend Mr Kenneth Rose. He always has the most perfect manners at teatime."

Crosland said: "Shut up and get me another plate of sandwiches. Don't you realise that I am a highly intelligent person?"

This story was told me by the Duke of Gloucester, so it may well be untrue. In any case, it will serve to illustrate the boorish manners and disgusting behaviour of the appalling brute Crosland.

## heathco
### For Better Value

### A message from the Managing Director

Hullo. Unpleasant things first. I have received a number of queries from some of our reps regarding the firm's policy on price reductions. I feel duty bound to clarify the position regarding this matter.

Briefly and simply the position is this. I know in the past the company forecast wide scale price reductions on a lot of our lines. We made this forecast in good faith, believe you me. But managing directors are not fortune tellers. They cannot see round corners. Like everyone else we are subject to our old friend Mr Unforeseen Circumstances!

Let me say at once that we are hoping in the long run to make reductions available to the public and I would be most grateful if you could all help to put the message across. But we shall have to wait until the general trading position has improved.

I know that I can rely on you all to bear with us over this temporary period.

Meanwhile, loose talk about "conning the housewife" which I hear is going around is hardly helpful and I hope will cease forthwith.

○

By the way I know some people for perfectly worthy motives are upset by the Heathco policy of resuming hardware sales in South Africa.

I sympathise very wholeheartedly with these people's misgivings about a country with such controversial practices as South Africa.

Be that as it may we are first and foremost a trading organisation. And like it or not, sentiment has no place in the world of commerce.

We pride ourselves on meeting our customers' requirements, whether they be black, white, purple or any other colour!

I hope what I say helps to put the record straight.

○

Incidentally, Christmas is only five weeks away. And we still have quite a few tickets remaining for our Grand Annual Fancy Dress Gala Evening.

I forgot to mention last time that Mrs Thatcher has agreed to organise a Bring and Buy stall in aid of the Pension Fund. I am sure there will be a good response.

Tickets are obtainable from Mr Barber, Room 11.

# COLOUR SECTION

The unfortunate Mr Peter Walker has become the subject of much abuse in the Conservative Party of Lancashire following his decision to overrule the considered opinion of his own planning inspector, Mr A G Harcourt, and to grant outline planning permission for the building of a 300ft high Whitbreads brewery in 55 acres of green belt between Preston and Blackburn.

Mr Walker reached his decision on August 27, but it was not announced until late on Saturday August 29th. As a result, it escaped the notice of a lot of national newspapers, and was only announced in Northern editions.

In recommending against planning permission for the brewery, Mr Harcourt concluded:

"The proposal would result in gross intrusion of industrial development into a pleasant rural area forming a valuable break of open country separating Preston and Blackburn ...

"The adjacent roads are totally unsuited to cater for the anticipated brewery traffic ... The provision of kerbs, paved footpaths and street lights, bearing in mind night work, would urbanise the area."

The provision of car parks for the brewery workers, the report went on, "would cause further detriment to the countryside and tend towards an undesirable coalescence of Preston and Blackburn."

The report recommends an alternative site for the brewery - in the area of a projected Central Lancashire new town - at Walton Le Dale. The site, said the report, would be suitable for the brewery, particularly if adequate attention be given to the sewage of the New Town." The planning consultants for the New Town, Robert Mathews, Johnson and Marshall Ltd, have also supported the New Town site for the brewery.

Whitbreads had argued that the site in the green belt would be cheaper for the company, with easier access for the company workers. This commercial argument, said the Inspector, was not strong enough to justify the desecration of a lovely stretch of countryside.

The area now proposed for the brewery has been jealously guarded against industrial development. Of 46 applications for planning permission previously submitted, only 12 were granted. Of these, 10 were for alterations to existing buildings, one was for housing and another for a sewage plant. Mr Walker's go-ahead for the brewery is bound to result in the swamping of the area with further industrial development.

According to the Housing Ministry's justification of Walker's decision, "He (Mr Walker) attaches more weight than the Inspector did to the evidence of the search conducted on behalf of the applicants, given the considerable restraints on their choice that are set by the requirements of the brewery."

The Inspector's report, however, was made, in its own words "after taking account of the special needs of the brewery."

"Nowhere" says a statement from the Council for the Preservation of Rural England, "has the Minister mentioned the needs of the environment. He has been concerned solely with the needs of the brewery and if this is to be typical of future decisions, the CPRE take it as a gloomy augury."

A week before Mr Walker's decision was announced, Whitbread and Company published its annual accounts. Colonel W H Whitbread, the chairman, said in his statement to shareholders:

"After nearly five years of government by professors and teachers with little commercial experience who do not believe in the profit motive, we breathed a sigh of relief on the morning on June 19th."

In 1968, Whitbreads donated £20,765 to the Conservative Party. In 1969-70 however, as the prospect of a Tory defeat loomed large, the donations slumped to £119.

Not all Tories share the Colonel's relief at the decision of Mr Walker further to desecrate Lancashire. Mr Edward Gardner, Tory MP for South Fylde, is among the protesters at the decision, as is Mr Charles Fletcher-Cooke, MP for Darwin. One leading Lancashire Tory was heard at a protest meeting lately to speak in distinctly unfraternal language about Mr Peter Walker and to declare his intention to "round up enough MPs to clobber the Grocer on this one and get the brewery out of here."

# Magistrates act to keep theatres open

*Evening Citizen*

# Mounting problems for young couples

Speaking at a social evening ...Wimborne St...

THE WESTERN GAZETTE.

Mr. Root said that although there might be evidence of premarital intercourse by young people there was little to suggest that this pattern persisted after marriage.

this is a COCK-UP

Raymonde

# THE WISLON MEMORANDUM

PRIVATE EYE IS PROUD TO PUBLISH THE AMAZING 750,000 WORD MEMORANDUM IN WHICH FOR THE FIRST TIME THE DISTINGUISHED STATESMAN AND THINKER, HAROLD WISLON, REVEALS THE TRUE STORY OF HIS RELATIONSHIP WITH THE YOUNG MAN, GERALD KAUFMAN, WHO WAS HIS CLOSEST AIDE AND CONFIDANT DURING THE LAST SIX EVENTFUL YEARS OF HIS CAREER.

KAUFMAN:
"Snake in the grass"

● I am writing this memorandum concerning Gerald Kaufman, not necessarily for publication (although I could do with the money) but because I have heard it put about that he is saying I am a "senile old megalomaniac who should never have been entrusted with the levers of power" and I wish to set the record straight.

I first met Gerald Kaufman when he called on me at my bungalow in the Scilly Islands in August 1964. He struck me immediately as being an impetuous and idealistic young man, with something of a chip on his shoulder. But anyone as old as myself is susceptible to flattery, and when he described me as "the most brilliant statesman in the entire history of the world since Winston Churchill" I was disposed to believe him.

Shortly afterwards when I came to power, I remembered this conversation, and invited him to Number Ten to become my secretary and amanuensis.

In those early days I found his ebullient sense of humour and natural charm as exhilarating as a breeze of wind on a muggy day. Throughout my "hundred days of dynamic action" when the eyes of the world were on my every move, he was always at my side, ready with a joke or a flattering remark to restore my sense of reality.

## Disillusion

My first doubts about Gerald arose at the time of my great Rhodesian initiative of 1965. It was Kaufman, with his customary impatience, who issued to the press in my name the famous claim that the crisis would be over in "a matter of weeks rather than months." I knew at the time that this was hopelessly idealistic, and the remark has often been held against me, but out of loyalty to Gerald I never issued a disclaimer.

But worse was to come. The financial crisis of 1966 was the first serious blow to our hopes, and it is a little known fact that the real cause of this run on the pound was the lack of confidence by foreign bankers in the advice Gerald had been giving me.

## More disillusion

By this time, many of my friends were writing to me, urging me to dissociate myself from Gerald's activities. They felt particular disquiet over his handling of the D-Notice affair, and the savage and heartless way in which, behind my back and entirely contrary to my wishes, he had engineered the dismissal of my old friend Col "Sammy" Lohan.

Perhaps it was foolish of me not to rid myself of Gerald's servies at this time, particularly in view of the embarrassment he caused me with his reckless initiatives over the devaluation of the pound, Anguilla, the White Paper on the Unions (which, contrary to popular belief was entirely his own idea) and his, I believe misguided attempt to abolish the House of Lords in 1969 which fortunately came to nothing, and derived in my opinion from his touchingly old-fashioned belief in Socialist militancy.

## Baldilocks

The last straw, however, came in the summer of 1970. It had always been my intention and that of my colleagues to hold a General Election in the autumn, when I was convinced that we would increase our majority to 300 seats. Imagine my horror when one night I learned that Gerald had issued a statement to the press, announcing that there would be an election on 18th June.

I called Gerald into my study, where I was sitting with my wife Gladys. She told him just what I thought of him, while I sat quietly sucking my pipe. When she had finished, I told Gerald frankly that I concurred with everything my wife had said, and he left our lives for ever.

Naturally enough, as I could have told him, we lost the election, and I am now living in retirement. Entirely as a result of Gerald's activities during the years when I looked upon him as a friend, my career is shattered, my reputation in shreds and I have become the laughing stock of the nation. But for all that, I must assure whoever may read this, that I bear him no ill will. I was very fond of him, and he had many good points, but I never regarded him as anything more than a joke, and I never listened to a word he said.

© H. Wislon Trustees 1970

# Nudist welfare man's model wife fell for the Chinese hypnotist from the Co-op bacon factory

*NEWS OF THE WORLD*

# O'Relli suspension shock

*by Our Man in the Casualty Department*

The soccer world was rocked to its foundations today by the shock news that Neasden's £100,000 white hope, Bert O'Relli, is to be suspended from playing for England in international matches.

The suspension follows O'Relli's controversial remarks on last night's Grampian TV "This And That" programme, in which he said: "I have a little book with the names of a few blokes I wouldn't mind standing up against a wall with a sub-machine gun and mowing them all down just like in the war."

### Shock

At a specially convened emergency meeting of the F A General Council in the small hours of this morning, the bosses of Britain's football lashed out at what one of them described as "the greatest blow the prestige of British football has suffered since Ted Groyne was sent off for 'behaving like a cad' in the second half of the 1889 Cup Final between Old Etonians and Royal Horse Guards Under-45's."

According to the FA, O'Relli's remarks are in flagrant contravention of Rule 734 (b) which states that "no player shall utter remarks on or off the television calculated to bring the noble art of self-defence into football."

### Horror

This morning, at a specially convened press conference, Neasden's tight-lipped manager Ron Knee, 59, lashed back at the FA's decision.

Said Knee: "This is fantastic, to my mind. After all, Bert was just saying in public what millions are thinking in private about football today.

"We have come a long way from the days when football was just a game." Added Knee, 59: "The better-educated, better-fed, better-clothed public of today don't pay good money just to see a few blokes kicking a ball about. What they want is a good old-fashioned punch-up like the Second World War."

### Disgusting

"If you ask me, it is the FA who are bringing soccer into disrepute, not lads like O'Relli. It is time these old-school tie fuddy-diddies woke up to the fact that we are living in the age of Vietnam and hijacking incidents of the type which recently led to the death of President Nasser. This is a violent world, and soccer must reflect this just like everything else."

Mr Knee is 59.

### LATE SCORE

Harlesden Wanderers 17 Neasden United 0

## with BAMBER GASKET

*Hello again! As Autumn comes on, lovers of motoring find themselves in contemplative mood. Winter is just around the corner and we'll soon be seeing our old friends icy and foggy patches back on the roads.*

*One of the clearest signs that autumn is upon us once more is the return to these islands of thousands of summer migrants making their way back from months of absence in sunnier climes. Just the other morning I was cruising along the B 4971 Feltham to Hanwell arterial when I espied one such wel-come returnee - a common Mini, still dusty from his long sojourn in Spain or Italy or some such tropical paradise.*

*His rear window was plastered over with colourful stickers bearing the names of his ports of call, each one evocative of distant parts in, as the poet has it, faery lands forlorn - Costa Del Sol, Torremolinos, Boulogne. Alas! My gaily coloured home-comer had yet to adapt to the conditions of his country of origin! Temporarily forgetting our native customs he drove out onto the right side of the road where he was soon in collision with an oncoming articulated lorry. Luckily not all our winter visitors meet a similar fate! As Old Jowett has it: "When coming back from France or Spain, Be sure to drive on the left again."*

*(AA Mobile Emergency Tent. Bath Road. Tuesday).*

"... AND ONCE AGAIN WE HAVE INTERRUPTION OF PLAY CAUSED BY
MOVEMENT BEHIND THE BOWLER'S ARM ..."

# GOVERNMENT TO BE SOLD?

## Shock plans imminent

by our Political staff

It now seems that present moves to sell off the more profitable parts of the government machine to private enterprise are far more extensive than has hitherto been realised.

Following recent announcements about airlines, local radio and the British Steel Corporation, it now seems certain that the Cabinet is actively considering the "hiving off" of many other spheres of government activity - in keeping with the view of Mr Heath and his colleagues that people have been depending on the government far too much and that they must "learn to stand on their own feet."

### Dynamic

Foremost among the plans now being drawn up, it is believed, is a scheme to sell off the police force to Securicor.

The prison service will be re-organised as a private corporation on a "Pay as you serve" basis and prisoners will be expected to pay an economic fee for board, loading and other services.

The Health Service, the BBC, the Post Office and the railways are all to be returned to the private sector and local government is to be administered by teams of local businessmen (as at present).

### Pragmatic

A specially imaginative solution has been devised to the problem of Britain's armed forces, which have been losing thousands of millions of pounds annually for centuries.

The only currently profitable department in this sector, the Household Brigade, is to be sold to Eric Morley's Mecca organisation, who plan to expand the Brigade's operation from its present limited role as a dollar-earner in central London, to cover all areas of the tourist drive.

The remainder of the armed forces, including the Polaris fleet, are to be sold by auction to the highest bidder. It is believed that "strong interest" has already been expressed by a mystery foreign consortium operating from behind the Iron Curtain.

If this deal comes off, it could be the biggest-ever of its kind and give a much-needed boost to Britain's export trade.

### Ruthless

But perhaps the most far-reaching of the Cabinet's proposals is one to sell off the whole of the Civil Service and Parliament to private enterprise management consultancy firms.

"It is scandalous" said a senior minister privately yesterday "that this tremendous pool of administrative talent is not being harnessed to the national need. British industry is crying out for the kind of expertise which can be found in Whitehall."

### Amazing

As for Parliament, many Ministers have long felt that this antiquated institution, costing the country many millions of pounds, no longer serves any useful purpose - besides occupying one of the most desirable and under-used sites in central London.

The Palace of Westminster, it is suggested, could be re-developed as a showpiece, multi-storey, hotel-cum-car-park complex.

With these changes in mind, the country will be run by a small group of businessmen, including Mr Peter Walker, Mr Robert Carr and Mr John Davies, under the chairmanship of Mr Edward Heath.

# Charge scheme for Royals

A new scheme to put Britain's Royal Family "on an economic footing," bringing it into line with other family businesses, was announced by the government today.

Under the scheme, the public will no longer have free access to the services provided by the Queen and her business associates, as they have in the past.

A token charge of 10s will be made, for instance, for all members of the public who wish to stand in the street outside Buckingham Palace, hoping to see the Duke of Gloucester driving in on his way to tea.

### SCANDALOUS

There will be a higher charge for watching full-dress state occasions. Says the Minister of Works, Mr Julian Amery: "People pay to watch a football match - why shouldn't they have to pay to see the Opening of Parliament?"

A scale of charges for many of the services at present performed for nothing by members of the Royal Family will be published shortly.

The fees (or "royalties" as they will be called) are believed to range from £5 for the unveiling of a plaque or ceremonial tree-planting by a minor member of the family (such as the Earl of St Andrews or Lord Snowdon) to £2,500 or over for a full-dress ship-launching ceremony attended by the Queen and the Duke of Edinburgh.

*"We've heard that you know of a way of smuggling people into Bradford?"*

# Mum gets the mess age

On Monday, 15th February, we change to decimal currency. Let's follow Betty Fisher as she takes her old (and rather crotchety) mother with her to the shops on D (for Decimal) Day.

*It said in the paper that a penny's going to be worth more than 2d. How can a penny be more than tuppence? I ask you!*

*It's all part of the new style of government mum. They said they would bring prices down and look, it's true!*

*Well I never! Beans are threepence a tin!*

*You see a penny's worth two pence halfpenny so naturally you get better value for money....*

*That means we'll be saving pounds on our grocery bills.*

*THINKS I'm glad I voted Conservative!*

A free copy of 'Your Guide to Decimal Money' is now being delivered to every home. It tells you all about shopping with the new money. Read it carefully and keep it by you for reference.

---

# Topes sues Turds **Legal Sensation**

*by Cyril Ray Connolly*

Mr Spiggy Topes, the popular singer, yesterday issued a high court writ against the three other members of The Turds, the former popular singing group.

The writ alleges libel, loss of earnings, defamation of character and gross indecency under the act of 1831.

### All my earnings

At a press conference in his Bagshot-style home Mr Topes told reporters: "The Turds have had it to my mind. Frankly they are a weight round my neck and I can't wait to get shot of them."

Lawyers however doubt whether any final settlement will ever be reached. Says Mr Jocelyn Weidenfeld, legal advisor to Nipple Ltd, the Turds business consortium: "The Turds are bound together by numerous contractual obligations. They cannot be separated. As I see it, the Turds will always be with us whether we like it or not."

### Oh Dear

Relations between individual members of the Turds have been described as "strained" by close friends.

When Spiggy Topes married the controversial Zen nudist, Okay Yoni, 47, a further split appeared in the Turds ranks.

In an interview in the American "pop" magazine *Rolling My Own* Spiggy revealed that fellow Turds had insulted his wife on more than one occasion.

"They said it spoilt the group's image to have her in tow" said Topes. "And they resented also very heavily the fact that I was in every way vastly superior to them both musically and intellectually. I also own 90% of the shares.

"I mean no disrespect to them when I say they are a trio of prize goons who would never have made it if it hadn't been for me pushing them from behind."

### Spiggy in his own Writ

The news came as no surprise at the Bond Street headquarters of Nipple. Says Turd manager, Len Greeb: "The Turds have been drifting apart for several months now. Each Turd is emerging as a personality in his own right. But I hope Spiggy will reconsider his legal action if only for the sake of my 27% stake in just about everything they do."

### Hard days cash

The writ which is entered in the name of Mr Leonard Barclay Tuft (Spiggy Topes) of 'The Old Grange,' Bagshot, Surrey, names Anthony Boxwood Strarbs of The Manor House, Chalfont St Giles, Bucks; Horace Grindley Kokoschka of The Old Rectory, Friars Balsam, Somerset; Terence de Vere Biggs of 'Ye Olde Hoose,' Weybridge, Surrey and Len Greeb, c/o Salvation Army, Whitechapel Road, London EC 1.

## Moving peacefully towards its close

## Lame Ducks

Already the soft-hearted and soft-headed brigade are bleating that the closure of the Daily Mail would be a tragedy. They are saying that it would be a black day for Fleet Street. Even a blow to our democratic way of life.

It would be nothing of the sort. In the harsh, competitive climate of the 70's, there can be no room for such wishy-washy sentimentality.

As the Prime Minister Mr HEATH has made clear on many occasions, the trouble with this country is that there are too many lame ducks, unable and unwilling to stand on their own feet.

If Britain is to stride forward into the future, her head held high and paying her way in the world, our captains of industry must be quite ruthless in rooting out inefficiency wherever it is to be found, whether in the board room or on the shop floor.

The facts about the Mail are clear. For many years this once great newspaper has been living entirely on its past. LORD NORTHCLIFFE's successors, each more incompetent than his predecessor, have reduced the paper to a pathetic sheet not even worthy to wrap up yesterday's chips.

Its slavish adherence to every tiny fluctuation in the Conservative Party line, its progression of vacillating editors, its third-rate staff and fourth-hand ideas, have all contributed to what is undoubtedly the dullest and most amateurish product that Fleet Street has ever known (barring only the Daily Sketch and the Evening News).

Nothing can be served by prolonging the grisly farce of the Mail's continued existence any longer. Remembering the inspiring words of the Prime Minister, Mr Edward Heath, that "there is no longer any place in the competitive Britain of tomorrow for obsolete ideas," Mr VERE HARMSWORTH should act now. It is high time that this particular lame duck was well and truly stuffed.

# The Final Hours

### by Vincent O'Mulled Claret

There are two rivers flowing through London tonight. And one of them is made up of unemployed journalists leaving the Daily Mail.

### Tragedy

All through the dark hours of yesterday the world held its breath. Would the great old paper last through the night?

The bulletin, when it came, was terse and unemotional:

"The Daily Mail is sinking fast."

Just six ordinary, familiar words. And yet, in that simple sentence, there seemed enough to bring even a strong man to brink of tears.

### Pathos

The day had been full of comings and goings. First to arrive in the morning was Mr Harry Krishner, 47, a South London bailiff. Grim-faced he told the waiting crowd of reporters: "I've come to take away the typewriters. No-one likes this job, but somebody has to do it."

Just after mid-day, a beaming Mr Rupert Murdoch arrived. His voice choking with laughter, he said: "I've just come to pay my last respects."

### Suffering

And so it continued all day, as the silent drama unfolded behind the closed doors of Carmelite House. From time to time anxious faces appeared at upper windows and once or twice the silence was broken by the thud of bodies falling to the pavement.

### Gloom

The usual laughter in the bars of Fleet Street was silent yesterday. The only sound the dull thud of bodies slumping to the floor, as hard-bitten journalists faced up to the reality that was too hard to bear.

The situation was perhaps best summed up in the words of a humble news-vendor whose pitch stands outside the Daily Mail's office: "It's a cryin' shame, gun'nor. In fact, it's worse than a shame, it's a ruddy crime. I tell you, Georgie's the best ruddy footballer in the whole ruddy world and I don't care who knows it."

### Nauseating

Of one thing, on this dank and dismal day, we can be sure. That no matter what happens here on earth, in heaven the presses will be waiting to roll tonight.

And tomorrow or the next day, the angels at least will be able to read the Daily Mail - "Celestial Edition."

# NO DAILY MAIL

The Postal Workers Strike Continues today.
(Pigeon News Service)

**A recent study**

"Y'know, it's sad to think that Jon could be out of work any day now"

# STOP PRESS

That was the order issued by Mr Vere Harmsworth last night.

**27**
Jonathan Crake bears a more than startling resemblance to Peter Cook.

**28**
Some early self-advertisement.

**29-32**
Parody of now extinct *Town* magazine.

**37**
Based on Huw Wheldon, then compere of BBC arts programme *Monitor*.

**40**
Original is Arnold Wesker, then busy founding Centre 42.

**41-3**
Inspired by vogue of films about working-class life in the North of England.

**45**
Tony Hancock, ill-fated BBC comedian.

**46**
Publication of *The Making of the President*, Theodore White's best-selling account of 1960 presidential election campaign.

**49**
Emergence of the Bishop of Woolwich alias John Robinson, the first blast of whose Godless Christianity was heard at about this time. The Eric Buttock column, written by Christopher Booker, ran intermittently in PE from March 1962 when Eric Lubbock to the surprise of all captured Orpington for the Liberals in a by-election.

**50**
Probably a reference to the case of Carmen Bryan deported under the new Immigration Act. The coloured gentleman is Dr Hastings Banda, Prime Minister of Malawi.

**52**
The great Macmillan cabinet purge of July 1962. Selwyn Lloyd, Chancellor of the Exchequer, is sacked.

**53**
Inspired by a spate of art thefts.

**54**
*Anatomy of Britain* by Anthony Sampson, bestseller of 1962, gave detailed analysis of interlocking Establishments.

**55**
Despite this savage attack, Stirling Moss asked to have the original to use as his Christmas card. This sort of thing happens with depressing frequency.

**56**
Ian Fleming, author of the famous Bond books.

**57 and 58**
Cuba crisis of November 1962. The photograph was what caused all the trouble.

**63**
Macmillan negotiates with U.S. to buy Polaris submarine.

**65**
De Gaulle vetoes Macmillan's application to join the Common Market.

**66 and 67**
Early attack on the *Sunday Times* colour section (founded 1962).

**68**
Fleet Street condemned by Vassall Tribunal. President Nkrumah, self-styled Messiah.

**69**
Resignation of Charles Fletcher-Cooke, Under-Secretary of State, Home Office.

**70**
Harold Wilson is favourite to succeed Hugh Gaitskell as Leader of the Labour Party. Gaitskell died January 1963.

**72**
Reprinted with apologies to the late Randolph Churchill. (See introduction.)

**73**
The full-page apology for the above which was printed in the *Evening Standard*. The list of signatories includes some joke nicknames copied from the credits in *Private Eye*.

**74**
Idle Talk is first mention of Profumo Affair.

**75**
Profumo had already issued a writ against a continental magazine.

**76 and 77**
Booker's swan song (see introduction). Tim Birdsall the artist died tragically in June 1963.

**78**
David Frost by Barry Fantoni. Trog cartoon refers to the famous headless man rumour in the Duchess of Argyll case. Rumour had it that the Duchess had photographed her friends in a state of undress. The matter was later investigated by Lord Denning.

**79**
Ward's letter to Brooke provoked the final downfall of Profumo. But the press are still keeping mum even at this late stage.

**82**
The *News of the World* publishes Christine Keeler's memoirs. Scarfe cartoon is based on famous photograph of nude Keeler.

**84**
The lovely Mandy Rice-Davies.

**85**
Claud Cockburn's issue includes the first account of the Harold Woolf case (see introduction).

**86**
Mervyn Griffith-Jones QC was Prosecuting Counsel in the trial of Stephen Ward.

**87**
Long-awaited publication of the Denning Report. After all the excitement the Report was actually an anti-climax.

**88**
The resignation of Harold Macmillan.

**91**
Earl of Home succeeds.

**93**
Exhibition of Goya in London. Scarfe pastiche shows Keeler, by now in prison, Home, Hailsham and shooting of Lee Harvey Oswald.

**94**
First appearance of Sir Basil Nardly Stoads.

**96**
Sir Cyril Osborne was Conservative MP for Louth.

**101**
Home announces date of General Election.

**102**
Publication of memoirs by Lord Kilmuir, Prosecuting Counsel at Nuremberg.

**103**
John Bloom, the washing-machine king, had now

gone into the holiday business. Once again he was not altogether successful.

**104**
The origin of *Private Eye*'s unusual nickname for Sir Alec Douglas Home.

**105**
Peter Cook and Claud Cockburn courageously name the Kray brothers.

**107-9**
Malcolm Muggeridge guest-editorship.

**110**
An early piece by Foot.

**112**
Arrival of the Labour Government.

**116 and 117**
Surprising as it may seem, this demonstration on behalf of Baillie Vass actually took place. It was totally ignored by the press, although it must have been one of the most extraordinary demonstrations ever to take place in London.

**118**
The Queen visits Germany.

**119**
Return of Christopher Booker, scourge of the Neophiliacs.

**121**
Edward Heath elected as Leader of the Conservative Party in succession to Home.

**124**
Swinging London and all that.

**127**
Wilson was busy dragging the Queen into the Rhodesian crisis.

**130**
On 7 January 1966 David Frost gave a notorious breakfast party at the Connaught Hotel.

**131**
Ian Smith makes UDI.

**133**
*The Times* starts printing news on the front page instead of classified advertisements.

**138**
A strike by the National Union of Seamen started on 16 May and lasted for six weeks. In a famous phrase, Wilson referred to a 'tightly knit group of politically motivated men' as being responsible for the failure to reach a settlement of the dispute.

**139**
Financial crisis of July 1966. Wilson freezes wages and prices for statutory six-month period. This cover was the subject of a complaint to the Press Council. The complaint was later dismissed. It is the only time this has happened.

**141**
George Brown had used the slogan 'Brothers, we're on our way' in 1962.

**142**
Chairman Mao went for a much-publicized swim in the Yangtse River.

**143**
Dr Verwoerd, Prime Minister of S. Africa, assassinated on 6 September.

**145**
Lord Thomson buys *The Times*.

**150**
Wilson makes exploratory Common Market probes.

**153**
Bertrand Russell's memoirs serialized in the *Observer*.

**154**
The oil tanker *Torrey Canyon* ran aground off the Scilly Islands on 18 March 1967. The fight to stop the pollution of beaches occupied the nation's and Mr Wilson's attention for several days.

**157**
Wilson announces intention to join Common Market. Calls for 'Great Debate'.

**159**
The devaluation of the pound in November 1967 sparked off renewed speculation about a possible coalition government.

**160**
A film version of *Dr Dolittle* was released.

**161**
The 50th anniversary of the Russian revolution was celebrated in October 1967.

**166 and 167**
Dr Emil Savundra, former head of the Fire, Auto and Marine Insurance Company, was sentenced on 7 March 1968.

**168**
The I'm Backing Britain campaign, masterminded by Robert Maxwell MP, advertised on these lines in the national press. All those mentioned lent their names to the campaign.

**170**
Mr Callaghan introduces his Bill to bar Kenyan Asians with British citizenship from entering Britain.

**174 and 175**
Enoch Powell made his first attack on coloured immigrants in Wolverhampton on 21 April.

**177**
Cecil King was dismissed from his post of Chairman of the International Publishing Co. at about this time.

**178**
Traditional strikes and rioting break out in France, May 1968.

**181**
Revolutionary student leaders come to London to appear on the telly.

**183**
Resignation of Ray Gunter, formerly Minister of Labour.

**190**
General Loan had personally executed a Vietcong prisoner in front of Press and TV cameras.

**191**
The Russians invade Czechoslovakia.

**194**
D'Oliveira omitted from MCC touring team to S. Africa.

**195**
Enormous anti-Vietnam demonstration called for 27 October.

**197**
John Lennon and Yoko Ono publicize their new record. An alternative bubble ran 'If your tits are right it's half past six.'

**198**
Sir Oswald Mosley's memoirs are published.

**199**
Jackie Kennedy marries Aristotle Onassis.

**206**
A leader in *The Times* called for the resignation of Harold Wilson and the establishment of a coalition government.

**212**
Train robber Bruce Reynolds arrested in Torquay.

**213**
Lord Mountbatten's memoirs are serialized on the telly.

**214**
Inspired by the BBC's decision to axe the long-running soap opera *Mrs Dale's Diary*.

**215**
Kray brothers sentenced to life imprisonment.

**216**
Maiden flight of the Concorde 2 March 1969.

**217**
Wilson invades Anguilla in March 1969.

**218**
Home Secretary James Callaghan dissociates himself from Wilson's Industrial Relations Bill.

**221**
Euthanasia controversy.

**223**
Sir Kenneth Clark's popular series on Civilization is broadcast on the telly.

**225**
More crudity.

**226**
See above.

**230**
Gnome column believed to be a reference to the Teddy Kennedy affair at Martha's Vineyard. *Oh Calcutta* opens in New York.

**231**
Wilson backs down on Industrial Relations Bill.

**233-235**
Royalty stages a comeback with Investiture of Prince Charles and lengthy TV documentary showing the Royal Family at work and play. The film is acclaimed by all.

**242 and 243**
Marathon TV show by David Frost covers man's landing on the moon.

**246**
Miss Bernadette Devlin tours America to raise money for the Ulster Catholics.

**248**
The collapse of Robert Maxwell's Pergamon publishing empire began when the American firm Leasco withdrew its takeover bid.

**249**
Panmure Gordon and Robert Fleming were Maxwell's brokers and merchant bankers.

**251**
Peter Knowles, a footballer, suffered a much publicised conversion to the Jehovah's Witnesses.

**252**
A balance of trade surplus of £42 million is recorded for August.

**253**
Speculation about the possibility of George Brown being taken back into the Cabinet. Lord Snowdon produced a film for television about people's dependence on pets.

**254**
Like many satirical items this subsequently came
true with the foundation in America and later in
Britain of the Gay Liberation Front.

**258 and 259**
In a letter published in *Eye* 207, Dr W. Visser
(sic) pointed out that his report did indeed
mention the Wisconsin research. He confirmed
that his researches were financed by the Dutch
sugar industry but said that he tried to remain
neutral.

**207**
It is revealed that the royal finances are in poor
shape.

**263**
Allegations are made about the massacre of
Vietnamese civilians at My Lai by US combat
troops.

**265**
President Nixon's ambassador in London,
Walter Annenburg, was one of the high spots of
the royal TV film (see page 233). His performance
was remarkable for its verbosity and
portentousness.

**270**
Wilson calls General Election.

**272**
The final instalment.

**273**
England's football team, coached by Sir Alf
Ramsey, lost to W. Germany in the World Cup.

**274**
More rumours in the American press about the
home life of our own dear Snowdons.

**275**
Auberon Waugh joined *Private Eye* as Political
Correspondent in February 1970 after being
sacked by the *Spectator* for disrespectful remarks
about Mr George Gale, now the Editor.
Visit to Britain of President Nixon.

**276**
Foreign Office criticism of George Brown, the
former Labour Foreign Secretary.

**278**
The Grocer was beginning to regret his pledge
to reduce prices, which had helped in no mean
way to win him the Election.
Mr Barber's mini budget reduced income tax by
6d but raised the price of school meals and
welfare services.

**279**
The anti-brewery campaign was unsuccessful and
the building went ahead. But shortly afterwards
Peter Walker started to adopt a more
conservationist stance.

**280**
A posthumous report by Bertrand Russell was
published concerning his former American aide,
Ralph Schoenman. Russell confessed that he had
been bamboozled by his lieutenant.

**285**
The merger of the *Daily Mail* and the *Daily
Sketch* was announced on 8 March 1971.